Strengthening SME Performance Through Social Media Adoption and Usage

Sikandar Ali Qalati
School of Finance and Economics, Jiangsu University, China

Dragana Ostic
School of Finance and Economics, Jiangsu University, China

Rohit Bansal
Vaish College of Engineering, Rohtak, India

A volume in the Advances in Business Strategy
and Competitive Advantage (ABSCA) Book Series

Published in the United States of America by
    IGI Global
    Business Science Reference (an imprint of IGI Global)
    701 E. Chocolate Avenue
    Hershey PA, USA 17033
    Tel: 717-533-8845
    Fax: 717-533-8661
    E-mail: cust@igi-global.com
    Web site: http://www.igi-global.com

Library of Congress Cataloging-in-Publication Data

Names: Qalati, Sikandar Ali, 1986- editor. | Ostic, Dragana, 1982- editor.
Title: Strengthening SME performance through social media adoption and
  usage / Sikandar Ali Qalati, and Dragana Ostic, editors.
Description: Hershey, PA : Business Science Reference, [2023] | Includes
  bibliographical references and index. | Summary: "This book focuses on
  different conceptions of factors and consequences influencing social
  media usage and SME performance"-- Provided by publisher.
Identifiers: LCCN 2022039908 (print) | LCCN 2022039909 (ebook) | ISBN
  9781668457702 (hardcover) | ISBN 9781668457740 (paperback) | ISBN
  9781668457719 (ebook)
Subjects: LCSH: Small business--Management. | Social media.
Classification: LCC HD2341 .S76 2023 (print) | LCC HD2341 (ebook) | DDC
  338.6/42--dc23/eng/20220906
LC record available at https://lccn.loc.gov/2022039908
LC ebook record available at https://lccn.loc.gov/2022039909

This book is published in the IGI Global book series Advances in Business Strategy and Competitive Advantage (ABSCA) (ISSN: 2327-3429; eISSN: 2327-3437)

British Cataloguing in Publication Data
A Cataloguing in Publication record for this book is available from the British Library.

For electronic access to this publication, please contact: eresources@igi-global.com.

Advances in Business Strategy and Competitive Advantage (ABSCA) Book Series

Patricia Ordóñez de Pablos
Universidad de Oviedo, Spain

ISSN:2327-3429
EISSN:2327-3437

MISSION

Business entities are constantly seeking new ways through which to gain advantage over their competitors and strengthen their position within the business environment. With competition at an all-time high due to technological advancements allowing for competition on a global scale, firms continue to seek new ways through which to improve and strengthen their business processes, procedures, and profitability.

The **Advances in Business Strategy and Competitive Advantage (ABSCA) Book Series** is a timely series responding to the high demand for state-of-the-art research on how business strategies are created, implemented and re-designed to meet the demands of globalized competitive markets. With a focus on local and global challenges, business opportunities and the needs of society, the **ABSCA** encourages scientific discourse on doing business and managing information technologies for the creation of sustainable competitive advantage.

COVERAGE

- Value Chain
- Innovation Strategy
- Joint Ventures
- Small and Medium Enterprises
- Business Models
- Differentiation Strategy
- Entrepreneurship & Innovation
- Strategy Performance Management
- Foreign Investment Decision Process
- Ethics and Business Strategy

IGI Global is currently accepting manuscripts for publication within this series. To submit a proposal for a volume in this series, please contact our Acquisition Editors at Acquisitions@igi-global.com or visit: http://www.igi-global.com/publish/.

Titles in this Series

For a list of additional titles in this series, please visit: http://www.igi-global.com/book-series/advances-business-strategy-competitive-advantage/73672

The Transformation of Global Trade in a New World
Bartolomé Marco-Lajara (University of Alicante, Spain) Ahu Coşkun Özer (Marmara University, Turkey) and Javier Martínez Falcó (University of Alicante, Spain)
Business Science Reference • © 2023 • 308pp • H/C (ISBN: 9781668459508) • US $250.00

Exploring the Economic Opportunities and Impacts of Migrant Entrepreneurship Success Stories and Case Studies
Meena Chavan (Macquarie University, Australia) and Sheba Nandkeolyar (Multiconnexions, Australia)
Business Science Reference • © 2022 • 231pp • H/C (ISBN: 9781668449868) • US $215.00

Analyzing the Relationship Between Corporate Governance, CSR, and Sustainability
Ayberk Soyer (Istanbul Technical University, Turkey) and Umut Asan (Istanbul Technical University, Turkey)
Business Science Reference • © 2022 • 315pp • H/C (ISBN: 9781799842347) • US $215.00

Handbook of Research on Digital Innovation and Networking in Post-COVID-19 Organizations
Ana Pego (Nova University of Lisbon, Portugal)
Business Science Reference • © 2022 • 539pp • H/C (ISBN: 9781668467626) • US $315.00

Antecedents and Outcomes of Employee-Based Brand Equity
Muhammad Waseem Bari (Government College University, Faisalabad, Pakistan) Muhammad Abrar (Government College University, Faisalabad, Pakistan) and Emilia Alaverdov (Tbilisi State University, Georgia)
Business Science Reference • © 2022 • 297pp • H/C (ISBN: 9781668436219) • US $250.00

Cases on Emerging Market Responses to the COVID-19 Pandemic
Raj K. Kovid (Sharda University, India) and Vikas Kumar (Central University of Haryana, India)
Business Science Reference • © 2022 • 332pp • H/C (ISBN: 9781668435045) • US $240.00

Impact of Digital Transformation on the Development of New Business Models and Consumer Experience
Maria Antónia Rodrigues (Polytechnic of Porto, Portugal & CEOS.PP, Portugal & SIIS Porto, Portugal) and João F. Proença (Faculty of Economics, University of Porto, Portugal & Advance/CSG, University of Lisbon, Portugal & ISEG, University of Lisbon, Portugal)
Business Science Reference • © 2022 • 347pp • H/C (ISBN: 9781799891796) • US $240.00

701 East Chocolate Avenue, Hershey, PA 17033, USA
Tel: 717-533-8845 x100 • Fax: 717-533-8661
E-Mail: cust@igi-global.com • www.igi-global.com

Table of Contents

Detailed Table of Contents

Chapter 1

An Unexpected Journey: Designing a Social Media Marketing Framework for Small and Medium
Enterprises (SMEs) 1

Bikramjit Rishi, Shiv Nadar Institution of Eminence (Deemed), India
Anushka Anand, Shiv Nadar Institution of Eminence (Deemed), India
Tejasvi Sharma, Shiv Nadar Institution of Eminence (Deemed), India

The chapter addresses how small-scale enterprises fundamentally use social media to leave a footmark of their brand and have a direct mode of interaction with customers. The chapter indicates the need for SMEs to develop a social media roadmap to come up with user-friendly ideologies and use of relevant social media platforms to cater to the needs of customers. The chapter also discusses the varied social media platforms that have become an integral part of the marketing function for SMEs and play an impeccable role in successful campaigns with the sole motive of adding value to a brand face. The chapter also provides some managerial guidelines to use social media marketing in the marketing function of SMEs.

Chapter 2

From Real-Time Marketing to Corporate Social Responsibility: The Impact of Social Media
Engagement on #womensday Posts by Companies 21

Cássia Liandra Carvalho, University of Aveiro, Portugal
Belem Barbosa, University of Porto, Portugal
Claudia Amaral Santos, University of Aveiro, Portugal

Social media strategies are commonly adopted by large and SMEs due to the expected impacts on customer engagement, branding, sales, and overall company performance. One particularly interesting strategy conducted on social media is real-time marketing (RTM) that enables the company to get involved in the discussion of trending topics. The main aim of this chapter is to analyze RTM impacts on user engagement in the case of socially relevant topics, particularly Women's Day. It provides an analysis of publications by the 25 most valuable brands in Brazil (comprising both large companies and SME) and explores the interconnections between RTM publications and CSR policies. One main conclusion is that companies should approach socially relevant dates in accordance with their CSR policies, and that successful RTM initiatives can comprise alternative approaches: promotional actions, tributes, and CSR. The findings of this chapter are particularly relevant for SMEs, considering the democratic nature of RTM and overall social media strategies.

Chapter 3

Poshan Yu, Soochow University, China & Australian Studies Centre, Shanghai University, China
Chenghai Li, Independent Researcher, China
Ramya Mahendran, Independent Researcher, India

In China, due to the rise of online literature and its derivative works, IP, which means intellectual property, refers to literary works with strong economic exploitation potential and the forms of exploitation include the adaptation of online literature into music works, film and animation, online games, etc. This chapter will analyze the development of Chinese online literature on social media and its IP creation and then focus on the case study of online literature company Jinjiang Literature and film company Daylight Entertainment. Both of them are famous SMEs in China, producing a lot of literature, films, and television works of high quality and meanwhile improving their business performance. In the end, this chapter will analyze the problems these companies face and find out the solutions.

Chapter 4

Poshan Yu, Soochow University, China & Australian Studies Centre, Shanghai University, China
Yue Pan, Independent Researcher, China
Melanie Bobik, Independent Researcher, China

This chapter aims to study whether and how e-commerce live streaming affects brand equity of the beauty industry in China. This chapter will explore the strategies of using e-commerce live broadcast to affect consumers' purchase behavior in China's beauty industry and study how these strategies will affect the brand awareness and brand loyalty of the industry. This chapter will investigate features of e-commerce live streaming on the social media and impacts on the related viewers. In addition, this chapter will use CiteSapce analysis to perform statistical and correlation analysis associated with e-commerce live streaming. Furthermore, this chapter will also analyze consumers' preference for e-commerce live broadcasting strategy through questionnaire survey. Cases from Douyin (the business outside China is called TikTok) will be used for explanations. This chapter will provide suggestions for the SMEs as to how to make use of e-commerce live streaming to enhance their brand equity.

Chapter 5

Kazi Turin Rahman, Coventry University, UK
Rohit Bansal, Vaish College of Engineering, Rohtak, India

The antecedents and consequences of choice overload, or overchoice, have been largely investigated. However, the aspect of comprehensively evaluating a large assortment of options and mitigating subsequent choice overload is absent. By adopting a growth mindset and comprehensively evaluating alternatives, it is possible to combat the menace known as overchoice. This chapter conceptualises a unique model that examines choice overload mitigation from a deeper psychological lens. Moreover, it also adds a new dimension to the concept by integrating the aspect of rigorous choice evaluation. Overall, future research propositions have been made that will enable researchers to validate the novel model. Implications of validating said model include strengthening the field of choice overload by offering comprehensive mitigation strategies.

Chapter 6

Niranjan Devkota, National Planning Commission, Government of Nepal, Kathmandu,
    Nepal
Amit Sigdel, Quest International College, Pokhara University, Nepal
Udaya Raj Paudel, Quest International College, Pokhara University, Nepal
Sahadeb Upretee, Central Washington University, USA
Devid Kumar Basyal, La Grandee International College, Nepal & Pokhara University, Nepal

There were numerous opportunities for small-medium businesses to gain more advantages by incorporating more ICT into their operations. Studying the effects of ICT use on organizational financial performance is an important research topic that has not been well described. Apart from the fact that ICT is underutilized in developing countries and the majority of empirical research focuses on large corporations, the researcher discovered that, as a result of the above literature findings and points, there is still a significant research gap between developed and developing country perspectives on ICT adoption and usage. Therefore, this research plans to see the exiting literature review and research gap for the context of developing country. ICT is a new concept, and there has been very little research and study in this field, with no research carried out in Nepal. This review can be instrumental for those who what to conduct ICT-linked SME performance and profitability.

Chapter 7

Vinay Pal Singh, Quantum University, Roorkee, India
Ram Singh, Maharishi Markandeshwar University (Deemed). Ambala, India

The backbone of any economy can be found in its small and medium-sized businesses (MSME). Over the past decade, they have made a major impact on GDP growth. They play a crucial part in bringing progress to underdeveloped regions. Every economy relies heavily on its small and medium-sized businesses (SMEs). Small and medium-sized enterprises (SMEs) bear the brunt of COVID-19. The goal of this study was to find out how SMEs respond to changes in their operating environment caused by COVID-19 by changing their business models with the help of digital technology.

Chapter 8

Ranson Sifiso Gwala, University of KwaZulu-Natal, South Africa
Pfano Mashau, University of KwaZulu-Natal, South Africa

This chapter explores how COVID-19 negatively impacted society and small-medium enterprises (SMEs) and how social media marketing, promoting, and influencing played a role in rescuing and resuscitating some of the SMEs during the COVID-19 pandemic. The chapter investigates the use of social media during the hard lockdown due to mitigation measures of COVID-19. It uses a desktop review of literature to qualitatively identify themes. The study aim was to understand how social media could be used by SMEs to improve and grow SMEs. The study identified five key themes during COVID-19, being social media adoption, employees layoffs, falling customer demand, government support, and online business adoption. The social media influencing is being adopted as part of social media marketing, and one of its positives is that it is affordable. The richness of data and literature could lead to the development of a conceptual framework for the use of social media by SMEs in Africa.

Chapter 9

Barkha, Maharshi Daynand University, India
Deepanshi Aggarwal, Maharshi Dayanand University, India

The fashion industry has become more globally competitive as a result of increased globalisation. The recent introduction of new technologies has presented opportunities as well as obstacles for the fashion industry, especially for small and medium-sized businesses (SMEs) whose low resources may make it difficult for them to adopt new technology. But, with the rise of social media, fashion SMEs have new opportunities that can help them become more visible and boost their sales. Accordingly, the present study attempts to analyse the efficacy of social media usage on the performance of SMEs in fashion industry. The study will use both qualitative and quantitative approach to examine the social media usage in terms of reach, richness, affiliation, and influence on SMEs performance. Data will be collected from 400 SMEs in Delhi through questionnaire and their respective social media account (Facebook). Results of the study show that most of the small and medium-sized enterprises used social media for business purpose, and their performance is improved after using social media.

Chapter 10

Roxie Ojoma Ola-Akuma, Bingham University, Nigeria
Desmond Onyemechi Okocha, Bingham University, Nigeria
Josiah Sabo Kente, Nasarawa State University, Nigeria

Nano, micro, small, and medium enterprises (NMSMEs) are still heavily reliant on the "brick-and-mortar" system or traditional street-side business methodology, which is no longer as efficient as it once was. In contrast to the foregoing, this study examined the effect of new media on nano and micro enterprises (MSSBs) in Nigeria. Hinged on the technology acceptance model (TAM) and theory of digital divide, the research employed a survey method to generate responses from micro business owners within 36 business categories in Bauchi Metropolis by deploying 100 questionnaires to a random sample size. Chi-Square test calculator and sample median test were used to examine the various hypotheses at a 5% level of significance. The analysis revealed that there was no significant positive relationship between new media products' usage and increased business performance in Bauchi. This is because the majority of NME owners were still unaware of what new media products could offer them. As such, NME owners need to be trained to adopt the new media tools in order to boost NMEs in this region.

Chapter 11

Riya Wadhwa, Maharashi Dayanand University, Rohtak, India

Rohit Bansal, Vaish College of Engineering, Rohtak, India

Aziza Chakir, FSJES AC, Hassan II University, Casablanca, Morocco

Reena Katyal, Sh. L.N. Hindu College, Rohtak, India

Small to medium enterprises (SMEs) are businesses that nourish revenues, assets, or number of employees below an unquestionable threshold. SMEs are the great altruist in developing the economy by employing vast numbers of people and helping in configuration through innovation as well as leading in global development of an economy. In emerging of market economies, SMEs are the engine of economic development because of their great entrepreneurial spirit. These will help to make an enterprise successful as well as bring new innovations for everyone. These days, SME entrepreneurs are coddling themselves on social media for amplifying their achievement, so this chapter will traverse the acquisition of social media and how the performance of SMEs is going while adopting these sites. Associating with these sites are helping people in linking with the world. Roles and challenges will also be narrated in this chapter.

Chapter 12

Shikha Singh, Maharshi Dayanand University, India

Nishita Pruthi, Maharshi Dayanand University, India

There is no denying that worldwide economic and environmental conditions have been affected by the COVID-19 pandemic. Small and medium-sized enterprises (SMEs) have been particularly impacted by the COVID-19 pandemic. With this research, the authors aimed to better comprehend the obstacles faced by small and medium-sized enterprises (SMEs) during a pandemic, the digital reforms that emerged as a result of COVID-19, and the preventive measures that SMEs can take to withstand the crisis. They reviewed a wide range of secondary materials, including scholarly journals, books, internet resources, and blogs. They conclude that small and medium-sized enterprises (SMEs) can benefit from digital transformation because it allows them to rethink their decision-making processes and their use of technology. To overcome the challenges posed by COVID-19 to SMEs, it is necessary to examine a set of policy measures that could aid the recovery of MSMEs.

Chapter 13

Amandeep Singh, Chitkara Business School, Chitkara University, Punjab, India

Amrinder Singh, Jain University (Deemed), Bangalore, India

The impact of social media can be seen everywhere. Now the success of a business depends upon how successfully it is able to handle its social media marketing. It is a new phenomenon that has changed how the business environment operates. Companies are able to gain access to resources that were otherwise not available to them. It has also helped businesses to increase their worthiness, cultivate strategic partnerships, and increase their contact with customers and suppliers. It has become important for business owners and marketers to understand how social media work as a communication and marketing tool and how they can significantly grow their businesses. The study focused on establishing the effect of social media on the growth of SMEs in India. The present study is theoretical research, based on the various literature available. Additionally, social media allows businesses to communicate speedily and cheaply with customers as well as allow them to construct a database that can be used to generate business leads that may translate to increased sales and thus grow the SMEs.

    Ankit Dhiraj, Lovely Professional University, India
    Sanjeev Kumar, Lovely Professional University, India
    Divya Rani, Patliputra University, India

The globe is experiencing a significant advancement in modern technology, particularly social networking sites that have been accessible in various industries, including travel and tourism. This makes it more difficult for tourism businesses to give people the best offers on tourist destinations. Tourism SMEs connect with customers, give support, and promotional activity through social media. These new media establish a stronger connection with consumers. Researchers collect data randomly through Google forms of 175 managers or owners from tourism SMEs to achieve their objectives. This chapter discusses the use of social media by tourism SMEs and social media promotion and other aspects like the development and advantages of social media.

    Rubina Nabin, Modern College of Business and Science, Muscat, Oman

Small and medium enterprises hold an utmost importance while considering any nation's growth, prosperity, and the betterment of its economy. This chapter aims to focus on the SMEs in Canada as a nation and how food chain as a SME can flourish successfully by using social media as a tool for its success. The types of food chain SMEs, the procedures for launching a food chain, acquiring license for food chain, possible challenges that could be faced in food chain SME are also discussed. Social media's adoption and usage to attract customers, promote products and services, market promotions are also intended to be discussed. Social media strategies for food chain SMEs including paid application sponsored advertisements, influencer-promoted paid promotions, food chain SMEs own page posts and promotions, and getting the food chain's social media verified officially will be the foci.

Preface

Improved globalization, digitization, technology advancement, and computerized systems substantially change the business environment. In addition, the COVID-19 pandemic has adversely affected social and business life. The fierce competition incurred due to globalization, free trade, and collaborations have created many challenges for small and medium-sized enterprises (SMEs). SMEs are recognized as the backbone of today's world economy. However, SMEs are well known for having limitations and acceptance barriers in adopting new technology even though the internet and communications channels revolution has changed the way people conduct business today. In addition, SMEs, especially in emerging countries, are at the periphery of advantages and disadvantages and vice versa. Besides, SMEs face a liability of smallness, which states that the smaller the firm, the fewer resources it typically controls. This enables them to be more vulnerable to internal and external events. In addition, they face several other challenges, such as a lack of resources (financial and non-financial), uncertainty due to rapid changes in the market, and an increase in competition.

To compete and satisfy the customer needs with limited resources, SMEs are required to adopt and use the technologies such as social media, which offer benefits of ease to use and technical manageability, and access to a large number of stakeholders (i.e., customers, partners, suppliers, etc.). In addition, it facilitates clear and rapid two-way communication, letting them understand the customer needs and monitor the competitors. Besides, social media adoption and use decisions enable SMEs to improve their knowledge and access to the global market. Although the challenges and opportunities offered by social media are clear, a comprehensive understanding of the challenges, factors, and impacts in the context of COVID-19 is required to guide practitioners, government agencies, scholars, and students.

Accordingly, the book title, *Strengthening SME Performance Through Social Media Adoption and Usage*, is self-explanatory. The adoption of and use of social media in SMEs is insufficient to improve performance. However, the right choice of social media platform (Facebook, Instagram, Twitter, WhatsApp, etc.), consistency and technicalities of using it, and successful implementation require integration of traditional and virtual practices and substantial changes in business models and strategies. In this way, the editors of this book invited practitioners and scholars from different industry backgrounds and counties to share their views on what could be hurdles SMEs face while adopting social media during the COVID-19 pandemic and how their impacts can be reduced. An outstanding number of proposals from different countries have been received, providing insights into the challenges faced by SMEs, designing a framework for SMEs, and their survival during a pandemic. This book provides students, universities, teachers, and practitioners with new perspectives on how social media usage has been dramatically changed due to COVID-19 and has greatly altered SMEs' ways of operation.

The book contains fifteen chapters that attempt to mirror the major areas of research on the topic and thus offer valuable findings to practitioners and readers.

The first chapter, titled "An Unexpected Journey: Designing a Social Media Marketing Framework for Small and Medium Enterprises (SMEs)," addresses how small-scale enterprises fundamentally use social media to leave a footmark on their brand and have a direct mode of interaction with customers. In addition, it indicates the need for SMEs to develop a social media roadmap to come up with user-friendly ideologies and use relevant social media platforms to cater to customers' needs. The second chapter, titled "From Real-Time Marketing to Corporate Social Responsibility: The Impact of Social Media Engagement on #womensday Posts by Companies," highlights the importance of real-time marketing for SMEs and analyzes its impact on user engagement in the case of socially-relevant topics, particularly Women's Day. The third chapter, titled "How Can SMEs Integrate Intellectual Property Rights Into Social Media Marketing Strategy to Achieve Brand and Business Development? A Case Study of Chinese Cultural Industry," analyzes the development of Chinese online literature on social media and its intellectual property creation. The fourth chapter, eitled "How to Improve the Brand Equity of Beauty Industry Through Effective E-Commerce Live Streaming Strategies: A Case Study of Douyin Live Broadcasting in China," explores the features of e-commerce live streaming on social media and its impacts on the related reviews. The fifth chapter, titled "Combating Choice Overload via a Growth Mindset in the Age of Social Media," examines choice overload from the perspective of social media. The sixth chapter, titled "Contribution of ICT on Small and Medium Enterprises Business Profitability: A Literature Review," highlighted the research gap among developed and developing countries from the perspective of ICT adoption and usage. Chapter 7, "COVID-19: A Disaster Master – Opportunities and Challenges for Small Medium Enterprises," focused on the issues and combat of SMEs from the COVID-19 viewpoint. Chapter 8, titled "COVID-19 and SME Adoption of Social Media in Developing Economies in Africa," explores how COVID-19 negatively impacted society and small and medium enterprises (SMEs) and how social media marketing, promoting and influencing played a role in reducing some of the SMEs during a COVID-19 pandemic. Chapter 9, titled "Efficacy of Social Media Usage on the Performance of SMEs in the Fashion Industry," uses both qualitative and quantitative approaches to examine social media usage in terms of reach, richness, affiliation, and influence on SME performance. Chapter 10, titled "Examination of the Effect of New Media in Revolutionizing Entrepreneurship in Bauchi State, Nigeria," explores the effect of new media on Nano, Micro, Small, and Medium Enterprises in Nigeria. Chapter 11, "Exploring Social Media Adoption and SME Performance: Role and Challenges," will traverse the acquisition of social media and how the performance of SMEs is going while adopting these sites. Chapter 12, titled "SME Survival During the COVID-19 Pandemic: An Outlook of Threats and Digital Transformation," aimed to better comprehend the obstacles faced by SMEs during a pandemic, the digital reforms that emerged as a result of COVID-19, and the preventive measures that SMEs can take to withstand the crisis. Chapter 13, titled "The Impact of Social Marketing on SMEs in India: A Theoretical Perspective," focused on establishing the effect of social media on the growth of SMEs in India. The second-to-last chapter, titled "Use of Social Media by SMEs in the Tourism Industry," discusses the use of social media by tourism SMEs and social media promotion and other aspects like the development and advantages of social media. The final chapter of the book, titled "Starting Food Chain as an SME in Canada: Adopting Social Media for Its Success," aims to focus on the SMEs in Canada as a nation and how the food chain as an SME can flourish successfully by using social media as a tool for its success.

We highly appreciate everyone involved in the publication of this book.

Sikandar Ali Qalati
School of Finance and Economics, Jiangsu University, China

Dragana Ostic
School of Finance and Economics, Jiangsu University, China

Rohit Bansal
Vaish College of Engineering, Rohtak, India

Chapter 1
An Unexpected Journey:
Designing a Social Media Marketing Framework for Small and Medium Enterprises (SMEs)

Bikramjit Rishi

Shiv Nadar Institution of Eminence (Deemed), India

Anushka Anand

Shiv Nadar Institution of Eminence (Deemed), India

Tejasvi Sharma

Shiv Nadar Institution of Eminence (Deemed), India

ABSTRACT

The chapter addresses how small-scale enterprises fundamentally use social media to leave a footmark of their brand and have a direct mode of interaction with customers. The chapter indicates the need for SMEs to develop a social media roadmap to come up with user-friendly ideologies and use of relevant social media platforms to cater to the needs of customers. The chapter also discusses the varied social media platforms that have become an integral part of the marketing function for SMEs and play an impeccable role in successful campaigns with the sole motive of adding value to a brand face. The chapter also provides some managerial guidelines to use social media marketing in the marketing function of SMEs.

DOI: 10.4018/978-1-6684-5770-2.ch001

INTRODUCTION

SMEs (Small and Medium Enterprises) play an essential role in many countries worldwide. It is due to their role in providing jobs and supporting regional development and innovation, all of which contribute to the economic well-being (Savlovschi & Robu, 2011, Epede & Wang, 2022). A thriving and productive SME sector is critical to a country's economic prosperity, and there appear to be opportunities for smaller enterprises to benefit from the usage of social media (Tiwasing, 2021). In emerging economies, formal SMEs generate up to 40% of national income (GDP) (Worldbank, 2022).

The internet's exponential growth has resulted in the rise of two critical phenomena: social media and online search engines. Social media is explicitly defined as a tool based on internet-based applications which best utilize the Web 2.0 ideology and technology, enabling rapid creation, exchange of content, interaction from a place of their comfort, garnering, and catering to humungous audiences, and building networks at fingertips (Andrade & Ruao, 2022). Web 2.0 technology and associated social media applications such as social network sites (SNSs), microblogging, weblogs, content communities, and wikis have been increasingly incorporated into organizational environments during the last few years (Boyd & Ellison, 2007). The use of social media apps has expanded beyond individuals to capture the attention of corporations. According to mounting evidence in this fast-paced world, small organizations can gain business value from using social media for internal and external objectives (Rishi & Bandyopadhyay, 2017).

It is critical for SMEs to develop a clear understanding of the business model to reflect on the target audience the business aims to capture and identify real problems that need to be addressed using social media as a powerful tool (Fang et al., 2021). Social media empowers strategies opted by SMEs for building brand recognition, addressing user review, understanding the areas of improvement, and building on constructive criticism received and giving a clear picture of the brand's performance. It broadens the horizon of customer relationships with the business (Popli & Rishi, 2021). It eases out the direct communication channel, bringing in revolutionary ideas and accelerating innovations in collaboration and building brands at affordable costs (Rishi & Kuthuru, 2021a). We know that SMEs predominantly have local clientele and prefer not to broaden their business beyond their region due to financial constraints (Lacho & Marinello, 2010).

Many SMEs use social media for branding, research, customer relationship management, services, and sales promotions, among other purposes. However, the central focus is on brand building (Das & Mondal, 2020). Similarly, SME customers can access various shared information sources from other customers regarding experiences and suggestions using social media (Qalati et al., 2020). The network built through social media for small businesses ultimately contributes toward business value. However, there is a range of instances where business models fail to implement it due to a lack of information related to technology (Rugova & Prenaj, 2016). At the same time, there are potential adverse effects of social media that require digging deep into the business model of SMEs. In SMEs, social media majorly contributes to customer relationships (Economist, 2009). However, the challenge lies in the fact that SMEs fail to realize business value from the use of social media due to a lack of identification of customer value proposition, henceforth underperforming in their use of the applications of social media to gain the best out of it and convert into results (Qalati et al., 2021; Qalati et al., 2022).

This chapter addresses how the growing popularity of social media can be helpful to SMEs in achieving their marketing objectives. With the help of the existing literature, the chapter establishes the use of social media as an essential tool for promotion. The chapter elucidates the social media guidelines that

SMEs can use to achieve their marketing objectives. The chapter proposes a theoretical framework that can be used to understand the consumers and design content to engage them effectively. It also provides a few examples that can be a reference point for SMEs to use social media for promotional purposes.

BACKGROUND

The constant notion of social media and its perception in SMEs has changed drastically over the past few years and, as a by-product, evolved the way people interact, participate, cooperate, understand, foster businesses and connect with each other, turning the traditional "one-to-many" into "many-to-many" (Odoom et al., 2017). Small-scale enterprises fundamentally use social media to interaction with customers. Different social media platforms have become a natural part of the marketing function, especially in small and medium enterprises, to achieve the marketing objectives. A plethora of opportunities exists for SMEs to gain advantages from the use of social media (Geho & Dangelo, 2012). At the same time, literature also provides evidence that organizations need to use social media wisely, or there is a considerable possibility for SMEs to suffer its adverse consequences. SMEs need to consider how they can effectively recognize and realize the business value of social media (Pervin & Sarker, 2021).

The usage of social media is frequently studied from a business-to-consumer perspective. Studies have looked into the impact of social media on consumer purchase decisions, brand awareness and buy intent, customer retention, electronic word of mouth, and purchase decision involvement, for example (Akar & Topçu, 2011; Mills & Plangger, 2015; Erkan & Evans, 2016; Rishi & Bandyopadhyay, 2017; Devereux et al., 2020; Dwivedi et al., 2020; Cao et al., 2021; Pfister & Lehmann, 2021; Rishi & Kuthuru, 2021b; Rishi & Mohammed, 2022). Despite social media's considerable impacts and perceived value, research on how SMEs adopt and use social media channels is scarce.

Social media platforms are not owned or controlled by organizations. Furthermore, experts claim that social media material is (typically) created collaboratively by businesses and their stakeholders, such as current and potential customers (Dalkir, 2011; Georgescu & Popescul, 2015, Saura, 2021). Specifically, various elements may aid in enlightening divergence in an SME's adoption of social media, including pressure from customers and competitors, which eventually influence an SME's decision to embrace or not (Wang et al., 2016). The pressure from key stakeholders could also impact the adoption decision. Social media marketing activities are emerging as a new way of conducting business, allowing firms to create a more intimate relationship with stakeholders (Kumar & Ayedee, 2018).

Extensive research on the applications of social media for businesses is varied. Richter and Riemer (2013) studied three typical cases of prime knowledge-intensive organizations which introduced corporate social networking sites as part of their marketing strategies. Drawing conclusions from their extensive study, they identified three modes of use of social media platforms, including the identification of experts from a similar field, building personal context, and fostering existing relationships. Meske & Stieglitz (2013) pointed out the vision of SMEs to increase the speed of access to knowledge, reduce communication costs, and increase the speed of access to internal experts as primary purposes for social media usage. Whereas for the non-social media user brands, the rise of problems related to the implementation and operation of social media played a crucial role in keeping them distant from their usage. The SMEs mostly scrutinized aspects of lack of support by employees, issues of corporate culture, and the lack of expected value and appropriate resources. It can also be noted that the personality of firm owners and their attitude toward doing business influence decision-making processes in SMEs to a visually large extent. Thereby the affinity of the CEO has a significant impact on social media initiatives by SMEs (Ainin et al., 2015). Another focus lies in the fact that SMEs should always consider the enterprise culture and mindset of the employees to be free with their work, and the adoption of social media should be constantly monitored (Brink, 2017). The impact of social media on the sales process is another relationship to be discussed as it showcases the relationship between the alignment of social media functionality and strategies with SMEs' performance (Bocconcelli et al., 2017).

SMEs are gaining significant value and insights from social media use. SMEs dive deep into the rapidly developing field of social media, which perhaps includes effective integration of customer channels within the limited resources of an SME and social computing (Tajvidi & Karami, 2021). Like other businesses, SMEs use several quantitative metrics to assess website traffic, visitors' time spent on the site, chart their expenditure on marketing activities, and note revenue or sales growth, which aligns with qualitative measures (McCann & Barlow, 2015).

Drawing comparisons to the traditional routes of audience connectivity has been converted to cheaper and more convenient resources for both companies and customers via social media platforms. One of the primary roles is to assist the company in accessing and assessing its periodic target customer quickly and at a faster pace (Sedalo et al., 2022). It overall enhances and grooms the customer base and proportion of market share, sales count, and brand awareness, henceforth holding a significant value, especially for the small - and medium-sized enterprises (SMEs). SMEs usually have their budget tight and face the common hurdle of lack of financial support and skilled employees at the initial stage of expanding their horizons (Karimi, & Naghibi, 2015; Nurfarida & Sudarmiatin, 2021).

Visualizing and studying models of various SMEs opting for social media as their core marketing strategy makes us conclude that social media has created a platform for research and new business opportunities. Social media enables one to overcome the geographic barriers, a larger domain of customers to interact, communicate, meet and gather information quickly, and utilize it to seek, share feedback, and exchange information in their everyday life (Atanassova & Clark, 2015; Cheng & Shiu, 2019). The perks and contribution of creating such partnerships and associations have helped individuals and brands establish new business relations, leading to long-lasting bonds and customer retention (Batista et al., 2022).

The rapid industrialization and dependency on technology have made the utilization of social media an irreplaceable option for SMEs. It improves the company's performance and may take it to new heights if clicked at the right spot (Basri & Siam, 2017). Social media comes in handy for SMEs as they are primarily deprived of resources; hence, their interest lies in the bandwidth of strategic plotting concerning budgeting, optimization, and technological partnering. Social media space is a continuously changing process, where customer preferences are changing and evolving with time (Bakri, 2017).

Drawing our attention to drawbacks, the flip side of the coin, several technological challenges adversely influence the sustainable business performance of SMEs (Pérez-González et al., 2017). There could be a possibility that these small-scaled enterprises fail to understand technology or use outsourcing. Therefore, brands need to understand their audience base and expectations from social media analytics and then proceed with drafting plans and leading to their execution.

A few of the critical conclusions from the existing research include:

- Dependency of the impact of social media on the nature and features of social media, along with other resources within SMEs. It nurtures a need to analyze the influence of reliable social media strategy on the performance of SMEs.

- Critical alignment between social media functionalities and social media strategy, which the SMEs aspire to achieve, directly correlates to improving SMEs' performance.
- Selection of the type of social media that the brand aims to target plays a crucial role as we know that different social media platforms have unique functionalities and strategies.
- Along with the implementation and execution of strategies, it is also vital to constantly proctor the perceived impact of social media used in SMEs to measure sales growth graphs.

SOCIAL MEDIA AND MARKETING STRATEGY OF SME'S

Successful small businesses have traditionally relied on word-of-mouth marketing to spread the word about their goods and services. Small businesses that use social media can now employ free tools to increase word-of-mouth while reducing their reliance on outbound advertising channels such as cable television ads, newspaper ads, yellow pages, etc. The cost and accessibility of Social Media Marketing technologies, combined with increased awareness of Social Media Marketing in general, have made social media marketing a viable avenue for smaller firms to identify and engage with their clients in recent years (Rishi & Bandyopadhyay, 2017; Popli et al., 2021).

Before developing an effective social media marketing strategy, SMEs need to understand the channels where their customers are present, ways to target the audience on those platforms, and the objectives and the return on investment they wish to achieve. In many ways, social media affects a broad segment of the population. The use of social media, driven by Facebook, Twitter, and LinkedIn, gives marketers significant capacity to execute precision targeting at a low cost. The best feature of these platforms is that they provide good data and analytics, allowing the executor to keep track of campaign success and make fast adjustments to improve campaign effectiveness and results (Roy & Dionne, 2015; Bocconcelli et al., 2017). The CEO's affinity has a significant impact on the social media activities in SMEs.

Social media directly impacts consumer attitudes, and decision-making is a major justification for having a social media presence. Social media, which has proliferated in recent years, is particularly significant for small businesses because it can be used to cut through the noise and engage with customers. Social media heavily influences consumer shopping decisions (Ming & Lam, 2012; Chen & Lin, 2021). SMEs can benefit indirectly from having a social media presence. In other words, it is utilized as a tool to create relationships with clients over time rather than directly leading to immediate decision-making or purchase behavior. The goal is to finally entice customers to the company's web page, which is totally under its control. The presence of social media has also been demonstrated to promote brand recognition and, as a result, search ranking on search engines like Google (Rugova, & Prenaj, 2016; Odoom et al., 2017).

Consumers' information satisfaction on social media sites impacts their behavioral intentions; thus, SMEs need to supply the most nuanced information possible to attract customers. It illustrates that social media has an extensive and growing influence on customer views and the significance of providing attractive information to the target customers (Jagongo & Kinyua, 2013; Ngammoh et al., 2021). Using social media to interact actively, engage target market customers, and influence customer behavior was a very effective tool for SMEs. The potential of social media to promote interactivity and debate is a great tool to engage customers and form long-term relationships with SME brands (Dutot, & Bergeron, 2016; Marolt et al., 2018).

SOLUTIONS AND RECOMMENDATIONS - DESIGNING SOCIAL MEDIA STRATEGY FOR SME'S

Social media plays a vital, indispensable instrument in marketing one's business idea, planning a roadmap for optimized market strategies, encouraging the development of dialogue, providing exclusive opportunity to be in direct contact with each client, and aiding their needs and feedback continuously (Effing & Spil, 2016; Vieira et al., 2022). Social media for business plays an effective tool in micro-targeting audiences, categorizing them into groups. Once we hit the right chord of the target segment, it becomes crucial to select the right platform to execute designed plans (Rishi & Mohammed, 2022). Diving and digging deep into social media analytics help expand the audience for local businesses. Social media requires a band of equipped management professionals who help the brand positioning and differentiation of products at pocket-friendly pricing across the varied social media resources and platforms (Qalati et al., 2020). Some of the social media goals include building trust and enriching loyal customer-brand relationships, acquiring customers, etc.

1. Setting Objectives

Developing a thriving community across social media platforms for small-scale enterprises is of vital utility these days. Understanding the challenging scenario and broader aspect of keeping customers engrossed across these platforms is a challenging endeavor, but equally, if not more important, to maintain and build trustworthy brands via the route of customer relationships with networks that one already has. (Barnhart, 2021). Failed review or poor customer experiences and feedback can spread through the client base like wildfire, leading to churn and making business costs hefty loss. Henceforth, keeping all these points in mind requires a consistent and strategic approach to setting goals at each step one takes (Effing & Spil, 2016; Vieira et al., 2022).

In the current scenario, finding customers on social media has a direct proportional impact on sales. Setting a crystal-clear objective for the social media market base must be driven with a vital purpose and calculated schedule. In the haste of building a brand name, enterprises often blast outposts or put promotions on social media pages (Kumar & Sharma, 2022). Predominantly to refine our purpose and objective, understand our users, publish relevant content, drive awareness, and expand the reach and overall brand awareness, three salient steps that should be employed by brands briefly involves (Barnhart, 2021):

- Plump goals based on funnel: One of the tactics employed by brands is the funnel approach. The idea of engaging with social media followers across every step of the funnel is paramount as it optimizes audience attention and grabs the eyeballs of people beyond the list of current clients. Precisely funnel perspective involves a series of formative stages to navigate prospects through the customer journey (Rishi & Popli, 2021). It enables marketing teams to plan and measure efforts to attract, engage, and converge prospects through varied/explicit/derived content involving other marketing aids, like landing pages and advertisements (Narayanaswamy & Heiens, 2022).
- Choosing goals specific to the industry: The purpose of increasing enrollment and retention, creating a positive reputation, building a tag name, and consistency across content for different target social media platforms involves espousing the right industry and developing the route of networking accordingly. To list a few of the target industries: could be educational institutions, health care

industry, non-profit organizations, the food and beverage industry, or the travel and hospitality sector (Zhang et al., 2022).

- Choosing goals by studying peers: Digging deep into social media might feel overwhelming at many points. Therefore, keeping an eye on competitors and peers enables one to stay on the right track for achieving respective targets. The alignment with brands helps achieve goals such as increasing brand awareness, increasing community engagement, or as basic as increasing website clicks (Saura, 2021).

Implementation of goals in the right direction must be meticulously tracked through social media analytics. The analysis such as t deeper analysis, cross-network analysis, cross-profile analysis, and more the same regard to keeping a regular proctor on the execution of plans and dig to the grass-root level of nurturing and developing the required persistency for investing in a social media management platform (Das & Mondal, 2020).

2. Know Your Consumer (Target Audience)

Before processing plans, narrowing down the audience or, in other words, setting up a brand's 'target audience' is a pivotal methodology of effective social media marketing. It helps cultivate a better understanding of budgeting, i.e., where to invest money and resources to connect with the pre-decided group of people. The small enterprises have their pockets fixed, and to make the most out of their marketing budget, an outline of expenditure entailing all requirements plays an indispensable role (Campaign Monitor, 2022; Rishi & Kuthuru, 2021a). Furthermore, it resolves the problem of identifying the right segment/audience and catering to their expectations of creating relevant and engaging content. In most cases, the absence of a specific user group would lead to generalized content that fails to spark the required enthusiasm among readers and a lack of traction or engagement online (Andrade & Ruao, 2022). One of the primary methods for getting familiar with customers is to create an email list with a vision of having a direct line of communication with the audience. It would allow small-scale brands to integrate social media audience insights with insightful media like email to create a well-rounded marketing strategy and gain a comprehensive understanding of the audience's demand (Campaign Monitor, 2022, Rishi & Kuthuru, 2021b).

Brands can often segregate their audience by brainstorming about target demographics and whom they eye as their ideal customer. Keeping a check on all these minute details, one can get details such as age, gender, education, work, income levels, locality, interests, and aspirations. It will help offer content curated to their needs and make individuals feel more connected to the brand and its motto. Eventually, this would help build a network with which the people would resonate and continue to make purchases in the long run (Geho & Dangelo, 2012; Kumar & Sharma, 2022). Once a general categorization is made for the users of products, one can start looking for them online and design pages/content accordingly. Instead of relying on platforms like Facebook, which gatekeep followers, leveraging social media presence through email lists comes handier these days (Jagongo, & Kinyua, 2013; Campaign Monitor, 2022). For instance, the Facebook audience insights tool offers endless research opportunities, and most social media sites offer specific profiles for businesses that use the platform. In short, brands can look to interact with potential audiences on niche pages and cumulate their marketing through social media according to the target audience.

3. Choice of Platform

After defining our target audience, the next step revolves around choosing the apt platform accordingly to drive sales by attracting customers. The utilization of social media varies across brands and depends on their individual goals and expectations from the varied platforms (Brink, 2017, Sprout Social, 2022). For instance, some brands use social media to drive brand recognition and develop friendly relationships with potential buyers, whereas others might use social media for customer support. One of the explicit examples showcasing what exactly is mentioned above is Netflix. Netflix uses the Twitter handle @ Netflixhelps to address customer service issues. Their ideal goal is simple not only does it free up their phone lines, but it allows satisfied customers to promote their brand. The platform grew its business exponentially within a decade of being on the floor due to the ingenious approach carried out by its founders. Few brands were working in the same sphere. However, Airbnb stood out from all its competitors by acquiring primarily two user acquisition strategies to focus on target audiences: people who were interested in renting out their houses or who wanted to rent houses while traveling, serving it as an alternative to hotels (von Hoffen et al. 2018; Liu & Mattila, 2017).

Twitter, the unconventional platform for promoting any business, was the first platform that helped Airbnb gather a massive reach. The strategy they employed for promoting the same served as USP for social media services. The process was an amalgamation of constantly tweeting for six days a 'shot list' and asking users' input to shoot one of the shots in the list (Liu & Mattila, 2017). Users would follow the director's instructions for a given shot and then share it. It received more than 750 submissions, of which about 100 were used in the short film. Some of the selected ones were offered $100. It got broad exposure gaining the attention of actors like Adam Goldberg and Ashton Kutcher. Further, they expanded their social media scope across platforms like Instagram and YouTube, bringing in features such as influencer marketing which helped them gain attractive engagement rates (Schivinski et al., 2020).

The methodology of turning an unconventional tool to promote brand business acted as USP for their social media presence. It can leverage the sales to an extensive end to reach its goal of becoming a household brand name. For creators, it is crucial to understand what target audience they are aiming for and plan their social media campaigns, portals, and marketing strategies in line with the same. The seamless user experience can only be enriched. Understanding business and local engagement with customers to go at the root level of understanding their needs irrespective of the platform utilized for the process would keep the result of creating brand awareness (Rishi & Bandyopadhyay, 2017).

4. Competitor Analysis (Marketing Strategy of Competitors)

Social media has become an indispensable part of most businesses' interaction with customers. SMEs must monitor their social media presence and their competitors' social media sites to gain valuable insights. It would allow large companies to critically identify situations or moves by their competitors at a preliminary stage and henceforth enable them to fabricate their position to initiate counteractive marketing measures (He et al., 2016). This measure comes in handy, especially in situations critical for SMEs when their peers use a new promotional technique. The customer's express negative opinions about the products or services through social media, and the publicity stunt goes in the wrong direction (Grégoire et al., 2015). Some SMEs use social media to derive data that can dig deep into competitive intelligence and further study the correlation of rival brand promotion events on sales data and consumer sentiments concerning the product and service. There are many techniques available that can be used to conduct competitive social media analytics. A few of the tactics that can be employed involve using a combination of traditional statistical analysis, content analysis, text mining, and sentiment analysis techniques (He et al., 2016). The collected data can be used to appraise and scrutinize the social media content collected from competing organizations and get to know more about customers' experiences and sentiments.

Popular social media sites such as Twitter, Facebook, and YouTube offer application programming interfaces (APIs) for data tracking, the first step while processing competitive analytics. The role of APIs is to allow organizations to create custom applications for more convenient data collection and ease the job (He et al., 2015). Once statistical analytics is performed based on data received, an understanding of social media content's patterns, trends, issues, and problems can be easily outlined. Drawing these analytics by making comparisons based on customer comments and sentiments about a particular competing product, a company could draft marketing strategies that eye precision, stand agile, and respond to consumer demands, thereby increasing its sales potential (He et al., 2016). By joining threads from the same, companies can make more informed recommendations and decisions on proper interventions and services that focus entirely on improving the customer experience and help achieve better business outcomes for the immediate future (Lee, 2018).

5. Content Creation and Engagement

With billions of social media users around the globe, the competition to build a brand online stands stiff amongst the people browsing a brand's profile, scrolling all day through the pages of a brand's competitor's content too or that of other businesses belonging to the same industry and providing similar quality as well as prices for the products (Cheng & Shiu 2019, Rishi & Bandyopadhyay, 2017; Huotari et al., 2015).

In the same regard, it becomes vital for businesses to create engaging social media content that stands out and provides viewers with a reason to click that "Follow" button, building ever-lasting relationships and spreading quality feedback about the service amongst natives and others.

The first step for creating engaging content on social media involves performing intense market research as content appreciation and liking depend only on the audience. Research involves considering the content of lead competitors and further understanding how to optimize resources and uniquely promote products by taking advantage of the features offered by the platform chosen by the business (Hardey, 2011).

Emerging platforms offer a new avenue and broad horizon to reach the target audience. For instance, they create short videos on YouTube to share the latest details about a product launch or conduct a giveaway to attract buyers (Cheng & Shiu 2019). Another such tactic could be re-posting content or encouraging current customers and promoters to generate organic content and requesting them to use hashtags to share their own experiences and pictures with the products (Bigley & Leonhardt, 2018).

Leveraging trends by staying updated with social media trends and organizing a schedule for posts to ensure that content is shared as planned can be quickly done using a social media management solution (Karimi & Naghibi, 2015). These tools grant captions, prepare pictures and videos, and schedule posts in advance, providing an edge by automatically sharing content on schedule and monitoring all post interactions and engagement. As a rule of thumb, brands should post quality content on social media. The beginning could be as simple as experimenting with fewer posts while considering factors such as the time of day of posting on social media and henceforth determining what time provides the highest level of engagement.

6. Brand - Consumer Synergy

A synergistic social media marketing strategy approach means 'using multiple marketing channels simultaneously and in harmony. It could be an amalgamation of social media platforms, websites, blog pages, etc (Dalkir, 2011, Brink, 2017).
Here are a few examples of how it can be carried forward and the way ahead:

- A short, seconds video on Facebook/YouTube/Instagram story describing the products of SME
- An informative blog with attractive captions and the use of relevant keywords to improve Search Engine Optimization.
- Metric employment such as Google AdWords displays ads that grab users' attention beyond boundaries.

Synergence of elements helps SMEs increase their brand awareness and the credibility of products, expand their reach following the route of multi-channel marketing, generate more leads, and retain older clients effectively (Qalati et al., 2021; Qalati et al., 2022).

7. Metrics and Analytics

Metrics act as an essential weapon to give a sneak peek of whether a strategy is a success over time. It provides an overall view of social media performance. Several metrics can be added to the current list relevant to businesses and the industry. Some of the most important metrics include engagement, impressions and reach, the share of voice, referrals, conversions, and response rate and time (Pérez-González et al., 2017).Some of the critical metrics include:

a. Engagement

Likes, comments, shares, and clicks: This showcases how actively a brand is involved with its content and caters to audience needs, defining how effective the planned brand campaigns are. A check on the engaged consumers can be sensed through interactions with brands through tools such as "likes," comments, and social sharing (Schivinsk et al., 2020).

b. Awareness

- Impressions The number of times a post shows up in someone's timeline
- Reach is usually defined as a summation of follower count plus accounts that shared the post's follower counts).

A post with a firm impression count but a low engagement number likely implies that the uploaded post failed to grab the attention of audiences and further act after seeing it in their feed. A post with a high reach count and high engagement rate will likely mean that the content went viral via Retweets and Shares (Tsimonis & Dimitriadis, 2014 & Vieira et al., 2022).

c. Share of Voice

It would likely give an overall view from the perspective of competitors as it measures information like how many people are talking about the brand online compared to competitors (Emerson et al., 2012; Hong & Kim, 2021).

d. Referrals and Conversions

It is primarily applicable for companies with websites or e-commerce platforms, social referral traffic, and conversions that connect to sales and marketing goals, ultimately leading to significant business goals. It could be done using a website traffic analytics program like Google Analytics or a built-in one like Shopify. Hand in hand with referrals and conversions is the click-through rate (CTR) in ads and posts. CTRs compare the number of times someone clicks on content to the number of impressions received (Kim, 2021).

Quoting the example of Uniqlo, among fiery competitors like ZARA (Inditex), H&M, Gap, and Forever21, Uniqlo has successfully established its brand name across global platforms. It is peculiarly known for quality, affordability, and fashionable associations, henceforth garnering support from a broad audience. It has established itself at an astounding pace due to the traffic generated via online buzz utilizing Pinterest (Hall & Jay, 2021). It is ubiquitous for brands to post pictures and eye-grabbing content about their brands on Pinterest and henceforth, with the vision to stand out from the crowd. Uniqlo intended to hijack the streams of pinners logged in at a particular time. They successfully created the buzz they aimed for as users scrolling through the pages of Pinterest, as a standard practice, experienced an eye-widening experience by having a glimpse of Uniqlo's T-shirts turning and flipping with distinguished colors. The unique proposition helped them gain a massive reach of about 55 million impressions and approximately more than 6,000 mentions on Twitter. The effective utilization of concept creation, ideation, designs, and customer-friendly prizes served as USP for the brand through the robust application of social media.

The brand optimizes the utility of social media to interact with the youth audience. It organizes small-scale events to keep the customers updated with recent products they launched. One such example includes the brand in collaboration with agency Dentsu establishing a special in-store event published across various digital channels to cater to their target audience, which revolves around the youth segment. The channel they used for pulling the digital event includes Facebook and Twitter. They used an inspiring marketing strategy announcing that they could "turn anyone into a model" and invited them to attend an event to prove it (Hall & Jay, 2021; Zhang et al., 2021).The social media messages encouraged customers to visit Shopping Avenue for an ongoing event running in one of the Uniqlo stores. The event allowed consumers to choose a color and strike poses for the instore camera, choose their favorite picture, and share it on social media- looking like a real model for a fashion brand. As an incentive, each consumer that participated received a Uniqlo shopping voucher. The event was a massive success in just 12 days. The brand achieved its KPI goal of 1000 people sharing their poses online, generating thousands of impressions on social media.

From the example above, one of the primary learnings showcases that a promising brand, constant commitment to innovation, adaptability, and a suitable social media model for the brand can fetch new customers most economically. The outstanding quality, performance, pricing, a robust social media buzz creation approach might exceed customers' expectations at any point and helps in establishing a position.

MANAGERIAL TOOLKIT FOR SOCIAL MEDIA INTEGRATION

Managerial toolkits help monitor and manage the social media networks of the organizations. It helps in the growth of the business by letting SMEs know the strengths and weaknesses of their strategy and the areas where they can find opportunities to grow. For a successful social media strategy, SMEs can use the following tool to their advantage (Rishi, & Kuthuru, 2021a, Vieira et al., 2022).

- Brand Guidelines: Brands have a personality that defines them and allows customers to relate to them. The customer is the key to creating a memorable brand, and the social media team may help with this by creating a set of brand rules. A mission statement, user personas, tone of voice, color schemes, the brand story, and a description of the brand personality are all included in brand guidelines. This type of formal report helps the team curate social media material consistent with the brand's identity and objectives (Hamzah et al., 2021).
- Social Media Calendar: Planning is essential for building a unique social media strategy. Social media calendars are an easy-to-use tool for organizing and managing social media content and ensuring consistency in communication by aligning marketing strategies with broader goals. A single document that helps manage all material would make the social media team's job more manageable (Bakri, 2017; Rishi & Mohammed, 2022).

FUTURE RESEARCH DIRECTIONS

Undertaking a comprehensive outlook of the role of adoption of social media on SMEs can be described in layman's terms as a tool that targets customers and is oriented according to their perspectives, respecting their sentiments for a product. The application of social media varies across platforms and has been embraced by SMEs and explored across many services that primarily promote products. It becomes a pertinent decision for SMEs to use social media wisely and effectively to achieve their marketing objectives.

Though the medium has a lot to offer, understanding the competition across companies, one cannot deny that it thoroughly relies on the small and medium-sized businesses and the firm's expertise and evaluation of social media to outshine and create their place amongst the humongous crowd. Social Media Marketing for SMEs necessitates knowledge and much effort, and it comes with its own set of problems and hazards to overcome before attaining success. Social media marketing is not always simple or cost-effective. Depending on the sort of firm, its size, age, and management style, extra work may be required in various areas. To begin, SMEs must devote human and time resources to managing their social media profiles. Employees involved in Social Media activities should be highly skilled and trained to effectively respond to every question and complaint that customers have daily and manage and control any potential negative comments before these are seen by hundreds or thousands of people.

In order to stay on the radar of consumers, social media staff must be very active and produce fresh content regularly, depending on the type of SMEs. It is vital because it allows SMEs to have a constant relationship with their customers. One of the most significant concerns for SMEs adopting social media marketing is reputational damage due to inefficient use of their social media platforms. Overuse of advertising, commercial presentation of products and services, and overzealous sales efforts are frequently seen negatively by audiences, who may become irritated and unfollow the business on social media.

Privacy, security, intellectual property, employment practices, and other legal risks are all possible with social media. Security risks occur when malware, viruses, or spyware is downloaded through Social Media sites; security concerns are a major negative factor because SMEs are afraid of financial risks from viruses and spyware.Before engaging in social media activities, social media personnel must comprehend information technology law. Security and operational risks are also high and may act as a deterrent to SMEs adopting Social Media Marketing.

CONCLUSION

Overall, we can understand that social media adoption is beneficial to SMEs and their business performances which can be studied in detail based on metrics. Social Media Marketing helps amplify word-of-mouth marketing, conducting market research, idea generation, visualizing promotional tactics of competitors, new product development, customer service, public relations, employee communications, and reputation management, among many other utilities. Social media can increase product and brand awareness, web traffic, and customer loyalty, improve a company's Search Engine Optimization, draft a tint of creativity, build future community, and network through relationships, achieving the foremost marketing objective for any brand. It would enable a brand to study in a more sophisticated manner what strategy works in favor of the company and their present customers' choice of promotional activities. Social media is primarily suitable to aid SMEs' budgeting and financial resources, understanding that their pockets are limited. The implication of the utility of social media on organizations is a significant growth predictor for sales, revenues, and feedback for a brand.

The utility of social media for SMEs leads to a clear display of promotion of brand awareness, brand recognition, a direct route of communication with audiences at affordable costs and being apprehensive of the notion that SMEs work at a circumscribed budget. It is predominantly a robust solution to enhance customer relationship management and accelerate sales promotion to a larger audience with an eye on building the brand provided we develop a holistic approach to visualize and simplify the technology for all. The only constraint which holds significance while framing the social media marketing framework for SMEs is to perfectly acknowledge the potential of the medium in the right direction according to the nature of the business model and the industry to which it belongs.

REFERENCES

Ainin, S., Parveen, F., Moghavvemi, S., Jaafar, N. I., & Mohd Shuib, N. L. (2015). Factors influencing the use of social media by SMEs and its performance outcomes. *Industrial Management & Data Systems*, *115*(3), 570–588. doi:10.1108/IMDS-07-2014-0205

Akar, E., & Topçu, B. (2011). An examination of the factors influencing consumers' attitudes toward social media marketing. *Journal of Internet Commerce*, *10*(1), 35–67. doi:10.1080/15332861.2011.558456

Andrade, J. G., & Ruao, T. (2022). *Navigating Digital Communication and Challenges for Organizations*. IGI Global. doi:10.4018/978-1-7998-9790-3

Atanassova, I., & Clark, L. (2015). Social media practices in SME marketing activities: A theoretical framework and research agenda. *Journal of Customer Behaviour, 14*(2), 163–183. doi:10.1362/14753 9215X14373846805824

Bakri, A. A. A. (2017). The impact of social media adoption on competitive advantage in the small and medium enterprises. *International Journal of Business Innovation and Research, 13*(2), 255–269. doi:10.1504/IJBIR.2017.083542

Barnhart, B. (2021). *Building Your Social Media Marketing Strategy for 2022.* Retrieved July 22, 2022, from https://sproutsocial.com/insights/social-media-marketing-strategy/

Basri, W. S., & Siam, M. R. (2017). Maximizing the social media potential for small businesses and startups: A conceptual study. *International Journal of Economic Perspectives, 11*(2), 241–245.

Batista, J. M., Barros, L. S., Peixoto, F. V., & Botelho, D. (2022). Sarcastic or Assertive: How Should Brands Reply to Consumers' Uncivil Comments on Social Media in the Context of Brand Activism? *Journal of Interactive Marketing, 57*(1), 141–158. doi:10.1177/10949968221075817

Bigley, I. P., & Leonhardt, J. M. (2018). Extremity bias in user-generated content creation and consumption in social media. *Journal of Interactive Advertising, 18*(2), 125–135. doi:10.1080/15252019.2018.1491813

Bocconcelli, R., Cioppi, M., & Pagano, A. (2017). Social media as a resource in SMEs' sales process. *Journal of Business and Industrial Marketing, 32*(5), 693–709. doi:10.1108/JBIM-11-2014-0244

Boyd, D. M., & Ellison, N. B. (2007). Social Network Sites: Definition, History, and Scholarship. *Journal of Computer-Mediated Communication, 13*(1), 210–230. doi:10.1111/j.1083-6101.2007.00393.x

Brink, T. (2017). B2B SME management of antecedents to the application of social media. *Industrial Marketing Management, 64*, 57–65. doi:10.1016/j.indmarman.2017.02.007

Cao, D., Maureen, M., Donna, W., & Senmao, X. (2021). Understanding consumers' social media engagement behaviour: An examination of the moderation effect of social media context. *Journal of Business Research, 122*, 835–846. doi:10.1016/j.jbusres.2020.06.025

Chen, Y. S., & Lin, H. H. L. (2021). Effect of Social Media Marketing Strategies on Competitive Advantage Among the SMEs in China. *Journal of Marketing Communications, 4*(1), 14–23.

Cheng, C. C., & Shiu, E. C. (2019). How to enhance SMEs customer involvement using social media: The role of Social CRM. *International Small Business Journal, 37*(1), 22–42. doi:10.1177/0266242618774831

Dalkir, K. (2011). Measuring the impact of social media: Connection, communication and collaboration. In *Social knowledge: using social media to know what you know* (pp. 24–36). IGI Global.

Das, S., & Mondal, S. R. (2020). *Innovations in Digital Branding and Content Marketing.* IGI Global.

Devereux, E., Grimmer, L., & Grimmer, M. (2020). Consumer engagement on social media: Evidence from small retailers. *Journal of Consumer Behaviour, 19*(2), 151–159. doi:10.1002/cb.1800

Dutot, V., & Bergeron, F. (2016). From strategic orientation to social media orientation: Improving SMEs' performance on social media. *Journal of Small Business and Enterprise Development, 23*(4), 1165–1190. doi:10.1108/JSBED-11-2015-0160

Dwivedi, Y. K., Ismagilova, E., Hughes, D. L., Carlson, J., Filieri, R., Jacobson, J., Jain, V., Karjaluoto, H., Kefi, H., Krishen, A. S., Kumar, V., Rahman, M. M., Raman, R., Rauschnabel, P. A., Rowley, J., Salo, J., Tran, G. A., & Wang, Y. (2020). Setting the future of digital and social media marketing research: Perspectives and research propositions. *International Journal of Information Management, 102168.* Advance online publication. doi:10.1016/j.ijinfomgt.2020.102168

Economist. (2009). *Small business, big problem.* Retrieved July 20, 2022, from https://www.economist.com/leaders/2009/12/10/small-business-big-problem

Effing, R., & Spil, T. A. (2016). The social strategy cone: Towards a framework for evaluating social media strategies. *International Journal of Information Management, 36*(1), 1–8. doi:10.1016/j.ijinfomgt.2015.07.009

Emerson, T., Ghosh, R., & Smith, E. (2012). Case study: Using the social share of voice to predict events that are about to happen. *Practical text mining and statistical analysis for non-structured text data applications,* 127-131.

Epede, M. B., & Wang, D. (2022). Global value chain linkages: An integrative review of the opportunities and challenges for SMEs in developing countries. *International Business Review, 31*(5), 101993. doi:10.1016/j.ibusrev.2022.101993

Erkan, I., & Evans, C. (2016). The influence of eWOM in social media on consumers' purchase intentions: An extended approach to information adoption. *Computers in Human Behavior, 61*, 47–55. doi:10.1016/j.chb.2016.03.003

Fang, G. G., Qalati, S. A., Ostic, D., Shah, S. M. M., & Mirani, M. A. (2021). Effects of entrepreneurial orientation, social media, and innovation capabilities on SME performance in emerging countries: A mediated–moderated model. *Technology Analysis and Strategic Management,* 1–13.

Geho, P. R., & Dangelo, J. (2012). The evolution of social media as a marketing tool for entrepreneurs. *The Entrepreneurial Executive, 17*, 61.

Georgescu, M., & Popescul, D. (2015). Social Media–the new paradigm of collaboration and communication for the business environment. *Procedia Economics and Finance, 20*, 277–282. doi:10.1016/S2212-5671(15)00075-1

Grégoire, Y., Salle, A., & Tripp, T. M. (2015). Managing social media crises with your customers: The good, the bad, and the ugly. *Business Horizons, 58*(2), 173–182. doi:10.1016/j.bushor.2014.11.001

Hall, C., & Jay, P. (2022, June 9). *Unpacking Uniqlo's India Strategy.* The Business of Fashion.

Hamzah, Z. L., Wahab, H. A., & Waqas, M. (2021). Unveiling drivers and brand relationship implications of consumer engagement with social media brand posts. *Journal of Research in Interactive Marketing, 15*(2), 336–358. doi:10.1108/JRIM-05-2020-0113

Hardey, M. (2011). Generation C: Content, creation, connections and choice. *International Journal of Market Research, 53*(6), 749–770. doi:10.2501/IJMR-53-6-749-770

He, W., Tian, X., Chen, Y., & Chong, D. (2016). Actionable social media competitive analytics for understanding customer experiences. *Journal of Computer Information Systems, 56*(2), 145–155. doi:10.1080/08874417.2016.1117377

He, W., Wu, H., Yan, G., Akula, V., & Shen, J. (2015). A novel social media competitive analytics framework with sentiment benchmarks. *Information & Management, 52*(7), 801–812. doi:10.1016/j.im.2015.04.006

Hong, H., & Kim, Y. (2021). What makes people engage in civic activism on social media? *Online Information Review, 45*(3), 562–576. doi:10.1108/OIR-03-2020-0105

Huotari, L., Ulkuniemi, P., Saraniemi, S., & Mäläskä, M. (2015). Analysis of content creation in social media by B2B companies. *Journal of Business and Industrial Marketing, 30*(6), 761–770. doi:10.1108/JBIM-05-2013-0118

Jagongo, A., & Kinyua, C. (2013). The social media and entrepreneurship growth. *International Journal of Humanities and Social Science, 3*(10), 213–227.

Karimi, S., & Naghibi, H. S. (2015). Social media marketing (SMM) strategies for small to medium enterprises (SMEs). *International Journal of Information, Business and Management, 7*(4), 86.

Kim, S. (2021). Mapping social media analytics for small business: A case study of business analytics. International Journal of Fashion Design. *Technology and Education, 14*(2), 218–231.

Kumar, A., & Ayedee, N. (2018). Social media tools for business growth of SMEs. *Journal of Management, 5*(3), 137–142.

Kumar, B., & Sharma, A. (2022). Examining the research on social media in business-to-business marketing with a focus on sales and the selling process. *Industrial Marketing Management, 102*, 122–140. doi:10.1016/j.indmarman.2022.01.008

Lacho, K. J., & Marinello, C. (2010). How small business owners can use social networking to promote their business. *The Entrepreneurial Executive, 15*, 127.

Lee, I. (2018). Social media analytics for enterprises: Typology, methods, and processes. *Business Horizons, 61*(2), 199–210. doi:10.1016/j.bushor.2017.11.002

Liu, S. Q., & Mattila, A. S. (2017). Airbnb: Online targeted advertising, sense of power, and consumer decisions. *International Journal of Hospitality Management, 60*, 33–41. doi:10.1016/j.ijhm.2016.09.012

Marolt, M., Zimmermann, H. D., & Pucihar, A. (2018). Exploratory study of social CRM use in SMEs. *The Engineering Economist, 29*(4), 468–477.

McCann, M., & Barlow, A. (2015). Use and measurement of social media for SMEs. *Journal of Small Business and Enterprise Development, 22*(2), 273–287. doi:10.1108/JSBED-08-2012-0096

Meske, C., & Stieglitz, S. (2013, June). Adoption and use of social media in small and medium-sized enterprises. In *Working conference on practice-driven research on enterprise transformation* (pp. 61-75). Springer.

Mills, A. J., & Plangger, K. (2015). Social media strategy for online service brands. *Service Industries Journal, 35*(10), 521–536. doi:10.1080/02642069.2015.1043277

Ming, T., & Lam, E. (2012). The Creativity of Social Media On Smes Brand Building. *ICSB World Conference Proceeding, 2*(1), 1.

Monitor, C. (2022). *Which Social Media Platform is Best for Marketing a Business.* Retrieved July 20, 2022, from https://www.campaignmonitor.com/resources/knowledge-base/which-social-media-platform-is-best-for-marketing-a-business/

Narayanaswamy, R., & Heiens, R. A. (2022). Finding the optimal social media marketing mix to drive customer attraction and sales performance: An exploratory study. *International Journal of Electronic Marketing and Retailing, 13*(1), 65–82. doi:10.1504/IJEMR.2022.119248

Ngammoh, N., Atthaphon, M., Sujinda, P., & Achariya, I. (2021). Enabling social media as a strategic capability for SMEs through organizational ambidexterity. *Journal of Small Business and Entrepreneurship*, 1–21. doi:10.1080/08276331.2021.1980682

Nurfarida, I. N., & Sudarmiatin, S. (2021). Use of social media marketing in SMEs: Driving factors and impacts. *Management and Entrepreneurship: Trends of Development, 2*(16), 70–81. doi:10.26661/2522-1566/2021-1/16-06

Odoom, R., Anning-Dorson, T., & Acheampong, G. (2017). Antecedents of social media usage and performance benefits in small- and medium-sized enterprises (SMEs). *Journal of Enterprise Information Management, 30*(3), 383–399. doi:10.1108/JEIM-04-2016-0088

Pérez-González, D., Trigueros-Preciado, S., & Popa, S. (2017). Social media technologies' use for the competitive information and knowledge sharing, and its effects on industrial SMEs' innovation. *Information Systems Management, 34*(3), 291–301. doi:10.1080/10580530.2017.1330007

Pervin, M. T., & Sarker, B. K. (2021). Benefits and challenges in adopting social media for SMEs: A case from Bangladesh. *Journal of Sustainable Tourism and Entrepreneurship, 2*(3), 171–185. doi:10.35912/joste.v2i3.783

Pfister, P., & Lehmann, C. (2021). Returns on digitisation in SMEs—A systematic literature review. *Journal of Small Business and Entrepreneurship*, 1–25. doi:10.1080/08276331.2021.1980680

Popli, Rishi, & Mathew. (2021). *Contemporary Marketing Regaining Ground: Perspectives from Research & Practice.* IMTG Report.

Popli, S., & Rishi, B. (2021). Customer Experience Management – The Road Ahead. In Crafting Customer Experience Strategy. Emerald Publishing Limited. doi:10.1108/978-1-83909-710-220211011

Qalati, S., Li, W., Ahmed, N., Ali Mirani, M., & Khan, A. (2020). Examining the factors affecting SME performance: The mediating role of social media adoption. *Sustainability, 13*(1), 75. doi:10.3390u13010075

Qalati, S. A., Ostic, D., Shuibin, G., & Mingyue, F. (2022). A mediated–moderated model for social media adoption and small and medium-sized enterprise performance in emerging countries. *Managerial and Decision Economics*, *43*(3), 846–861. doi:10.1002/mde.3422

Qalati, S. A., Yuan, L. W., Khan, M. A. S., & Anwar, F. (2021). A mediated model on the adoption of social media and SMEs' performance in developing countries. *Technology in Society*, *64*, 101513. doi:10.1016/j.techsoc.2020.101513

Richter, A., & Riemer, K. (2013). *The contextual nature of enterprise social networking: A multi-case study comparison*. ECIS.

Rishi, B., & Bandyopadhyay, S. (Eds.). (2017). *Contemporary issues in social media marketing*. Routledge. doi:10.4324/9781315563312

Rishi, B., & Kuthuru, N. R. (2021a). A Review for Managerial Guidelines for Social Media Integration of IMC in Digital Era. In Digital Entertainment (pp. 187-212). Palgrave Macmillan. doi:10.1007/978-981-15-9724-4_10

Rishi, B., & Kuthuru, N. R. (2021b). Leveraging Social Media to Create Socially Responsible Consumers. In *Social and Sustainability Marketing* (pp. 415–432). Productivity Press. doi:10.4324/9781003188186-15

Rishi, B., & Mohammed, J. (n.d.). Design, Execute, and Manage Promotions: Study on Social Media Platforms. In Promotional Practices and Perspectives from Emerging Markets (pp. 226-245). Routledge India.

Rishi, B., & Popli, S. (2021). Getting Into the Customers, Shoes: Customer Journey Management. In Crafting Customer Experience Strategy. Emerald Publishing Limited. doi:10.1108/978-1-83909-710-220211002

Roy, A., & Dionne, C. (2015). How SMEs evaluate their performance in reaching and attracting customers with social media. In *ECSM2015-Proceedings of the 2nd European Conference on Social Media* (390-397). Academic Press.

Rugova, B., & Prenaj, B. (2016). Social media as marketing tool for SMEs: Opportunities and challenges. *Academic Journal of Business*, *2*(3), 85–97.

Saura, J. R. (2021). *Advanced Digital Marketing Strategies in a Data Driven Era*. IGI Global. doi:10.4018/978-1-7998-8003-5

Savlovschi, L. I., & Robu, N. R. (2011). The role of SMEs in modern economy. *Economia. Seria Management*, *14*(1), 277–281.

Schivinski, B., Langaro, D., Fernandes, T., & Guzmán, F. (2020). Social media brand engagement in the context of collaborative consumption: The case of AIRBNB. *Journal of Brand Management*, *27*(6), 645–661. doi:10.105741262-020-00207-5

Sedalo, G., Boateng, H., & Kosiba, J. P. (2022). Exploring social media affordance in relationship marketing practices in SMEs. *Digital Business*, *2*(1), 100017. doi:10.1016/j.digbus.2021.100017

Tajvidi, R., & Karami, A. (2021). The effect of social media on firm performance. *Computers in Human Behavior, 115*, 105174. doi:10.1016/j.chb.2017.09.026

Tiwasing, P. (2021). Social media business networks and SME performance: A rural-urban comparative analysis. *Growth and Change, 52*(3), 1892–1913. doi:10.1111/grow.12501

Tsimonis, G., & Dimitriadis, S. (2014). Brand strategies in social media. *Marketing Intelligence & Planning, 32*(3), 328–344. doi:10.1108/MIP-04-2013-0056

Vieira, V. A., Severo de Almeida, M. I., Gabler, C. B., Limongi, R., Costa, M., & Pires da Costa, M. (2022). Optimising digital marketing and social media strategy: From push to pull to performance. *Journal of Marketing Management, 38*(7-8), 709–739. doi:10.1080/0267257X.2021.1996444

von Hoffen, M., Hagge, M., Betzing, J. H., & Chasin, F. (2018). Leveraging social media to gain insights into service delivery: A study on Airbnb. *Information Systems and e-Business Management, 16*(2), 247–269. doi:10.100710257-017-0358-7

Wang, W. Y., Pauleen, D. J., & Zhang, T. (2016). How social media applications affect B2B communication and improve business performance in SMEs. *Industrial Marketing Management, 54*, 4–14. doi:10.1016/j.indmarman.2015.12.004

World Bank. (2022). *Small and Medium Enterprises (SMEs) Finance*. Retrieved July 20, 2022, from https://www.worldbank.org/en/topic/smefinance

Zhang, H., Zang, Z., Zhu, H., Uddin, M. I., & Amin, M. A. (2022). Big data-assisted social media analytics for business model for business decision making system competitive analysis. *Information Processing & Management, 59*(1), 102762. doi:10.1016/j.ipm.2021.102762

KEY TERMS AND DEFINITIONS

Brand Synergy: The perfect branding is based on a clear understanding of what a company does, what it stands for, and who its customers are. This concept should be reproduced throughout all sales channels, and the business should focus on building stronger brand loyalty, more trust, and, as a result, increased sales.

Industrialization: Industrialization is the gradual transition of an economic system from primitive to more complex production processes. It is a systematic reform aimed at reshaping a country's productive forces.

Microblogging: A form of web service which allows users to post short messages or videos primarily on the mobile web for the audience to interact with them more frequently and with great ease like Twitter.

Social Media Integration: Involving the utility of social media as a part of employed marketing strategy for a brand and in turn extending its reach to its target audience and customers.

Social Media Marketing: Social media marketing, often known as use of social media to market the brands, is the promotion of brands through the use of the social media platforms to interact with potential clients.

Target Audience: A target audience is a group of people who share specific characteristics and behaviors. User personas are frequently created by firms based on what they know about their target audience. These personalities govern their marketing campaign decisions.

Text Mining: To classify and segregate the unstructured text passages into literal meaning giving quality outputs such as summary or in-depth analysis with the help of software tools.

Web 2.0: Web 2.0 defines the current state of the internet, which contains more user-generated content and end-user usability than its previous form.

Website Traffic: It refers to the number of users who visit a website determining the potential, loyal and regular customers a brand has on average.

Chapter 2
From Real-Time Marketing to Corporate Social Responsibility:
The Impact of Social Media Engagement on #womensday Posts by Companies

Cássia Liandra Carvalho
University of Aveiro, Portugal

Belem Barbosa
(iD) https://orcid.org/0000-0002-4057-360X
University of Porto, Portugal

Claudia Amaral Santos
(iD) https://orcid.org/0000-0003-2630-294X
University of Aveiro, Portugal

ABSTRACT

Social media strategies are commonly adopted by large and SMEs due to the expected impacts on customer engagement, branding, sales, and overall company performance. One particularly interesting strategy conducted on social media is real-time marketing (RTM) that enables the company to get involved in the discussion of trending topics. The main aim of this chapter is to analyze RTM impacts on user engagement in the case of socially relevant topics, particularly Women's Day. It provides an analysis of publications by the 25 most valuable brands in Brazil (comprising both large companies and SME) and explores the interconnections between RTM publications and CSR policies. One main conclusion is that companies should approach socially relevant dates in accordance with their CSR policies, and that successful RTM initiatives can comprise alternative approaches: promotional actions, tributes, and CSR. The findings of this chapter are particularly relevant for SMEs, considering the democratic nature of RTM and overall social media strategies.

DOI: 10.4018/978-1-6684-5770-2.ch002

INTRODUCTION

Social media are in their essence spaces of dialogue and interaction, where people engage in conversations with their peers, share opinions and discuss topics of interest. Aligned with the bidirectional nature of the dialogue, the success of social media marketing strategies is dependent on the ability to generate interaction, and being part of the ongoing conversations is of utmost importance for brands and companies' integration on the different social media such as Facebook, Instagram, Twitter, and YouTube, to name but a few.

One popular tactic of social media marketing is to associate brand messages to trending topics and events. In this regard, real time marketing (RTM), defined as the publication of messages as a reaction to ongoing trending topics and events (Busch, 2016; Scott, 2011), is a strategy aligned with the immediacy of the digital world we live in. The main focus of this communication model is engagement with the public and generating conversations (Willemsen et al., 2018). RTM focuses on taking advantage of trends in social media discussions to generate user engagement, and ultimately generate post interaction and increase brand messages' reach.

Obviously, trending topics and events can have very diverse nature, from cultural and sports achievements, national dates, entertainment gaffs, and social relevant issues. One of such examples is International Women's Day celebrated on March 8. In recent years, brands have embraced this date as an opportunity to show their alignment with female empowerment, gender equity and women's causes. This activity has been increasingly noticed in the market and brands are linked to narratives and speeches that are trends in social networks. The annual celebration of women's day is often related to the brands' involvement with feminist values and with corporate social responsibility (CSR) practices, while simultaneously associating it with a social relevant issue, namely considering the Sustainable Development Goals proposed by the United Nations (i.e., Goal 5 – gender equality).

Indeed, gender issues have proliferated along with brands' CSR. CSR comprises actions aimed at sustainability, responsibility and ethical performance (Cho et al., 2017), and organizations understand that CSR programs have a significant impact on women's lives (Ozkazanc-Pan, 2018) and companies use their social networks to also publish their actions and initiatives in favor of women's causes, equity and even deeper issues such as femicide and violence against women (Grosser & Moon, 2019).

Despite the relevance of RTM for practitioners and the fact that RTM actions are often related to social-relevant topics, the literature on RTM is still very scarce. For instance, Web of Science database only lists one journal article on the topic by Pereira et al. (2022). As for the wide database of Google Scholar, a total of 85 articles are listed as in April 2022. Clearly, this is an emerging research topic, still lacking comprehensive studies. One of the gaps in the literature regards the possible synergies with the values and social-relevant practices embraced by the company whenever the topic connected to RTM is associated with a socially-relevant issue.

Thus, the main objective of this chapter is to contribute to the explanation of the engagement of brand publications on social networks on women's day, exploring how it is influenced by the brand's involvement with feminist values and CSR practices. To better understand how brands have positioned themselves on social networks during Women's Day, a study was carried out with 25 most valuable brands in Brazil (Sutto, 2021). The research explored the posts of each of the brands on Instagram on Women's Day and compared the CSR actions in favor of women that each company publishes on its platforms. The analysis was guided by the literature on RTM and the main aspects associated with CSR practices, which are presented in the next section.

BACKGROUND

Real-Time Strategic Marketing as a Competitive Advantage

Social media have brought a new rhythm to the market (Gruber et al., 2015; Killian & McManus, 2015). Facts and events quickly spread amidst social media platforms and among user profiles with shares and likes. Brands noticed this new consumption movement (Chu et al., 2016) and understood that they should add strategies aligned with the digital world (Yasmin et al., 2015). In addition, consumer behavior has also changed due to the influence of social networks (Akar & Dalgic, 2018; Gironda & Korgaonkar, 2014). The consumer has become more demanding and seeks immediacy with promotions and offers. According to the Salesforce Research (2020) report, 80% of consumers expect companies to respond and interact with them in real time. The survey also shows that 67% of consumers expect an email response within an hour, and 15% actually expect an immediate response. This new scenario spurred/propelled the marketing areas to add "real-time" actions to their brand and product plans.

RTM refers to associating messages from timely events in the dissemination of products and brands (Busch, 2016; Scott, 2011), that is, marketing actions adapt according to what is happening at the current moment. Essentially, RTM focuses on current events, trends or even conversations with consumers (Willemsen et al., 2018). Marketing planning also aims at customer satisfaction (Zajas; & Zotz, 1995) and focuses on following market trends. This is because social networks have allowed companies and brands to establish agile and secure communication channels with their customers, creating important relationship bonds. RTM seeks to bring customers and companies closer together (McKenna, 1995) and also requires brands and companies to actively engage in listening to their consumers to discover customer data and identify competitor actions or even new consumer trends (Reece, 2010; Scott, 2011).

The Gartner report (Blum & Omale, 2019) indicates that most RTM use cases focus on demand generation, advertising, promotion, sales and services. The survey also reports that brands are combining behavioral analytics and marketing automation to deliver RTM efforts based on specific customer behaviors. RTM can be an effective model because it understands your consumer behavior (Kallier Tar & A Wiid, 2021) and consequently helps companies stay ahead of the competition. When a company is the first to react to news and events, it can naturally gain a competitive advantage over its competitors. RTM has been widely used as it allows companies to react quickly to the latest news and events. By being able to respond quickly, companies can take advantage of the latest trends and capitalize on opportunities as they arise. According to the article published by Gesenhues (2020), RTM is based on 4 pillars: detection, data, decision and delivery. Detect what the customer wants to know or even trends that are circulating on the internet and then combine this information with data that stimulate feelings or sensations. With these two actions taken, it is easy to decide which action to deliver to the customer, whether it's a personalized offer or a post about specific content.
The RTM strategy is composed of 5 main factors:

- **Benefit for the Target Audience**: you need to understand your target audience and what their needs are. Not all topics will catch the attention of consumers. It is necessary to listen and understand what consumers are looking for, and understand how your brand can fit into consumer interests. According to (Kallier, 2017), the ideal is to take advantage of the moment when the user is active and engage him in the best possible way, presenting benefits that he sees as important.

- **Relevance**: it is necessary to be very attentive to situations, trends and news to understand which ones can be multiplied in brand communication. According to Chu et al. (2016), content relevance responds to the needs of the audience. To provide a connection between brand and consumers, it is necessary that the publicized action impacts the consumer and makes sense to their consumption behavior.

- **Agility**: Scott (2011) reinforces the importance of agility in the RTM processes. The first step of the strategy is to closely monitor the conversations, understanding the behavior of users. The speech needs to be fast and active and this is because the audience seeks narratives that communicate at the moment she is talking about the topic.

- **Dialogue**: it is necessary to enable conversation between brand and audience. Kwon & Sung (2011) state that interaction between brand and consumer is essential because it generates positive results in terms of engagement with the target audience. The audiences seek to engage with brands that provide an open conversation and appreciate their suggestions, comments and opinions.

- **Mindset**: Scott (2011) also highlights that there are a number of tools available to bring the consumer closer to the company and generate real-time marketing. But, at the same time, the tools won't make sense if the company doesn't apply an agile and connected mindset to the audience's culture. The author also emphasizes that no matter which tool, the important thing is to follow the profile of this new consumer, which is much more immediate.

A summary of the main contributions in the literature regarding RTM objectives and the expected impacts for the company is presented in Table 1. The popularity of RTM could be explained by its ability to approach several of the most relevant social media marketing objectives, particularly user engagement. Additionally, the literature suggests that RTM can be also associated with brand Involvement and even sales.

Table 1. Real time marketing objectives and outcomes

Factors	Objectives	Outcomes	Authors
Benefit for the target audience	Engagement Sales	"The current research found that RTM campaigns, which offered personalized marketing offerings at the time of purchase and discount vouchers based on what the customer purchased most frequently at the time of purchase and discount vouchers received immediately, had an influence on the respondents' purchase behavior"	Kallier, 2017, p.131
Relevance	Engagement Brand involvement	"Brands can generate interesting and provocative content to create engagement or to highlight important information"	Chu et al., 2016, p.427
Agility	Reach Engagement	"What counts today is speed and agility"	Scott, 2011, p.33
Dialogue	Engagement	Consumers expect a dialogue in social media, in which brands listen to what they have to say rather than simply pushing promotional marketing messages without taking into account what customers think, feel, and want.	Kwon & Sung, 2011, p.13
Mindset	Active participation Engagement	"Social media are tools? Real time is a mindset?"	Scott, 2011, p.55

From well-designed strategies, RTM can be effective in its objective to generate engagement. According to Pereira et al. (2022), brands that use RTM as a strategy obtain greater sharing on social networks than messages that do not. Another point that influences consumer engagement on social media is the type of content. Posts with videos, gifs or moving images generate greater interaction on social platforms (Aydin, 2020). Regarding the type of content, emotional appeals influence customer engagement more than informational appeals (Rietveld et al., 2020). In addition, content production needs to be continuous (Gummerus et al., 2012), be relevant (Read et al., 2019) and generate benefits for the consumer (Bilro et al., 2020; Dessert et al., 2015).

CSR and Purpose: Important Pillars for Brand Equity

In many companies, CSR is a way to generate customer engagement. Through voluntary environmental, ethical and even global challenges (Clenger & Macgregor, 2019; Eteokleous et al., 2016), companies seek to play an active and strategic role with their stakeholders. CSR demonstrates that the company is interested in broader societal issues, not just those that affect its profit margins. That is, CSR refers to the strategies that companies put into action as part of corporate governance and that are designed to ensure an ethical and positive view of the community (Knox, 2004). It is closely linked to the creation of economic, social and environmental value for society.

CSR initiatives and campaigns have a direct effect on consumer behavior and purchase intentions (Kuokkanen & Sun, 2019; Öberseder et al., 2013) and this is because consumers like to relate to companies and brands that have ethical, balanced and sustainable initiatives. Moreover, it is understood that companies investing in CSR initiatives generate a positive essence in addition to intangible assets such as credibility and reputation (Hur et al., 2014). According to Krisch and Grabner-kra (2017), supporting worthy causes and communicating them to their consumers increase brand visibility and generate positive social impact.

Social platforms have been great channels for CSR disclosure (Capriotti, 2017; Zou et al., 2018), they offer great opportunities for companies to establish a deeper connection with stakeholders. More and more companies and brands use their digital profiles to report on their CSR actions and activities. Through social networks, brands express their understanding of CSR, their actions and also, through interactions with customers, they can promote engagement with their consumers (Farache et al., 2014). Promoting CSR on platforms like Twitter, Facebook or Instagram can increase consumer loyalty and trust. When they post on social media about their actions, companies and brands are committed to transparency and honesty, accepting the views, comments and criticisms of online stakeholders. Despite this, some studies say that explicit communication is not welcomed by consumers. According to Schmeltz (2012), it is inappropriate for organizations to communicate and unleash their own "good deeds". In other words, you don't have to advertise that you're good. This type of behavior can even alienate consumers and generate a negative reputation for the brand and company.

Some brands have invested in CSR actions related to diversity and gender equity (Grosser & Moon, 2005; Sterbenk et al., 2021) because this theme has been increasingly requested among employees and consumers (Hur et al., 2016). Companies have invested in corporate diversity practices because they recognize their crucial role in advancing gender equality, and understand that female empowerment is a fundamental step in the evolution of the market. The UN's 5th Sustainable Development Goals (United Nation, 2022) refers to gender equality, and UM research shows that even with the evolution of global indicators, female representation is still insufficient in several areas of the economy, such as technology, mathematics and design, which impacts a series of transformative benefits for society. Studies show that there are more and more CSR initiatives focused on women's development and empowerment (Grosser & Moon, 2019; Mccarthy, 2017; Ramya, 2019).

In many companies, CSR is a derivation of the company's purpose. Purpose is the reason for the company's existence, that is, what is the meaning of work beyond measures of financial results (Gartenberg et al., 2019). Currently, purpose has become one of the strategic trends that can boost business growth as well as brand and product value (Hurth et al., 2018; Jimenez et al., 2021). According to Bhattacharya et al., (2022), the purpose of a company needs to be pluralized and decoded by all stakeholders, only in this way will a common understanding be possible about the meaning of why the company exists. Based on its purpose, the company manages to align how it will work with the CSR, that is, what initiatives it will generate to improve social damage and promote quality of life for society. However, recently researchers have separated CSR and Purpose. According to Fleischer (2021), there are supporters of the principle that CSR focuses on profit and social benefit, whereas the purpose is an instrument of direction for all activities of a company, since the purpose is the protagonist.

CSR and Purpose are big drivers of brand equity. Brand equity refers to the added value of a product by virtue of a brand (Yoo & Donthu, 2001). Considered an indicator linked to the success of organizations (Tasci, 2021), it represents how customers view the brand, as it is this perception that will make the biggest difference in profits and in the valuation of the company as a whole (Keller & Brexendorf,

2019). It is measured by the perception, judgments, thoughts and intangible beliefs about the quality of a product or service (Foroudi et al., 2018). From there consumers classify whether their perception was positive or negative.

Expected Relationship Between RTM and Social Corporate Strategy

As mentioned above, the literature on RTM is still very scarce, and the relationship between the topics it approaches and CSR have not yet been explored. Based on the previous sections, it is clear that the main objective of RTM is user engagement. Considering the importance of relevance (Chu et al., 2016) to the success of this tactic, one would expect that the fit of the topic to the brand, considering its alignment with the company's values and CSR practices, will benefit the ability of the message to generate user engagement and to overall generate benefits to the brand.

METHODOLOGY

An empirical research was carried out to answer the question: how does CSR drive marketing actions in real time? The research used netnography as a form of analysis and combined the content published on social networks together with the information available on the companies' websites. Netnography is used for studies focusing on human behavior in digital environments, as it is an extension of the more web-specific ethnography (Kozinets, 2002). According to Kozinets & Gambetti (2021), netnography collects and explores all online material - whether conversations, comments, posts, shares - and all forms of communication generated by online individuals within social platforms. The analysis uses ethnographic research techniques to understand people's behavior, interactions, narratives and messages online. It has become a way of mapping consumer narratives and discourses with brands (Kozinets et al., 2018). The netnographic analysis consists of exploring conversations carried out on platforms, such as Instagram, to build a scenario that translates the feeling and behavior of an audience regarding a product, service or theme.

For data collection, a study was carried out with 25 most valuable brands in Brazil. The posts related to Women's Day, which took place on March 8, 2022, were collected from their Instagram profiles. The ranking of the 25 most valuable brands in Brazil is produced by the company Intelbrand, which uses a methodology that combines financial performance, perception and the influence of the most valuable national brands among consumers (Sutto, 2021). For the analysis, the posts available on Instagram profiles were collected and the webpages of each company were explored.

The list of analyzed companies is presented in Table 2.

Table 2. List of companies analyses in this chapter

Brand	Segment	Instagram	Followers	Comments	Likes
Itáu	Bank	https://www.instagram.com/itau/	792,000	no posts	
Bradesco	Bank	https://www.instagram.com/bradesco	436,000	no posts	
Skol (Ambev)	Beverages	https://www.instagram.com/skol	580,000	no posts	
Brahma (Ambev)	Beverages	https://www.instagram.com/brahmacerveja/	668,000	no posts	
Natura	Cosmetic	https://www.instagram.com/naturabroficial	3,400,000	350	3,228
Banco do Brasil	Bank	https://www.instagram.com/bancodobrasil	495,000	113	431,295
Petrobras	Oil industry	https://www.instagram.com/petrobras/	170,000	67	401
Magazine Luiza	Retailer	https://www.instagram.com/magazineluiza	5,900,000	374	1,084,587
Vivo	Telecom	https://www.instagram.com/vivo/	592,000	525	70,288
Americanas	Retailer	https://www.instagram.com/americanas	13,000,000	99	3740
XP Inc.	Finance	https://www.instagram.com/xp.inc	171,000	26	794
Renner	Fashion	https://www.instagram.com/lojasrenner	7,900,000	201	2,025
Ipiranga	Oil industry	https://www.instagram.com/ipiranga	80,000	64	756
Claro	Telecom	https://www.instagram.com/clarobrasil	431,000	no posts	
Cielo	Electronic payment	https://www.instagram.com/cielooficial/	80,000	40	93
Drogasil	Drugstore	https://www.instagram.com/drogasiloficial	245,000	124	2,136
Porto Seguro	Insurance	https://www.instagram.com/portoseguro	198,000	no posts	
Havaianas	Fashion	https://www.instagram.com/havaianas	3,000,000	240	9,921
Casas Bahia	Retailer	https://www.instagram.com/casasbahia	3,100,000	125	7,576
Assaí	Supermarket	https://www.instagram.com/assaiatacadistaoficial	2,200,000	47	5,890
Atacadão	Supermarket	https://www.instagram.com/atacadaosa.oficial/	1,400,000	39	1,123
PagSeguro	Electronic payment	https://www.instagram.com/pagseguro	545,000	85	223
SulAmerica	Insurance	https://www.instagram.com/sulamerica	90,000	47	345
Localiza	Car rental	https://www.instagram.com/localiza	194,000	23	62,740
Hering	Fashion	https://www.instagram.com/hering_oficial/	3,200,000	35	967

The research analyzed 16 posts, due to the fact that ten brands did not make any post in celebration of International Women's Day. The study analyzed the post text, image and comments next to the post and correlated with RTM or CSR actions. In the research, the objective of netnography was to understand the reactions of consumers to publications on social networks. In addition, based on the literature review, the main items for RTM planning were analyzed along with the companies' posts. It also researched CSR actions aimed at gender equity and female empowerment available on the companies' websites.

RESULTS

Among the 16 companies that had posts, the content of the posts was classified as:

- Promotional actions: posts that promote products or services to attract and retain consumers. Three companies received this classification.
- Tributes: posts that express admiration and respect for women and have content of congratulations and celebration. Eight companies received this classification.
- CSR: posts that reveal the company's social responsibility actions with the female audience and corporate activities that seek gender equity. Five companies received this classification.

These categories are analysed in detail in the next sections.

Promotional Actions

Hering, Localiza and Banco do Brasil used their Instagram profiles on Women's Day to promote their products to their consumers. Table 3 presents a summary of the findings.

The retail company Hering released a campaign "the basics for Brazil", which seeks to portray stories of people who symbolize their communities in the north and northeast regions of Brazil and who have creativity as a craft.

@hering_oficial: Today is @sambaqueelasquerem. 🎶

Meet the samba circle formed by women musicians who make their talent a representative tool.

#OBásicoPeloBrasil #NossasMulheres

Localiza, a car rental company, announced a partnership with the organization Sisterwave, a platform that seeks to reduce the obstacles faced by female travelers and increase female freedom.

@localiza: We wish more and more women to hit the road and live incredible experiences. So, on this International Women's Day, we're announcing our new partnership with @sisterwave, a community that brings together women passionate about travel and helps others to do the same - encouraging, giving tips or even connecting and creating a network that makes them more confident to travel.

In the comments, tag your friend's @ and share this news. Take advantage of the fact that Localiza will give two months of Sisterwave free to all customers who use the LOCALIZAMULHER coupon now, this March.

Stay on top of this partnership through the bio link.

#MêsDaMulher #LocalizaESisterwave #MulheresQueViajam

Banco do Brasil released the website bb.com.br/bbpraelas, where women can find a series of products and services that facilitate and support female entrepreneurship:

@BancodoBrasil: BB has arrived for Elas. The Bank of Brazil, l created to enhance the strength of Brazilian women. Go to #linknabiobb and find out. #PraTudoQueVoceImaginar #BBpraElas

Video description: The film shows several women looking confidently towards the camera, while the voiceover says the text. Among the women, there are of all origins and ages, including one with hearing impairment. At the end, he invites you to access the website bb.com.br/bbpraelas and signs with the Banco do Brasil brand.

Table 3. Main findings – Promotional actions

Company	Benefit for the Target Market	Relevance	Agility	Dialogue	Mindset	Engagement Likes
Hering	Low	Low	Medium	High	High	967
Localiza	High	High	High	High	High	62,740
Banco do Brasil	High	High	High	High	High	431,295

Of the three companies with promotional actions, only Banco do Brasil and Localiza presented the benefit to the consumer/target market in their posts. Both companies clearly displayed in their posts the advantages for the consumer with their service or product. As Kallier (2017) points out, the customer needs to understand the advantage of being associated with a brand. In the analysis of relevance, Hering's post was not as expressive. Localiza and Banco do Brasil had content that was more relevant to consumers.

In the agility analysis, Localiza and Banco do Brasil presented arguments that are highly pluralized in social networks with the female audience. Willemsen et al. (2018) highlight the importance of brands linking their content to moments or events that are publicly discussed on social media in real time. Banco do Brasil brought female entrepreneurship and Localiza the freedom of women who travel alone, topics that are well accepted on social platforms. Hering's argument, on the other hand, talks about a group of women who dance samba, a segmented argument for a consumer profile. In the dialogue item, we researched through the comments next to the posts how consumers reacted:

For the Hering brand, consumers were engaged in the cause:

@barbara.llouise: 😍 *they shine too brightly* ✨

@mariacarmenmoraes: I love it so much♡

For the Localiza brand, consumers also expressed themselves positively about the promotional action:

@flavyannesouza: The partnershiiipppp 😍 ♡

@giovannabayara: Sensational 😍

For Banco do Brasil, consumers also expressed themselves positively and celebrated the action:

@leidianecastroserafim: Is this a credit for women entrepreneurs?

@dilzascarpa: ♡ ♡ ♡ 😍 😍

The three brands under analysis have a high mindset about RTM. All bet on ways to be in line with the trend of the moment: Hering approached with the hashtag #OurWomen in addition to content, Banco do Brasil and Localiza provided content aligned with female trends. That is, according to Scott (2011), the brands behaved as if they have entered conversations that are already happening quickly and organically.

When it comes to engagement, posts that directly presented a consumer benefit had the most engagement. Banco do Brasil with more than 400 thousand likes and Localiza with more than 60 thousand likes, provided customers with a differentiated digital experience, presenting relevant content and a specific benefit to the target audience. According to Dessert et al. (2015), in order to establish a solid and trusting relationship with consumers, it is necessary for brands to understand the needs of their audience. Banco do Brasil and Localiza presented posts aligned with the needs of their customers, unlike Hering, who made an informative post, without any commercial appeal or in celebration of Women's Day.

Tributes

Seven brands paid tribute on their social networks in celebration of Women's Day. Table 4 presents a summary of the findings.

The insurer SulAmerica bet on a campaign that addressed what women want to hear to celebrate women's day. The company seeks to discuss the topic widely in digital media and give voice to important debates for all women through words of support and recognition, whether at work, on public transport or at home.

@sulamerica: Is there anything better than a "Happy International Women's Day"? In fact, there is: what they most want today – and always – is to feel respected and recognized. Follow our social media this month and understand what women really like to hear.

#whattheyliketolisten

#ParaTodosVerem This content has accessible text #SulAmericaAccessible

PagSeguro, an electronic payments' company, celebrated women's historic moments in their female financial independence.

@PagSeguro: International Women's Day is a date to celebrate the struggle of women around the world for equality and freedom, to celebrate what has been achieved and to reflect on the obstacles that still need to be overcome.

Therefore, this March 8, we recall here some important milestones in the search for women's autonomy and financial independence.

Access the special article we prepared to let you know about this story and understand the importance of this date. https://bit.ly/34oHrkf

#InternacionalDaMulher #8M #pagbank

The Atacadão supermarket chain paid tribute to the company's employees and women.

@atacadaosa.oficial: More than flowers, on International Women's Day, give the Partner you love real actions for equal rights! May men and women have equal responsibilities in caring for the home, children, and life, and may this struggle continue for all generations to come. 😉 🖤 *#DiaInternacionalDaMulher #DiaDaMulher*

The supermarket chain Assaí also celebrated women's day with a tribute:

@assaiatacadistaoficial: Today is International Women's Day! ♡ 👧 ⌖

Behind every woman there is always a story. Of overcoming and conquests. Starts and restarts. Of discoveries and achievements. Assaí honors all women who own their own history.

#DiaDaMulher #MulherEmpoderada #DiaDelas #DiaInternacionalDaMulher #TodasAsMulheres #Assai #AssaiAtacadista #MondialÉNoAssaí #AssaiDonasdaPropriaHistoria

The electronic payments' company Cielo also honored women:

@Cielo: Today, March 8, we celebrate International Women's Day, so we want to reinforce the importance of female empowerment for society and how it increasingly strengthens business in the world. 🚀

We want all women to continue performing and occupying spaces every day! Tag here businesses that are led by women who make it happen 😍

The Ipiranga gas station network paid tribute to the women of its company and featured the first owner of a gas station in Brazil in its campaign.

@Ipiranga: On this #Woman'sDay, Ipiranga is honoring Maria Athênice, the first woman to own a gas station in Brazil. A woman ahead of her time who overcame barriers with a lot of determination and courage, and went down in history. An inspiration for all Marias and women who also struggle to conquer their space, anywhere.

The Americanas retail chain also honored women on their day. The campaign, which lasted throughout March, presented the story of 3 Brazilian entrepreneurs who also told how they started their businesses and gave tips on how to increase sales.

@we know that there is no Brazilian like any other.

so we invite @camiladelucas to introduce you to women who are transforming their realities.

Follow our networks to meet Maria Nilde, the sisters Leite and Ana Eliza, and discover how #ElasConquistamTudo

The oil company Petrobras paid tribute to women and published the story of a collaborator. A good example of a woman who believes, overcomes barriers and inspires other women in the company.

@petrobras: Ana Lucia's path was based on her passion for Geology. And on curiosity. She started her career at our Research Center, and now works in Exploration. Ana is one of the many female oil women who contribute to making our company stronger and stronger. One of the many women who transform barriers into drivers and who inspire us today and every day. Happy International Women's Day.

Table 4. Main findings - Tributes

Company	Benefit to the Target Market	Relevance	Agility	Dialogue	Mindset	Engagement Likes
SulAmerica	Low	Low	Medium	Medium	Low	345
PagSeguro	Low	Medium	Medium	Low	Medium	223
Atacadão	Low	Low	Low	Low	Low	1,123
Assaí	Low	Low	Low	Low	Low	5,890
Cielo	Low	Low	Low	High	Low	93
Ipiranga	Low	Medium	Low	Low	Low	756
Americanas	Medium	Medium	HIgh	Low	High	3,740
Petrobrás	Low	Medium	Low	Low	Low	401

When we analyzed the benefit for the consumer in the posts of the companies, we noticed that only one company, Americanas, was able to present an argument with a emphasis for the consumer. The company shared success stories of Brazilian entrepreneurs on how they grew and increased their profits. The remaining companies did not show any benefit to the consumer in their content, only celebrated women's day. In the item relevance, PagSeguro, Ipiranga, Americanas and Petrobras showed relevance in their content, posting examples of inspiring women or telling how women empowered themselves. The rest of the brands did not bring any relevance to their content.

Chu et al., (2016) reinforces that to engage and gain the trust of followers, companies need to invest in interesting content that generates connection and adds value. When we analyzed the agility of each of the companies, PagSeguro and SulAmerica were able to present a speech aligned with trends discussed on social networks. In particular, SulAmerica opted for a feminist hashtag and PagSeguro campaign addressed women's financial independence. Americanas presented a higher index because it brought about female entrepreneurship. The rest of the companies did not address any content related pluralized narratives on social platforms. Busch (2016) reinforces the importance of listening to your audience and activating your network at the right time, so that the narrative is high among your consumers.

In the dialogue item, for SulAmerica, consumers congratulated the action but with low intensity.

@psicanalistavanessafernandes: Congratulations for making a conscious post.

@ Danncastilho: 👏👏👏👏

For PagSeguro there was no post congratulating the action. The Instagram profile is a contact channel for customers and they use it for complaints.

@thairan_tsj: I'm not able to transfer via pix

@Luanacantom: I DO NOT RECOMMEND ANYONE TO HIRE THE WORK OF VCS

For Atacadão there was a low rate of dialogue and only congratulations.

@monica_neves24: Congratulations to the whole team at atacadao, a happy women's day to all of you. 😍

@mariasoares8981: Congratulations on your women's day.

The same happened for Assaí, very little interaction and only congratulations.

@Carolinefanti: 😍😍😍

@mariadasdoressanti: 👏👏👏👏👏

The company Cielo had interactions due to its post, encouraging women to post profiles of entrepreneurs:

@karolpramires: @_docesdaclaudinha Entrepreneurial women who make it happen! The best sweets 🤩🤍

@anasilvasocialmedia: @pridascanio, the best aesthetic professional!!! 👩‍🔧♀️

Ipiranga had few interactions, most congratulating the action:

@carolinaeschneider: Wow!!! 👏😍💪

@jussara_palieraqui: A beautiful life story with lots of determination and love! 😍👏👏👏👏👏👏👏👏👏

Americanas had a high interaction with its consumers:

@carlagodoygabriel: Long live the women who fight every day to improve the lives of other women. ♡🌼🌼🌼🌼

@joanaportugal: @anaelizaangelieri so proud!!! 👏👏👏👏

For Petrobras, the interaction was low and only with congratulations:

@maria.nunes.999999: ♡♡♡👏👏👏👏

@neusa.fonseca.1257: Congratulations on your inspiring work!!! 👏👏

PagSeguro had an average mindset, because it created an action aligned with feminist trends. Americanas had a high mindset for its speed and attention to market conversations. The rest of the companies had a low mindset, without connecting with the public during crucial and important moments.

When analyzing the engagement of brands that carried out tributes on women's day, it is clear the low engagement of the audience, even with brands with a large number of followers. Consumers do not connect with brands or engage with the tributes. Social media users tend to share more emotional content (Rietveld et al., 2020) unlike posts made by companies that bet on more informative and direct content.

CSR Actions

Finally, regarding the CSR actions, the engagement generated tended to be much higher, as shown in Table 5.

The network Varegista Casas Bahia communicated in its post the actions that Fundação Casas Bahia has taken in favor of female empowerment. The Foundation's campaign gives visibility to initiatives that foster female entrepreneurship and features several female entrepreneurs in a series of videos on how to leverage their businesses.

@CasasBahiaFor us, women's month is all year round! ♡

In the last 3 years, Fundação Casas Bahia has supported projects that seek to encourage and bring more autonomy to entrepreneurs across the country - more than 15 thousand of them have already benefited. And if it depends on us, the future holds even more transformative initiatives for these women.

Life calls for female empowerment all year round, #PedeCasasBahia 🏬

XP Inc. chose to communicate about gender equity actions within the company. The campaign presents all the initiatives that the company develops to reach 50% of women in its staff and leadership. In addition, the campaign also addresses the numbers of promotions and salary equitaty between genders, the launch of exclusive vacancies for women and training and mentoring for career and leadership.

@xp.inc: We believe that transformation happens when people with great potential and the will to make it happen find the right place and create a movement for change. On today's date we want to share some of the many achievements in our history, which were carried out by women from our team. We are proud to say that from time to time they have occupied more and more positions in different areas here at XP Inc., contributing to the growth of our business, the well-being of our collaborators, the satisfaction of our customers and many other transformations that are yet to come. ☺

Want to discover more inspiring stories? Follow the hashtag #MulheresQueTransformam on social media and check out the testimony of amazing women.

Vivo, the telephone company, opted for one of its gender diversity programs. The campaign focuses on boosting female presence in the Customer Services area, promoting diversity and encouraging the presence of women in activities that used to be typically male, such as repair and installation functions at the customer's home.

@vivo: To celebrate International Women's Day, @xanravelli came to our base to meet the technician @jullyanemarquez, one of more than 300 women hired in Vivo's Women in Technical Areas Program. The project is an initiative that helps to break with stereotypes and increase female representation in an area still dominated by men. After all, around here, if there's one thing we believe, it's that a woman can be exactly everything she wants to be!

Magazine Luiza, a retail chain, used the date to launch a women's financial empowerment program for women who suffer from domestic violence.

@Magalu:Today is #InternationalWomen'sDay. There are many reasons to celebrate! But it is also necessary to remember that, in 2021, 46% of women would not report a situation of violence because they are financially dependent on the aggressor (DataSenado, survey 2021). It's a situation that needs to change! That's why Magalu launches #MeEmpodera today. A project that aims to help women achieve their financial independence. We are going to donate 10,000 scholarships for professional training courses from ComSchool, through a partnership with 9 NGOs that work on the front lines of the fight against violence. The course will have 4 modules, with 10 lessons in total. The content ranges from basic concepts and techniques of how to sell on the internet, to financial education and female empowerment. Financial independence is an important step in breaking the cycle of violence against women. And Magalu wants to help make that happen.

Natura, a cosmetics company, used the date to reinforce its CSR actions and publicize some consulting companies who have been at the forefront of progress and promoting transformations in their communities and their families:

@naturabroficial: Who will you choose to echo? Every time we give a voice to a woman, we give a voice to all And to the construction of something new. #MulheresEcoamMulheres

#PraTodosVerem

The post is a carousel with five images. In all, we have the text "#MulheresEcoamMulheres" and the Natura logo. In the first image, we have a photo of a woman smiling, looking to the side, with sunbeams on her face, with the texts "Echoe the strength of March 8" and "Mara Ester, Natura Beauty Consultant". In the second image, we have a photo of a woman in a field of flowers with the texts "It's time to echo what unites us" and "Aline Roelens, Natura Beauty Consultant". In the third image, there is a photo of another woman on a boat with the texts "Echoing what is ours is echoing affection." and "Maria do Socorro Valente Alves, Associate of the CART cooperative". In the fourth image, we have a photo of another woman looking to the side with the texts "March 8 is conquest. It's a journey. It's affection." and "Pamela da Costa, Natura Beauty Consultant". To close, in front of a red background, we have the invitation "Use the comments and tag women who inspire you. #MulheresEcoamMulheres".

Table 5. Main findings - CSR

Company	Benefit to Consumer	Relevance	Agility	Dialogue	Mindset	Engagement Likes
Casas Bahia	High	High	HIgh	HIgh	HIgh	7,576
XP Inc.	High	High	High	HIgh	HIgh	794
Vivo	High	High	High	HIgh	HIgh	70,288
Magazine Luiza	High	High	High	HIgh	HIgh	1,084,587
Natura	HIgh	High	High	HIgh	HIgh	3,228

All companies that promoted CSR actions achieved high scores in all levels of the table. As for the benefit to the consumer, all companies showed important advantages for their consumers when relating to the brand. The relevance of all companies was high because both campaigns brought up important themes for the cause of women: female entrepreneurship, gender equity actions, support for victims of violence against women and boosting the chain of workers. Öberseder et al. (2013) highlight that CSR actions directly impact the audience and have a positive value for the consumer as he sees the company as a force in raising awareness about important social causes. In addition, agility was also high for all companies, since the topics addressed by the companies make up the main topics of conversations of women that permeate social networks. According to Kwon & Sung (2011), actions need to generate engagement with the public and generate conversations, that is, show the audience that the brand follows the main social agendas. The mindset of all companies is aligned with the immediacy of the world we live in today.

The fashion company Havaianas, the insurance company Porto Seguro, the drugstore chain Drogasil, the telecommunications company Claro, the fashion retailer Lojas Renner, the beer brand Brahma and Skol and the banks Bradesco and Itaú did not hold any posts in celebration of the women's day on Instagram profiles.

RTM is an important factor in audience engagement (Pereira et al., 2022). The analyzed brands achieved high rates of likes with their content. Magazine Luiza, a brand with a history of working for women's causes, surpassed one million likes with its post. Vivo, which promoted its program in favor of gender equality, had great involvement from the target audience and exceeded 70 thousand likes. CSR actions promoted by the brands during Women's Day were well accepted by the public and generated a high level of engagement.

Companies' CSR Strategy Focus

Some brands work their accountability activities through their institutes and foundations and use the brands to replicate the news. Table 5 shows us that all companies, with the exception of PagSeguro, have information about their social responsibility actions available on their webpages, or on the webpages of their parent brands or even in their companies' institutes or foundations. In some cases, the dissemination of the action is the sole responsibility of the foundation and often the brand does not distribute its social content.

Table 6. CSR strategy focus

Brand	Segment	CSR	Focus
Itaú	Bank	Itaú Foundation	Culture and Education
Bradesco	Bank	Bradesco Bank	Sustainable Finance, Education and Sports
Skol (Ambev)	Beverages	Ambev	ESG
Brahma (Ambev)	Beverages	Ambev	ESG
Natura	Cosmetic	Natura Institut	Education
Banco do Brasil	Bank	Banco do Brasil Foundation	Socioproductive Inclusion
Petrobras	Oil	Company	ESG
Magazine Luiza	Retailer	Company	Value Chain, Society
Vivo	Telecom	Telefônica Vivo Foundation	Education
Americanas	Retailer	Company	Sustainability, Engagement, Social Projects, Value Chain
XP Inc.	Finance	Company	Education, Culture, Sports and Health
Renner	Fashion	Lojas Renner Institut	Fashion and Women Empowerment
Ipiranga	Gas	Company	Diversity
Claro	Telecom	Claro Institut	Education
Cielo	Electronic payment	Company	Corporate Sustainability
Drogasil	Drugstore	Company	Community
Porto Seguro	Insurance	Porto Seguro Institut	Education
Havaianas	Fashion	Alpargatas Institut	Social Sustainability
Casas Bahia	Retailer	Casas Bahia Foundation	Social Enterpreneurship
Assaí	Supermarket	Company	Corporate Sustainability
Atacadão	Supermarket	Carrefour Institute	Diversity
PagSeguro	Electronic payment	Non-existent	Non-existent
SulAmerica	Insurance	Company	Sustainability and Environment
Localiza	Car rental	Company	Sustainability and Environment
Hering	Fashion	Cia Hering	Sustainable Fashion

Banco Itaú, for example, did not post any content on its institutional profile on Instagram. But Itaú Social, a profile referring to the bank's social actions, paid tribute to women who work with educational projects supported by the bank:

@itausocial: This week, we celebrate International Women's Day.

We leave here our recognition to them, who continue to overcome barriers and fight to conquer rights and spaces over the years. To mark the date, we highlight the work of some women who make a difference in Brazilian education and contribute to the integral development of children and adolescents. Visit the link in bio and learn more about these stories and actions.

Ambev, parent brand of Skol and Brahma beers, celebrated Women's Day and shared a series of actions for female professional development:

@Ambev: Hey, woman! Your opportunity to work in the technology area has already become a reality.

Z-Tech and Bees will offer 200 scholarships in the "Eu progr{amo}" course, for women who want to start their professional career in the field of technology.

Applications are open until March 23.

Come and be part of a more diverse and representative market.

Lojas Renner also did not make any post in celebration of women's day, but Instituto Renner published a video explaining its work with women's empowerment and change in communities:

@institutolojasrenner: Empowered women are transformative. 👩 👧 *Whether in lives, communities or their own realities, the positive impacts that result from this stimulus to the power they already have are gigantic. Therefore, our work is for and for them, generating employment and income and investing in their training and business. All this so that better living conditions become a reality for all. Long live the #EstiloQueEmpodera all the honorees on this Women's Day.*

It can be concluded that Table 6 shows a perfect fit between RTM and promotional actions. First, because the audience can perceive a value in communication and a clear benefit, which influences consumer behavior (Kallier Tar & A Wiid, 2021) and engages them in the cause. In addition, brands were able to use the immediacy (Willemsen et al., 2018) and agility that RTM needs to create connections with their consumers. Localiza, a car rental company, partnered with Sisterwave and was able to take advantage of women's day to discuss an important argument: female independence in travel. In addition, he invited women to comment on the post and tag their friends to organize trips, generating organic engagement. In other words, the brand knew how to combine the importance of the date with a feminist argument and even delivered a benefit to its consumer, following the step by step of the RTM. Banco do Brasil did no different, released BBpraelas, a specific webpage for female entrepreneurs with all the services and products available for women. The company understood the need to talk about one of the main topics covered by Google Trends (2022) in line with what its consumers are looking for (Reece,

2010). Banco do Brasil's consumers perceived an important advantage with the brand exactly in the period in which the Women's Day is celebrated, a perfect combination for the RTM.

CSR actions were also right with RTM, because they aimed to strengthen the bond between brands and their customers (McKenna, 1995). With the celebration of Women's Day, companies selected CSR actions that generate engagement with their audience and at the same time are topics that are part of feminist trends (Gesenhues, 2020). Casas Bahia brought in its text the actions that its institute has carried out in favor of women's causes. Magazine Luiza launched a campaign to support women who suffer some type of violence. XP Inc and Vivo highlighted the internal actions they have carried out in search of corporate gender equity and the search for diversity in all business sectors. Natura brought the stories of consultants who have been protagonists in their communities and promoted women and their needs. All companies brought much more than CSR actions to their posts, they also showed their purpose, what makes them unique in the market and can differentiate themselves from the multitude of existing brands (Hurth et al., 2018). The communication of CSR as an RTM strategy is extremely effective since there is an increase in the credibility and generation of brand value (Krisch & Grabner-kra, 2017), that is, using women's day to pluralize what the company has been doing well with the female audience is extremely positive for the brand.

Promotional actions and CSR were positive and generated consumer engagement. Both actions had positive comments through texts or even emogis of hearts, palms or faces with hearts in their eyes. Consumers approved the actions and were positively impacted by the brands, because it is understood that respect and admiration are some of the consequences generated by the CSR with the consumer (Kuokkanen & Sun, 2019). Some companies encouraged consumer participation as a form of engagement, which was favorable and had a positive response from participants.

Table 7. Likes generated by each company

Brand	Followers	Likes	Likes/Followers Rate
Magazine Luiza	5,900,000	1,084,587	18,38%
Banco do Brasil	495,000	43,1295	87,13%
Vivo	592,000	70,288	11,87%
Localiza	194,000	62,740	32,34%
Havaianas	3,000,000	9,921	0,33%
Casas Bahia	3,100,000	7,576	0,24%
Assaí	2,200,000	5,890	0,27%
Americanas	13,000,000	3,740	0,03%
Natura	3,400,000	3,228	0,09%
Drogasil	245,000	2,136	0,87%
Renner	7,900,000	2,025	0,03%
Atacadão	1,400,000	1,123	0,08%
Hering	3,200,000	967	0,03%
XP Inc,	171,000	794	0,46%
Ipiranga	80,000	756	0,95%
Petrobras	170,000	401	0,24%
SulAmerica	90,000	345	0,38%
PagSeguro	545,000	223	0,04%
Cielo	80,000	93	0,12%

As shown in Table 7, it is evident that the brands that had the highest number of likes were the ones that opted for promotional actions and CSR approaches. Magazine Luiza led with more than one million likes and demonstrated that the combination talking about your work together with the women's cause on women's day generates a good engagement of the target audience, that is, presenting your CSR purpose and actions with RTM (Pereira et al., 2022) is a way to connect with the audience. Banco do Brasil, with a specific promotional action for women, also brought relevant content (Chu et al., 2016) and benefit to the consumer (Kallier, 2017), being seen as a positive initiative by women. Promotional messages and CSR were reliable, transparent, and meaningful, essential attributes in generating RTM value. Brands with promotional posts and CSR produced creative content, without losing the immediacy of the date, and explored important scenarios for women's causes.

SOLUTIONS AND RECOMMENDATIONS

The celebration of Women's Day has gained more and more prominence over the years. The analyzed companies have developed actions for women's empowerment, diversity, women's financial education and women's entrepreneurship. Much more than honoring women, companies have focused on generating CSR with a focus on gender equity (Grosser & Moon, 2019; Hur et al., 2016). Casas Bahia, Magazine Luiza, XP Inc, Natura and Vivo collaborated to reduce gender inequality by recognizing women as an economic agent and looking for ways to increase gender equity and provide tools for women's financial, social and cultural growth. In other words, companies have generated CSR actions to face social inequalities and create a more inclusive, healthy and productive community environment. Through the study, it is clear that brands understood that, in addition to promoting women's causes and empowering women (Ramya, 2019), brands also add value to their brand equity (Foroudi et al., 2018) with RTM actions focused on Women's Day.

During the netnographic analysis, along with the comments of the brands that did not make any post referring to women's day, no consumer questioning was found. Lojas Renner and Havaianas announced their e-commerce products. Itaú, Bradesco, Skol, Brahma, Drogasil and Porto Seguro did not make any postings on the date. However, these companies have CSR shares. Some communicate through other profiles (institutes or foundations), others assessed the need to communicate the CSR action with their target audience (Schmeltz, 2012).

Hence, this study provides highlights on several solutions to approach social relevant dates on social media. Clearly, these publications need to be aligned with the overall strategy of the company, namely its values and CSR. Within an adequate balance between the topic approached and the characteristics of the company, these RTM strategies can generate impressive levels of engagement as shown in Table 7, particularly for companies such as Magazine Luiza, which consistently communicate values associated to the topic approached by RTM.

FUTURE RESEARCH DIRECTIONS

The results of this study should be seen as a first step towards understanding RTM strategies on social platforms, especially on issues of gender equity. The study indicated how CSR can be combined with the RTM strategy in companies. Future research should explore which CSR issues are analyzed together with diversity or even social inclusion and RTM on other commemorative dates. Another important point to be discussed would be to understand how companies that did not make any post in celebration of Women's Day highlighted the date and what is the vision of these companies regarding gender equality.

CONCLUSION

Consumers are increasingly influencing brand communication strategies (Willemsen et al., 2018) and their awareness of brands' social and environmental impacts and their interaction with trending topics. Corporations that invest in customer interaction through social media have gained market share and market voice, as their content is more consumed and shared. Amongst social media communication strategies, RTM stands out for generating good digital marketing results, as consumers want to have real conversations and realize that the company really connects with their causes (Pereira et al., 2022). Naturally, cause involvement needs to be consistent with CSR strategies. Brands that share their social concerns and how they have been agents of change in their communities (Grosser & Moon, 2005) gain competitive advantages as a result of their ability to connect with and involve their target audiences.

Many companies still consider March 8th, International Women's Day, just a date to honor women and use their brands to congratulate their female employees and customers. Apparently, these companies disregard the evolution of digital content consumption and do not follow the contemporary societal discussions about women's causes. Considering that the relevance of content plays a key role in the consumption of online content (Read et al., 2019), other brands have embraced International Women's Day as an opportunity to show their alignment with female empowerment. These brands presented a more in-depth look at what women want and need to know and opened a debate on gender equity, misogyny, harassment have been important agendas were more consumed. Hence, Women's Day is no longer a date of celebration to become an important reminder of how to persevere in the struggle of women. Overall, socially-relevant dates provide interesting opportunities for social media communication and the involvement on RTM, as demonstrated by this chapter. Still, this strategy should be carefully planned and, as stressed in this article, conveniently aligned with the overal values and CSR strategies of the company.

REFERENCES

Akar, E., & Dalgic, T. (2018). Understanding online consumers ' purchase intentions: A contribution from social network theory. *Behaviour & Information Technology, 37*(5), 473–487. doi:10.1080/0144 929X.2018.1456563

Aydin, G. (2020). Social media engagement and organic post effectiveness: A roadmap for increasing the effectiveness of social media use in hospitality industry. *Journal of Hospitality Marketing & Management, 29*(1), 1–21. doi:10.1080/19368623.2019.1588824

Bhattacharya, C. B., Sen, S., Edinger-Schons, L. M., & Neureiter, M. (2022). Corporate Purpose and Employee Sustainability Behaviors. *Journal of Business Ethics.* Advance online publication. doi:10.100710551-022-05090-5

Bilro, R. G., Maria, S., & Loureiro, C. (2020). A consumer engagement systematic review : synthesis and research agenda. *Spanish Journal of Marketing, 24*(3), 283–307. doi:10.1108/SJME-01-2020-0021

Blum, K., & Omale, G. (2019). *Gartner Identifies Four Emerging Trends That Will Transform How Marketers Run Their Technology Ecosystems.* https://www.gartner.com/en/newsroom/press-releases/2019-08-2 9-gartner-identifies-four-emerging-trends-that-will-tra

Busch, O. (2016). *Programmatic Advertising: The Successful Transformation to Automated, Data-Driven Marketing in Real-Time.* Springer. doi:10.1007/978-3-319-25023-6

Capriotti, P. (2017). The World Wide Web and the Social Media as Tools of CSR Communication. In Handbook of Integrated CSR Communication (pp. 193–210). doi:10.1007/978-3-319-44700-1_11

Cho, M., Furey, L. D., & Mohr, T. (2017). Communicating corporate social responsibility on social media: Strategies, stakeholders, and public engagement on corporate facebook. *Business and Professional Communication Quarterly, 80*(1), 52–69. doi:10.1177/2329490616663708

Chu, S. C., Chen, H. T., & Sung, Y. (2016). Following brands on twitter: An extension of theory of planned behavior. *International Journal of Advertising, 35*(3), 421–437. doi:10.1080/02650487.2015.1037708

Clevenger, M. R., & Macgregor, C. J. (2019). Stakeholder Management and Corporate Social Responsibility (CSR). *Business and Corporation Engagement with Higher Education,* 67–81. doi:10.1108/978- 1-78754-655-420191003

Dessart, L., Veloutsou, C., & Morgan-Thomas, A. (2015). Consumer engagement in online brand communities: A social media perspective. *Journal of Product and Brand Management*, *24*(1), 28–42. doi:10.1108/JPBM-06-2014-0635

Eteokleous, P. P., Leonidou, L. C., & Katsikeas, C. S. (2016). Corporate social responsibility in international marketing: review, assessment, and future research. In International Marketing Review (Vol. 33, Issue 4). doi:10.1108/IMR-04-2014-0120

Farache, F., Tetchner, I., & Kollat, J. (2014). CSR Communications on Twitter: An Exploration into Stakeholder Reactions. In Corporate Responsibility and Digital Communities. Palgrave Studies in Governance, Leadership and Responsibility (pp. 145–163). Academic Press.

Fleischer, H. (2021). Corporate Purpose : A Management Concept and its Implications for Company Law. European Corporate Governance Institute.

Foroudi, P., Jin, Z., Gupta, S., Foroudi, M. M., & Kitchen, P. J. (2018). Perceptional components of brand equity: Configuring the Symmetrical and Asymmetrical Paths to brand loyalty and brand purchase intention. *Journal of Business Research*, *89*(January), 462–474. doi:10.1016/j.jbusres.2018.01.031

Gartenberg, C., Prat, A., & Serafeim, G. (2019). Corporate purpose and financial performance. *Organization Science*, *30*(1), 1–18. doi:10.1287/orsc.2018.1230

Gesenhues, A. (2020). How real is your real-time marketing? *MarTech*, 1–9. https://martech.org/how-real-is-your-real-time-marketing/

Gironda, J. T., & Korgaonkar, P. K. (2014). Understanding consumers ' social networking site usage. *Journal of Marketing Management*, *30*(5–6), 571–605. doi:10.1080/0267257X.2013.851106

Google Trends. (2022). *Dia Internacional da Mulher*. Google.

Grosser, K., & Moon, J. (2005). The role of corporate social responsibility in gender mainstreaming. *International Feminist Journal of Politics*, *7*(4), 532–554. doi:10.1080/14616740500284524

Grosser, K., & Moon, J. (2019). CSR and Feminist Organization Studies: Towards an Integrated Theorization for the Analysis of Gender Issues. *Journal of Business Ethics*, *155*(2), 321–342. doi:10.100710551-017-3510-x

Gruber, D. A., Smerek, R. E., Thomas-Hunt, M. C., & James, E. H. (2015). The real-time power of Twitter: Crisis management and leadership in an age of social media. *Business Horizons*, *58*(2), 163–172. doi:10.1016/j.bushor.2014.10.006

Gummerus, J., Liljander, V., Weman, E., & Pihlström, M. (2012). Customer engagement in a Facebook brand community. In Management Research Review (Vol. 35, Issue 9). doi:10.1108/01409171211256578

Hur, W. M., Kim, H., & Jang, J. H. (2016). The Role of Gender Differences in the Impact of CSR Perceptions on Corporate Marketing Outcomes. *Corporate Social Responsibility and Environmental Management*, *23*(6), 345–357. doi:10.1002/csr.1380

Hur, W. M., Kim, H., & Woo, J. (2014). How CSR Leads to Corporate Brand Equity: Mediating Mechanisms of Corporate Brand Credibility and Reputation. *Journal of Business Ethics*, *125*(1), 75–86. doi:10.100710551-013-1910-0

Hurth, V., Ebert, C., & Prabhu, J. (2018). Organisational purpose: The construct and its antecedents and consequences. *Cambridge Judge Business School*. https://www.jbs.cam.ac.uk/fileadmin/user_upload/research/workingpapers/wp1802.pdf

Jimenez, D., Franco, I. B., & Smith, T. (2021). A review of corporate purpose: An approach to actioning the sustainable development goals (SDGs). *Sustainability (Switzerland)*, *13*(7), 3899. Advance online publication. doi:10.3390u13073899

Kallier, S. M. (2017). International Review of Management and Marketing The Influence of Real-time Marketing Campaigns of Retailers on Consumer Purchase Behavior. *International Review of Management and Marketing*, *7*(3), 126–133. http:www.econjournals.com

Kallier Tar, S. M., & A Wiid, J. (2021). Consumer perceptions of real-time marketing used in campaigns for retail businesses. *International Journal of Research in Business and Social Science, 10*(2), 86–105. doi:10.20525/ijrbs.v10i2.1075

Keller, K. L., & Brexendorf, T. O. (2019). Measuring Brand Equity. In S. R. Wirtschaft (Ed.), *Handbuch Markenführung*. Springer Gabler. doi:10.1007/978-3-658-13342-9_72

Killian, G., & McManus, K. (2015). A marketing communications approach for the digital era: Managerial guidelines for social media integration. *Business Horizons*, *58*(5), 539–549. doi:10.1016/j.bushor.2015.05.006

Knox, S., & Maklan, S. (2004). Corporate Social Responsibility: Moving Beyond Investment Towards Measuring Outcomes. *European Management Journal*, *22*(5), 508–516. doi:10.1016/j.emj.2004.09.009

Kozinets, R. V. (2002). The Field Behind the Screen: Using Netnography For Marketing Research in Online Communities. *JMR, Journal of Marketing Research*, *39*(1), 61–72. doi:10.1509/jmkr.39.1.61.18935

Kozinets, R. V., & Gambetti, R. (2021). *Netnography Unlimited - Understanding Technoculture Using Qualitative Social Media Research*. Routledge.

Kozinets, R. V., Scaraboto, D., & Parmentier, M. A. (2018). Evolving netnography: How brand auto-netnography, a netnographic sensibility, and more-than-human netnography can transform your research. *Journal of Marketing Management*, *34*(3–4), 231–242. doi:10.1080/0267257X.2018.1446488

Krisch, U., & Grabner-kra, S. (2017). Insights into the Impact of CSR Communication Source on Trust and Purchase Intention. In *Handbook of Integrated CSR Communication* (pp. 449–469). CSR, Sustainability, Ethics & Governance. doi:10.1007/978-3-319-44700-1_25

Kuokkanen, H., & Sun, W. (2019). Companies, Meet Ethical Consumers : Strategic CSR Management to Impact Consumer Choice. *Journal of Business Ethics*. doi:10.1007/s10551-019-04145-4

Kwon, E. S., & Sung, Y. (2011). Follow Me! Global Marketers' Twitter Use. *Journal of Interactive Advertising*, *12*(1), 4–16. doi:10.1080/15252019.2011.10722187

Mccarthy, L. (2017). Empowering Women Through Corporate Social Responsibility: A Feminist Foucauldian Critique. *Business Ethics Quarterly*, *27*(4), 603–631. doi:10.1017/beq.2017.28

McKenna, R. (1995). Real-Time Marketing. *Harvard Business Review*.

Öberseder, M., Schlegelmilch, B. B., & Murphy, P. E. (2013). CSR practices and consumer perceptions. *Journal of Business Research*, *66*(10), 1839–1851. doi:10.1016/j.jbusres.2013.02.005

Ozkazanc-Pan, B. (2018). CSR as Gendered Neocoloniality in the Global South. *Journal of Business Ethics*, 1–14. doi:10.100710551-018-3798-1

Pereira, T., Loureiro, S. M. C., & Sarmento, E. M. (2022). Achieving Brand Engagement and Brand Equity Through Co-creation Process. *Journal of Creative Communications*, (3), 303–318. Advance online publication. doi:10.1177/09732586221083862

Ramya, V. (2019). Corporate Social Responsibility Towards Women Empowerment. *Quarterly Journal*, *22*(4), 10732–10739.

Read, W., Robertson, N., McQuilken, L., & Ferdous, A. S. (2019). Consumer engagement on Twitter: Perceptions of the brand matter. *European Journal of Marketing*, *53*(9), 1905–1933. doi:10.1108/EJM-10-2017-0772

Reece, M. (2010). *Real-Time Marketing for Business Growth*. FT Press.

Rietveld, R., Van Dolen, W., Mazloom, M., & Worring, M. (2020). What you feel, is what you like. Influence of message appeals on customer engagement on Instagram. *Journal of Interactive Marketing*, *49*(1), 20–53. doi:10.1016/j.intmar.2019.06.003

Salesforce Research. (2020). *State of thee connected customer*. https://www.salesforce.com/content/dam/web/pt_br/www/documents/e-books/stateoftheconnectedcustomer/Salesforce State of the Connected Customer 4th Ed_BR.pdf

Schmeltz, L. (2012). Consumer-oriented CSR communication: Focusing on ability or morality? *Corporate Communications*, *17*(1), 29–49. doi:10.1108/13563281211196344

Scott, D. M. (2011). *Real-Time Marketing and PR: How to Instantly Engage Your Market, Connect with Customers, and Create Products That Grow Your Business Now*. John Wiley & Sons.

Sterbenk, Y., Champlin, S., Windels, K., & Shelton, S. (2021). Is Femvertising the New Greenwashing? Examining Corporate Commitment to Gender Equality. *Journal of Business Ethics*, *2015*. Advance online publication. doi:10.100710551-021-04755-x

Sutto, G. (2021). *As 25 marcas mais valiosas do Brasil em 2021, segundo a Interbrand*. InfoMoney. https://www.infomoney.com.br/negocios/as-25-marcas-mais-valiosas-do-brasil-em-2021-segundo-a-interbrand/

Tasci, A. D. A. (2021). A critical review and reconstruction of perceptual brand equity. *International Journal of Contemporary Hospitality Management*, *33*(1), 166–198. doi:10.1108/IJCHM-03-2020-0186

United Nation. (2022). *Goal 5: Achieve gender equality and empower all women and girls*. Sustainable Development Goals. https://www.un.org/sustainabledevelopment/gender-equality/

Willemsen, L. M., Mazerant, K., Kamphuis, A. L., & van der Veen, G. (2018). Let's Get Real (Time)! The potential of real-time marketing to catalyze the sharing of brand messages. *International Journal of Advertising, 37*(5), 828–848. doi:10.1080/02650487.2018.1485214

Yasmin, A., Tasneem, S., & Fatema, K. (2015). Effectiveness of Digital Marketing in the Challenging Age: An Empirical Study. *The International Journal of Management Science and Business Administration, 1*(5), 69–80. doi:10.18775/ijmsba.1849-5664-5419.2014.15.1006

Yoo, B., & Donthu, N. (2001). Developing and validating a multidimensional consumer-based brand equity scale. *Journal of Business Research, 52*(1), 1–14. doi:10.1016/S0148-2963(99)00098-3

Zajas, J., & Zotz, L. Jr. (1995). Integrating Customer Satisfaction into the Strategic Marketing Plan. *Journal of Customer Service in Marketing & Management, 1*(3), 51–66. doi:10.1300/J127v01n03_05

Zou, H., Xie, X., Meng, X., & Yang, M. (2018). The diffusion of corporate social responsibility through social network ties: From the perspective of strategic imitation. *Corporate Social Responsibility and Environmental Management, 26*(1), 186–198. doi:10.1002/csr.1670

Chapter 3

How Can SMEs Integrate Intellectual Property Rights Into Social Media Marketing Strategies to Achieve Brand and Business Development?
Case Study of the Chinese Cultural Industry

Poshan Yu
https://orcid.org/0000-0003-1069-3675
Soochow University, China & Australian Studies Centre, Shanghai University, China

Chenghai Li
Independent Researcher, China

Ramya Mahendran
https://orcid.org/0000-0001-9585-9077
Independent Researcher, India

ABSTRACT

In China, due to the rise of online literature and its derivative works, IP, which means intellectual property, refers to literary works with strong economic exploitation potential and the forms of exploitation include the adaptation of online literature into music works, film and animation, online games, etc. This chapter will analyze the development of Chinese online literature on social media and its IP creation and then focus on the case study of online literature company Jinjiang Literature and film company Daylight Entertainment. Both of them are famous SMEs in China, producing a lot of literature, films, and television works of high quality and meanwhile improving their business performance. In the end, this chapter will analyze the problems these companies face and find out the solutions.

DOI: 10.4018/978-1-6684-5770-2.ch003

INTRODUCTION

Definition and Classification

Social media are internet-based programs that allow users to create and share user generated content (Kaplan and Haenlein, 2010). They can be classified into different categories (Hanafifizadeh et al., 2021). WhatsApp, Line, Telegram and WeChat are examples of networking sites. Youtube, Tiktok and Vimeo are examples of content communities. Twitter and Blogspot are examples of blogs. TripAdvisor, Yelp and FourSquare are examples of online forums & discussion. Organizational usage of social media is changing organizational communication and public relations (Farzana et al., 2018). Social media enables open communication, which helps organizations to understand customer needs and motivates them to respond proactively and efficiently to those needs (Farzana et al., 2016).

Small and Medium-sized Enterprises (SMEs) are important contributors to any nation's economy. Globally, in developing countries, SMEs constitute about 90% of businesses and over 50% of employment, representing a major portion of GDP (World Bank, 2020). SMEs' prominence lies in the innovation, poverty alleviation, job creation, economic growth and social cohesion. It has contributed over 40% to GDP and created over 70% jobs in emerging economies (Sheshadri & Arpan, 2020).

While large organizations dominate the use of social media, research has proven that social media are crucial tools for SMEs (Rahmawati et al., 2020). Social media can be employed by SMEs because of its low cost, technical manageability and ease of use, and its capability to connect with and reach consumers in scale (Farzana et al., 2018).

The Special Meaning of IP in China

China, as a developing country with a high social media penetration rate, has valuable experience in the organizational usage of social media. One of the examples is the creation of online literature IP. IP originally refers to intellectual property rights. In China, it has almost become a synonym for a particular form of cultural production—original internet fiction (Wu, 2022). It typically refers to web novels with strong economic exploitation potential, and the forms of exploitation include the adaptation of online literature into music works, film and animation, online games, etc. (Zeng & Du, 2021).

China's online IP literature and film industry are very well developed. Jinjiang Literature and Daylight entertainment, as SMEs, are one of the forerunners in the literature and film industries respectively. They produce high-quality literary works, film and television works, and receive rich financial returns. Meanwhile, it also helps them enhance their corporate image.

Research Questions

In this chapter we are going to explore the following questions.

Question 1. What types of SMEs in China are suitable for social media marketing?
Question 2. Why is it possible for these types of SMEs in China to create IP through social media and improve their performance?
Question 3. What kind of social media did each of these two companies use and how did they become successful?

Question 4. Do SMEs in China encounter any problems when using social media? If so, how can they be solved?

This chapter will first present a global and Chinese perspective of usage of social media, SMEs, IP industry, etc. Next, this chapter will analyze the development of Chinese online literature on social media and its IP creation, and then focus on the case study of online literature company Jinjiang Literature and film company Daylight Entertainment. Both of them are famous SMEs in China, producing a lot of literature, films and television works of high quality and all the while, work on improving their business performance. In the end, this chapter will analyze the problems these companies face and find out the solutions.

LITERATURE REVIEW

Organizational Use of Social Media

There has been considerable interest in the impact of social media on businesses among researchers, policymakers, and management of corporate organizations in the recent years (Suryani et al., 2021). Previous research mainly focuses on two areas, one is the role that social media plays in brand and marketing strategies, and the other is how they are promoting interaction and contact with customers and audience. Certain marketing objective can be obtained by using social media, including creating brand affinity, increasing sales prospects, and improving customer service (Haudi, 2022; Misirlis & Vlachopoulou, 2018; Wood and Khan, 2016).

Some studies have focused on the role that social media can play in obtaining relationship marketing goals (Sedalo et al., 2022; Abeza, O'Reilly, & Reid, 2013; Williams & Chinn, 2010). Their use goes beyond simple social communication (Ngai, Tao, & Moon, 2015). Social media assists firms in improving contact with their customers, increasing the level of trust and relationship building and facilitating the identification of possible business partners (Jaini, 2023; Misirlis & Vlachopoulou, 2018; Meske and Stieglitz, 2013; Kelleher and Sweetser, 2012; Michaelidou et al., 2011).

Some scholars have found that social media usage has positive effects on SMEs' performance (Qalati, 2022; Judy & Peter, 2019). Borah et al. (2022) explore the relationships between social media usage and innovation capabilities to improve sustainable SME performance. Leonardi and Vaast (2016) review existing academic research on social media and organizations, emphasizing social media diffusion, use, and its implications for organizational processes of communication, collaboration, and knowledge sharing.

There are also some studies on the use of social media by SMEs in developing countries. Nguyen et al. (2022) examined the effects of entrepreneurial orientation, social media, and managerial ties on the business performance of SMEs in Vietnam. Their study suggests practical implications for Vietnamese SMEs to improve firm performance effectively and efficiently. Bruce et al. (2022) investigates the impact of social media usage on the long-term sustainability of SMEs in Ghana. Wibawa et al. (2022) explore why and how SMEs in Indonesia use social media and its impact on marketing performance by using an explanatory pilot study as a research method. Zeng, Xu and Wu (2022) demonstrate how social media content reaches and impresses more users. Using a sample of 345 articles released by Chinese small and medium-sized enterprises (SMEs) on their official WeChat accounts, they employ the self-determination theory to analyze the effects of content optimization strategies on social media visibility.

However, most of the social media platforms covered by these studies are social networking sites, content communities and blogs. There are few studies on online literature platforms, not to mention studies on the online literature IP established by SMEs. There are many different types of SMEs. As online literature and its IP are well developed in China, this chapter will examine how online literature companies and film & TV companies can use social media to build IP and obtain better performance.

Intellectual Property Rights in China

Intellectual property rights (IPRs) have been recognized in Europe for more than 300 years (Sherman & Bently, 1999). China's IPR laws started late relatively, and there is some literature devoted to its development process. Yu (2018) discusses the system's evolution from its birth all the way to the present. Hong, Edler and Massini (2022) also illustrate the evolutionary changes of the Chinese IPR system and analyze the changes introduced in four revisions. China's current IPR system has been developed through the transplantation of the concept and models from the Western world since the end of the 1970s. The direct transplantation leads to divergence and the divergence thus leads to difficulty in the enforcement of IPRs (Zhang & Bruun, 2017). Shen and Wen (2016) point out that there are still many problems in the Chinese intellectual property protection regime. The most essential one is the implementation of the law. China's intellectual property protection laws are not yet perfect, not to mention the early 21st century, when online literature was just emerging. Chinese people's awareness of copyright is also not strong during that time. In the process of creation, the writers of online literature do not consider whether their works can be protected, but more out of the need to share and socialize. The rise of online literature has further contributed to the improvement of China's intellectual property protection laws.

DATA: SOCIAL MEDIA USAGE AND IP INDUSTRY IN CHINA

The Usage of Social Media Worldwide and in China

China is one of the world's largest social media markets with highly engaged and mobile-savvy users (Statista, 2022. Social networks in China - statistics & facts).

Figure 1. Leading iPhone social media apps in the Apple App Store worldwide in February 2022, by number of downloads (in millions)
Source: Statista

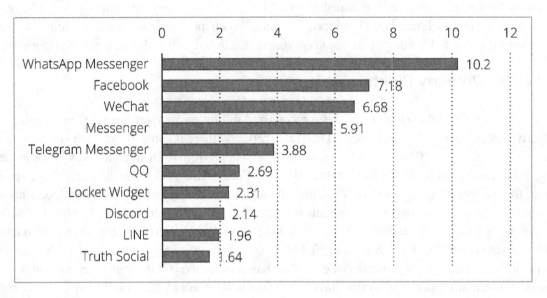

As is shown in Figure 1, considering only the number of social media downloads in the Apple Store, three of China's social media applications are ranked in the top positions. China's media landscape in terms of social networks almost mirrors that of the rest of the world, except that these sites are domestically engineered platforms.

Figure 2. Active user base of top-tier influencers in China 2021, by platform
Source: Statista

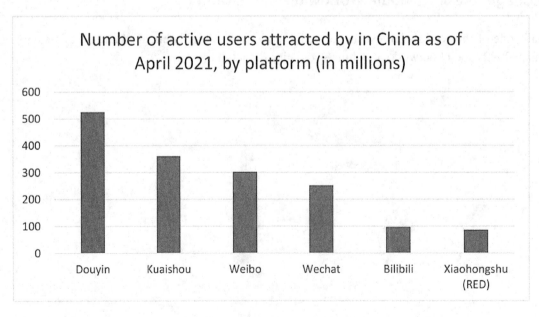

Figure 2 illustrates that as of April 2021, Douyin - TikTok's Chinese sister app - attracted around 525 million active users in China. Its local rival Kuaishou was another active platform with 361 million active users. In terms of the time spent on social media apps, Douyin was among the most used social media apps in China as well. Weibo, as a social media often used by literature companies and film companies to conduct publicity, comes in the third place. It will be mentioned in the case study below.

Figure 3. Monthly time spent on main social media apps in China 2020
Source: Statista

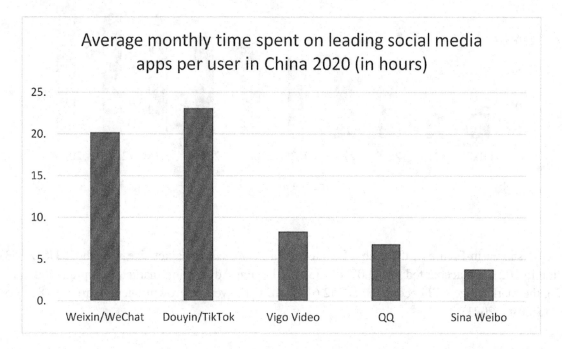

Figure 3 shows that Chinese users spend a lot of time on social media every month, with the content community Douyin and the social networking site Wechat being two of the most frequently used social media. It is also worth mentioning that Sina Weibo ranks fifth.

Overall, social media in China is mature, with a large number of active users and a long average usage time. This makes the organizational usage of social media possible.

The Social Media Advertising Market Worldwide and in China

Social media is a very effective advertising platform (Yu et al., 2022) due to the presence of a large number of active users.

Figure 4. Global revenue forecast in billion US$ and mobile/desktop distribution
Source: Statista Digital Market Outlook 2021

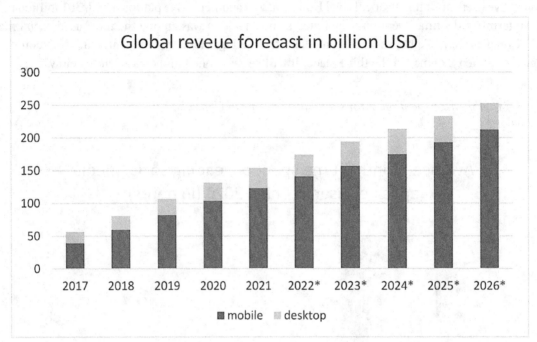

As is shown in Figure 4, the global Social Media Advertising market size was about USD 153.7 billion in 2021 and accounted for 33.0% of the total Digital Advertising market. It is predicted that in 2026, the market size will become USD 252.6 billion, with average growth rates of around 18.1% per year (Statista, 2021).

Figure 5. Revenue forecast in billion USD
Source: Statista Digital Market Outlook 2021

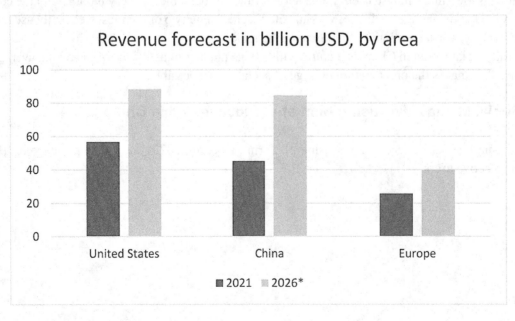

As is shown in Figure 5, the U.S. market leads in Social Media Advertising and generated revenues of about USD 56.7 billion in 2021. That is a 29.8% share of the total U.S. Digital Advertising market. The market in Europe was about USD 25.7 billion in 2021, half the size of the U.S. market and the segment share is 29.2% of the whole European Digital Advertising market.

In China, Social Media Advertising is the largest segment of the Digital Advertising revenue. Expressed in absolute figures, Social Media Advertising generated USD 45.1 billion in 2021 and accounted for 43.7% of Digital Advertising in China (Statista, 2021).

With the revenue of USD 45.1 billion in 2021, China's social media advertising market accounts for nearly 30% of the global market. Social media advertising is an effective marketing method with high returns in China.

The IP Industry in China

The figure below (Figure 6) shows that China's IP licensing industry witnessed an increase from 48.5 billion yuan in 2015 to 84.4 billion yuan in 2019. The market size of the intellectual property licensing industry, as measured by retail value, was projected to reach 156.1 billion yuan in 2024.

Figure 6. Market size of the IP licensing industry in China 2015-2024
Source: Statista

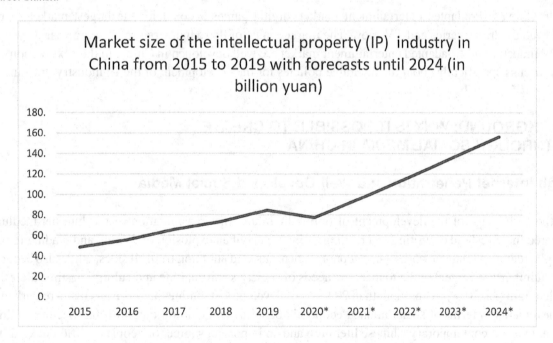

As is shown in Figure 7, in 2019, the market size of intellectual property-adapted entertainment industry totaled 308 billion yuan, increasing from 263.9 billion yuan in the previous year. It is expected to rise at an even faster rate.

Figure 7. Market size of the IP-adapted entertainment market China 2015-2024, by entertainment
Source: Statista

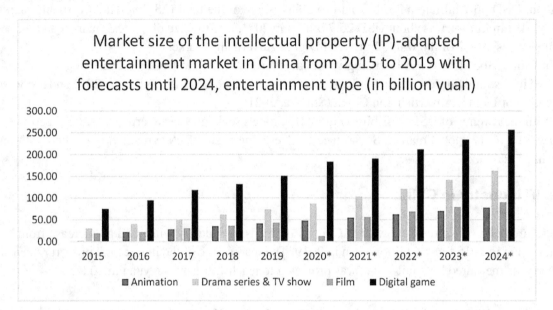

In China's IP-adapted entertainment market, digital games account for the largest market share, followed by drama series and TV show. The market value of these industries is growing year on year.

IP industry and IP-adapted entertainment market are well developed in China. In the next section we will discuss specifically about the favorable policies for the development of the IP industry in China.

BACKGROUND: WHY IS IT POSSIBLE TO CREATE IP THROUGH SOCIAL MEDIA IN CHINA

High Internet Penetration and Well-Developed Social Media

At the early stage of the development of online literature, the transmutation of the Internet medium lowered the threshold of writing and reading, bringing about an explosion of writing and reading for all people, reaping abundant works, huge economic benefits, and attention from all sides, while also becoming an important content outlet to meet the needs of society's spiritual life and cultural pastime after the millennium (Li, 2018). After more than 20 years of development, online literature has made remarkable achievements in terms of social impact, economic benefits, and cultural output. It has become an important part of contemporary Chinese literature and an important source for people of different kinds to read, profoundly influencing the way we read and the dissemination of culture in contemporary society.

In China, online literature holds an absolute advantage in the literature reading and digital reading market. The 49th Statistical Report on the Development of the Internet in China (CNNIC[1], 2022) shows that by the end of December 2021, the total size of China's Internet users was 1.032 billion, the Internet penetration rate reached 73.0%, and the scale of Internet applications ranked first in the world. By the end of December 2021, the total scale of online literature users in China reached 502 million, an increase of 41.45 million over the same period last year, accounting for 48.6% of the total number of Internet users, and the number of readers reached the highest level ever.

Online literature has cultivated the good habit of using smart phones and other electronic devices to make full use of fragmented time for reading activities. The idea of promoting "reading for all" is not just to "encourage more people to fall in love with reading", but also to "broaden the scenes and time periods in which reading takes place". Nowadays, the readership of online literature has covered all provinces, municipalities, and autonomous regions in China, both in terms of the absolute number of readers and in terms of distribution, the wave of "reading for all" has become unstoppable.

2020 Report on the development of Chinese Internet literature (2022) pointed out some characteristics of the development of Chinese online literature. It points out that writers of online literature have continued to grow younger and more professional. Readers of Internet literature, mostly Generation Z, have a strong willingness to pay and interact. Author and reader characteristics promote the development of online literature IP.

Policies Conducive to the Development of Online Literature

China has introduced many policies that are favorable to the development of online literature, which can be mainly divided into financial support, talent cultivation and technical support.

In terms of financial support, the State Administration of Radio Film and Television of China issued guidance on promoting the healthy development of online literature (SARFT, 2014). The guidance suggested policy support, such as seeking financial support for the development of online literature at all levels, improving relevant publishing funds and special funds, and implementing preferential value added tax (VAT) policies for online literature publishing.

In terms of talent cultivation, guidance on deepening the reform of the title system for art professionals (2020) issued by the Ministry of Human Resources and Social Security. The Ministry of Culture and Tourism proposes to open up channels for the assessment of titles for online writers and promote the interface between the title system and the talent cultivation system.

In terms of technical support, relevant policies mainly support the development or application of technical standards for work management, product technical standards, as well as content distribution technology, information application technology, digital copyright protection technology, AR/VR technology, and content regulation technology, to improve the capacity of online literature work management, distribution, copyright protection and online literature regulation.

Policies for the Protection of Intellectual Property

The policies and laws on copyright protection are improving in China. The government cracks down on plagiarism, piracy, and infringement. The National Copyright Administration, in conjunction with the State Internet Information Office, the Ministry of Industry and Information Technology and the Ministry of Public Security, has been conducting the "SwordNet" special campaign for 17 years. The "SwordNet 2021" focuses on combating online copyright infringement and piracy, and rectifies the copyright order in five areas, further strengthening the supervision of copyright on social networking platforms and knowledge-sharing platforms, and consolidating the results of special treatment in areas such as news works, online music and online literature (Zhang, 2020).

China has made significant progress in the protection of intellectual property rights. The Copyright Law (National People's Congress Standing Committee, 2020), which has been amended three times, the recent revision came into force in June 2021 and addresses the previous problem of insufficient punishment for infringement by optimizing the calculation of damages and raising the upper limit of compensation, which has a deterrent effect on piracy infringement. It also provides the most authoritative and professional protection for authors and the industry as a whole. In line with the implementation of the new law, the China Writers' Association has revised the "Practical Guide for Writers to Safeguard Their Rights", which contains judicial interpretations such as the "Interpretation of the Supreme People's Court on the Application of Punitive Damages in Civil Cases of Infringement of Intellectual Property Rights" and the interpretation of common provisions in the "Book Publishing Contract" and "Information Network Dissemination Rights Licensing Contract", which are more suitable for the needs of copyright protection under the new situation and provide a basis for authors to safeguard their rights and interests.

THE CASE STUDY OF SMEs IN CHINA

In China, there is a vast market for online literary IPs and their IP adaptations. This process can be called "IP operation", which is the process of maximizing the commercial value of the original work by creating outstanding online literary works to gather popularity, forming a "fan effect" through Internet operation, and then adapting the original work into movies, TV series, games, plays and peripheral products. Publishing physical books, producing audio books, creating games and adapting films, TV dramas, animation or stage plays are all forms of "IP operation".

Prior to the widespread use of IP operations, online literature websites mainly relied on membership fees, physical book publishing and advertising for their profits, while the rise of the IP adaptation trend has brought about new ways of profitability, with online literature websites relying on IP rights trading for higher profits.

The process of IP operation is one of media convergence, and its operation as a whole is an industrial value chain. Online literature is the foundation and most important link in this industry's value chain, and the quality of its content affects the subsequent value-added space. A good story and a fan base are essential elements of an "IP", so IP operation requires the selection or cultivation of "IPs".

Online literature is at upstream of the entire pan-entertainment industry, and with its rich content reserves, it is constantly delivering content and stories to the entire industry chain, linking different forms of content such as film, television, games, and animation through online IPs, meeting the individual needs of different users with diversified forms of expression and development, and promoting the linkage effect of various links in the pan-entertainment ecological chain. This section takes two typical cases from upstream and midstream of the IP industry chain to analyze how they have used IP to gain better performance.

The Case of Jinjiang Literature

Introduction to Jinjiang Literature and Its IP Resources

History of Jinjiang Literature

Jinjiang Literature was established in 1999. At that time, it was still a forum on the Jinjiang World Wide Web. Huang Yanming, who loved literature, took over the forum by chance and established Jinjiang Original in 2003, which was later renamed Jinjiang Literature. Now, Huang is the CEO of Jinjiang Literature, and her husband Liu Xudong is the President of the company.

In 2005, many of the similar online reading sites have gone commercial and paid authors for their work. As a result, Jinjiang has passively started its own commercialization process in order to retain authors and readers (Shu, 2019). It launched paid reading business in 2008 and the subscribers quickly exceeded 5.8 million (Shi, 2021).

Unlike the majority of websites that are directly acquired by capital, Huang and Liu only sold half of Jinjiang's equity, maintaining its independence while receiving investment. After years of development, it has become increasingly influential in the field of online literature. In 2021, Jinjiang Literature earned RMB 1.25 billion in revenue and RMB 418 million in profit for the year (ChinaLiterature, 2022).

Main Business of Jinjiang Literature and Its Development

The main business of Jinjiang Literature includes film, television, games and other copyright business, overseas copyright cooperation, electronic copyright business and Physical publishing business (Jinjiang Literature, 2022). The first business mentioned above is where IP plays an important role.

As one of the leading online literature websites, Jinjiang Literature has a large number of high-profile and influential online literary works, which have been developed into film and television works and games since the beginning of the popularity of "IP" (Du, 2018). In 2011, the TV series "Treading On Thin Ice", adapted from a novel of the same name by Jinjiang author Tong Hua, became popular, showing the strong potential of the film and television adaptation of high-quality online novels. Later, many original novels of popular TV series were all first published in Jinjiang Literature and are representatives of the "IP" of Jinjiang Literature, such as "The Legend of Zhen Huan", "The Journey of Flower" and "Silent Separation". The TV series Reset, which was a hit in China in early 2022, was also adapted from a novel in Jinjiang Literature.

According to its official website (Jinjiang Literature, 2022), as of May 2022, Jinjiang Literature has over 4.91 million online novels and nearly 10,000 published novels. It has over 250,000 contracted copyrighted works, with an average of over 2,800 new contracted copyrighted works every month. The number of registered authors exceeds 2.19 million, the average daily update word count exceeds 36 million, and the cumulative word count published on the website exceeds 116.6 billion.

Since the launch of the website's paid reading business in January 2008, the number of registered users has exceeded 54.28 million by May 2022, with an average daily online time of up to 80 minutes. Users from nearly 200 countries and regions around the world visit Jinjiang, with developed countries such as the United States, Canada and Australia accounting for a large proportion, and the proportion of overseas user traffic exceeding 10%.

Nowadays, more than 600 novels have been adapted into film and television dramas or have been sold for film and television rights in Jinjiang Literature, making it a leader among literature websites. The copyright fees for a single novel by a well-known author can reach up to ten million CNY.

Table 1. Works that sold for over CNY10 million in copyright in Jinjiang Literature

Title of the Work	Author	Copyright Transaction Amount
Heavenly God blesses the people	Smell of ink and copper coin	40 million
Fire to drown sorrows	Priest	10 million
Non-polluting	Priest	10 million
Breaking through the clouds 1	Huai Shang	10 million
Breaking through the clouds 2	Huai Shang	10 million
Tian Bao subdues demons	Fei tian	10 million
Epic of Divinity Light	Fei tian	10 million
Capture the Dream	Fei tian	10 million
Turing Code	Fei tian	10 million
You are more beautiful than Beijing	Jiu Yue Xi	10 million
The stars are shining brightly	Concern is confusing	10 million
Silent Reading	Preist	10 million

Source: Jinjiang Literature

Jinjiang has cooperated with over fifty publishers in Hong Kong, Macau, Taiwan (China), over twenty Vietnamese publishers, several Thai publishers and copyright partners in Russia, Hungary, Germany, the United States, Japan, Korea, Malaysia and Myanmar. The company has exported more than 2,000 online literary works overseas and is continuing to actively explore new copyright export channels to promote more outstanding works to more countries.

As the global competition for cultural soft power becomes more and more intense, online literature has been widely noticed as a part of cultural soft power, where copyright development and IP operation have great potential for development. Focusing on and studying the copyright development and IP operation of online literature websites not only helps to study the development and profitability of online literature, but also has profound contemporary significance and long-term strategic value.

The Reasons for Jinjiang Literature's success

Focus on the Social Attributes of the Online Literature Platform

As is mentioned above, Jinjiang evolved from a literary community, and it retains the format of forum.

The Jinjiang forum, called "Riverside", began as a forum for communication between authors and readers, or readers and readers. Nowadays, it has evolved into a powerful means of building a fan base (Shi, 2021). This format allows authors to freely share their creative ideas and get feedback from readers, while readers can recommend their favorite books. What more, the forum gathers fans of an author or "book fans" of a particular work. The community-based trend of "Riverside" strengthens user bonding and enables readers to gradually form a sense of belonging and identification with Jinjiang Literature, which is very beneficial to the marketing of content in the fan circle nowadays.

For example, the book fans of Magician Ancestor, a work in Jinjiang Literature, have a core group of users who spontaneously made the re-creation in "Riverside". Moreover, the fans also draw relative artwork and music on other social media such as Weibo and LOFTER (an online content community). This progressive model also allows the work to bring further effect to the masses (Shi, 2021). Jinjiang Literature themselves helps to promote popular IPs to the fans, thus further exploring the development path of IP marketing and better achieving the purpose of the distribution of quality content.

The founders of Jinjiang, Huang and Liu, know how to develop the social attributes of online literature platforms. Liu is concerned about interaction between readers and authors (Shu, 2019). For example, if a work is collected or reviewed by readers, the author's work will be recommended; if there are negative comments, the recommendation will be reduced. They use mathematical models to create a multi-latitude evaluation system, which can take advantage of the low cost and social attributes of the Internet to improve performance.

Attract Mobile Users of Online Literature

Jinjiang Literature has grown rapidly and steadily from a hub for literature lovers to an industry-leading website covering all kinds of terminals including personal computer (PC) terminal, wireless application protocol (WAP) terminal and mobile phone application (App) terminal. Its mobile reading App "Jinjiang Novel Reader" has versions for Android and iOS and can be downloaded from all major application stores.

Since its inception, online literature has been mainly available on the PC side. However, with the popularity of mobile phones, mobile users have gradually surpassed PC users. According to CNNIC (2015), as of June 2014, the number of mobile internet users in China reached 527 million, and the proportion of internet users using mobile phones to access the internet increased from 81.0% in 2013 to 83.4%, with the scale of mobile internet users surpassing that of traditional PC internet users for the first time. In order to respond to the trend of mobile users of online literature, Jinjiang Literature gave priorities to development of mobile terminal. In August 2014, the Android version of the mobile client was launched, and in November 2015, the iOS version of the mobile client was launched.

At the same time, Jinjiang Literature cooperates with platforms to further expand content distribution channels and attract mobile users of online literature. Since October 2008, Jinjiang Literature has cooperated with mobile internet service content providers such as China Mobile and China Unicom and mobile phone terminal companies such as Samsung and Nokia to provide quality genuine works to their mobile phone reading programs, further promoting and publicizing Jinjiang's quality (Du, 2018). Since 2013, Jinjiang Literature has cooperated with mobile reading Apps such as iReader, Duokan Reader and iQIYI Reader, expanding the mobile reading client channel. The format of multiple channels for one work effectively enhances the publicity effect and revenue of the work.

Capture Social Media Users' Preference

There are a large number of online literature websites in China, and Jinjiang Literature stands out from the rest because of the high quality and variety of its works. Jinjiang Literature attaches importance to the cultivation of quality works and its editors do not interfere too much with the genre of works (Shu, 2019). What more, Jinjiang Literature fully captures the preference of social media users.

When using social media, people seek the quick access to information and pleasure. The literature works in Jinjiang are shorter than those of other literary sites, with most of its works concentrated in the 3,00,000 – 8,00,000 word range while other online literature are often more than a million words. The paid-reading system, which is based on the number of words the reader reads, makes readers spend more when reading long works. However, in other literary sites, many novels with millions of words are of low quality and the plot is slow. It is not uncommon to see a dozen chapters updated without any progress in the plot. Authors increase their word count by over-describing the setting and appearance. These behaviors and phenomena are not only detrimental to the interests of readers, but also to the production of good works. Jinjiang Literature avoids these problems and attract readers. The fan base is the key to its ability to build an IP.

Overall, online literature is in the upstream of the IP industry chain, which is a copyright reserve trading segment (Fan, 2017). Online literature has the largest volume of copyright trading, and the market size has reached the tens of billions of yuan, which is profitable through licensing or independent development. Jinjiang Literature is able to capture the preferences and social needs of readers, continuously cultivating original IP, integrating quality IP resources, building brand image, and improving performance.

The Case of Daylight Entertainment

Introduction to Daylight Entertainment

Daylight Entertainment was established in 2011. In the highly competitive TV drama industry, the TV dramas produced by Daylight Entertainment have always maintained a high standard. From *The Legend of Zhen Huan*, *Nirvana in Fire* and *The Disguiser*, to *Ode to Joy*, *The Story of Minglan*, and then to the web drama *Reset*, which was a hit at the beginning of this year, this company has won both ratings and reputation due to these adaptations. It has also become a representative film brand of innovative break-throughs and a model of using IP of online literature.

From 2015 to 2020, the company has produced a total of 15 works, 13 of which were adapted from IP literature (Ma & Zhang, 2021). In terms of content selection, Daylight Entertainment prefers to adapt the stories of existing works, the so-called IP adaptations, which not only saves time in script creation but also attracts a group of fans of the original. On the basis of deciding on a suitable subject, the choice of scriptwriter is also key to the quality of an IP project. Unlike original scripts, IPs come with their own base of original fans, so in the process of film and television, the audience's restoration of the novel's characters, lines and plot often becomes the focus of attention for IP dramas. How to balance the plot of the novel with the rationalization of the film and television has become an important part of the test for IP scriptwriters.

In a situation where the film industry is constantly disputing the concept of IP and many IP projects are underachieving, the IP dramas of Daylight Entertainment have been making great strides. According to the previous works, the primary condition for the success of its IP film and television is to choose the type of subject matter that suits you. Daylight Entertainment has a unique eye for choosing IPs (Shi, 2021). In terms of genres, they cover elements such as espionage, power struggles, romance, house battles, court, time loops, family, and commercial warfare. On the other hand, Daylight Entertainment does not buy so-called big IPs, but rather small ones with potential for development.

The dramas produced by Daylight Entertainment, are renowned for their choice of subject matter and their knack for being topical dramas, which generate a lot of discussion and strong interaction between the whole media, both online and offline, as soon as they are broadcast. What's more, "Men's dramas" was the most obvious labels attached to Daylight Entertainment in the early days (Zhang, 2021). The top 5 high-scoring dramas from Daylight Entertainment, which are *Nirvana in Fire*, *Like a Flowing River*, *The Disguiser*, *Two Families in Wenzhou*, show the style of the old times and expresses heavy emotions. This is the strength of Daylight Entertainment and is also directly related to the aesthetic preferences of the team.

Behind the many successful IP projects, Daylight Entertainment has also continued to export value for its own brand image through quality content. Today, the words "Daylight Entertainment" have become the new IP symbol of the domestic TV drama industry in China.

Reasons for Daylight Entertainment's Success

Exploit the Fan Effect

As mentioned above, online literature is in the upstream of the IP industry chain (Fan, 2017). Meanwhile, the film & TV industry is in the midstream or downstream of this industry. Just as Jinjiang Literature retains its forum format, many online literary platforms themselves act as social media. Daylight entertainment is good at using the fan effect from upstream companies.

Daylight Entertainment is good at exploiting fan effect and uniting the power of fans, to stimulate their participation and thus enhance the influence of products. The Internet era is also the era of fan economy. In the TV drama industry, fans, as the most enthusiastic audience group, can not only provide airtime for TV dramas, but also provided positive communication and spontaneous publicity (Feng & Xiao, 2018).

Film & TV creators have been working on adaptations of online literature, as the literature itself has a fan base that cannot be ignored for the overall promotion of the TV series. Fans are an important customer group and can lead to better results (Scott & Scott, 2020). As for TV dramas, fans of the original work are the main audience for TV dramas in the Internet era, not only providing the drama's airtime, but also playing a role in positive communication.

For example, the main actors in *Like a Flowing River*, had accumulated a huge fan base before, and the broadcast of *Like a Flowing River*, the interaction of fans on social media platforms such as Weibo triggered the "crowd effect", and the expanding fan ecosystem generated high ratings for the drama, making the drama gain widespread attention (Wei, 2021).

Take another example. When Daylight Entertainment announced that it would be filming *When a Snail Falls in Love*, it raised the expectations of a large number of fans of the original author Ding Mo's books (Feng, 2018). The suspense and romance theme of *When a Snail Falls in Love* is also popular in 2014, meeting the audience's demand. At the same time, the lead roles already have a very large and loyal fan base, and this is their third time for them to act as a couple, which has generated a lot of interest from CP fans (i.e., fans who like them to act as a couple).

Apply Social Thinking

Daylight Entertainment not only made use of online literature IP, but also made full use of various mobile terminals and social networks to create various topics and opportunities to stay interactive with viewers and boost the heat and attention of the TV series (Wei, 2021).

In the production and marketing of TV dramas, social thinking means making full use of various mobile terminals and social networks to create various topics and opportunities to stay engaged with viewers and raise attention of the drama. Generating interactive discussions requires two things: firstly, the drama itself can cater to a wide range of viewership groups in order to provide the drama with a viewership base; secondly, the drama should be able to capture hot topics in its marketing so that viewers have room to discuss them (Feng & Xiao, 2018).

As mentioned above, Daylight Entertainment is very good at producing topical dramas, which generate a lot of buzz once they are broadcast. If social media is used to interact with the audience at this time, it will increase audience engagement and further enhance the popularity of the work.

Take the TV series *Ode to Joy* as an example. Firstly, the five girls in *Ode to Joy* all live a different life, which is very accurate in catering to a wide range of viewing groups. Secondly, prior to the start of the show, the official Weibo account of *Ode to Joy* built up momentum in advance, releasing posters of the main cast and teaser footage of the show one after another. At the same time, it worked closely with major video sites to recommend the TV series on their home pages. These all aroused a strong sense of curiosity and anticipation.

After the start of the series, the team worked with micro-bloggers on Weibo and adopted a multi-level marketing approach, driving audience discussion and continuously following up with official bloggers. This marketing approach kept the number of Weibo topics for *Ode to Joy* high, reaching a total of 3.5 billion at its peak (Feng & Xiao, 2018). As seen from the Weibo Hot Search Index, every peak of *Ode to Joy* is a hot topic with a high degree of concentration, and it is a "storyline" that has been planted by the cast and crew during the preparation and production process, generating interactive discussions. The interaction between the creators and viewers was also very strong, with frequent interactions between the main cast and viewers on Weibo both during and after the series, maintaining the follow-up buzz.

Daylight entertainment uses social media in two ways. On the one hand, it takes full advantage of the upstream online literature sites' own social media properties and uses the fan effect to raise popularity of its own work. On the other hand, it builds momentum for its works in social media commonly used by the general public and interacts with its audience. Both of them help develop good reputation of its works and also of the company itself.

PROBLEMS AND SOLUTIONS

The Problems Online Literature Companies and Film Companies Face

As online literature plays an important role of IP for the cultural industry, copyright protection has a direct impact on the passion and quality of creation. Due to the popularity of social media and the ease of digital text copying and transcription, piracy becomes increasingly easier, which seriously affects the development of the industry.

The growing scale of piracy has seriously dampened creative enthusiasm. According to *the White Paper on Copyright Protection of Chinese Online Literature 2021,* in 2020, the overall market size of Chinese online literature was RMB 28.8 billion, and the scale of piracy losses rose 6.9% year-on-year to RMB 6.028 billion in 2019, with the scale of piracy losses accounting for 21% of the overall market size. At the same time, 85.4% of writers have experienced infringement and piracy, and the proportion of those who suffer from frequent infringement and piracy is as high as 42%. About 60% of writers believe that infringement seriously damages the interests of both creators and platforms, and severely discourages creative enthusiasm (Chinese Academy of Social Sciences, 2022).

The speed at which pirate sites steal genuine version continues to rise. Due to technological advances, it is common for pirate sites to quickly steal and synchronize genuine content.

In February 2021, the TV series adapted from the online literature IP *My Heroic Husband* hit the airwaves, and the original novel reading on ChinaLiterature platform (Tencent Holdings' online novel platform) increased by nearly 17 times. At the same time, however, pirate platforms quickly launched the novel, with up to 4 million pirate links for the keyword "My Heroic Husband TXT". The pirate platform converts some of the new readers into pirate readers through search traffic, and even more so, the pirate website will release the new book of the author first to induce fans to read it.

The Solutions to the Problems

Measures That Companies Can Take

The relevant companies should insist on the specialization and normalization of rights protection. ChinaLiterature's IP management team constantly improves its technical monitoring mechanism, monitoring key channels, including PC, App, WeChat public number, online disk, and audio, etc., In 2020, a total of 12.08 million web links were taken down in complaints by its legal department, with an average of more than 2,00,000 infringing links per week in search engine channels alone. For third-party piracy platforms, ChinaLiterature has taken evidence and archived all infringements of piracy in its daily monitoring, so as to be prepared for subsequent rights protection (Chinese Academy of Social Sciences, 2022).

Since 2021, special piracy scans and rights defense actions have also been added for the original books of popular IP dramas. IReader (an online reading platform) has designed and built a copyright support system that can manage massive amounts of content copyright, with a 3 early warning mechanism, 17 copyright risk identification and 5 risk response plans. Websites such as iQIYI, Chinese Online and Migu, have also professionalized and regularized their monitoring and rights protection services.

Policies That the Government Should Develop

Policies on copyright issues have been mentioned in 4.3. The government should strictly implement these policies and continuously improve the relevant laws and regulations. With the help of relevant laws and policies, there is also a need to further strengthen the publicity, supervision, and crackdown on copyright protection of online literature and to form a top-down comprehensive governance norm. The online literature industry should join forces with government agencies to strengthen the supervision of service providers such as search engines, mobile application markets and online advertising alliances, urge platforms to conduct regular self-examination and self-correction, and hold relevant platforms jointly and severally liable for spreading pirated content.

CONCLUSION AND FUTURE RESEARCH DIRECTIONS

Conclusion

Because of the well-developed social media and IP industry in China, it is suitable for SMEs in online literature and film & TV industry to use social media and improve their performance. What's more, high internet penetration rate and favorable policies make it possible for SMEs to create IP through social media.

Online literature company Jinjiang Literature ranks among the top online literature websites in terms of the number of film and television copyright deals. It is good at creating and cultivating online IP literature. This chapter attributes its success to retaining the forum format and social attributes, attracting mobile users of online literature, and capturing user preferences. Film company Daylight Entertainment stand out in the television and film industry. It is good at making IP adaptations. This chapter attributes its success to its ability to exploit the fan effect and the usage of social thinking. Both of these companies use platform which are in forum like formats for collecting and sharing online literature platform, and other social media platforms such as Weibo, LOFTER and so on to expand the publicity and connect with the audience.

However, there are also some difficulties for these companies. The main problem these companies face is piracy. This chapter gives ways to respond to the problems from both government and companies.

Huang Yanming, the CEO of Jinjiang Literature, points out that before the concept of online literature IP was established, film and television productions have mostly followed the traditional approach of screenwriters writing scripts. Although some works of online literature have been adapted into film and television, it was not because of their special status as online literature. It is the fact that a famous or excellent work has been adapted, and it happens to be online literature (Yan, 2017).

Perhaps this is also the case in other developing countries, and managers of online literature platforms or the film industry in those countries are not yet aware of the huge market of IP. The cases discussed in this chapter can inspire some SMEs in other developing countries, especially SMEs in online literature and film & TV industry, to find their way to build brand image and gain better performance.

Future Research Directions

The IP industry in China has been able to grow (e.g. Yu et al., 2022) because of the high coverage of social media in China and the younger generation's preference for entertainment through social media. China started relatively late implementation of its intellectual property laws, and it is yet to be perfected in many ways. However, they have made significant progress since its implementation, especially when it comes to IP online literature. The Chinese users were also not aware of intellectual property rights until the beginning of the 21st century, authors and users alike. Authors paid little attention to where they uploaded their completed works, whether their works could be well protected on the SMEs developed platforms. The author's primary intention remained at sharing their stories and connecting with their fans. As the industry is developing however, these works are getting more attention from not just readers (and fans) but also investors who want to appropriate popular stories into media adaptations. With adaptations the talk about rights, needs to protect against plagiarism, distribution of power and compensation starts to shift dynamics. These online platforms have to grow both their business and also protect their writers against many online and offline forces from inside and outside the industry.

While we covered two very important case-studies of SMEs from China, there is a lot left to be explored in this space as it further evolves, here are some suggested future research directions,

1.   For authors What were the reasons that authors chose to publish on an online platform like Jinjiang Literature in the beginning? This paper states that their motivation was simply to share, but whether there were other reasons besides it, such as to get revenue, remains to be proven. When the law was not strong at the beginning of 21st century, were they worried about their articles being plagiarized and how did they defend their rights? How did they balance between the convenience of online literature platform and risks of being plagiarized.

2.   For large companies in this industry China's largest online writing platforms are basically those owned by large social media companies or affiliated with them. For example, two of the major social media, QQ and WeChat, which owned by Tencent, also operate IP industry. The online literature platforms of them are called QQ Reading and WeChat Reading. ByteDance, the parent company of TikTok, also has its online literature platform called Tomato Novel. This chapter is about SMEs, so it does not talk about these online literary platforms which belongs to the large companies. But this phenomenon is worth thinking about, as it represents a close connection between the online literary IP industry and social media. It is worth studying the online literary platforms owned by large Chinese social media companies, and explore what lessons SMEs can learn from them.

3.   For SMEs How does an SME like Jinjiang Literature continue to exist in a situation where online literary platforms owned by large corporations are popular? How are they different and which one is more popular?

As an SME, how much money does a film company like Daylight Entertainment spend on social media to interact and promote itself to the audience? Is this experience replicable and can other SMEs have this capability? Do SMEs face more difficulties compared to some large film companies, such as in terms of funding and intellectual property protection?

4.   For government China's intellectual property right laws are improving, but it is worth looking into which areas need to be improved. What's more, should relevant SMEs be helped by the government, or should large social media companies be enabled to develop their own online writing platforms?

5.   For consumers and fans When downstream industry, like film and TV industry, adapt web novels into film and television works, this action often causes the fans of the original work dissatisfied with the adaption. Are they more satisfied with the IP transformation of small and medium-sized film and television enterprises, or more satisfied with the large ones? And what are the reasons? How should film and television companies pay attention to make the works get audience's preference and get higher ratings and revenue?

6.   For other developing countries In countries with better IPR laws, it is a question of future research to investigate whether authors can trust small and micro enterprises and will be willing to publish their works on their platforms. Meanwhile, whether IP industry can be generated in countries with imperfect IP laws also needs to be further tested.

In other countries, should SMEs use the existing social media for IP industry development or set up their own forums like Jinjiang Literature? Do they have such ability to operate and manage the platform and protect intellectual property rights? In different countries, we need to discuss it on a case-by-case basis. SMEs in other developing countries must be careful when learning from the successful experience of the Chinese IP industry.

ACKNOWLEDGMENT

The authors extend sincere gratitude to:
- Our colleagues from Soochow University, the Australian Studies Centre of Shanghai University, The European Business University of Luxembourg and Krirk University as well as the independent research colleagues who provided insight and expertise that greatly assisted the research, although they may not agree with all of the interpretations/conclusions of this chapter.
- China Knowledge for supporting our research.
- The Editor and the International Editorial Advisory Board (IEAB) of this book who initially desk reviewed, arranged a rigorous double/triple blind review process and conducted a thorough, minute and critical final review before accepting the chapter for publication.
- All anonymous reviewers who provided very constructive feedbacks for thorough revision, improvement, extension and fine tuning of the chapter.

REFERENCES

Abeza, G., O'Reilly, N., & Reid, I. (2013). Relationship marketing and social media in sport. *International Journal of Sport Communication*, *6*(2), 120–142. doi:10.1123/ijsc.6.2.120

Borah, P. S., Iqbal, S., & Akhtar, S. (2022). Linking social media usage and SME's sustainable performance: The role of digital leadership and innovation capabilities. *Technology in Society*, *68*, 101900. Advance online publication. doi:10.1016/j.techsoc.2022.101900

Bruce, E., Shurong, Z., Egala, S. B., Amoah, J., Ying, D., Rui, H., & Lyu, T. (2022). Social media usage and SME firms' sustainability: An introspective analysis from Ghana. *Sustainability (Switzerland)*, *14*(15), 9433. Advance online publication. doi:10.3390u14159433

Cao, Y., Ajjan, H., Hong, P., & Le, T. (2018). Using social media for competitive business outcomes: An empirical study of companies in China. *Journal of Advances in Management Research*, *15*(2), 211–235. doi:10.1108/JAMR-05-2017-0060

China Internet Network Information Center. (2022). *The 49th Statistical Report on the Development of the Internet in China.* http://www.cnnic.cn/hlwfzyj/hlwxzbg/hlwtjbg/202202/P020220407403488048001.pdf

ChinaLiterature. (2022). *ChinaLiterature Annual Report 2021.* https://max.book118.com/html/2022/0419/5111024204004214.shtm

Chinese Academy of Social Sciences. (2022). *2021 Research Report on the Development of Online Literature in China.* http://lit.cssn.cn/wx/wx_yczs/202204/t20220407_5402451.shtml

CNNIC. (2015). *Ten highlights of China's Internet development in the 12th Five-Year Plan.* http://www.cnnic.com.cn/AU/MediaC/rdxw/2015n/201511/t2015110 5_52985.htm

Du, Y. (2018). *A Study on Jinjiang Literature City IP Operation.* Shanxi Teacher Training University.

Fan, W. (2017). The Sense of Internet of Online Literature is Important in the IP Era. *International Publishing Weekly*, 11.

Farzana, P. T., Noor, I. J., & Sulaiman, A. (2016). Social media's impact on organizational performance and entrepreneurial orientation in organizations. *Management Decision, 54*(9), 22080–22234.

Farzana, P. T., Noor, I. J., & Sulaiman, A. (2018). Understanding the impact of social media usage among organizations. *Information & Management, 55*(3), 308–321. doi:10.1016/j.im.2017.08.004

Feng, S.S., & Xiao, Y.Y. (2018). Internet thinking in the production of Daylight Entertainment TV series. *Film and Television Production, 24*(12), 79-82.

Hanafifizadeh, P., Shafifia, S., & Bohlin, E. (2021). Exploring the consequence of social media usage on firm performance. *Digital Business, 1*(2).

Haudi, H., Handayani, W., Suyoto, M. Y. T., Praseti, T., Pitaloka, E., Wijoyo, H., Yonata, H., Koho, I. R., & Cahyono, Y. (2022). The effect of social media marketing on brand trust, brand equity and brand loyalty. *International Journal of Data and Network Science, 6*(3), 961–972. doi:10.5267/j.ijdns.2022.1.015

Hong, J., Edler, J., & Massini, S. (2022). Evolution of the Chinese intellectual property rights system: IPR law revisions and enforcement. *Management and Organization Review, 18*(4), 755–787. Advance online publication. doi:10.1017/mor.2021.72

Jaini, A., Md Dahlan, J., Suhadak, N., & Zainuddin, N. A. (2023). *Leveraging digital marketing to empower SME competency: A conceptual paper.* doi:10.1007/978-3-031-08093-7_4

Jinjiang Literature. (2022). www.jjwxc.net

Kaplan, A. M., & Haenlein, M. (2010). Users of the world, unite! The challenges and opportunities of social media. *Business Horizons, 53*(1), 59–68. doi:10.1016/j.bushor.2009.09.003

Kelleher, T., & Sweetser, K. (2012). Social media adoption among university communicators. *Journal of Public Relations Research, 24*(2), 105–122. doi:10.1080/1062726X.2012.626130

Leonardi, P. M., & Vaast, E. (2016). Social media and their affordances for organizing: A review and agenda for research. *The Academy of Management Annals, 11*(1), 150–188. doi:10.5465/annals.2015.0144

Li, Y. Q. (2018). Virtual Experience and Literary Imagination - New Essays on Chinese Internet Literature. *Chinese Social Sciences, *(1), 156-178+207-208.

Ma, L. J., & Zhang, X. N. (2020). An analysis of the reasons for the success of Daylight Entertainment TV series. *Contemporary Television, 2020*(3), 94-96. DOI:. doi:10.16531/j.cnki.1000-8977.2020.03.025

Meske, C., & Stieglitz, S. (2013). Adoption and use of social media in small and medium-sized enterprises. *Working Conference on Practice-Driven Research on Enterprise Transformation*, 61-75. 10.1007/978-3-642-38774-6_5

Michaelidou, N., Siamagka, N. T., & Christodoulides, G. (2011). Usage, barriers and measurement of social media marketing: An exploratory investigation of small and medium B2B brands. *Industrial Marketing Management*, *40*(7), 1153–1159. doi:10.1016/j.indmarman.2011.09.009

Misirlis, N., & Vlachopoulou, M. (2018). Social media metrics and analytics in marketing–S3M: A mapping literature review. *International Journal of Information Management*, *38*(1), 270–276. doi:10.1016/j.ijinfomgt.2017.10.005

National People's Congress Standing Committee. (2020). The Copyright Law.

Ngai, E. W., Tao, S. S., & Moon, K. K. (2015). Social media research: Theories, constructs, and conceptual frameworks. *International Journal of Information Management*, *35*(1), 33–44. doi:10.1016/j.ijinfomgt.2014.09.004

Nguyen, A. T. H., Nguyen, P. V., & Do, H. T. S. (2022). The effects of entrepreneurial orientation, social media, managerial ties on firm performance: Evidence from Vietnamese SMEs. *International Journal of Data and Network Science*, *6*(1), 243–252. doi:10.5267/j.ijdns.2021.9.004

Qalati, S. A., Ostic, D., Sulaiman, M. A. B. A., Gopang, A. A., & Khan, A. (2022). Social media and SMEs' performance in developing countries: Effects of technological-organizational-environmental factors on the adoption of social media. *SAGE Open*, *12*(2). Advance online publication. doi:10.1177/21582440221094594

Rahmawati, T. Y., Dewi, M. K., & Ferdian, I. R. (2020). Instagram: Its roles in management of Islamic banks. *Journal of Islamic Marketing*, *11*(4), 841–861. doi:10.1108/JIMA-11-2018-0213

Scott, D. M., & Scott, R. (2020). *Fanocray: Turning Fans into Customers and Customers into Fans*. Portfolio.

Sedalo, G., Boateng, H., & Kosiba, J. P. (2022). Exploring social media affordance in relationship marketing practices in SMEs. *Digital Business, 2*(1).

Shen, H., & Wen, X. (2016). The reform of the Chinese intellectual property trial system. *Global Journal of Comparative Law*, *5*(1), 68–90. doi:10.1163/2211906X-00501004

Sherman, B., & Bently, L. (1999). *The making of modern intellectual property law: the British experience, 1760–1911*. Cambridge University Press.

Sheshadri, C., & Arpan, K. K. (2020). Why do small and medium enterprises use social media marketing and what is the impact: Empirical insights from India. *International Journal of Information Management*, *53*, 1–42.

Shi, Z. M. (2021). From Literary Creation to Copyright Sale: A Study of the Platform Ecology of Jinjiang Literature City in the New Media Perspective. *New Media Research*, *7*(05), 49–52. doi:10.16604/j.cnki.issn2096-0360.2021.05.015

Shu, J. Y. (2019). 20 Years of Jinjiang Literature. *China Reading News*, 17.

Suryani, T., Fauzi, A. A., & Nurhadi, M. (2021). SOME-Q: A model development and testing for assessing the Consumers' perception of social media quality of small medium-sized enterprises (SMEs). *Journal of Relationship Marketing*, *20*(1), 62–90. doi:10.1080/15332667.2020.1717277

The Ministry of Human Resources and Social Security & the Ministry of Culture and Tourism. (2020). *Guiding Opinions of the Ministry of Human Resources and Social Security, the Ministry of Culture and Tourism on Deepening the Reform of the Title System for Artistic Professionals*. http://www.mohrss.gov.cn/SYrlzyhshbzb/rencairenshi/zcwj/zhuanyejishurenyuan/202009/t20200928_391837.html

The State Administration of Radio Film and Television of China. (2014). *Circular of the State Administration of Press, Publication, Radio, Film and Television on Printing and Distributing the Guiding Opinions on Promoting the Healthy Development of Internet Literature*. https://www.nppa.gov.cn/nppa/contents/772/76567.shtml

Wanyoike, J., & Kithae, P. P. (2019). Social media networks and SME performance in the international arena: A case of SMEs operating in Kamukunji area of Nairobi County, Kenya. *European Journal of Business & Management Research*, *4*(5). Advance online publication. doi:10.24018/ejbmr.2019.4.5.122

Wei, J. (2021). An interpretation of the innovative thinking of Daylight Entertainment's TV series. *News Enthusiasts*, *2021*(01), 49–51. doi:10.16017/j.cnki.xwahz.2021.01.013

Wibawa, B. M., Baihaqi, I., Nareswari, N., Mardhotillah, R. R., & Pramesti, F. (2022). Utilization of social media and its impact on marketing performance: A case study of SMEs in Indonesia. *International Journal of Business and Society*, *23*(1), 19–34. doi:10.33736/ijbs.4596.2022

Williams, J., & Chinn, S. J. (2010). Meeting relationship-marketing goals through social media: A conceptual model for sport marketers. *International Journal of Sport Communication*, *3*(4), 422–437. doi:10.1123/ijsc.3.4.422

Wood, J., & Khan, G. F. (2016). Social business adoption: An empirical analysis. *Business Information Review*, *33*(1), 28–39. doi:10.1177/0266382116631851

World Bank. (2020). *Small and Medium Enterprises (SMEs) Finance*. https://www. worldbank.org/en/topic/smefinance

Wu, S. (2022). Television adaptation in the age of media convergence: Chinese intellectual property shows and the case of all is well. *Adaptation*, *15*(2), 187–206. doi:10.1093/adaptation/apab002

Xiao, J., Chen, D., Tang, Q., Suo, L., Zhou, X., Wang, W., Zheng, W., & Zhou, M. (2022). 2020 Report on the development of Chinese Internet literature. *New Techno Humanities*, *2*(1), 1–12. doi:10.1016/j.techum.2022.100004

Yu, P., Liao, Y., & Mahendran, R. (2022). Research on Social Media Advertising in China: Advertising Perspective of Social Media Influencers. In I. Krom (Ed.), *Handbook of Research on Global Perspectives on International Advertising* (pp. 88–122). IGI Global. doi:10.4018/978-1-7998-9672-2.ch006

Yu, P., Tang, H., Tang, H., & Hanes, E. (2022). Using "Digitalization + Intellectual Property" Management to Realize Cultural Economy: Case Study of Chinese Museums. In R. Pettinger, B. Gupta, A. Roja, & D. Cozmiuc (Eds.), *Handbook of Research on Digital Transformation Management and Tools* (pp. 236–264). IGI Global. doi:10.4018/978-1-7998-9764-4.ch011

Yu, P. K. (2018). When the Chinese intellectual property system hits 35. *Queen Mary Journal of Intellectual Property*, *8*(1), 3–14. doi:10.4337/qmjip.2018.01.01

Zeng, X., Xu, X., & Wu, Y. J. (2022). Learning social media content optimization: How can SMEs draw the users' attention on official WeChat accounts? *Frontiers in Psychology*, *12*, 783151. Advance online publication. doi:10.3389/fpsyg.2021.783151 PMID:35095669

Zeng, Y. G., & Du, Z. W. (2021). Rethinking IP Adaptation of Online Literature in the Era of Digital Media. *Chinese Editorials*, *6*, 75–78.

Zhang, H. (2020, June 18). "SwordNet 2020" to combat online piracy. *People's Daily Online*. http://politics.people.com.cn/n1/2020/0618/c1001-31750923.html

Zhang, L., & Bruun, N. (2017). Legal transplantation of intellectual property rights in china: Resistance, adaptation and reconciliation. *IIC International Review of Intellectual Property and Competition Law*, *48*(1), 4–41. doi:10.100740319-016-0542-1

Zhang, L. Y. (2021). Analysis and lessons learned from the experience model of Daylight Entertainment's film & TV drama production. *Western Radio and Television*, *42*(14), 99–101.

ENDNOTE

[1]   CNNIC stands for China Internet Network Information Center.

Chapter 4

How to Improve the Brand Equity of the Beauty Industry Through Effective E-Commerce Live Streaming Strategies:
A Case Study of Douyin Live Broadcasting in China

Poshan Yu

https://orcid.org/0000-0003-1069-3675

Soochow University, China & Australian Studies Centre, Shanghai University, China

Yue Pan

https://orcid.org/0000-0001-5101-0813

Independent Researcher, China

Melanie Bobik

Independent Researcher, China

ABSTRACT

This chapter aims to study whether and how e-commerce live streaming affects brand equity of the beauty industry in China. This chapter will explore the strategies of using e-commerce live broadcast to affect consumers' purchase behavior in China's beauty industry and study how these strategies will affect the brand awareness and brand loyalty of the industry. This chapter will investigate features of e-commerce live streaming on the social media and impacts on the related viewers. In addition, this chapter will use CiteSapce analysis to perform statistical and correlation analysis associated with e-commerce live streaming. Furthermore, this chapter will also analyze consumers' preference for e-commerce live broadcasting strategy through questionnaire survey. Cases from Douyin (the business outside China is called TikTok) will be used for explanations. This chapter will provide suggestions for the SMEs as to how to make use of e-commerce live streaming to enhance their brand equity.

DOI: 10.4018/978-1-6684-5770-2.ch004

INTRODUCTION

Affected by the new crown pneumonia epidemic, offline activities have been restricted, and China's small and medium-sized enterprises have been hit a lot, especially in the beauty and consumer goods industry, which relies on consumers' offline purchases to generate profits. The backlog of inventory poses challenges to the development of enterprises. Live streaming, also known as live streaming e-commerce, has become an important means for Chinese companies to survive and seek stability. E-commerce live broadcast is a new model based on the network platform, in which one or more anchors transmit product information to the audience to promote e-commerce sales. E-commerce is the foundation, and live broadcast is a tool. E-commerce uses live broadcast to obtain customer traffic, thereby Achieve the goal of increasing sales (Luo, 2020). In the face of weak consumption under the epidemic, in April 2022, the General Office of the State Council issued an opinion on further releasing consumption potential and promoting the continuous recovery of consumption, proposing to adapt to the needs of normalized epidemic prevention and control, promote new consumption, and accelerate the organic integration of online and offline consumption, expand and upgrade information consumption(National Development and Reform Commission, 2022, April 26).

According to the 49th "Statistical Report on the Development of Internet Networks in China", as of December 2021, the number of online live broadcast users in my country reached 703 million, an increase of 86.52 million compared with December 2020, accounting for 68.2% of the total netizens, of which e-commerce live broadcasts The number of users ranked first, reaching 464 million, an increase of 75.79 million compared with December 2020, accounting for 44.9% of the total netizens.

Figure 1. Webcast User Scale and Utilization Ratio (2017.12 - 2021.12)
Source: National Bureau of Statistics

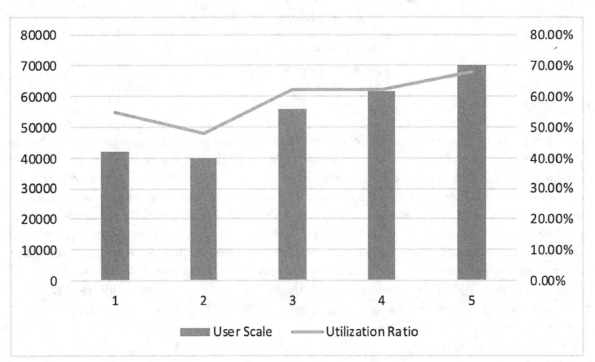

From the data in the figure 1, we can see that although the epidemic has greatly reduced offline consumption, the use and consumption of online platforms have not been significantly affected. From 2020 to 2021, both the user scale and usage rate of webcasting will show a continuous upward trend. This shows that in order to further expand the audience, Chinese companies used the form of live webcasting to expand their brand influence.

In general, 2017-2020 is a period of great development of Chinese brand e-commerce live broadcasts. During this period, the new users of live broadcast are mainly post-95s and post-00s. They tend to be more demanding of interest, interactivity, and content value. Therefore, in the live broadcast products, the Guochao brand is the new bright spot. According to Baidu's "2021 Guochao Search Big Data Report", the attention of the Guochao brand has increased by 528% in the past ten years, and its core paying users are "post-90s" and "Post-00" accounts for 74.4% of all its users. Among them, the national trendy beauty brands such as Perfect Diary and Huaxizi are very popular among consumers in the generation Z. Generation Z refers to people born between 1995 and 2009, also known as the Internet generation and Internet generation, which collectively refers to a generation greatly influenced by technological products such as the Internet, instant messaging, SMS, MP3, smartphones and tablet computers. According to 2018 data from the National Bureau of Statistics, Generation Z accounts for about 19% of my country's total population, and this group contributes 40% of the overall consumption. Their brand choices are more diverse, and niche is their favorite word. They are keen to post their tastes on social media. Their spending on electronic equipment, training and learning, makeup and toiletries far exceeds other categories.

In addition to bringing better online experience to consumers by virtue of its strong immediacy and good interactivity, live e-commerce also comprehensively displays product information and communicates with users in depth to gain user trust, which has the effect of expanding publicity(Yang, 2021). Therefore, while being loved by consumers, live e-commerce is also more favored by enterprises.

Brand is a key factor for enterprises to gain competitive advantage, and consumers' purchase intention and behavior ultimately serve the development of brands (Wang, 2021). As a dedicated platform for product sales and brand display, the brand live broadcast room is used for consumer interaction and brand communication on social media. The interactivity of the live broadcast room highlights the concept of consumer participation (Helme, 2019). This process of consumer participation enables consumers to more actively express their needs and understand brands, which in turn contributes to consumer behavior and brand recognition through active consumer participation. More and more companies use live broadcast e-commerce to collect demand information and strengthen interactive communication, so that users can obtain value satisfaction from the interactive experience of live broadcast, form brand recognition and support, thereby accumulating high-quality word of mouth and increasing brand equity (Meng, 2020). In marketing theory, brand equity refers to the marketing benefits or incremental revenue that a brand brings to a product or enterprise (Keller et al., 2006). What this paper discusses is the brand equity evaluation of opportunity consumer survey, which is reflected in the endogenous value of the brand. Aaker proposed that brand equity is a multi-dimensional concept. He proposed that the five models of brand equity evaluation consist of five parts: brand loyalty, brand recognition, perceived quality, brand image and other brand proprietary assets (1991).

Specifically, consumer word of mouth and media reports have a direct impact on the establishment of brand image, and advertising, as an important channel of communication with consumers, also has an important impact on the formation of brand image (Zhao, 2005). Therefore, this paper uses consumer word-of-mouth as an indicator to measure brand image. Yo and Donthu believe that brand loyalty is a purchase tendency, so this paper uses product repurchase rate to measure brand loyalty (2001). Considering the previous theoretical discussion, we propose the following hypothesis that livestreaming e-commerce has a positive impact on beauty brand equity.

Most of the current literature research on live broadcast e-commerce and brand equity only stays on the status quo, mode, advantages and limitations of live broadcast delivery, and only briefly describes the impact of live broadcast e-commerce on brand equity. But mostly research are qualitative research, lack of relevant empirical research. At the same time, these studies did not compare the changes in specific industries before and after the introduction of live e-commerce.

Therefore, this chapter aims to conduct certain quantitative research on the basis of qualitative research, and explore the impact mechanism of live broadcast e-commerce on brand equity in the context of the development of China's beauty industry. The research structure of this paper is as follows. The next section will explore scholars' research on the relationship between social media and brand equity and the development of live-streaming e-commerce. Next, we will introduce the development status and characteristics of China's beauty industry under the influence of the new crown pneumonia. Next, we will analyze the results of our questionnaire, discuss the development opportunities and challenges of live-streaming e-commerce, explore the strategies of using live-streaming of e-commerce to influence consumers' purchasing behavior in China's beauty industry, and study how these strategies will affect the industry's brand awareness and Brand Loyalty. Finally, we will draw the research conclusions of this paper, and put forward suggestions on how small and medium-sized enterprises can use e-commerce live broadcast to enhance brand equity.

This chapter aims to study how and whether e-commerce live streaming affects brand equity of the beauty industry in China. This chapter will explore the strategies of using e-commerce live broadcast to affect consumers' purchase behavior in China's beauty industry, and study how these strategies will affect the brand awareness and brand loyalty of the industry. This chapter will investigate features of e-commerce live streaming on the social media Douyin and impacts on the related viewers. In addition, this chapter will use CiteSapce analysis to perform statistical and correlation analysis associated with e-commerce live streaming. Furthermore, this chapter will also analyze consumers' preference for e-commerce live broadcasting strategy through questionnaire survey. Cases from Douyin will be used for explanations. This chapter will provide suggestions for the SMEs as to how to make use of e-commerce live streaming to enhance their brand equity.

BACKGROUND

Social Media and Brand Marking in China

With the upgrading of the Internet to socialization, a new development trend of network media has been formed, and social media has gradually become the main carrier for people to obtain and disseminate information. Antony Mayfield believes that participation, openness, communication, dialogue, community, and connectivity are the characteristics of social media. Among them, creating content for each individual and disseminating it independently is its most obvious feature. The core basis of the research direction of the later researcher is his proposal to "give everyone the ability to create and disseminate content". In addition, he classified social media sites, blogs, wikis, forums, podcasts, content communities and Weibo into seven types of social media, and explained the operation modes of these forms respectively (2007).Social media provides a platform for people to communicate and share with each other. The early forms of media include search engines, forums, portals, and videos. There are also many forms of media that flood our lives today, such as: Weibo(A local Chinese social platform similar to Facebook), short videos platforms like Douyin, and social networking sites like WeChat. The emergence of these social media has greatly changed people's lives and also changed the brand marketing model.

With the improvement of people's living standards, people's consumption attitudes and purchasing patterns have also changed, and people pay more attention to the additional feelings brought by products. With the emergence of this demand, various social media with their own characteristics have appeared one after another. At the same time, with the increase of consumers' personalized needs, the original large-scale market has been subdivided into countless small markets. In order to promote products, enterprises need to master the characteristics of different social media, and formulate brand marketing strategies according to the needs of different consumers (Shan, 2016). Secondly, the traditional marketing model is passive and compulsory information acceptance, which can no longer attract consumers. The emergence of social media undoubtedly provides a new idea for corporate brand marketing, and establishes a relationship between enterprises and consumers. A two-way interactive communication channel. Enterprises have changed from being pure sellers in the past to being friends of consumers. While pursuing profits, they also pay more attention to consumers' feelings. At the same time, consumers' trust in enterprises has gradually increased, and enterprises have obtained more and more valuable information through consumer feedback, and they are more aware of consumers' preferences and preferences. The emergence of social media also provides consumers with an opportunity to participate in the entire process of corporate product marketing, enabling consumers to enhance their sense of self-identity and belonging, and at the same time enhance users' brand loyalty. Brand loyalty refers to the frequency of consumers repeatedly purchasing the same brand products (Jacoby & Kyner, 1973). Through social media, brands have high flexibility in operation, and brand-related suggestions can be fed back to enterprises through social platforms, thus realizing the realization of enterprise-to-consumption It is necessary to accurately grasp the brand attitude and cognition of consumers, and take effective feedback measures (Zhou, 2020). Social media itself is interactive and topical, and it is an effective carrier for brand emotional communication, which facilitates the interaction and dialogue between the brand and consumers, and is the emotional recognition of consumers to the brand.

In addition, the emergence of social media has also highlighted the importance of word-of-mouth marketing. Consumers' purchasing decisions are divided into five stages, namely: finding problems, collecting information, evaluating alternatives, making purchasing decisions and post-purchase behaviors (Wu, 2007). In the era of social media, consumers can autonomously search, post, rate or share information on social media. Consumers use social media to inquire and pay attention to online word of mouth, and the evaluation of others on social media will affect their attitude towards the original brand. According to a global report by Nielsen, few consumers today pay attention to corporate-directed advertisements or use them to guide their purchases. About 90% of consumers trust products recommended to them by acquaintances or friends, and about 70% of consumers trust the opinions of customers on the Internet (Hu, 2012).

According to data from Weiboyi, China's mainstream social media traffic scale is huge. The short video platforms represented by Douyin and Kuaishou have an average of more than 10 million new users per month, and the number of users has maintained rapid growth, of which Douyin has doubled. This shows the huge potential of Chinese social media.

Figure 2. Volume of traffic on major social media platforms
Source: Weiboyi Database

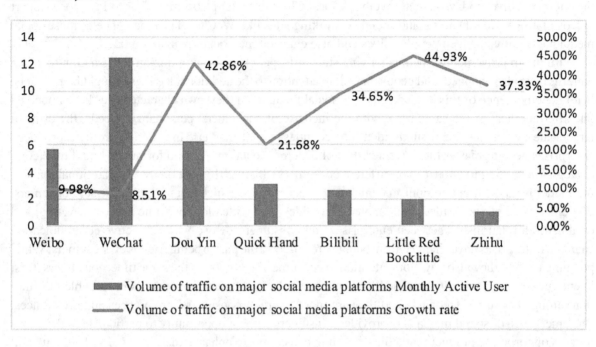

From the data in the figure 2, we can see that the average monthly new users of short video platforms represented by Douyin and Kuaishou are more than 10 million, and the number of users has maintained rapid growth, of which Douyin has doubled; The increase of new users is obvious, among which the substantial growth of WeChat does not rule out the rapid development of video accounts; other social media platforms based on UGC content like Bilibili, Xiaohongshu, and Zhihu all maintain the monthly increase of new users in the order of one million. Huge platform traffic provides a broad market for brand marketing.

China's E-commerce Live Broadcast Industry

With the gradual transfer of consumers' shopping methods to online platforms, users' demand for detailed understanding of commodity information is increasing. China's e-commerce is also developing new forms while the Internet is constantly upgrading. The introduction of commodities It has also gradually developed from the original single pictures and texts to short videos and live broadcasts.

E-commerce live broadcast is a new model based on the network platform, in which one or more anchors transmit product information to the audience to promote e-commerce sales. E-commerce is the foundation and live broadcast is a tool. E-commerce uses live broadcast to obtain customer traffic, thereby Achieve the goal of increasing sales (Luo, 2020).

The early Internet was born in the United States, and the emergence of Meerkat and Periscope opened the era of mobile Internet live broadcast, but the development of these two live broadcast platforms did not continue. However, due to cultural differences, China's online live broadcast industry is booming.

From 2016 to 2017, it was the early stage of the development of online live broadcasting in China, and the live broadcast of the show, represented by the face-value anchors, became the mainstream form of online live broadcasting at that time. However, the profit of this kind of live broadcast mainly comes from fans' rewards, and a relatively stable profit model has not been formed. And this attention-oriented economy is bound to make live content develop in a vulgar direction. Therefore, in December 2016, the State Internet Information Office, the Ministry of Culture, the State Administration of Press, Publication, Radio, Film and Television and other departments jointly implemented management and control to guide the online live broadcast industry and find a balance between regulating development and chasing profits (CAC, 2016). E-commerce live broadcast came into being.

Internet communication has the characteristics of timeliness, scene, and visualization, so live broadcast e-commerce has built a platform that is more in line with consumer needs. From the perspective of the supply side, live e-commerce has realized the real-time realization of user needs and accelerated the speed of product development. Secondly, traditional enterprises increase their popularity through marketing models such as celebrity endorsements and advertising communication, but for small and medium-sized enterprises, a large amount of publicity costs have formed a greater financial pressure on them, and e-commerce live broadcasts have broken through traditional publicity. Ways to attract consumers' attention through brand self-broadcasting or traffic anchors bringing goods. It allows consumers and merchants to complete the transaction of goods more smoothly, and shorten the straight-line distance between people and the source of goods. The live streaming of goods completes a more thorough "Internetization" of supply and demand transactions, which further eliminates consumption barriers (Wang, 2022). From the perspective of consumption, live broadcast e-commerce takes advantage of consumers' unplanned shopping needs to build a consumption experience similar to offline shopping, narrowing the gap between online and offline shopping experience. In particular, under the influence of the new crown pneumonia epidemic in 2020, physical shopping has been affected, while online shopping has hardly been affected.

From a micro perspective, the emergence of live-streaming e-commerce has brought about the rapid transformation of orders, and from a macro perspective, it is profoundly shaping the current operating model of China's Internet economy.

The combination of live broadcast media and product marketing, e-commerce live broadcast is not the first. At the earliest, the promotion of the product was carried out by means of live TV, which promoted the sales of the product to a certain extent. However, in this method, the process of introducing the product by the anchor is dominant, and the channel for instant feedback is lacking, and the interaction between consumers and merchants is greatly reduced. With the development of information technology, Internet information carriers have become more diverse, and live broadcast, a more timely and convenient medium, has gradually been accepted by users.

From the perspective of brand marketing, live e-commerce is a type of influencer marketing. The concept of influencer marketing was originally proposed by Brown and Hayes, who pointed out that influencer marketing is "the formulation and implementation of marketing strategies and activities by individuals who have influence on customers and potential customers", and proposed that social media is a new influence to promote author's point of view (Brown, 2008). In the e-commerce live broadcast, the network anchor is the influencer in influencer marketing, and the user, the viewer of the live broadcast, is the affected party. With their professionalism, popularity, and influence, anchors establish consumer identity with consumers during the live broadcast process, thereby influencing consumers' purchasing behavior (Li, 2020). Customers may not buy immediately while watching the live broadcast, but the process of live broadcast can attract more traffic for merchants, some of which are converted into actual purchase behavior, and the other part also cultivates a large number of potential audiences for the brand.

In the future, these potential Audiences may be converted into actual buyers, ultimately achieving the purpose of increasing brand equity.

CHINESE BEAUTY BRANDS DURING THE COVID-19 PANDEMIC

The new crown epidemic in 2020 has become a major global public health event. The WTO has raised the global risk level to the highest level. The Institute of International Finance released a report predicting that the global economy will drop to 1.5% in 2020 (2020).

The International Monetary Fund also predicts that the global economy will fall into negative growth, and the Oxford Institute for Economic Research estimates that if the epidemic spreads to the world, global GDP will drop by 2.8% (2020). Our economy has also been hit hard. The consumption data in 2020 verifies the impact of the epidemic on the total consumption and structure. According to data from the National Bureau of Statistics, my country's investment and consumption both fell by more than 20% from January to February 2020. The epidemic prevention and control has severely impacted the production and consumption of my country's secondary and tertiary industries (2020).

The industries most affected by the epidemic are culture, sports, tourism, catering, accommodation, exhibitions, transportation and other industries. These industries are precisely the areas where small, medium and micro enterprises are concentrated. From the perspective of cash flow, more than 70% of small, medium and micro enterprises are mainly distributed in wholesale and retail, catering and accommodation, cultural tourism, commerce and other industries. Among them, 85.01% of enterprises have a cash balance on their accounts for up to three months, and 34% of them only Can last for a month. The beauty industry is a typical type of small, medium and micro enterprises in China. According to data from iiMedia Research, the market size of China's cosmetics market in 2020 has declined compared to 2019 due to the epidemic, reaching 395.8 billion yuan (2021). After the epidemic situation gradually improved, according to the data of the National Bureau of Statistics, the national cosmetics retail sales exceeded 400 billion yuan for the first time in 2021, a year-on-year increase of 14.0%, which was higher than the growth rate of 9.5% in the same period last year, but the growth was mainly concentrated in the first half of the year, and the month-on-month growth rate continued Monthly decline, the year-on-year growth rate in the second half of the year fell to single digits, and there was zero growth in August (2021). Many brands have innovated their marketing ideas to save themselves during the epidemic. For example, skin care brands take advantage of the need to wear masks during the epidemic to carry out marketing planning for people's skin problems, while color cosmetics brands focus on the emerging concept of "mask makeup", packaging eye makeup products and anti-makeup products as epidemics Popular products below.

In the post-pandemic period, consumers will be more cautious about shopping decisions than they were before the pandemic. The new crown pneumonia epidemic has had a major impact on my country's consumption, reducing consumption ability and willingness, and causing consumption structure and consumption. There has been a major shift in consumption (Chen, 2020). Keynes's "Absolute Income Hypothesis" (Absolute Income Hypothesis) points out that current consumption has a great dependence effect on current income, and the epidemic has had a huge impact on the income of employees in many industries, greatly reducing social consumption ability and willingness. According to the "2020 New Crown Epidemic Consumer Behavior Attitude Impact and Trend Report" released by CCTV Market Research (2020), due to the epidemic, people could not go out to work from home, and consumers' overall spending on beauty consumption dropped by 55.4%, and some consumers even said that they

Beauty-related spending has been eliminated during this period. The report data shows that consumers affected by this after the epidemic have shown two completely different consumption intentions. Some consumers (33.8%) said that they will increase their spending on beauty, while others (41.4%) Indicate that they will be affected and reduce this expenditure.

In addition, the epidemic has made people's choice of cosmetics more rational, people have become more concerned about cosmetic ingredients, and the party of ingredients has suddenly emerged. The so-called ingredient party is a group that emphasizes the ingredients that play a significant role in the product. According to iResearch's survey data, 53.2% of beauty consumers value product ingredients and efficacy the most when choosing products, rather than taking "whether the brand is from abroad" as an important factor in purchasing decisions in the past (2022). This provides the possibility for local brands focusing on the efficacy and beauty track to quickly develop new iterations and grab the market share of international brands based on their understanding of domestic consumers.

The pandemic has prompted Chinese consumers to be more sustainable than ever and to make greener choices. According to Accenture's research report "2021 Chinese Consumer Research - Post-pandemic", 77% of Chinese respondents said that the environment is becoming a more important issue, while only 53% of global respondents hold the same view. At the same time, they believe that governments and businesses should play a greater role in promoting sustainable and ethical consumption – 83% of Chinese respondents believe that brands should do more to facilitate sustainable buying and consumption behaviours;55% of Chinese respondents said that after the epidemic, they will place more emphasis on the sustainable development and ethical values of their companies. This shift naturally also mirrors their choice of brands and products. While price, quality and convenience remain the top three factors considered by Chinese consumers, sustainability is accelerating in importance to consumers' purchasing decisions. Therefore, after the epidemic, the development of credit economy and quality economy has become the path for beauty brands to pursue sustainable development.

The epidemic has made consumers more aware of health, and the performance of men is more prominent. Compared with women, men pay more attention to the efficacy and ingredients of beauty products, and are more cautious about the choice of skin care products. More and more men are also beginning to pay attention to personal care and grooming. Many men are beginning to take care of their skin and even use makeup products to correct their flaws. The male beauty market has become more and more popular. According to Ipsos survey data (2021), male consumers' psychological needs for skin care and beauty products are mainly "exquisiteness and a sense of ritual to make them better" (37%), and "beautiful can bring them positivity" positive energy" (32%). For male consumers, the pursuit of beauty is no longer an expression of femininity, but a pursuit of self-image. In addition, compared with the high-frequency and impulsive consumption characteristics of female consumers, although men consume less frequently, they pay more attention to quality, high single consumption price, and higher brand loyalty. Therefore, once men pay attention to a domestic beauty Makeup brands often contribute more to the value of the brand than women.

The COVID-19 epidemic has had a huge impact on the consumer market, leading to a block in global consumption momentum, impacting traditional consumer markets such as offline retail, breaking the original balance of supply and demand, and forcing the market to seek a new equilibrium amid fluctuations (Guan Lixin, 2020). The development of the digital economy has provided new momentum for the consumer market, spawned new consumption that can resist the impact of the epidemic, realized the upgrading and updating of traditional consumption, and neutralized the negative impact of the epidemic on traditional consumption (Zhang Jingwei, 2020). According to Accenture's research report "2021 China Consumer Research - Post Epidemic", as consumers spend more time at home and gradually adapt to the "stay at home" lifestyle, people are turning more to digital and virtual ways to satisfy Important daily needs, the explosive growth of digital needs in various fields has also released huge business opportunities to platforms and enterprises. If a few years ago, digital tools were only the decoration of life, now people have entered the era of comprehensive digitalization of life. In 2020, the e-commerce penetration rate of beauty and personal care in China will reach 33%. In the post-epidemic era, major beauty brands are actively embracing online channels and looking for new growth points. Accelerating the development of e-commerce and improving online retail experience services are the keys for beauty brands to attract online consumers. It is worth mentioning that 71% of Chinese consumers are happy to shop directly on social media platforms, which is nearly 30 percentage points higher than the global average; this proportion is as high as 80% among young and middle-aged 18-39 year olds (2021). In response, many leading social media platforms in China have also launched their e-commerce businesses during the epidemic, hoping to take the lead. New formats such as the sharing economy, live broadcast economy, and platform economy emerge rapidly and are gradually on the right track (Zuo P, 2021). Among many social media, the importance of e-commerce live broadcast is particularly prominent. During the epidemic, consumers' minds of "going to live broadcasts" were further cultivated and strengthened, and they continued to be maintained after the epidemic subsided. It can be said that live broadcasts led the recovery of traffic. On the one hand, it is because the live broadcast format can holographically explain the characteristics of products, which can compensate for offline counter sales suppressed by the epidemic; on the other hand, it is also because consumers have relatively ample leisure time during the epidemic, and watching e-commerce live broadcasts can effectively pass the time.

To sum up, the Chinese beauty market, like other industries, has been hit by the new crown pneumonia epidemic. The beauty industry has shown new market characteristics after the epidemic. The epidemic is both a challenge and an opportunity for China's beauty industry.

METHODOLOGY

This paper aims to explore the impact mechanism of live e-commerce on the brand equity of the beauty industry. This paper selects the Questionnaires method in the Survey Method on the data collect method. It is conducted in order to gather large size of information in a short period of time. The advantages of this approach are as follows. First, Members of the sample group can remain anonymous. Second, Considerably cheaper than most of the other primary data collection methods. Third, Possibility of generating large amount of data.

In this paper, the quantitative data analysis method is selected in the data analysis. Quantitative data analysis turn raw numbers into meaningful data through the application of rational and critical thinking. Quantitative data analysis includes the calculation of frequencies of variables and differences between variables. A set of analytical software can be used to assist with analysis of quantitative data. The analysis software used in this chapter is Microsoft Excel and SPSSAU.

In addition, in terms of questionnaire design, this paper conducts a visual analysis of the research hotspots of live delivery and brand influence based on CiteSpace, and uses computer to search the core collection database of web of Science and CNKI. Documents in Chinese and English on live broadcast delivery and brand influence, the time range is from January 2015 to May 2022, using CiteSpace5.8.R3 software for visual analysis and knowledge map drawing. A total of 147 Chinese literatures and 217 English literatures were included. The specific analysis is shown in Figure 3 and Figure 4.

Figure 3. Keyword Clustering Map (WOS)
Data Source: Web of Science

CiteSpace, v. 5.8.R3 (64-bit)
May 8, 2022 11:59:54 AM CST
WoS: /Users/mac/WOS/Data
Timespan: 2015-2022 (Slice Length=1)
Selection Criteria: g-index (k=25), LRF=3.0, L/N=10, LBY=5, e=1.0
Network: N=217, E=1010 (Density=0.0431)
Largest CC: 212 (97%)
Nodes Labeled: 1.0%
Pruning: None

behavior health
beauty
eating disorder
facebook
adolescent
self-objectification
social satisfaction internalization
dissatisfaction
adolescent girl
appearance

Figure 4. Keyword Clustering Map (CNKI)
Data Source: China National Knowledge Infrastructure

CiteSpace, v. 5.8.R3 (64-bit)
May 7, 2022 10:29:17 PM CST
CSSCI: /Users/mac/CNKI/Data
Timespan: 2015-2022 (Slice Length=1)
Selection Criteria: g-index (k=25), LRF=3.0, L/N=10, LBY=5, e=1.0
Network: N=147, E=258 (Density=0.024)
Largest CC: 95 (64%)
Nodes Labeled: 1.0%
Pruning: None

The keywords of a document are the concentration and refinement of the core content of the article, and the research topics it presents are the research hotspots in the field (Yang, 2010). From the high-frequency keyword analysis of figure 3 and figure 4, it can be seen that the current research hotspots on live streaming and branding mainly focus on social media, self-media, internet celebrity, gender and word of mouth. Therefore, when designing the questionnaire, we refer to these research hotspots for question setting.

Basic Information of the Questionnaire

From May 10 to May 20, 2022, the questionnaire will be distributed to the public according to the random statistical design with Questionnaire Star. Finally, the IP addresses of 645 respondents from 24 provincial administrative regions in China completed the questionnaire. Respondents who said they have watched Douyin live broadcasts continue to answer the channels through which they understand beauty products, whether they will make impulse purchases when watching live broadcasts, the factors that affect their purchase of live broadcast beauty products, and the factors that affect their non-purchasing live broadcasts. The effective rate of the questionnaire was 80%. From the preliminary results of the

Figure 5. Geolocation Analysis of Source of Answer
Data Source: SPSSAU

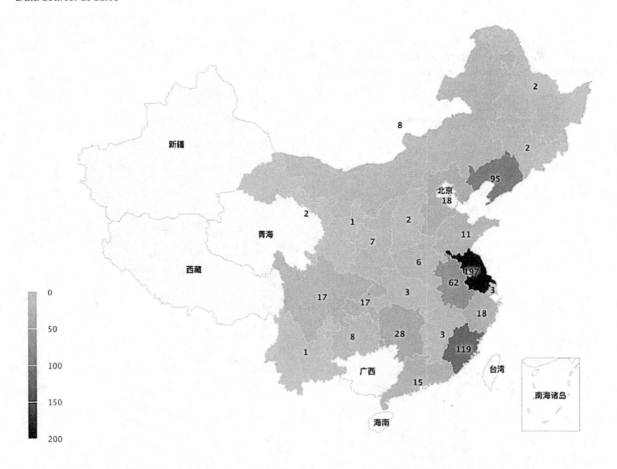

questionnaire, 62.64% of the respondents were women and 37.36% were men; the age was concentrated in 18-25 years old, accounting for 69.41%, and the marital status was mostly unmarried, accounting for 65.74%. This reflects that the audience for live streaming is still relatively young. 90.77% of the respondents have watched Douyin live streaming, and 88.99% have the need to understand beauty products. This shows that live streaming has indeed played a role in the purchase of beauty products. Figure 5 shows the Geolocation Analysis of Source of Answer.

From the figure 5, from 24 provincial administrative regions in China completed the questionnaire. However, it is worth noting that the results of the questionnaire have limitations. The results of the questionnaire survey only covered 26 of China's 34 provincial levels, and lacked data for Xinjiang, Qinghai, Tibet, Guangxi, Hainan, Taiwan, Beijing, and Tianjin. The graph shows the IP source of the respondents. The darker the color, the more respondents were from that provincial administrative region. It can be seen that the color of Jiangsu Province is relatively dark, but the color of some areas is very light, indicating that the distribution of respondents across the country is uneven, which may have a certain impact on the results of the questionnaire.

OPPORTUNITIES AND CHALLENGES FOR THE DEVELOPMENT OF LIVE E-COMMERCE IN THE BEAUTY INDUSTRY

When talking about the channels through which consumers learn about beauty products, most respondents said they learned about beauty products through social media, of which social media such as short video platforms and Weibo, which are dominated by public domain traffic, accounted for 58.71% respectively. and 63.59%. And social media dominated by private domain traffic such as WeChat accounted for 48.26%. Table 1 shows the different channels through which consumers know about beauty products.

Table 1. Channels through which consumers know about beauty products

Categories	Response		Polularity rate (n=50)
	n	Response rate	
Shopping platform (Taobao, Jingdong, etc.)	396	28.80%	61.40%
Short video platforms (Tik Tok, Kuaishou, etc.)	337	24.51%	52.25%
Mass meida (Xiaohongshu, Weibo, Bilibili, etc.)	365	26.55%	56.59%
Social media (WeChat, QQ, etc.)	277	20.15%	42.95%
Total	1375	100%	213.18%
Goodness of fit: χ^2=22.350 p=0.000			

Data Source: SPSSAU

Private domain traffic refers to the fans and customers accumulated in personal accounts. The characteristic of private domain traffic is that users can directly access and use it repeatedly. Private domain traffic has many advantages over public domain traffic. For example, private domain traffic is owned by individuals and has controllable traffic without charging. Public domain traffic is generally the traffic that first participates in content exposure on the platform, while private domain traffic comes from customers, that is, as a group of groups that give information and even likes, they exist in the community (Hu, 2022). Through this form of traffic spread and converted with the help of user word of mouth, marketing costs are effectively reduced, and a certain emotional connection is established between merchants and users. Such emotional connection can improve the emotional value of consumers, thereby maintaining the formation of brand relationships (Steth, 1991).

According to iiMedia's research report "Analysis report on the development status and trend of private domain traffic in China from 2021 to 2022", online retail sales in 2016-2020 showed an upward trend, but due to the saturation of the market, its year-on-year growth rate increased year by year decline. In 2020, online retail sales will account for 30% of total retail sales of social goods. Based on big data and new technologies, digitalization continues to empower all channels in the retail industry, offline channels are transforming to intelligence, online channels have significant advantages in terms of convenience and personalized recommendations, and the role of private domain traffic is becoming more and more important (2022). Take Douyin and Quick hand, the two major Internet short video platforms in China, as examples. Douyin pays more attention to the expansion of public domain traffic, while Kuaishou pays more attention to the cultivation of private domain traffic. Douyin's recommendation algorithm has an obvious "Matthew effect". This "information flow funnel algorithm" builds a centralized content creator. Fans gather in the head, and Douyin's 3% head video accounts for 80%. Users play, 5% of content creators cover 98% of the total number of fans. A large amount of traffic from the head anchor is conducive to expanding the exposure of the brand, causing large-scale attention and expanding brand awareness. The Kuaishou platform, on the other hand, pays more attention to de-neutralized operations, and the platform is committed to allocating more traffic resources to personal accounts, thereby bringing about a strong social relationship between the platform and users (Wang, 2021). Therefore, private domain traffic can bring stronger user stickiness and brand loyalty.

When it comes to another question, whether they have impulse purchase intentions when watching live broadcasts, 62.91% of the respondents said that they often have impulsive consumption intentions when watching live broadcast e-commerce. Rook D W believes that impulse spending is a complex buying process that is sudden, irresistible and hedonic, in which a purchasing decision is made quickly without careful consideration of all relevant information and choices.

Table 2. The most important factors in purchasing beauty products

Categories	Response		Polularity rate (n=50)
	n	Response rate	
The actual use value of the product	338	24.07%	52.40%
Beauty product quality	313	22.29%	48.53%
Cost-effective beauty products	301	21.44%	46.67%
Beauty product appearance	226	16.10%	35.04%
To support the anchor	226	16.10%	35.04%
Total	1404	100%	217.67%
Goodness of fit: χ^2=38.187 p=0.000			

Source: SPSSAU

Stimulated by the authenticity, visibility, and entertainment of the Internet, consumers may have a strong emotional response, which in turn triggers shopping behavior (Liu, 2020). Therefore, immersed consumers often ignore the sense of time and pay more attention to the online marketing activities of merchants, resulting in more impulsive consumption. This impulsive consumption reflects that in the post-epidemic era, people have turned to online e-commerce platforms because offline consumption is restricted. The traditional e-commerce platform only pushes the products that consumers are interested in on the homepage of the software according to the big constraints. However, in the live broadcast, there are special anchors explaining and introducing products, acting as a shopping guide in offline consumption, giving consumers a better shopping experience and product introduction, and increasing brand awareness.

When talking about the most important factors in purchasing beauty products in the live broadcast room (Table 2), 64.88% of the respondents said that the actual use value of the product is more important, and the quality of the product and the price of the product accounted for 60.08% and 57.77% respectively. The respondents who value the appearance of beauty products only accounted for 43.38%.

It can be seen that consumers of live e-commerce are not only irrational and impulsive consumer groups. If the product only has a refined appearance, but lacks strict quality control, most consumers will not make a purchase decision. In addition, it is worth noting that 43.38% of the respondents purchased products in order to support the anchor. It can be seen that anchors in live broadcast e-commerce can have a positive impact on consumers' brand awareness and consumption behavior. This will be analyzed in detail in the next section.

Table 3. Expected characteristics of live broadcast e-commerce anchors

Categories	Response		Polularity rate（n=50）
	n	Response rate	
Personal image that matches the brand	325	21.34%	50.39%
Possess extensive background knowledge in beauty makeup	352	23.11%	54.57%
It will mobilize fans' emotions and liven up the atmosphere	285	18.71%	44.19%
Timely feedback and dialogue with the audience	276	18.12%	42.79%
Ability to make fair and objective evaluations of products	285	18.71%	44.19%
Total	1523	100%	236.12%
Goodness of fit：χ²=13.950 p=0.007			

Source: SPSSAU

When talking about the expected characteristics of live broadcast e-commerce anchors (Table 3), 67.56% of the respondents believe that anchors with professional beauty knowledge background are more attractive. 62.38% of the respondents expect the image of the anchor to match the beauty brand. 54.7% of consumers expect the anchor to mobilize the atmosphere of the live broadcast room and make fans emotional. 52.98% of the respondents expect the live broadcasters to be able to communicate with fans in a timely manner, which will make the live broadcast more interactive. 54.7% of the respondents hope that the anchor can make a fair evaluation when introducing the product.

In the interaction in the context of live broadcast with goods, not only the anchor displays product information to consumers in real time through the live broadcast platform, but consumers can also consult the anchor in the form of barrage at the same time, thus forming a two-way real-time interaction (Zhao, 2021). In the e-commerce live broadcast, the anchor gives a comprehensive introduction to beauty brand products, and provides information about the brand and products, which meets the needs of consumers for informational content about product cognition. In the research of Hananto A (2012) et al., it is proposed that informational content is direct, practical, and reliable. That is to say, consumers expect that the anchor needs to clarify the relevant information of the product in the live broadcast, so as to help consumers better understand the product.

Table 4. Factors that affect the repurchase of beauty products in live broadcasts

Categories	Response		Polularity rate（n=50）
	n	Response rate	
Timely feedback to understand product details	333	23.08%	51.63%
Interact with the anchor to relieve loneliness	279	19.33%	43.26%
There are fan discounts, big discounts	308	21.34%	47.75%
Quality of the products recommended by is guaranteed	282	19.54%	43.72%
Interesting and entertaining content	241	16.70%	37.36%
Total	1443	100%	223.72%
Goodness of fit：χ²=16.456 p=0.002			

Source: SPSSAU

When talking about the factors that affect the repurchase of beauty products in live broadcasts (Table 4), 63.92% of the respondents expect the host to provide product information in a timely manner; 53.55% of the respondents hope to relieve loneliness by interacting with the host; 59.12% of the respondents value the benefits and discounts of fans; 54.13% of the respondents expect the product quality of the brand to be guaranteed; 46.26% of the respondents expect the live broadcast content to be highly entertaining.

It can be seen from the table 4 that consumers' requirements for brand repurchase are significantly higher than those for initial purchases. Consumers not only consider product quality and price factors important, but also have higher requirements for the entertainment and emotional value of e-commerce live broadcasts. According to the U&G theory of communication, in content marketing, the information it conveys includes functional information, entertainment information, self-concept, social interaction, and brand interaction (Floreddu et al., 2016).

The anchors in the live broadcast e-commerce attract a large number of users to gather in the live broadcast room through their individual characteristics, and gather a high degree of emotional energy through brand interaction, so that consumers have a sticky behavior of long-term participation in the live broadcast room purchase. This increase in user stickiness increases consumer brand loyalty (Gai, 2021).

In addition to brand interaction, entertainment information is another factor that increases consumers' online stickiness. In his research, Hananto A believes that entertainment information is content that can make consumers feel happy, or can attract consumers to be curious, and then be interested in continuing to watch live broadcasts, which can also help consumers reduce stress to a certain extent., gain attention, and also have a positive impact on the final behavior of consumers. In the live broadcast, the anchor sends consumers the content they are interested in, such as makeup skills, skin care knowledge, and cross-dressing videos. The attention of consumers increases the online stickiness of consumers.

In addition to entertainment content increasing brand loyalty, emotional content in live e-commerce is also conducive to mobilizing consumers' brand attitude identification and generating purchase behavior. Zeng (2021) found in his research that the current society has entered the era of perceptual consumption, reflecting the real state and emotional needs of the public, which can better impress consumers.

In addition to brand recognition and brand loyalty, consumer perceived value also affects brand equity. In addition to expressing their opinions through the barrage, consumers also see the barrage of other consumers. Wongkitrungrueng and Assarut (2018) found that consumers will read bullet screens while watching live broadcasts. These bullet screens will make them feel the attitudes of other consumers and affect consumers' perceived value and behavioral intentions. This result is also in line with the influence of brand reputation in Guan's research. He believes that when consumers watch the live broadcast of brand stores, the brand has a better reputation and it is easier to enhance the perceived value of customers (Guan, 2021). This perceived value increases consumers' online word-of-mouth, which in turn influences their attitudes toward branded products.

Table 5. Factors that are not conducive to the purchase of goods in live broadcast

Categories	Response		Polularity rate (n=50)
	n	Response rate	
Think the product is of poor quality	56	9.03%	8.68%
Poor after-sales service of the platform	120	19.35%	18.60%
Do not trust the beauty brand	80	12.90%	12.40%
No offline experience is more direct	67	10.81%	10.39%
Do not trust internet celebrity bloggers	96	15.48%	14.88%
Buying steps are complicated	117	18.87%	18.14%
more directly from the e-commerce platform	84	13.55%	13.02%
Total	620	100%	96.12%
Goodness of fit: χ^2=39.197 p=0.000			

Source: SPSSAU

The questionnaire mentioned 7 main factors that are not conducive to the purchase of goods in live broadcast (Table 5), namely poor product quality, poor after-sales service of the platform, distrust of beauty brands, no direct offline experience, no e-commerce platform convenience, do not trust bloggers, and the purchase steps are complicated. Among them, the two factors with the highest proportion are poor after-sales service of the platform and complicated purchasing steps. This is also reflected in the question of expecting the improvement direction of live broadcast delivery. 50.29% of the respondents hope that live broadcast e-commerce can provide more convenient operation methods in the future.

This involves the issue of group discrimination. Although most of the subjects who watch e-commerce live broadcasts in the questionnaire survey are young people, there are many elderly people who also watch live broadcasts and bring goods. The new crown pneumonia epidemic has changed a lot of the elderly's lifestyle. In the past, the elderly were used to shopping offline, but because of the epidemic, many Chinese elderly have learned to shop online and browse short videos. The operational complexity of e-commerce live broadcasts also hinders some middle-aged and elderly consumers. According to data from the National Bureau of Statistics, in 2019, China's population over the age of 65 accounted for 14.2% of the total population, entering a deeply aging society (2019). This data shows that China's middle-aged and elderly beauty market has huge potential. According to the e-commerce platform Taobao, in May 2020, Taobao's monthly sales of middle-aged and elderly cosmetics were 15.23 million yuan, doubling from 7.16 million yuan a year ago. The average transaction price of middle-aged and elderly cosmetics on Taobao reached 169 yuan, compared with 143 yuan last year, an increase of 18.2%. The increase in the average transaction price shows that middle-aged and elderly women still have a lot of room to develop their consumption power, and they are willing to accept higher prices for better products.

The Douyin live broadcast section is embedded in the Douyin short video, and users can browse the live video randomly during the process of browsing the short video. Therefore, the service entrance of the current Douyin e-commerce part is not obvious. Not only is it difficult for the elderly to find shopping entrances, but even young people feel that the platform design is insufficient in this regard. Secondly, the current after-sales service of Douyin can only be communicated in the form of typing, which is undoubtedly difficult for many elderly people who cannot type, if there is a transaction dispute, it is undoubtedly difficult to seek after-sales protection.

Second, the high returns good rate of Douyin live broadcast is due to its lack of a complete e-commerce system at present. On October 9, 2021, Douyin E-commerce announced the cancellation of third-party connections with professional e-commerce platforms such as Taobao and Tmall, and plans to build an independent e-commerce system. However, Douyin's marketing, payment, logistics and supply chain are not yet perfect, so there are after-sales problems such as returns.

To sum up, although Douyin's current live-streaming e-commerce model provides beauty brands with opportunities for rapid development, there are also problems such as group discrimination and imperfect supply chains that need to be improved urgently.

SOLUTIONS AND RECOMMENDATIONS

Therefore, in the context of the huge impact of the new crown pneumonia epidemic on the global economy, it is particularly important for small and medium-sized enterprises to seek digital transformation. Based on the above conclusions, the following suggestions are put forward for the brand development of SMEs:

1. Enhance consumer perceived value through brand reputation.

On the one hand, enterprises should strengthen the training of anchors, improve their awareness of the brands they broadcast live, so that they can accurately and timely explain the quality of the brand, product functions and culture in the process of live broadcast delivery, so as to improve their awareness of the brand. Improve consumers' awareness and trust in the brand; on the other hand, to improve the quality of after-sales service, it is necessary to abide by the relevant regulatory policies promulgated by the state, and strictly control all links from production, transportation to after-sales to ensure consistency of product quality and promotion.

2.   Efforts to improve consumer trust in the brand.

Although brand stores rely on their own brand reputation to enhance consumer trust, false marketing still exists in live broadcast delivery, which makes consumers question the overall credibility of the live broadcast delivery industry. Therefore, the live broadcast room of the brand store should use the bullet screen comment content to echo the explanation of the anchor to enhance the trust of consumers.

3.   Consider consumer groups that have been overlooked in the past.

We can see that the current live-streaming delivery target groups are still young women aged 20-35, ignoring other groups with stronger spending power, such as male consumers and middle-aged and elderly groups, whose consumption power is still very high. Large development space, they are more willing to accept higher prices for better products. Therefore, enterprises should fully conduct market research, fully consider the characteristics of each consumer group, adopt differentiated marketing, and expand the radiation range of brand influence.

CONCLUSION

Based on the questionnaire survey method, this paper studies and analyzes the Chinese Douyin platform as a case, and discusses the impact mechanism of live broadcast e-commerce on brand equity. The results show that, livestreaming e-commerce dose have a positive impact on beauty brand equity. With its features of high interactivity and high cost performance, live streaming can meet the needs of consumers to the greatest extent, and it has played a huge role in enhancing the functional value of the product and the perceived value of consumers.

The specific impact mechanism is as follows. Live e-commerce first attracts consumers through highly interesting short video content, which improves brand awareness. As a result, consumers pay attention to products and brands. Secondly, live e-commerce further improves consumers' perceived value through the celebrity effect of Internet celebrities and highly interactive scene simulation. Finally, the brand image of consumers is strengthened through word-of-mouth communication, which further strengthens brand loyalty and makes consumers and potential consumers have the possibility of continuous consumption of the brand. Under the combined effect of this series of influences, live e-commerce finally increases brand equity.

This article is different from previous studies on the impact of live e-commerce on consumers. Previous studies focused on the media behavior. This article focuses more on the impact of live e-commerce on enterprises, also called brands. This article discusses the background of the development of live streaming in China, as well as the development characteristics of the beauty industry, the subject of this study, and compares the change of China's beauty industry before and after the introduction of live streaming, so as to highlight the emerging trend of live streaming. The emerging role of social media in brand development.

REFERENCES

Ajitha, S., & Sivakumar, V. J. (2017). Understanding the Effect of Personal and Social Value on Attitude and Usage Behavior of Luxury Cosmetic Brands. *Journal of Retailing and Consumer Services*, *39*(11), 103–113. doi:10.1016/j.jretconser.2017.07.009

Alibaba. (2021, April 28). *Taobao Live 2021 Annual Report*. https://tbd.wshang.com/home

Baidu. (2021, May 10). *Baidu 2021 National Tide Pride Search Big Data*. https://baijiahao.baidu.com/s?id=16993346422733339852&wfr=spider&for=pc

Bao, L. J., Zhong, W. J., & Mei, S. (2021). The influence of social media "like" sharing advertisements. *Journal of Southeast University*, *37*(4), 429–435.

Boonghee, Y., & Naveen, D. (2001). Developing and validating a multidimensional consumer-based brand equity scale. *Journal of Business Research*, *52*(1), 1–14. doi:10.1016/S0148-2963(99)00098-3

Brown, D., & Hayes, N. (2008). *Influencer marketing*. Elsevier Ltd. doi:10.4324/9780080557700

Cao, J. X., Chen, G. J., Wu, J. L., Liu, B., Zhou, T., Xu, S., & Zhu, Z. Q. (2016). Mining of Social Network Opinion Leaders Based on Multidimensional Feature Analysis. *Journal of Electronics (China)*, *44*(04), 898–905.

Chen, J. (2020). The Dynamic Mechanism of "Double Upgrading" of Industry and Consumption in the Post-epidemic Era. *Journal of Shanghai Jiaotong University*, *28*(5), 100-111. Doi:10.13806/j.cnki

China Internet Network Information Center. (2022, February 25). *The 49th Statistical Report on Internet Development in China*. http://www.cnnic.net.cn/hlwfzyj/hlwxzbg/hlwtjbg/202202/P020220311493378715650.pdf

CTR Market Research. (2020, June 9). *2020 New Coronary Pandemic Consumer Behavioural Attitude Impact and Trend Report*. https://www.ctrchina.cn/static/upload/20210225108xf_20210511175945559.pdf

David, A. Aaker. (1991). Managing brand equity. Macmilan.

First Financial Daily. (2012, March 16). *Internet word-of-mouth influences consumer buying behavior*. https://www.yicai.com/news/1531334.html

Floreddu, P. B., & Cabiddu, F. (2016). Social media communication strategies. *Journal of Services Marketing*, *30*(5), 490–503. doi:10.1108/JSM-01-2015-0036

Gai, S. N. (2021). Research on the influence of e-commerce anchors on college students' consumption behavior: Based on the perspective of interactive ritual chain theory. *Southeast Communication*, (4), 114-118. doi:10.13556/j.cnki.dncb.cn35-1274/j.2021.04.032

Guan, H., Wu, H. W. (2021). Research on the Influence Mechanism of Brand Store Live Streaming on Consumers' Purchase Intention. *Price Theory and Practice*, (10), 125-128. doi:.2021.10.335 doi:10.19851/j.cnki.cn11-1010/f

Guo, S. H., & Lv, X. (2020). A review of data mining and behavior analysis of online live broadcast platforms. *Wuli Xuebao*, *69*(8), 117–126. doi:10.7498/aps.69.20191776

Hi, D., & Guo, Z. (2018). An Empirical Study on the Impact of Product Crisis Response Strategies on Consumers' Purchase Intentions—Based on the Moderating Role of Corporate Reputation. *Journal of Shanghai Jiaotong University*, *52*(02), 247–252. doi:10.16183/j.cnki.jsjtu.2018.02.019

Hi, J. Y. (2022). The innovation path of social e-commerce model from the perspective of private traffic. *Business Economics Research*, (9),87-90.

Hu, J., Li, L., Zhang, H., Zhu, X. Z., & Yang, W. S. (2022). Dynamic pricing decision of online live broadcast platform considering reference effect and anchor influence. *System Engineering Theory and Practice*, *42*(03), 755–766.

iiMedia Research. (2021, March 31). *2021 China Cosmetics User Survey and Development Forecast Research Report*. https://www.iimedia.cn/c460/78987.html

Ipsos. (2021, October 9). *2021 Men's Skincare and Grooming Market Insights*. https://coffee.pmcaff.com/article/13750893_j

Li, J., Yu, M. Y., & Wang, Q. (2007). Overview of Brand Competitiveness. *Journal of Shanghai Jiaotong University*, (6), 1035–1044. doi:10.16183/j.cnki.jsjtu.2007.06.039

Li, X., & Cui, B. J. (2020). "E-commerce live broadcast" from the perspective of the domestic economic cycle. *Ideological Front*, (6), 56-63.

Li, X., Huang, B., & Shen, L. (2020). WeChat marketing strategy of clothing brands. *Textile Journal*, *41*(12), 130–136. doi:10.13475/j.fzxb.20200302607

Liu, Y., Li, Q., & Yin, M. (2020). Research on the influence of online shopping characteristics on consumers' purchasing behavior. *Soft Science*, *34*(06), 108–114.

Lou, Q. Q. (2020). Analysis on the development of live broadcast e-commerce. *China Convention and Exhibition*, (23), 108-113.

Ma, Y. (2021). The impact of the digital economy on the consumer market: mechanism, performance, problems and countermeasures. *Macroeconomic Research*, (5), 81-91. doi:10.16304/j.cnki.11-3952/f.2021.05.008

Meng, L., Liu, F. J., Chen, S. Y., & Duan, S. (2020). Can I Arouse You—Research on the Influence Mechanism of Different Types of Live Streaming Influencer Information Source Characteristics on Consumers' Purchase Intention. *Nankai Management Review*, *23*(1), 131–143.

National development and Reform Commission. (2022, April 25). *Opinions on Further Unleashing Consumption Potential and Promoting Sustainable Recovery of Consumption*. https://www.ndrc.gov.cn/xxgk/jd/jd/202204/t20220425_1323087.html?code=&state=123

Oxford Economics. (2020, April 22). *Global GDP forecast to fall 2.8% in 2020, only China to grow in Q2*. https://baijiahao.baidu.com/s?id=1664638512861311500&wfr=spider&for=pc

Peters, L. D., Pressey, A. D., Vanharanta, M., & Johnston, W. J. (2013). Theoretical developments in industrial marketing management: Multidisciplinary perspectives. *Industrial Marketing Management, 42*(3), 275–282. doi:10.1016/j.indmarman.2013.02.001

Shan, J. J. (2016). Corporate Brand Marketing Strategy under the Background of Social Media. *Journal of Southeast University, 18*(S1), 23-25. doi:.2016.s1.008 doi:10.13916/j.cnki.issn1671-511x

Sheth, J. N., Newman, B. I., & Gross, B. L. (1991). Why we buy what we buy. *Journal of Business Research*, (2).

Wang, F. Q., & Jiang, J. H. (2021). How does the Internet short video business model realize value creation? A Double Case Study of Douyin and Kuaishou. *Foreign Economics and Management, 43*(2), 3–19. doi:10.16538/j.cnki.fem.20210103.101

Wang, J. L., & Feng, K. (2022). From the performance economy to the traffic e-commerce: the instrumental transformation of the online live broadcast function. *Media*, (3), 51-54.

Wang, S., Xuan, Z. N., Sun, L., & Wang, H. L. (2021). Research on the value co-creation mechanism of social e-commerce brand equity based on user-generated content. *Science and Science and Technology Management, 42*(7), 35–52.

Weiboyi Database. (2022, May 27). *2022 Mainstream Social Media Platform Trend Insights Report*. https://coffee.pmcaff.com/article/13779262_j

Wongkitrungrueng, A., & Assarut, N. (2020). The role of live streaming in building consumer trust and engagement with social commerce sellers. *Journal of Business Research, 117*, 543–556. doi:10.1016/j.jbusres.2018.08.032

Wu, J. A. (2007). *Marketing*. Higher Education Press.

Xing, P., You, H. Y., & Fan, Y. C. (2022). Quality Effort Strategy of Live E-commerce Service Supply Chain Considering Platform Marketing Efforts. *Control and Decision, 37*(1), 205-212. doi:.kzyjc.2020.1205 doi:10.13195/j

Yang, G. L., Li, P., & Liu, J. (2010). Scientific Knowledge Graph: A New Field of Scientometrics. *Science Popularization Research, 5*(4), 28-34. doi:.1673-8357.2010. 04.004 doi:10.19293/j.cnki

Yang, Y., Liu, S., Li, Y. W., & Jia, J. M. (2020). Big Data Marketing: Review and Prospect. *System Engineering Theory and Practice, 40*(08), 2150–2158.

Zhang, B. G., & Wang, Y. F. (2021). The influence of the characteristics of e-commerce anchors on consumers' purchase intention. *Business Research*, (1), 1-6.

Zhang, Y. R., & Y, X. T. (2021). On the new marketing model of "e-commerce + live broadcast". *Academic Exchange Quarterly, 04*, 100–110.

Zhao, S. M., & Liang, B. (2021). Characteristics, challenges and development trends of live streaming delivery. *China Circulation Economy*, *35*(8), 61–71. doi:10.14089/j.cnki.cn11-3664/f.2021.08.006

Zhao, Z. B. (2005). An Exploratory Study on the Dimension of Brand Equity. *Management Science*, (5), 12–18.

Zhou, W. (2020). Analysis of Content Marketing, Customer-Brand Engagement, Brand Loyalty Relationship. *Business Economics Research*, (11), 77-81.

Zhou, Y., Meng, W. D., Du, H. Y., & Wu, P. Y. (2008). A Study on Purchase Intention of Mobile Data Service Based on Perceived Value. *Journal of Communication*, (9), 97–102.

Chapter 5
Combating Choice Overload via a Growth Mindset in the Age of Social Media

Kazi Turin Rahman
https://orcid.org/0000-0001-5585-7034
Coventry University, UK

Rohit Bansal
https://orcid.org/0000-0001-7072-5005
Vaish College of Engineering, Rohtak, India

ABSTRACT

The antecedents and consequences of choice overload, or overchoice, have been largely investigated. However, the aspect of comprehensively evaluating a large assortment of options and mitigating subsequent choice overload is absent. By adopting a growth mindset and comprehensively evaluating alternatives, it is possible to combat the menace known as overchoice. This chapter conceptualises a unique model that examines choice overload mitigation from a deeper psychological lens. Moreover, it also adds a new dimension to the concept by integrating the aspect of rigorous choice evaluation. Overall, future research propositions have been made that will enable researchers to validate the novel model. Implications of validating said model include strengthening the field of choice overload by offering comprehensive mitigation strategies.

INTRODUCTION

Marketers and retailers strive to offer numerous product and service options to their customers. Technological advancement and product innovation have contributed to an abundance of choices for consumers (Rahman 2021a; Rahman 2021b). Offering more choices to consumers has benefits like stimulating variety-seeking behaviour and boosting enjoyment of shopping (Herpen and Pieters 2002). However, more is not always merrier as too many choices can result in choice overload among consumers. Also known

DOI: 10.4018/978-1-6684-5770-2.ch005

as overchoice, this concept refers to the feeling of being cognitively overwhelmed from an abundance of choice options (Toffler 1971). Since the coinage of the term, many studies have confirmed that too many choices can be detrimental (Settle and Golden 1974; Keller and Staelin 1987; Iyengar and Lepper 2000; Misuraca and Teuscher 2013; Greenwood and Ramjaun 2020). Choice overload also leads to negative consequences like suffering from post-choice decision regret or deferring the choice indefinitely (Noguchi and Hills 2016; Pilli and Mazzon 2016). Overchoice has been a mainstay in academic literature for quite some time. While the consequences have been documented and theorized, research focusing on conceptualising the mitigation of choice overload is quite scarce. At present, only few authors like Malone and Lusk (2018) have dealt with mitigation of choice overload. There have been renewed calls to investigate the psychological processes involved in picking from large assortments (Benoit and Miller 2017). Since the problem of choice overload is a cognitive aspect, a psychological investigation into the mindset of a consumer can help in alleviating the problem. Therefore, this paper proposes to use growth mindset (the belief that human traits are malleable) as a mechanism to combat choice overload and develop a novel model towards mitigating this problem.

The conceptualization of said model is preceded by a literature review of choice overload, growth mindset and existing research gaps. With regards to novel theoretical development, there are a number of ways this can be achieved. First of all, new theories can be synthesised based on context like the agency and reactance theory of crowding (Lim, 2021). Another way is theoretical integration like the integrated information systems-consumer behaviour model for e-shopping (Lim, 2015). Novel theories emerging from systematic reviews are another possibility as demonstrated by Lim and Weissmann (2021) in their development of the theory of behavioural control. Altogether, this paper has chosen to follow a hybrid route towards novel theoretical development. Theoretical integration (of choice overload and growth mindset) was achieved after a systematic review of maiden evidence to support the core tenets of the new theory. Subsequently, research propositions have been made so that future studies can validate the proposed model. The paper concludes with a discussion on the implications of authenticating the novel model of overchoice mitigation. Analysing on-going debates, identifying gaps in literature and synthesising new relationships have been the primary focus of this conceptual study. Altogether, these components are essential in the formation of any theoretical/conceptual articles as narrated by Yadav (2014) and Jakkola (2020). Altogether, the sections below will present a comprehensive overview of the literature before proposing a novel model to mitigate choice overload.

LITERATURE REVIEW

Overview on Choice Overload

Initially, the antecedents and consequences of choice overload were fragmented across literature. Chernev et al. (2015) integrated these elements into one, comprehensive theoretical framework. According to said framework, four moderating factors (antecedents) contributed towards overchoice; decision task difficulty, choice set complexity, preference uncertainty and decision goal. In turn, choice overload lead to seven different consequences; choice satisfaction, decision regret, decision confidence, choice deferral, switching likelihood, assortment choice, and option selection. Among the antecedents, decision task difficulty refers to the structural attributes of the decision problem at hand. Said attributes consist of consumer time constraints, physical properties of the available options (colour, design, etc.) and presentation format.

Therefore, depending on the time at hand and various options presented, a large assortment of choices is likely to overwhelm consumer decision-making (Adriatico et al. 2022). Choice set complexity encompasses those factors which affect the value of the options available. These factors include the presence of a dominant option and overall attractiveness of all options at hand. Hence, consumers will experience choice overload when a dominant option is missing and when overall options are of low quality (Thai and Yuksel 2017). Preference uncertainty indicates the degree to which consumers have articulated preferences with respect to the decision at hand. This factor is operationalized in terms of the product expertise consumers possess and their articulated ideal point. Thus, when individuals are less knowledgeable on products and they do not have an ideal product in mind, they are likely to face the problem of overchoice (Inbar et al. 2011). Decision goal is the degree to which consumers tend to minimize cognitive effort in decision-making. Intent, focus and level of construal affect this factor. Therefore, if consumers with low level construal intend to buy a specific product from a large assortment, they will face choice overload (Goodman and Malkoc, 2012). As for the consequences of experiencing overchoice, consumers will feel less satisfied and confident with the option selected and suffer more from post-decision regrets (Iyengar and Lepper, 2000; Inbar et al. 2011). That is not all; consumers facing choice overload are likely to defer making a choice, more likely to reverse an initial choice, feel discouraged at larger assortments and more likely to choose something that is easily justifiable (Chernev 2003; Sela et al. 2009).

What Is Growth Mindset?

A growth mindset refers to the belief that human traits are changeable (Dweck 1988). For instance, some people may be angry by nature. But, they will believe this is corrigible through yoga or mediation over time. Such is the idea of having a growth mindset. This concept has been a mainstay in social psychology for decades. Developed by Dweck and Leggett (1988), the initial scope of the concept involved the academic performance of young students. It was proven that the growth mindset orientation was linked to increased academic results through consistent effort (Yeager et al. 2016). Gradually, the application of growth mindsets expanded into multiple avenues like the impact of such mindsets on athletic performance, leadership styles and weight regulation (Chen et al. 2008; Hoyt et al. 2012; Burnette and Finkel, 2012). Across many of these aforementioned contexts, it is well documented that individuals with growth mindsets are process driven and effort-oriented (Sharifi and Palmeira 2017). Moreover, growth mindset-oriented customers prefer options (like exercise programs) which offer long-term results (Murphy and Dweck 2015). Growth mindsets are gradually making inroads into consumer behaviour literature. This is due to the fact that exploration of this concept in the domain of consumer behaviour has the potential for fruitful theoretical development (Wheeler and Omair 2015). Studies like that of Song et al. (2019), Kim et al. (2018) and Kwon et al. (2016) have already incorporated growth mindset into social networking, branding and advertising, respectively.

Implications of Growth Mindset in Choice Overload

The existing concerns within overchoice literature warrant discussion. It must be understood that marketers and retailers will offers as many choices as possible to consumers. Hence, avoiding choice overload is very difficult and consumers will inevitably evaluate multiple alternatives along the way. Iyengar et al. (2006) stressed that extra effort is required to sift through all options and it is impossible to make a thorough comparison. This inevitably leads to an overload of the consumer's cognitive resources.

Moreover, consumers do not always form concrete preferences prior to shopping and make choices on-the-go. Based on limited time and resources, consumers tend to make a decision with little expertise and information processing capacity (Scheibehenne et al. 2010). Hence, finding ways of combating choice overload is needed. Benoit and Miller (2017) suggested the need to further examine factors that decrease the negative effects of overchoice. Chernev et al. (2015) also recommended that more research is needed to uncover effects of the decision-maker's goals and goal-related factors that impact choice overload. Moreover, the consumer's ability to anticipate choice overload is another area that needs further investigation. Saltsman et al. (2020) stressed that future work should consider various decision-making strategies involving multiple choices. Overall, this paper argues that adopting a growth mindset can help in alleviating choice overload. Jain and Weiten (2020) highlighted that examining mindsets can help us gauge how consumers process their surroundings and make choices. Moreover, growth mindsets are ideal for information processing. Growth mindset-oriented individuals consider a plethora of variables that are behavioural, psychological and contextual in nature (Murphy and Dweck 2016). Thus, it can be concluded that such individuals possess the ability of holistic thinking, a process of analysing the 'whole picture'. Holistic thinking plays a mitigating role in choice overload as proven by Benoit and Miller (2017). Growth mindset-oriented individuals also have higher choice satisfaction and goal-setting standards (Cho and Johar 2011). Furthermore, growth mindset-oriented individuals focus on choosing options containing functional and developmental benefits (Kim et al. 2013). As a whole, this paper strongly proposes that the malleability and holistic thinking capacity that accompanies growth mindsets are adequate to mitigate choice overload.

Conceptualization of the Novel Model

Based on the aforementioned literature review, the proposed model has been conceptualized and illustrated in Figure 1. Said model demonstrates combating choice overload via a growth mindset. It is comprised of components adapted and modified from the original choice overload framework conceptualised by Chernev et al. (2015); growth mindset, no choice overload, less choice set complexity, less decision task difficulty, high preference certainty, long-term decision goals, choice satisfaction, decision confidence, decision regret, choice deferral, switching likelihood, assortment size and option selection. The first component illustrates the growth mindset of the consumer, which is adapted from Dweck and Leggett (1988). Such consumers strongly believe that effort fosters growth and have a plan to develop themselves over time (Murphy and Dweck 2015; Sharifi and Palmeira 2017). Since they are certain in what they want to achieve, this strengthens their preferences and long-term decision goals. Hence, traditional antecedents of choice overload like 'decision uncertainty' and 'decision goal' are eliminated. Growth mindset-oriented individuals also exhibit a mastery over coping strategies in tough situations (Jain and Weiten 2020). In a difficult situation like choosing from a large assortment, they are likely to use their holistic thinking capabilities; a technique known to mitigate choice overload as discovered by Benoit and Miller (2017). This eliminates the antecedents of choice overload known as 'choice set complexity' and 'decision task difficulty' since growth mindset-oriented individuals focus more on the underlying process of winnowing out less-desirable options rather than getting the choice 'right' (Mathur et al. 2013). Altogether, choice overload does not occur due to a growth mindset along with its four new antecedents (less choice set complexity, less decision task difficulty, high preference certainty and long-term decision goals). Since overchoice is mitigated, the accompanying negative consequences identified by Chernev et al. (2015) are also eliminated.

Figure 1. Proposal model of combating choice overload via growth mindset

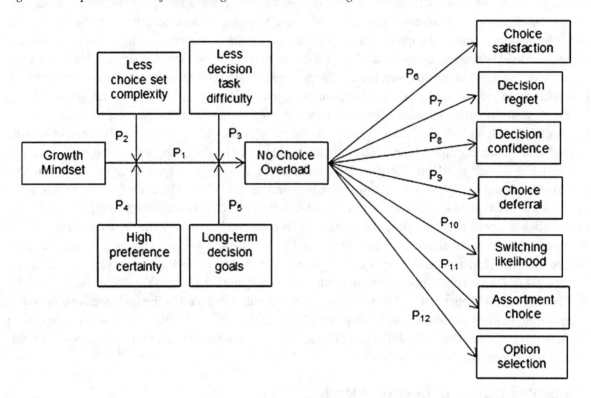

As discussed earlier, choice satisfaction and goal standards are high for the growth mindset orientation along with focus on self-growth and development (Kim et al. 2013; Cho and Johar 2011). Therefore, a high degree of choice satisfaction and decision confidence is expected with the absence of choice overload. It must also be noted that growth mindset-oriented individuals focus on choosing options containing functional and developmental benefits (Kim et al. 2013). Thus, pursuing the path to self-development is predicted to avert decision regrets and choice deferrals. The likelihood of switching or reversing an original choice is also decreased since growth mindset-oriented individuals are firm in their decisions. Additionally, exposure to large assortments does not discourage such individuals. Instead, they will use their holistic thinking capabilities to sift through available options and choose the best possible alternative, not just an easily justified one (Sela et al. 2009; Benoit and Miller 2017).

P1: Growth mindset is positively associated with 'no choice overload'

P2, 3, 4, 5: Less choice set complexity, less decision task difficulty, high preference certainty and long-term decision goals positively moderate the relationship between growth mindset and 'no choice overload'.

P6, 7: 'No choice overload' is positively associated with choice satisfaction and decision confidence

P8, 9, 10, 11, 12: 'No choice overload' is negatively associated with decision regret, choice deferral, switching likelihood, and assortment size and option selection.

As a whole, many intriguing future research propositions have emerged from the analyzed literature and discussions above. Said propositions have been outlined above for future researchers to empirically validate.

CONCLUSION

Limitations

Before discussing the contributions of this theoretical paper, the limitations of it must be brought to light. Firstly, one search engine, Mendeley, was used to extract papers relevant to choice overload. Although it is an extensive database of indexed publications developed by Elsevier, some papers may have been ignored in this study. Secondly, some of the keywords pertaining to this field may have been overlooked. However, the keywords used to obtain papers were adopted from overchoice literature reviews like that of Scheibehenne et al. (2010) and Chernev et al. (2015) so the chances of missing out were minimized. Finally, expert suggestions were sought about this subject via email but no responses were received.

Implications

To reiterate, striving to validate the proposed model in this paper has many implications for researchers. Firstly, the development of relatively scarce literature on overchoice mitigation can be achieved since most studies have focused on its antecedents and consequences so far. This paper also responds to the call that it is crucial to introduce new psychological theories into the field of consumer research (Block et al. 2021). The concept of growth mindsets is one such novel introduction that has been made in this paper. Fortifying the newly introduced concept of holistic thinking in the field of choice overload is also achievable (Benoit and Miller 2017). Theoretically, this paper offers a new perspective into the concept of overchoice as well. Analysing the phenomenon from a growth mindset perspective can mitigate many of the negative effects found in existing literature. Said effects include preference uncertainty, decision regrets and more (Inbar et al. 2011; Noguchi and Hills 2016). That's not all; the issue of how many choices to offer still irks marketers and retailers to this day. Hence, close collaboration is necessary between psychology and marketing researchers to tackle this problem. Pursuing the empirical validation of the proposed model will benefit both parties and further overchoice literature considerably.

Final Remarks

Although more choices attract the interest of potential consumers, they are likely to be overwhelmed by the sheer abundance of alternatives and experience choice overload. Primarily, the central objective of this paper was to develop a novel model of overchoice mitigation. The foundation of said model presented in this study is based on growth mindsets. Extant literature showed a dearth in mitigation strategies of choice overload since maximum studies only focused on the antecedents and consequences. Therefore, this study was aimed at filling the aforementioned research gap by introducing a model that tackles overchoice using growth mindsets. Marketers and retailers have a responsibility to ensure that customer experience is as smooth as possible. However, 'how much is too much?' is a question that is still being investigated by researchers and practitioners. In this era of consumerism and excessive choice options, the modern-day customer must evaluate available options smartly and reach a concrete decision (Grandi and Cardinali 2021).

REFERENCES

Benoit, I. D., & Miller, E. G. (2017). The mitigating role of holistic thinking on choice overload. *Journal of Consumer Marketing, 34*(3), 181–190. doi:10.1108/JCM-07-2016-1889

Bhoi, N. K. (2018). Mendeley data repository as a platform for research data management. *Marching Beyond Libraries: Managerial Skills and Technological Competencies*, 481-487.

Block, L., Argo, J., & Kramer, T. (2021). The Science of Consumer Psychology. *Journal of Consumer Psychology, 31*(1), 3–5. doi:10.1002/jcpy.1205

Broniarczyk, S. M. & Griffin, J. G. (2014). Decision difficulty in the age of consumer empowerment. *Journal of Consumer Psychology, 24*(4), 608-625.

Chernev, A. (2003). When more is less and less is more: The role of ideal point availability and assortment in consumer choice. *The Journal of Consumer Research, 30*(2), 170–183. doi:10.1086/376808

Chernev, A., Böckenholt, U., & Goodman, J. (2015). Choice overload: A conceptual review and meta-analysis. *Journal of Consumer Psychology, 25*(2), 333–358. doi:10.1016/j.jcps.2014.08.002

Cho, C. K., & Johar, G. V. (2011). Attaining satisfaction. *The Journal of Consumer Research, 38*(4), 622–631. doi:10.1086/660115

Choi, I., Koo, M., & Choi, J. A. (2007). Individual differences in analytic versus holistic thinking. *Personality and Social Psychology Bulletin, 33*(5), 691–705. doi:10.1177/0146167206298568 PMID:17440200

Dweck, C. S. (1988). Goals: An approach to motivation and achievement. *Journal of Personality and Social Psychology, 54*(1), 5–12. doi:10.1037/0022-3514.54.1.5 PMID:3346808

Dweck, C. S. (2000). *Self-theories: Their role in motivation, personality, and development*. Psychology Press.

Dweck, C. S., & Yeager, D. S. (2019). Mindsets: A view from two eras. *Perspectives on Psychological Science, 14*(3), 481–496. doi:10.1177/1745691618804166 PMID:30707853

Fasolo, B., McClelland, G. H., & Todd, P. M. (2007). Escaping the tyranny of choice: When fewer attributes make choice easier. *Marketing Theory, 7*(1), 13–26. doi:10.1177/1470593107073842

Grandi, B., & Cardinali, M. G. (2021). Choice Overload in the Grocery Setting: Results from a Laboratory Experiment. *International Business Research, 14*(1), 1–94.

Greenwood, E., & Ramjaun, T. R. (2020). Exploring choice overload in online travel booking. *Journal of Promotional Communications, 8*(1), 86–104.

Inbar, Y., Botti, S., & Hanko, K. (2011). Decision speed and choice regret: When haste feels like waste. *Journal of Experimental Social Psychology, 47*(3), 533–540. doi:10.1016/j.jesp.2011.01.011

Iyengar, S. S., & Lepper, M. R. (2000). When choice is demotivating: Can one desire too much of a good thing? *Journal of Personality and Social Psychology, 79*(6), 995–1006. doi:10.1037/0022-3514.79.6.995 PMID:11138768

Iyengar, S. S., Wells, R. E., & Schwartz, B. (2006). Doing better but feeling worse: Looking for the "best" job undermines satisfaction. *Psychological Science, 17*(2), 143–150. doi:10.1111/j.1467-9280.2006.01677.x PMID:16466422

Jain, S. P., & Weiten, T. J. (2020). Consumer psychology of implicit theories: A review and agenda. *Counselling Psychology Review, 3*(1), 60–75. doi:10.1002/arcp.1056

Kahneman, D. (2013). *Thinking, fast and slow*. Farrar, Straus and Giroux.

Keller, K. L., & Staelin, R. (1987). Effects of quality and quantity of information on decision effectiveness. *The Journal of Consumer Research, 14*(2), 200–213. doi:10.1086/209106

Kim, H., Kulow, K., & Kramer, T. (2013). The interactive effect of beliefs in malleable fate and fateful predictions on choice. *The Journal of Consumer Research, 40*(6), 1139–1148. doi:10.1086/674196

Kim, P., Vaidyanathan, R., Chang, H., & Stoel, L. (2018). Using brand alliances with artists to expand retail brand personality. *Journal of Business Research, 85*, 424–433. doi:10.1016/j.jbusres.2017.10.020

Kwon, J., Seo, Y., & Ko, D. (2016). Effective luxury-brand advertising: The ES–IF matching (Entity–Symbolic versus Incremental–Functional) model. *Journal of Advertising, 45*(4), 459–471. doi:10.1080/00913367.2016.1226995

Lim, W. M. (2015). Antecedents and consequences of e-shopping: An integrated model. *Internet Research, 25*(2), 184–217. doi:10.1108/IntR-11-2013-0247

Lim, W. M. (2018). Dialectic antidotes to critics of the technology acceptance model: Conceptual, methodological, and replication treatments for behavioural modelling in technology-mediated environments. *AJIS. Australasian Journal of Information Systems, 22*, 22. doi:10.3127/ajis.v22i0.1651

Lim, W. M. (2021). Toward an agency and reactance theory of crowding: Insights from COVID-19 and the tourism industry. *Journal of Consumer Behaviour, 20*(6), 1690–1694. doi:10.1002/cb.1948

Lim, W. M. (2021a). A marketing mix typology for integrated care: The 10 Ps. *Journal of Strategic Marketing, 29*(5), 453–469. doi:10.1080/0965254X.2020.1775683

Lim, W. M., & Weissmann, M. A. (2021). Toward a theory of behavioral control. *Journal of Strategic Marketing*, 1–27. doi:10.1080/0965254X.2021.1890190

Malone, T., & Lusk, J. L. (2019). Mitigating choice overload: An experiment in the US beer market. *Journal of Wine Economics, 14*(1), 48–70. doi:10.1017/jwe.2018.34

Manolică, A., Guță, A. S., Roman, T., & Dragăn, L. M. (2021). Is Consumer Overchoice a Reason for Decision Paralysis? *Sustainability, 13*(11), 5920. doi:10.3390u13115920

Mathur, P., Jain, S. P., Hsieh, M.-H., Lindsey, C. D., & Maheswaran, D. (2013). The influence of implicit theories and message frame on the persuasiveness of disease prevention and detection advocacies. *Organizational Behavior and Human Decision Processes, 122*(2), 141–151. doi:10.1016/j.obhdp.2013.05.002

McCabe, S., Li, C., & Chen, Z. (2016). Time for a radical reappraisal of tourist decision making? Toward a new conceptual model. *Journal of Travel Research*, *55*(1), 3–15. doi:10.1177/0047287515592973

Misuraca, R., Ceresia, F., Teuscher, U., & Faraci, P. (2019). The role of the brand on choice overload. *Mind & Society*, *18*(1), 57–76. doi:10.100711299-019-00210-7

Misuraca, R., & Teuscher, U. (2013). Time flies when you maximize—Maximizers and satisficers perceive time differently when making decisions. *Acta Psychologica*, *143*(2), 176–180. doi:10.1016/j.actpsy.2013.03.004 PMID:23584103

Misuraca, R., Teuscher, U., & Faraci, P. (2016). Is more choice always worse? Age differences in the overchoice effect. *Journal of Cognitive Psychology*, *28*(2), 242–255. doi:10.1080/20445911.2015.1118107

Monga, A. B., & John, D. R. (2010). What makes brands elastic? The influence of brand concept and styles of thinking on brand extension evaluation. *Journal of Marketing*, *74*(3), 80–92. doi:10.1509/jmkg.74.3.080

Murphy, M. C., & Dweck, C. S. (2016). Mindsets and consumer psychology: A response. *Journal of Consumer Psychology*, *1*(26), 165–166. doi:10.1016/j.jcps.2015.06.006

Noguchi, T., & Hills, T. T. (2016). Experience-based decisions favor riskier alternatives in large sets. *Journal of Behavioral Decision Making*, *29*(5), 489–498. doi:10.1002/bdm.1893

Paul, J., Lim, W. M., O'Cass, A., Hao, A. W., & Bresciani, S. (2021). Scientific procedures and rationales for systematic literature reviews (SPAR-4-SLR). *International Journal of Consumer Studies*, *45*(4), O1–O16. doi:10.1111/ijcs.12695

Paul, J., & Mas, E. (2020). Toward a 7-P framework for international marketing. *Journal of Strategic Marketing*, *28*(8), 681–701. doi:10.1080/0965254X.2019.1569111

Pilli, L. E., & Mazzon, J. A. (2016). Information overload, choice deferral, and moderating role of need for cognition: Empirical evidence. *Revista de Administração (São Paulo)*, *51*(1), 36–55. doi:10.5700/rausp1222

Polman, E. (2012). Effects of self–other decision making on regulatory focus and choice overload. *Journal of Personality and Social Psychology*, *102*(5), 980–993. doi:10.1037/a0026966 PMID:22429272

Rahman, K. T. (2021a). Applications of Blockchain Technology for Digital Marketing: A Systematic Review. *Blockchain Technology and Applications for Digital Marketing*, 16-31.

Rahman, K. T. (2021b). Driving Engagement on Instagram: A Comparative Analysis of Amazon Prime and Disney+. *SEISENSE Business Review*, *1*(3), 1–11. doi:10.33215br.v1i3.676

Rucker, D. D., & Galinsky, A. D. (2016). Growing beyond growth: Why multiple mindsets matter for consumer behavior. *Journal of Consumer Psychology*, *26*(1), 161–164. doi:10.1016/j.jcps.2015.06.009

Saltsman, T. L., Seery, M. D., Ward, D. E., Lamarche, V. M., & Kondrak, C. L. (2021). Is satisficing really satisfying? Satisficers exhibit greater threat than maximizers during choice overload. *Psychophysiology*, *58*(1), e13705. doi:10.1111/psyp.13705 PMID:33107043

Scheibehenne, B., Greifeneder, R., & Todd, P. M. (2010). Can there ever be too many options? A meta-analytic review of choice overload. *The Journal of Consumer Research, 37*(3), 409–425. doi:10.1086/651235

Schwartz, B. (2004). *The paradox of choice: why more is less*. Harper Perennial.

Settle, R. B., & Golden, L. L. (1974). Attribution theory and advertiser credibility. *JMR, Journal of Marketing Research, 11*(2), 181–185. doi:10.1177/002224377401100209

Sharifi, S. S., & Palmeira, M. (2017). Customers' reactions to technological products: The impact of implicit theories of intelligence. *Computers in Human Behavior, 77,* 309–316. doi:10.1016/j.chb.2017.09.013

Song, Y. A., Lee, S. Y., & Kim, Y. (2019). Does mindset matter for using social networking sites?: Understanding motivations for and uses of Instagram with growth versus fixed mindset. *International Journal of Advertising, 38*(6), 886–904. doi:10.1080/02650487.2019.1637614

Thai, N. T., & Yuksel, U. (2017). Choice overload in holiday destination choices. *International Journal of Culture, Tourism and Hospitality Research, 11*(1), 53–66. doi:10.1108/IJCTHR-09-2015-0117

Toffler, A. C. (1971). Learning to Live with Future Shock. *College and University Business, 51*(3), 55–57.

Wheeler, S. C., & Omair, A. (2015). Potential growth areas for implicit theories research. *Journal of Consumer Psychology, 26*(1), 137–141. doi:10.1016/j.jcps.2015.06.008

Yadav, M. S. (2014). Enhancing theory development in marketing. *AMS Review, 4*(1-2), 1–4. doi:10.100713162-014-0059-z

KEY TERMS AND DEFINITIONS

Choice Overload: Also known as overchoice, it is a cognitive impairment in which people have a difficult time making a decision when faced with many options.

Growth Mindset: People who have a growth mindset believe that even if they struggle with certain skills, their abilities aren't set in stone. They think that with work, their skills can improve over time.

Psychology: It is the scientific study of mind and behavior. Psychology includes the study of conscious and unconscious phenomena.

Social Media: Social media are interactive technologies that facilitate the creation and sharing of information, ideas and interests.

Chapter 6

Contribution of ICT on Small and Medium Enterprise Business Profitability:
A Literature Review

Niranjan Devkota

iD https://orcid.org/0000-0001-9989-0397

National Planning Commission, Government of Nepal, Kathmandu, Nepal

Amit Sigdel

Quest International College, Pokhara University, Nepal

Udaya Raj Paudel

Quest International College, Pokhara University, Nepal

Sahadeb Upretee

Central Washington University, USA

Devid Kumar Basyal

iD https://orcid.org/0000-0002-8363-8581

La Grandee International College, Nepal & Pokhara University, Nepal

ABSTRACT

There were numerous opportunities for small-medium businesses to gain more advantages by incorporating more ICT into their operations. Studying the effects of ICT use on organizational financial performance is an important research topic that has not been well described. Apart from the fact that ICT is underutilized in developing countries and the majority of empirical research focuses on large corporations, the researcher discovered that, as a result of the above literature findings and points, there is still a significant research gap between developed and developing country perspectives on ICT adoption and usage. Therefore, this research plans to see the exiting literature review and research gap for the context of developing country. ICT is a new concept, and there has been very little research and study in this field, with no research carried out in Nepal. This review can be instrumental for those who what to conduct ICT-linked SME performance and profitability.

DOI: 10.4018/978-1-6684-5770-2.ch006

SMALL MEDIUM ENTERPRISES (SMEs): HISTORY AND EVOLUTION

The existence of many nations, organizations, and people is impacted by globalization, the information society, and economics (Martin, 2017). Likewise, the proliferation of the aforementioned processes was significantly impacted by the quick development of information and communication technologies, or ICT (further), which transforms the established corporate structures and communication channels. It is well recognized that the adoption and use of ICT represents basics of economic growth and competitiveness for businesses, organizations, and even nations that are able to utilize them (Myovella et al., 2020).

In the twenty-first century, information and communication technology (ICT) has become an integral part of human life (Devkota & Phuyal, 2018). ICT devices, in particular, have helped businesses increase productivity and manage inter-organizational affairs. However, customers may also use the technology to perform more versatile and reliable personal communications, business transactions, and banking operations (Zhang & Kizildag, 2018). Likewise, small and mid-size enterprises (SMEs) are businesses that maintain revenues, assets or a number of employees below a certain threshold (Adhikari et al., 2021). SMEs affect both the geographical placement of SMEs and country-specific legislation (Yolande Smit, 2012), and diversity of small business (Chittithaworn et al., 2011). In addition to micro-enterprises with just a few workers, the group of small and medium-sized enterprises (SMEs) includes profitable businesses with a large number of employees (Devkota et al., 2022). The Federal Ministry of Economic Affairs and Energy in Germany describes SMEs as companies with less than 500 workers or an annual turnover of up to EUR 50 million (Noorali & Gilaninia, 2017). Likewise, the business environment is becoming increasingly dynamic, complex and unpredictable with technology, globalization, knowledge and changing competitive approaches affecting overall performance (O'Regan et al., 2006). Small and medium-sized enterprises (SMEs) form an important part of both developed and emerging countries' economies. They build jobs, develop new business models and goods, minimize poverty, inflation and income inequality and solve the issue of balance of payments(Athapaththu & Nishantha, 2018).

Historically, because small and medium-sized enterprises were not considered economically viable enterprises, they were either encouraged to grow into much larger enterprises or, for other non-economic considerations, considered worthy of protection from external competition (Juradoa & Battisti, 2019). However, governments have introduced legislation to protect SMEs (and, in the specific case of New Zealand, all businesses) from external competition and to protect long-standing values of independence and self-reliance in largely immigrant-based societies such as the United States, Australia and New Zealand, epitomized by the right to 'make their own way' (Anglund, 2000; Hunter & Morrow, 2006; Lundström et al., 2014). Additionally, SMEs were also shielded from the arrival of big business in older, more developed cultures, but this protection was articulated in terms of maintaining traditional ways of manufacturing products and focus was also put on the effect that a shift in the production scale would have on lifestyles and the quality of the product itself (Landes, Mokyr & Baumol, 2010).

In the 1980s, many large-scale industrial operations closed and collapsed in the developing world, resulting in high levels of unemployment concentrated in regional centers which sparked greater policy-makers' interest in self-employment policies, particularly after research revealed that SMEs play an important role in generating employment (Birch, 1979; Karki et al., 2021). Indeed, public policy on SMEs was very scarce up to this point in the UK when the focus shifted to promoting self-employment (Greene, Mole, & Storey, 2008). Interest in the role of SMEs and entrepreneurial activity in stimulating regional growth was also stimulated by the decrease in large-scale industrial operations (Reynolds, Storey & Westhead, 1994). For example, SMEs owner-man-agers were encouraged to develop networking opportunities based on the logic that spillovers of knowledge and enhanced networks would boost regional economic development. SMEs were widely accepted at the beginning of the 1990s as a credible and significant contributor to economic growth (Loveman & Sengenberger, 1991).

As the economy moved towards more agile and versatile knowledge-based economic operation (Kharel et al., 2022), because of their ability to react and respond rapidly to changes in their climate, SMEs were considered to have a new role in adding value to the evolving knowledge-based economy (Audretsch, 2009). In addition, globalization challenged existing policy tools as obsolete, especially given the emerging emphasis on entrepreneurship as a new paradigm (Gilbert, Audretsch, & McDougall, 2004; Devkota et al., 2020). In the latter phase of SMEs policy creation, main policies such as innovation have been an important priority for governments in their attempts to improve competitiveness and other policies aimed at developing an atmosphere for SMEs that will contribute to growth (Audretsch & Aldridge, 2014; Devkota et al., 2022).

In the context of developing countries, ICT was generally accepted during the three decades after the Second World War (1945-1970) that multinational corporations enjoyed greater economies of scale, promoted more competition and improved productivity in world markets. As a result, the agenda of the UK government was supposed to promote the growth of big companies (Acs & Audretsch, 1990; Griffiths et. al. 2004). While the SMEs suffered a long period of declining share, they remained alive and then a revived interest in them took place in the early seventies. This new interest was created because the policymaker noticed that, not through internal expansion, big corporations frequently expanded from mergers. Moreover, small businesses have proven themselves to be more creative than believed and very significant providers of work (Griffith's et.al. 2004; Johnson, 2008). The revival of SMEs can be explained by several variables, according to Storey (1994), the most important being the reaffirmation of an enterprise tradition, the increase of outsourcing, subcontracting and vertical disintegration of enterprises and, eventually, privatization. Therefore, there is still a significant digital divide between developed and developing countries, and theories developed in the developed world might not be sufficient for addressing this. However, developed countries have become ICT-dependent to perform various functions such as government, industry, education, and services (for individuals and organizations) through their high Internet penetration. Likwise, developing countries may have more access to the Internet than developed ones and this could pave the way for a more diverse use and utilization of ICT in developing countries-grew significantly faster than developed countries in terms of Internet use (Alshubiri et al., 2019).

The empirical evidence from around the world indicates that the ubiquity of SMEs has drawn the interest of the world. Since the 1950s, the initial premise established at the end of the 19th century that large corporations are the biggest support for the economy has been questioned. Nowadays, the important role played by SMEs in the economy cannot be overlooked. Ayyagari, Demirguç-Kunt, & Maksimovic (2011) examined the role of SMEs in job creation and showed that in many countries, SMEs with fewer than 250 employees are the engine of growth. Beck, Demirguc-Kunt, & Levine (2005) added that in most developed countries, SMEs account for over 60% of total manufacturing jobs. SMEs accounted for 99.4 percent of all companies in China in 2012, contributing to 59 percent of China's GDP and accounting for 60 percent of overall revenue, according to data from the Chinese National Bureau of Statistics (Wang, 2016). In summary, SMEs have always been important; the way they have been concerned has changed over time (Audretsch, 2009). However, this evolution, which manifests itself in evolving SMEs policies, can only be narrowly traced as business historians have largely overlooked SMEs and, in particular, SMEs policy. There is a lack of comprehensive historical accounts of SMEs policy development that take into account the role and interaction over time between actors, contexts, and events.

LINKAGES OF ICT AND SMEs

Information and communication technologies' stands for ICT, refers to technologies which, through telecommunication, provide access to information which primarily focuses on communication technologies, such as the internet, mobile phones, wireless networks, and other mediums for communication (Ratheeswari, 2018). However, in today's world, organizations of all kinds use information and communication technology (ICT) not only to minimize costs and boost performance, but also to provide better customer service. Governments around the world are now implementing ICT to provide their residents with quality facilities. Organizational adoption of ICT requires a business climate that facilitates free competition, confidence and security, interoperability and standardization, and the availability of ICT finance (Ashrafi & Murtaza, 2008).

The use of information and communication technology (ICT) by organizations of all sizes is very common. In both developed and emerging countries, many small and medium-sized enterprises (SMEs) are rapidly implementing ICT (Agboh, 2015). The rapid evolution of information and communication technology (changing current business structures and ways of communicating) has had a significant effect on the diffusion of the processes. The adoption and use of ICT is considered to be the cornerstone of competitiveness and economic development for businesses, organizations and even countries capable of leveraging it (Tarutė & Gatautis, 2014). ICT has introduced what is referred to as the 'Networked Economy,' where successful Companies are connected in real-time with their suppliers, internal production processes, shippers and customers. Today, businesses are able to transfer data and communicate in real time with each other. This has changed the way corporations treat themselves. ICT has the ability to reduce coordination, communication and data processing costs and many companies have taken advantage of this (Sewanyana & Busler, 2007).

Information and communication technologies and e-business applications provide many advantages across a broad variety of business processes and transactions in intra- and inter-firm.ICT technologies facilitate the management of information and expertise within the organization and can minimize transaction costs and improve the speed and reliability of business-to-business and business-to-consumer transactions. In addition, they are also effective instruments for enhancing external relations and the quality of services for existing and new clients (Digital & Papers, 2004). Almost all industries, including education, health, banking and entertainment, have been affected by information and communication technologies (ICT), to name a few Business companies are investing rapidly in ICT because there are so many benefits attached to it. Many researchers have shown that ICT and business performance have a significant impact on (Athapaththu & Nishantha, 2018). According to surveys conducted by OECD countries, the use of ICT by SMEs is becoming increasingly common. A survey conducted by Euro stat on e-commerce shows that at the end of 2000/early 2001, nine out of ten SMEs were equipped with computers. Access to the internet is also commonplace among SMEs. While Internet penetration in larger businesses is usually higher, the gap between larger companies and SMEs is narrowing(Digital & Papers, 2004).

Through competitiveness and innovation, IT adoption is also measured. Innovation generally occurs when firms strive to move forward with the inspiration being growth and profitability. Survival, on the other hand, means remaining competitive in the market, becoming stable or simply fitting in (Nguyen, 2009). Bharadwaj's (2000) study demonstrates the value of a strong IT capability, including the basic ICT skills of small business owners/managers, showing that companies with a strong IT capacity outperform those on profitability and cost-based performance measures (Shiels et al., 2003). From entire study, it can be seen that internet access is typically higher in larger firms, the distance between larger businesses and SMEs is shrinking, indicating that companies with a strong IT capability perform better with profitability and cost-based efficiency measures.

ROLE OF ICT ON SMEs PERFORMANCE AND PROFITABILITY

According to Ashrafi and Murtaza (2008) shows that Omani SMEs are investing appropriately in ICT and that there is some rivalry among them. The key motivators for ICT investment were to improve and speed up customer service, keep ahead of the competition, and adhere to top management strategy. The majority of SMEs' strategic strategy was to deliver high-quality goods and services to their customers while establishing long-term relationships. Nearly half of the respondents said that ICT adoption has resulted in strengthened consumer relationships, increased sales, and cost reduction.

According to Nyangarika and Ngasa (2020), concludes that ICT use is critical in Tanzanian small businesses, especially in their daily activities in terms of competitiveness, market accessibility, and profitability, which includes increased business functionality, increased profit margins, and the ability to advertise their products and services globally. However, there were many ways for small companies to achieve additional benefits by integrating more ICT into their operations. However, they faced challenges that prevented them from completely using ICT, such as a lack of resources, such as capital to purchase high-cost ICT systems and the expertise to operate the systems. Lack of skills applied in both, the technical and business areas and makes the IT strategy approach gaining advantage largely unworkable to Small Enterprises.

According to Maguire et al. (2007) is expected to be a significant step forward in the creation of a reference structure and management model for SMEs to analyze, manage, and use current and new e-business resources and information in the e-business and knowledge management era. Since they lack the tools and expertise to do so, SMEs are not completely using ICT to achieve a competitive advantage. In its current form, the IS/IT strategy approach to gaining competitive advantage in SMEs is essentially unworkable due to a lack of expertise in both the technological and business fields.

According to Favaretto (2015) state modern companies have emerged in a world that continuously demands the assessment of new technology's competitive impact, and they must increasingly concentrate on optimizing ICT output to remain competitive in their industries. They have been forced to re-organize and re-profile themselves on a continuous and organic basis, with ICT playing an important role in promoting these changes (see table 1).

Table 1. Role of ICT in SMEs Performance

Author and Study Area	Methods	Variable Used	Result	Conclusion/ Recommendation
Ashrafi & Murtaza (2008)	Exploratory study	Independent variable ICT infrastructure, use of internet, website, drivers for ICT investment, barriers to ICT adoption, competition, and benefits of ICT Dependent variable ICT adoption	According to the findings, only a small percentage of SMEs in Oman are aware of the advantages of ICT adoption. The primary motivations for ICT investment are to improve and speed up customer service and to stay ahead of the competition. The majority of SMEs surveyed reported improved performance and other benefits as a result of incorporating ICT into their operations.	A thorough investigation should take a more comprehensive approach, taking into account a wide range of ICT adoption topics. These findings are based on a small sample of 51 SMEs, with 80 percent of them being Micro and Small Businesses. Data was gathered from SMEs that use ICT in some way in their operations. The study did not include any organizations that did not use computers.
Nyangarika et al. (2020) Tanzania	Quantitative Methodology	Independent variables Contribution of ICT on Productivity Role of ICT on Market accessibility Contribution of ICT on Profitability Dependent variable SMEs performance	The findings of the study show that ICT is used in SBEs' daily activities and is beneficial to productivity, market accessibility, and profitability, including increased business functionality, increased profit margins, and the ability to advertise their products and services globally.	According to the findings, ICT usage is critical in SBEs, and as a result, SBEs must support knowledge management in order to meet their business objectives. The study recommended ICT training and a well-articulated policy that focuses on ICT usage in SBEs, specifically on lowering the costs of ICT-related equipment.
Maguire & Magrys (2007) UK	Questionnaire survey and semi-structured interviews was	Independent variables SCM (supply chain management) Knowledge management ERP (enterprise resources planning) CRM (customer resource planning) Dependent variables Competitive advantage	This paper provides solid evidence that ICT can help SMEs gain a competitive advantage. ICT was cited by more than 70% of respondents as assisting their business in one or more of the accepted competitive areas. However, SMEs can gain even more advantages by taking a more integrated and strategic approach to their ICT use.	The findings have direct implications for SMEs in the United Kingdom. It would be interesting to conduct an international comparison of SMEs' ICT adoption.
Favaretto, (2015)	Theoretical concepts and methodological rules	Independent variables Applications Portfolio (AP), ICT/ IS Resources (IR), ICT/IS Management practices (IM), User Community (UC) – and a new process, Emerging ICT/IS (EG), Dependent variables Stage of growth of ICT/IS	According to this model, each of the six stages is evaluated differently based on the five growth processes. The mean value obtained from the five growth processes in each stage is the appropriate level of ICT/ IS alignment for that stage when evaluating the level of alignment of all processes in each of the respective stages.	Further research is possible, and the data collected from the questionnaire developed in this study could be used to investigate the relationships between ICT/ IS initiative stage level alignment and other organizational variables (dependent variables), such as business performance, organizational learning, business innovation, business analytics, and so on.

Therefore, table 1 conclude that SMEs are making the proper ICT investments, and there is some competition among them. However, to enhance and expedite customer service, stay ahead of the competition, and follow top management strategy were the primary drivers for ICT investment. The IT strategy method is often impractical for small businesses due to a lack of skills employed in both the technical and commercial domains.

CONTRIBUTION OF SMEs IN BUSINESS

According to Alhajeri (2012) state that concerning the main administrative and authoritative issues contrarily affecting the achievement elements of private ventures in Kuwait, these include: absence of preparing programs that assist staff with building up their administrative abilities, absence of the experience needed for proprietors of such tasks, especially with regards to the readiness of legitimate achievability considers, the contention among entrepreneurs for running exercises, and absence of administrative abilities required for the individuals who do such activities. These managerial problems account for 75.8% of variations taking place in the success factors affecting small businesses in Kuwait.

Lee (2010) revealed that positive effects of innovation include the recruitment of a more professional staff, higher in-house skills that support future innovation, better SMEs' reputation and brand, increased operating efficiency and cost advantages, and more. Likewise, costs, unmanageable market growth, a decline in firm credibility and image, issues with employees and customers, and effects on health, safety, and the environment are just a few of the drawbacks of innovation. In addition to this, instead of restricting organizational innovation to a single company, based on system-wide innovation, unintended results can be clearly defined, overcomes, or applied for each of the companies' innovation activities or innovation category. As a result, the effects of innovation can only be analyzed overall whereas the impact of each type of innovation is overlooked.

According to Yazdanfar & Öhman (2018) on average, the employment level of the sampled firm's is substantially positively linked to sales growth, implying that rising SMEs recruit more employees than other firms. This finding is consistent with findings from other studies conducted in different countries (Birch & Medoff, 1994; Funke et al., 1999; Schreyer, 2000; Voulgaris et al., 2005; Moneta et al., 2013). SMEs who obtain a competitive advantage have more opportunities to invest in recruiting workers, according to the report. Furthermore, the size and age control variables used in the estimations have a positive impact on the degree of jobs. This means that larger, existing, high-growth SMEs are more likely to recruit employees than other companies.

According to Eggers et al., (2013) customer orientation, interpreted as a purely sensitive construct, cannot be considered a strategy that leads to long-term firm growth. If a small business wishes to expand, it will need entrepreneurial orientation to help it achieve its goals. These findings are backed up by our findings, which show that scoring high on entrepreneurial orientation and low on customer orientation leads to the most progress (see table 2).

Table 2. Contribution of SMEs on Business

Author and Study Area	Methods	Variable Used	Result	Conclusion/ Recommendation
Abdullah et al. (2012) Kuwait	Quantitative survey	Independent variable financial problems, marketing problems, organizational and administrative problems, and legislative problems Dependent variable Success factors Small business	There were major variations between the perspectives of relevant study groups on the success factors of small projects in Kuwait, according to the findings. Furthermore, it was discovered that there was a connection between the problems that small projects in Kuwait face and the success factors for those projects. These issues account for 75.8% of the variation in the performance factors. However, there was a poor connection between the difficulties that small projects in Kuwait face and the desire to pursue the project; these issues explained just 2.6 percent of the variance in the dependent variable.	Finally, detailed guidelines for policymakers and managers who would benefit from this research have been introduced.
Lee (2010) UK	Quantitative survey	Independent variables Process innovation New product development New ways of working Dependent variable Financial performance	Improved SMEs' credibility and brand, increased operating efficiency and cost benefits, resulting in improved financial results, recruitment of a more professional workforce, and increased in-house skills contributing to further innovation are all positive outcomes of innovation. The negative consequences of innovation include costs, uncontrollable market development, loss of company credibility and reputation, employee and consumer problems, as well as health, safety, and environmental consequences.	Future research is needed to assess the financial cost and profit of having a company-wide innovation program, as well as how negative results can be handled in general and explicitly for various types of innovation.
Yazdanfar & Öhman (2018) Sweden	Panel data	Independent variable growth Size Age Dependent variable Employment level	The findings show that the number of workers recruited by the sampled companies is positively linked to revenue growth as a competitive advantage. Furthermore, the variables of size and age are also positively related to the number of workers employed. The findings support the resource-based view's suitability for explaining job development by SMEs.	Future studies should also look at other industries. Other countries' research is also welcomed. Due to data limitations, the current analysis only covers four-year duration. Future researchers should suggest longer periods of time to resolve problems related to the time effect if they are effective in collecting empirical data.
Eggers at al., (2013)	Quantitative Empirical Approach	Independent variables Customer orientation entrepreneurial orientations Dependent variables SMEs growth	Entrepreneurial orientation is positively related to SMEs development, while customer orientation is negatively related to growth, according to this study. Furthermore, according to this study, SMEs that have a high entrepreneurial orientation and a low consumer orientation grow the fastest.	According to the findings, further research into the relationships between customer orientation and Entrepreneurial orientation is required. Future research should look into the interplay between customer orientation and Entrepreneurial orientation across wider dimensions of firm success to better understand the circumstances under which customer orientation and Entrepreneurial orientation can be beneficial or destabilizing to a business.

Table 2 depicts that innovation has several disadvantages, including costs, uncontrollable market expansion, a deterioration in corporate credibility and image, problems with employees and consumers, and a host of others. Additionally, each of the businesses' innovative activities or categories may be employed to explicitly define, avoid, or use unintended effects. Likewise, SMEs that have a competitive edge have more chances to spend in hiring personnel. Large, established, high-growth SMEs are more likely to hire workers than other businesses.

SMEs IN THE CONTEXT OF NEPAL

Nepal is renowned for craftsmanship. In 648 AD, Chinese travelers such as Wanghunshe and Huansang admired Nepalese arts and crafts and the skills of Nepalese craft SMEs and artisans. It is also mentioned in Kautilya's Economics during the time of Chandra Gupta Mouriya, in the fourth century, about an exported product from Nepal. From the beginning until the mid-nineteenth century, national industries and trade were promoted by the country's rulers to various measures of production, promotion and advancement. Except for those that were not produced locally, commodities were not allowed to be imported to save the domestic industry. Due to the general liberal import policy of the government, the Nepalese arts and crafts industry and the entire home-based industries generally suffered a great deal towards the end of the nineteenth century. Nepal was perceived as the primary route to Tibet for external trade with other countries prior to the establishment of the British regime over India and the conclusion of a peace treaty with Tibet in 1904 AD. Nepal has also entered the Rana regime's era of industrialization (Ghimire, 2011).

Nepal's history of industrial revolution goes back to 1936. Jute Mill was established this year in Biratnagar as a joint venture with an Indian industrialist. Thirty-five new joint companies were established in 1940 until 1951, but after that, due to social and political unrest, no businesses were established for a decade. In 1940, the Cottage Skill Awareness Office (Gharelu Ilam Prachar Adda) was created under the Rana regime (1836 to 1951). After the elected government was established in 1958, new industrial policy was announced and the government also realized that Nepal would play a very important role in the economy as a hilly topographic country, small and cottage industries. Different district training centers have been set up to promote the cottage industry in the private sector. From 1970 to 1990, the development program for the cottage industry began in various forms, such as the program for industrial and technical service, the program for handicraft design, the program for village industries, the program for sales management, the training program (GON, 1970). The Department of Cottage and Small Industries (DCSI) has been established to promote and promote various types of cottage and small industries that increase their industrial productivity and create a friendly environment for industrial investment in accordance with policy. During the Sixth Plan (1980-1985), the cottage and small industries were emphasized. The aim of the plan was to reduce income inequality by helping people with low incomes and increasing employment (Ghimire, 2011).

The majority of Nepalese SMEs are engaged in the processing and production of consumer and home items, food products, commodities for export and import, and other things (Meinhold & Darr, 2019). Hereby, household necessities and consumer goods such rice, pulses, oil and flour mills, dairy, aerated soft drinks, fruit juices, processed goods, noodles, cookies, and sweets have dominated SME activity in Nepal. Industries based on wood and metal fibers, wooden and textile handicrafts, clothing and accessories, woolen carpets, pashmina shawls, and rugs, as well as leather are other sectors which dominates in SMEs in Nepal (Paudel & Devkota, 2018; Paudel et al., 2018). In certain areas, there has also been investment in micro hydropower, tourism destinations, and infrastructure development. A sizable number of unregistered firms run seasonally off-farm at the micro, community, and family levels. The bulk of these unregistered firms manufacture consumer and domestic items using agro- and forestry-based raw materials.

CONCLUSION AND RESEARCH GAP

To study the effects of ICT, use on organizational financial performance is an important research topic that has not been well described. ICT receives nearly 30% of all research and development budgets (in both the private and public sectors) in industrialized countries (Nyangarika, 2020). Existing diffusion theories' applicability to developing countries is also debatable. Researchers want to examine all of the important aspects of the ICT diffusion observable fact in a comprehensive and in-depth manner (Azam, 2014). According to existing research, small and medium-sized businesses are a vital and dynamic part of the economy in most countries (Chien et al., 2021). According to Alam and Noor (2009), the majority of empirical research focuses on large corporations, while SMEs are characterized as lacking knowledge about the actual benefits of ICTs. There were numerous opportunities for small medium businesses to gain more advantages by incorporating more ICT into their operations (Lu et al., 2020). However, they faced obstacles that prevented them from fully utilizing ICT, such as a lack of resources, such as capital to purchase high-cost ICT systems and the skills to operate the systems (Nyangarika, 2020).

Earlier research has looked into a variety of aspects of innovation diffusion using a variety of theoretical frameworks. The majority of them have looked into one aspect of the contextual and environmental factors at a time in order to avoid analytical complexity by developing a lean research model (Hervás-Oliver et al., 2021). It is well known that including a large number of important and relevant variables improves model fit and increases the variation explained by the model. Variables (endogenous or exogenous) are likely to have different effects in different contexts, as well as with the number of variables included in the model (Azam, 2013).

Apart from the fact that ICT is underutilized in developing countries and the majority of empirical research focuses on large corporations, the researcher discovered that, as a result of the above literature findings and points, there is still a significant research gap between developed and developing country perspectives on ICT adoption and usage. As a result, researchers are interested in learning more about this topic because it is a relatively new phenomenon, and previous research had to focus on both large corporations and individuals. Several studies on ICT adoption have been conducted, mostly in an international context rather than in Nepal, but no studies on prior knowledge imprint have been conducted to date.

This research is helpful for SMEs performance and its profitability, this research helpful to others SMEs to utilization of ICT, this research helpful to the government of Nepal for promoting utilization of ICT. However, study does not clearly clarify how the first-order variables (the variables that make up a higher-order hybrid variable) affect ICT use and business outcomes. Moreover, the impact of many social institutions and the organizational characteristics, as well as country-specific characteristics, may aid in the development of policies and initiatives to encourage SMEs to use ICT. Future research could compare the aggregated results to the specific outcomes of several profitability aspects including return on assets, return on equity, and net profit margin.

REFERENCES

Adhikari, D. B., Shakya, B., Devkota, N., Karki, D., Bhandari, U., Parajuli, S., & Paudel, U. R. (2021). Financial hurdles in small business enterprises in Kathmandu Valley. *Modern Economy*, *12*(6), 1105–1118. doi:10.4236/me.2021.126058

Agboh, D. K. (2015). Drivers and Challenges of ICT Adoption by SMES in Accra Metropolis, Ghana. *Journal of Technology Research*, *6*, 1–16.

Alhajeri, A. S. (2012). *The financing and success factors of small business in Kuwait* [Doctoral dissertation]. University of Portsmouth.

Alshubiri, F., Jamil, S. A., & Elheddad, M. (2019). The impact of ICT on financial development: Empirical evidence from the Gulf Cooperation Council countries. *International Journal of Engineering Business Management*, *11*, 1847979019870670. doi:10.1177/1847979019870670

Ashrafi, R., & Murtaza, M. (2008). Use and impact of ICT on SMEs in Oman. *Electronic Journal of Information Systems Evaluation, 11*(3).

Athapaththu, J. C., & Nishantha, B. (2018). Information and Communication Technology Adoption in SMEs in Sri Lanka; Current Level of ICT Usage and Perceived Barriers. *International Journal of E-Entrepreneurship and Innovation*, *8*(1), 1–15. doi:10.4018/IJEEI.2018010101

Azam, M. S. (2013). Towards Digital Communication and transaction: An inquiry into the individuals' Internet acceptance and usage behaviour in Bangladesh. *Journal of International Technology and Information Management*, *22*(1), 123–140.

Azam, M. S. (2014). *Diffusion of ICT and SME Performance: The Mediating Effects of Integration and Utilisation.* Curtin University.

Bock, G., Zmund, R. W., Kim, Y., & Lee, J. (2005). Behavioral Intention Formation in Knowledge Sharing: Examining the Roles of Extrinsic Motivators, Social- psychological Forces, and Organisational Climate. *Management Information Systems Quarterly*, *29*(1), 87–111. doi:10.2307/25148669

Chien, F., Ngo, Q. T., Hsu, C. C., Chau, K. Y., & Iram, R. (2021). Assessing the mechanism of barriers towards green finance and public spending in small and medium enterprises from developed countries. *Environmental Science and Pollution Research International*, *28*(43), 60495–60510. doi:10.100711356-021-14907-1 PMID:34156623

Chittithaworn, C., Islam, M. A., Keawchana, T., & Yusuf, D. H. M. (2011). Factors affecting business success of small & medium enterprises (SMEs) in Thailand. *Asian Social Science*, *7*(5), 180–190. doi:10.5539/ass.v7n5p180

Devkota, N., Paudel, U. R., & Bhandari, U. (2020). Does westernization influence the business culture of a touristic city? *Economia e Sociologia*, *13*(4), 154–172. doi:10.14254/2071-789X.2020/13-4/10

Devkota, N., & Phuyal, R. K. (2018). Adoption practice of climate change adaptation options among Nepalese rice farmers: Role of information and communication technologies (ICTs). *American Journal of Climate Change*, *7*(2), 135–152. doi:10.4236/ajcc.2018.72010

Devkota, N., Shreebastab, D. K., Korpysa, J., Bhattarai, K., & Paudel, U. R. (2022). Determinants of successful entrepreneurship in a developing nation: Empirical evaluation using an ordered logit model. *Journal of International Studies*, *15*(1), 181–196. doi:10.14254/2071-8330.2022/15-1/12

Eggers, F., Kraus, S., Hughes, M., Laraway, S., & Snycerski, S. (2004). Implications of customer and entrepreneurial orientations for SME growth. *ICT, E-Business and Small*, (86). doi:10.1787/232556551425

Favaretto, J. E. R. (2015). *Stage level measurement of information and communication technology in organizations* (Doctoral dissertation).

Ghimire, R. (2011). Micro and Small Level Enterprises in Nepal. *Journal of Finance and Management Review*, *2*(2), 257–269.

Hervás-Oliver, J. L., Parrilli, M. D., Rodríguez-Pose, A., & Sempere-Ripoll, F. (2021). The drivers of SME innovation in the regions of the EU. *Research Policy*, *50*(9), 104316. doi:10.1016/j.respol.2021.104316

Jurado, T., & Battisti, M. (2019). The evolution of SME policy: The case of New Zealand. *Regional Studies. Journal of Regional Science*, *6*(1), 32–54.

Karki, D., Upreti, S., Bhandari, U., Rajbhandari, S., Devkota, N., Parajuli, S., & Paudel, U. R. (2021). Does the Formal Financial Sector Enhance Small Business Employment Generation in Nepal: Evidence from Cross-Sectional Data. *Journal of Social Economics Research*, *8*(2), 155–164. doi:10.18488/journal.35.2021.82.155.164

Kharel, S., K C, A., Devkota, N., & Paudel, U. R. (2022). Entrepreneurs' Level of Awareness on Knowledge Management for Promoting Tourism in Nepal. *Journal of Information & Knowledge Management*, *21*(02), 2250023. doi:10.1142/S021964922250023X

Lee, S. (2010).. . *The Electronic Library*, *34*(1), 1–5.

Lu, J., Ren, L., Zhang, C., Rong, D., Ahmed, R. R., & Streimikis, J. (2020). Modified Carroll's pyramid of corporate social responsibility to enhance organizational performance of SMEs industry. *Journal of Cleaner Production*, *271*, 122456. doi:10.1016/j.jclepro.2020.122456

Margues, S., & Simon, S. C. L. (2007). The adoption of e-business and knowledge management in SMEs. *Benchmarking*, *14*(1), 37–58. doi:10.1108/14635770710730928

Martin, W. J. (2017). *The global information society*. Routledge. doi:10.4324/9781315239385

Meinhold, K., & Darr, D. (2019). The processing of non-timber forest products through small and medium enterprises—A review of enabling and constraining factors. *Forests*, *10*(11), 1026. doi:10.3390/f10111026

Myovella, G., Karacuka, M., & Haucap, J. (2020). Digitalization and economic growth: A comparative analysis of Sub-Saharan Africa and OECD economies. *Telecommunications Policy*, *44*(2), 101856. doi:10.1016/j.telpol.2019.101856

Nguyen, T. H. (2009). Information technology adoption in SMEs: an integrated framework. International *Journal of Entrepreneurial Behavior & Research*.

Nyangarika, A., & Ngasa, Z. J. (2020). *Profitability of ICT Usage towards Productivity of Small Business Enterprises in Tanzania*. Academic Press.

O'Regan, N., & Ghobadian, A. (2006). Perceptions of generic strategies of small and medium sized engineering and electronics manufacturers in the UK: The applicability of the Miles and Snow typology. *Journal of Manufacturing Technology Management, 17*(5), 603–620. doi:10.1108/17410380610668540

Paudel, U. R., & Devkota, N. (2018). Socio-Economic influences on small business performance in Nepal-India open border: Evidence from cross-sectional analysis. *Economia e Sociologia, 11*(4), 11–30. doi:10.14254/2071-789X.2018/11-4/1

Paudel, U. R., Devkota, N., & Bhandari, U. (2018). Socio-cultural and economic factors in cross-border purchase: A study of customers' perspective in Sunauli-Nepal/India Border. *Modern Economy, 9*(6), 1089–1102. doi:10.4236/me.2018.96070

Ratheeswari, K. (2018). Information Communication Technology in Education. *Journal of Applied and Advanced Research, 3*(S1), 45. doi:10.21839/jaar.2018.v3iS1.169

Sewanyana, J., & Busler, M. (2007). Adoption and usage of ICT in developing countries: Case of Ugandan firms. *International Journal of Education and Development using ICT, 3*(3), 49-59.

Sharma, S. (2019). Article. *Descriptive Statistics., 18*(5). Advance online publication. doi:10.32964/tj18.5

Shiels, H., McIvor, R., & O'Reilly, D. (2003). Understanding the implications of ICT adoption: Insights from SMEs. *Logistics Information Management, 16*(5), 312–326. doi:10.1108/09576050310499318

Wang, Y. (2016). What are the biggest obstacles to growth of SMEs in developing countries?–An empirical evidence from an enterprise survey. *Borsa Istanbul Review, 16*(3), 167–176. doi:10.1016/j.bir.2016.06.001

Yazdanfar, D., & Öhman, P. (2018). Growth and job creation at the firm level: Swedish SME data. *Management Research Review, 41*(3), 345–358. doi:10.1108/MRR-03-2017-0093

Zhang, T., Lu, C., & Kizildag, M. (2018). Banking "on-the-go": Examining consumers' adoption of mobile banking services. *International Journal of Quality and Service Sciences, 1*(1), 1–20. doi:10.1108/IJQSS-07-2017-0067

Chapter 7
COVID-19:
A Disaster Master – Opportunities and Challenges for Small-Medium Enterprises

Vinay Pal Singh

Quantum University, Roorkee, India

Ram Singh

ⓘ https://orcid.org/0000-0002-6565-3091

Maharishi Markandeshwar University (Deemed). Ambala, India

ABSTRACT

The backbone of any economy can be found in its small and medium-sized businesses (MSME). Over the past decade, they have made a major impact on GDP growth. They play a crucial part in bringing progress to underdeveloped regions. Every economy relies heavily on its small and medium-sized businesses (SMEs). Small and medium-sized enterprises (SMEs) bear the brunt of COVID-19. The goal of this study was to find out how SMEs respond to changes in their operating environment caused by COVID-19 by changing their business models with the help of digital technology.

1. INTRODUCTION

COVID-19 causes economic and societal damage worldwide. News publications call it the worst worldwide crisis since WWII. Despite being highly transmissible, this virus has expanded slowly globally. COVID-19 is a health emergency, but it's more. This is a systemic shock with long-term effects. This virus caused a short-term economic crisis that resulted to the closure of many enterprises, the loss of jobs for tens of millions of people, and other business effects. Small and medium-sized firms can and should help stop global unemployment, poverty, and food insecurity.

Almost every sector of the economy has been affected by COVID-19, and that includes small and medium-sized enterprises (SMEs). Rapid shifts in customer preferences, product availability, and buying habits have forced small enterprises to adapt quickly. Many businesses have been deprived of not only direct consumers but also of the raw materials, inputs, and export opportunities they once had. Lockdowns

DOI: 10.4018/978-1-6684-5770-2.ch007

and other forms of restricted movement have often rendered essential employees unavailable for their jobs. It's no secret that the economy as a whole has been hit hard by the recent job losses. Sadly, sales have dropped. There have been a lot of closures in supply networks overall. Demand for many goods and services made or sold by MSMEs has dropped even more because people are spending less because they don't know how the pandemic will turn out in the future.

Companies of all sizes, as well as national economies and societies around the world, are feeling the effects. As the pandemic has spread, it has disrupted international commerce and travel around the world. The greatest exporters and major actors in global value chains, including China, the European Union, and the United States, have either stopped or significantly reduced their cross-border commerce, causing widespread disruption to supply chains. Many small and medium-sized enterprises (SMEs) have been severely impacted by this, both as exporters and consumers of imported commodities. There has been a global decline in the number of micro, small, and medium-sized enterprises (MSMEs), and many more are in danger of going out of business or are already in the process of closing. Numerous traditional patterns of sales, distribution, and consumption have been drastically and irrevocably transformed, and this presents a new challenge for surviving businesses. These shifts present difficulties for the owner-managers of such businesses, difficulties that are magnified in economies with a high concentration of micro and small enterprises. Long-term uncertainty about the future is also having an effect on businesses and customers. The "recovery" period that follows deconfinement has historically been associated with a temporary uptick in economic activity, but historical evidence suggests that this trend is unlikely to be maintained. Prevalent production and demand patterns, as well as distribution methods and customer tastes, have undergone significant shifts that are difficult to quantify. For some micro, small, and medium-sized enterprises (MSMEs), a recovery may signify a "new normal," while for others it may be a more challenging transition.

Estimating the complete impact of COVID-19 on the SME sector is difficult since it varies with infection and recovery rates, current travel limits in different locations, and governmental measures in different nations. Concern about COVID-19 has prompted comparable research and analysis of small and medium-sized enterprises (SMEs), although up-to-date global statistics on this topic are few. Multiple government departments need to work together to solve the numerous issues that small and medium-sized enterprises (SMEs) face. Many of these are already well under way. However, authorities should not ignore the connection between competition policy and M&S enterprises' access to markets.

2. REVIEW OF LITERATURE

In many countries, small and medium-sized enterprises (SMEs) are seen as the primary drivers of national and regional development (Keskn et al., 2010). The importance of small and medium-sized businesses to a nation's GDP has been widely recognised (Perker, 2011; Henning, 2003; Miller, Besser, Gaskill and Sapp, 2003). As a result of their superior performance, these industries have garnered the backing of governments, NGOs, and international organisations around the world (2011). However, small and medium-sized enterprises (SMEs) are optimistic about the future, according to Perks and Struwig (2005). According to a assessment by the Organisation for Economic Co-operation and Development (OECD), SMEs are an important factor in the industrialization of emerging nations. According to the survey, small and medium-sized enterprises (SMEs) account for as much as 90% of all businesses located outside of the agriculture sector. In addition, the OECD report (2004) states that the expansion of small and medium-sized enterprises (SMEs) is the primary driver of sustainable economic growth in Africa. Poor infrastructure, insufficient funding, insufficient knowledge and skills, restricted access to the market, and rapid technological development are just some of the obstacles that small and medium-sized enterprises (SMEs) face on the road to success (Haider Syed, M., Khan, S., Raza Rabbani, M., & Thalassinos, Y. E. 2020). According to Wanjohi and Mugure (2008), corruption and an unfavourable regulatory environment are two more significant hurdles, Gachara, Hottensiah N., and Munjuri (2018), SMEs play a crucial role in the economy. As a result, a number of recent studies have looked at what variables encourage SMEs to innovate and improve their performance in Europe, Asia, and Brazil. They have not only found evidence for the importance of encouraging creativity within organisations, but they have also written extensively on the subject. Several authors, including Mitra (2000), Terziovski (2003), Massa and Testa (2004). Many countries' economic growth and GDP are attributed to their small and medium-sized enterprises (SMEs), as found in a study by (Dev and Sengupta, 2020). Small and medium-sized enterprises (SMEs) across the globe have felt a significant impact from COVID 19. As a result of the COVID 19 pandemic, millions of SMEs have been forced to abandon their original business strategies, a large portion of their personnel has been laid off, and the bulk of SMEs' stakeholders have been hit hard. The extended duration of the COVID 19 pandemic crisis has led to widespread layoffs, impaired business finances, and a reliance on the Coronavirus Aid, Relief, and Economic Security Act by the vast majority of small and medium-sized enterprises (SMEs) (Alexander W. Bartik, Glaeser, Luca, and Stanton, 2020). COVID 19 has had a negative impact on 82 percent or more of small and medium-sized enterprises (SMEs), and 70 percent or more of SMEs believe it will take another year to recover losses and achieve demand before COVID 19. Over half of small and medium-sized enterprises (SMEs) are counting on help from the government and other organisations (The Economic Times, 2021). The COVID 19 outbreak resulted in a lockdown and it has severely impacted SMEs of China. The imposed lockdown has decreased the demand for products and unavailability of labor was the common phenomenon, in the first wave of the COVID 19 pandemic approximately 80% of SMEs were temporarily closed (Dai, et al., 2021) The study conducted by (Mirza, Naqvi, Rahat, and Rizvi, 2020) found that due to COVID 19 pandemic more than 5800 businesses are closed, and organizations have downsized their workforce by almost 40%. This situation is responsible for an increase in the unemployment rate and affected the performance of the country's economy. The study conducted by (Sun, Zhang, Dinca, and Raza, 2021) concluded that there is a significant effect of COVID 19 on SME's profit margin, innovative practices of operations, hybrid work, and satisfaction and safety of stakeholders. According to the survey of (Dimson and Sharma, 2021), different sectors of SMEs have shown a dropped in revenue by 30-90% in 2020, and 40% of SMEs have applied or planning to apply for Government support due to COVID 19 pandemic. The study conducted by (Pedauga, Sáez, and Delgado-Márquez, 2021) found that due to COVID 19, there is a decline of 43% of SME business activities and two-thirds of the decline in employment. According to the study of (Hebert, 2021), there was a scarcity of raw materials to produce goods by SMEs during the COVID 19 pandemic, and the spending capacity of consumers was decreased, as a result, the revenue generation of SMEs was also decreased. Such a loss of revenue is hampering the capability of SMEs to their business commitments. According to the study of (Bhalerao and Patil, 2021) SMEs have faced issues like employee layoff, issues of health, very poor business operations, available jobs are at risk, and chances of the permanent or temporary closure of businesses due to the COVID 19 pandemic. The technology is enabling the organization to achieve sustainable development. Organizations can use various recent technologies in various functional areas of the business (Bhalerao, Mahale, Jyothi, and Yelikar, 2021). Product innovations may enable SMEs to improve their performance (Abubakar, Abdullahi, and Ibrahim, 2021). Indidustry 4.0 is enablling businesses enhance work life balance, productivity, reduction in production cost and minimization of waste (Kenge and Khan, 2021)

3. OBJECTIVES OF THE STUDY

1. To explore SME business scenario during COVID 19 pandemic.
2. To examine and discuss opportunities and Challenges of COVID 19 on SMEs.

4. RESEARCH METHODOLOGY

The foundation of this paper is a literature review. The secondary data is collected from various sources, research journals, conference proceedings, reports, and websites. The collected data is used for analyzing and understanding COVID 19 situation and its impact on SMEs.

5. IMPACT OF COVID 19 PANDEMIC ON SMALL AND MEDIUM ENTERPRISES

In the world, where the COVID 19 appeared, many SMEs had to shut down in a lockdown period which varies from country to country and region to region. However, after lockdown, SMEs were permitted to reopen but SMEs were found difficult to resume business operations. This situation results in further financial losses by SMEs. SMEs are playing significant roles in most economies. They are the drivers of growth, the largest provider of employment, and create new markets. However, during COVID 19 crisis SMEs are the most affected element of the economy.

5.1 Manufacturing Disruption

Many small and medium sized enterprises (SMEs) in areas where COVID 19 has been detected have been forced to close for a period of time that varies widely by country and region. After the lockdown was lifted, however, small and medium sized enterprises (SMEs) were allowed to reopen, but many found it challenging to get back into business. This circumstance causes further losses in capital for SMEs. In most economies, SMEs represent a major driving force. They generate new opportunities and markets, and are the primary engines of economic expansion. Small and medium sized enterprises (SMEs) are hit the hardest amid the current COVID 19 crisis.

5.2 Employment

Millions of employees are under lockdown while firms struggle to replenish supplies and return to normal operations (Smith-Bingham and Hariharan, 2020; Sneader and Singhal, 2020). Despite government attempts, the majority of SMEs in South Africa have enacted widespread layoffs, and 70% of all SMEs have cut back on company spending (Agesan, Nomfanelo, and Shakeel, 2020). McKinsey's (2020) research on small and medium-sized enterprises (SMEs) in Europe concluded that at least two out of every three jobs there are at risk.

They estimate that across Europe, over 59 million jobs, or 26% of employment, are at risk of reduced hours, reduced compensation, temporary layoffs, or permanent elimination. According to research conducted by Welter, Wolter, and Kranzusch (2020), most small and medium-sized enterprises (SMEs) are able to weather the current economic crisis without having to shut down operations, even if the lockout caused by COVID lasts for two and a half months. Small and medium-sized enterprises (SMEs) may lose millions of jobs if the shutdown lasts more than six months. According to Michael (2020), during the lockdown in New Zealand in March and April of 2020, small businesses lost 4% of their jobs. Mexico News Daily (2020) cites a BBVA report that estimates 1 million formal sector employment have been lost because to the COVID 19 pandemic, and that the labour market will not be able to recover before 2024.

5.3 Closures of SMEs

Kyodo News (2020) reports that in Japan the impact of COVID 19 has led to a sudden 15% surge in bankruptcies among SMEs, particularly in the accommodation and tourism sectors. There are around 10,000 closed and 12,000 unorganised enterprises in Mexico as a result of the COVID 19 pandemic lockdown, and another 600,000 are at risk of closing as a result (Mexico News Daily, 2020). According to Fairlie's (2020) research, as a result of the spread of COVID 19 in the United States, about 22% (3.3 million) business owners have shut down their operations; 41% of African-American business owners have seen a decline in business; 26% of Asian-owned businesses have seen a decline in business; and 25% of businesses owned by women have been affected. About 59% of MSMEs in India may reduce operations, sell their company, or cease operations altogether if the COVID 19 pandemic continues unchecked (Dave, 2021).

5.4. Challenges Related to Cost and Finance for SMEs

Rental or mortgage payments, utility bills, and insurance premiums are all examples of fixed operating costs that can be challenging for small and medium-sized enterprises to budget for. Given the company's past and present limitations, the possibility of it continuing to operate if these costs are not met was called into serious question. There were many obstacles that stopped small and medium-sized businesses (SMEs) in China's Sichuan Province from carrying on their usual business. A shortage of resources, a lack of demand, and a reluctance to return to work were all factor. The lack of, or delay in, reimbursement of permanent operational costs is a major source of stress for small and medium-sized businesses, as was revealed by the research.

Small and medium-sized enterprises (SMEs) are impacted by the shortage of human resources and the rise in the rate of human cost due to low employee turnout. Hoorens et al. found that self-employed business owners (i.e., those without employees) had an easier time dealing with the challenge than their employed counterparts because they did not have to bear the additional costs and difficulties of supporting their employees and/or laying them off to reduce costs. It was found that the outbreak in Masvingo, Zimbabwe had a major impact on the financial performance of SMEs due to work stoppage and layoffs during the lockdown. Small and medium-sized businesses (SMEs) have been begging the government for help in reviving after the lockdown due to the pandemic's effects on financial management and supply chain disruptions. Macau's SMEs fared better economically following a natural disaster because they were better equipped to adjust to new conditions than large businesses were.

5.5 SME Operations Interrupted by Covid-19 Pandemic

The spread of COVID-19 has made it difficult for small and medium-sized businesses to operate. Increasing adaptation calls for managerial know-how, resilience, and perseverance. Hadi, an authority on Yogyakarta's creative sector and the revival of SMEs in Indonesia's tourism industry, thinks that primary resources cannot be overestimated for the performance of critical business operations aimed at offering additional value to clients. Small and medium-sized enterprises (SMEs) in the tourism industry benefit from a diverse network of business travel partners, which includes agents and communities. In order to stay in business, small and medium-sized enterprises (SMEs) can contribute to and engage with regulatory organisations to implement a wide range of projects.

5.6. Significant Challenges Facing SMEs

Lu et al. surveyed 4807 SMEs in Sichuan Province, China, and found that COVID-19 had a negative impact on the return of employment, income, and confidence among SMEs and posed a serious existential danger to the sector. However, several studies have shown that small and medium-sized enterprises (SMEs) can employ COVID-19 to enhance product quality and prepare for future product releases. Additionally, analysed 171 SMEs in the MENA area and Turkey and found that 15% of SMEs see potential to enhance domestic demand, and 14% are displaying substantial demand for new products or services.

6. COVID-19 POSITIVE OUTCOME FOR SMEs

Literature emphasises SMEs as a source of economic viability, however the COVID19 epidemic has cast doubt on this. This section provides advice on how small and medium-sized enterprises (SMEs) might survive the effects of COVID-19 and other challenges, recoup from the past, and revitalise their operations to minimise damage to their resources.

Figure 1. Cycle of Enhancing SMEs' competitiveness
Sources: Authors Compilation

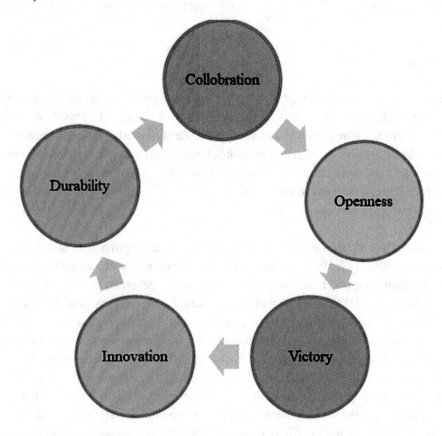

First, there must be cooperation between all involved parties, with an emphasis on producing outcomes that are beneficial to all. Remembering one's social network (coworkers, friends, and family) is crucial at this time, as it may be used to forge alliances and contribute to the success of the business.

As part of this resilient strategy, some of the following are proposed measures:

1. Promote locally owned businesses: small and medium-sized enterprises (SMEs), in conjunction with other businesses and local councils (or equivalent), should increase promotion to attract and encourage customers to buy local. Businesses in the food and lodging industries, for example, can easily promote themselves to a neighbourhood clientele.
2. **Regulatory Bodies:** It is particularly difficult for the SME sector to comply with government policies and laws. To reduce bureaucratic and, consequently, administrative costs, regulatory authorities should engage with businesses and vice versa. The model proposed which based on Vietnam's Thanh Hoa province after the COVID-19 period, can be used in the current setting where SMEs are operating. This policy framework helps small and medium-sized enterprises (SMEs) thrive by incorporating input from all levels of government. Even if SMEs are working at a reduced capacity due to a lack of resources, they still require help paying for things like interest and salaries, as well as keeping records and paying rent. Small and medium-sized enterprises (SMEs) may suffer in the long run as a result of government-enforced operational constraints. When it comes to taxes,

financing, and subsidies for employment and operations, SMEs have asked governments for help. However, the demand for and uptake of government services beyond the realm of finance were relatively low.

6.1. Openness

The second element is openness, which is being honest and forthright with the stakeholders by maintaining open lines of communication and permitting two-way input and feedback. Together, honesty and open lines of communication can help businesses keep good standing with both their internal and external constituents. To alert stakeholders of potential issues being faced and constructively explore solutions, openness is predicated on using various communication tactics. The current state of digitalization provides a great deal of uniqueness to the problems presented by COVID-19 and the subsequent solutions centred on digital adoption and integration.

1. **Social Media:** The emergence of the new techno-centric paradigm may make a firm grasp of social media a prerequisite for SMEs' resiliency. Beyond the confines of any lockdowns, this may also affect the marketing of goods and services through the widespread proliferation of social media.
2. **Digital Technologies (DT) and Innovation:** Modern digital technologies' and more complex networking processes might improve SMEs' communication channels. Innovation and DT: Strategic adoption can improve competitiveness, productivity, and performance while also encouraging the development of new competencies and access to online learning opportunities. These qualities can give SMEs an edge in the marketplace and help them weather storms when up against larger rivals. There is a dearth of empirical evidence indicating the efficacy of the use of digital technologies in both developed and developing countries, despite an apparent growth in the SME literature relating to their use of digital technology in boosting competitive advantage. Despite these technological advancements, a number of social, political, and legal restrictions still exist and make it difficult for SMEs to succeed and thrive.
3. Adaptability and suppler responsiveness: There must be transparency on a scale never before seen, regardless of whether a company is itself a supplier or simply buying raw materials from one. Over-dependence on a small number of providers has come into focus as state and international borders have closed (Rajagopaul, A., Magwentshu, N., & Kalidas, S. 2020). For the success of any commercial endeavour, it is essential to establish and maintain lasting connections with all parties involved. Yet, in the absence of these reliable associates, there has been no backup plan established. As the regulatory landscape shifts, suppliers must be nimble and adaptable or risk being left behind. A company should also do a thorough review of its supply chain at this time and, if necessary, find new partners to replace any suppliers found to be too rigid, if required, replace their inflexible suppliers with new partners.

6.2. Victory

Recognizing the threats from the outside world is essential for success, but so is actively seeking and seizing opportunities. Again, this calls for concerted effort from a wide range of stakeholders and the development of creative approaches like:

1. **Initiatives by Government:** It was found that SMEs/firms with a lengthy history, a large employee number, and a strategy of formal catastrophe mitigation can recover within 4 months after the onset of the crisis, while businesses with no strategy and fewer resources can take much longer to get back on their feet. Loan guarantees and direct subsidised loans are two forms of debt financing that the United Kingdom and other OECD countries have been providing to small and medium sized firms (SMEs) to help them weather the financial storm of the COVID-19 outbreak. The analysis in suggests a number of further alternatives, including wage subsidies and loan programmes. Local small and medium-sized businesses (SMEs) rely large on technology and telecommunication; hence increasing government investment in technology is necessary during disasters. Certain sectors that rely largely on technology and the internet, like those dealing with life sciences, medical equipment, online delivery, software, and application development, look set to flourish in the wake of the pandemic.

2. **Variations of Employment Contracts and Recruitment**: Reduced job vacancies could give businesses with diversity, but temporary business closures can lead to permanent job loss. Unprecedented difficulties, such as a shift in business, a decrease in the company's ability to repay loans, a shift in personnel, and insufficient resource gain, can arise for SMEs under these situations. Numerous American businesses, according to research by Bartik et al. have either temporarily shut down or reduced their workforce since January 2020. None of the surveyed groups had a favourable impression of the federal government's fiscal stimulus package (CARES Act loan program). Brown et al. advocated for programmes like the Scottish Jobs Guarantee Scheme to help millennials break into the workforce. A series of unusual policies, including the Scottish Government's absorption of failed organisations, was proposed by Brown et al.

3. **Economic Structure Flexibility:** Financial institutions on a national, regional, and global scale will feel the effects of the COVID-19-caused economic disaster. Substantial shifts in SME behaviour can be prompted by quite modest financial aid, even in times of high uncertainty. Examples of this include measures that offer stimulus packages for established and aspiring business owners, such as loan forgiveness and the legal protection of existing enterprises. Additionally, web-based advertising and the teaching of digital skills are required. Firms' efforts to learn about electronic and social media marketing, as well as other strategies that call for sales sub-agents in every state, bear this out. Business objectives and the improvement of SME products or services necessitate optimal digitalization strategy. Governments and SMEs alike need to be responsive and adaptable in order to create innovative business platforms. SMEs are a part of the digital economic ecosystem, which requires adaptability and innovation in digital skills to ensure its continued success. Accelerating these transformations after COVID-19 is encouraged, and government policies and village officials in Yogyakarta, Indonesia, are backed to do so.

6.3. Innovation

This involves putting different pieces of the jigsaw puzzle together and learning about and investing in transferable skills and resources from individual to organisational levels. The potential options here include:

1. **Business Transactions Support:** The economically affected sector of SMEs is dependent on the money transactions in the sale and purchase of products. In the research conducted by [30], it was found that there is a requirement to support services to avoid SMEs from closing business before the

end of this year. There is also a need for cash grants and similar kinds of support. Many European governments quickly protected SMEs' employees by providing plans relating to jobs retention and wages support (Omar, A. R. C., Ishak, S., & Jusoh, M. A. 2020). Tsilika et al. highlighted that policymakers need to assist organizations in responding to harmful environmental conditions caused because of disasters and examine entrepreneurial breakage and its particularities. These innovative alternatives can contribute towards invigorating human creativity. Policymakers need to have conversations besides providing financial aid and discuss regulations and methods to manage organizations cropping from human creativity.

2. **Circular Economy:** Discussions about the circular economy are beginning at the national and Corporate Levels (CE). While it's still early, the foundations of CE may be put in place now to guarantee a more productive and economical use of resources. Refusing, Reducing, Reusing, Reforming, & Recycling (5R) resources (raw and end product) are the cornerstones of CE since they lead to less waste, which benefits the environment. These 5R concepts are applicable to enterprises of all sizes (including micro) and in all industries in the present COVID-19 environment, characterized by limited resources and constant change. Moreover, it's important to recognise that some people and enterprises will encounter difficulties along the way. The biggest challenge is shifting from a "throw-away" and "make-or-break" economic structure to a "make-to-keep" one. According to the authors, many families have started down the path to CE by doing things like getting resourceful with their food sources and finding novel ways to prevent food waste in the COVID-19 climate. Since the future of their jobs is uncertain, people are cutting back on discretionary expenditure in areas like takeout and eating at home less frequently.

6.4. Durability

SME owners should adopt a long-term perspective that includes unconventional thinking and careful implementation to ensure their success. While this is described last due to the circular nature of the process, it may also be the first step with resilience, i.e. durability being developed at the individual level before being transferred to other groups and the entire organization.

The spectrum of initiatives includes:

1. **SWOT of the Owner/Manager/Decision Maker:** Every business owner or manager should conduct a SWOT analysis of themselves and, preferably, the people they work with (both personally and professionally). The preceding discussion of how they should work together with their support system will be reflected in this review. Since the decision-maker is more likely to have a well-rounded understanding of the other stakeholders' perspectives thanks to the objective nature of the SWOT analysis, the method also benefits long-term partnerships. Skill sets that can be used in a variety of contexts will be uncovered throughout the course of this exercise.

2. **Balance in Life Dimensions:** Maintaining a healthy work-life balance is important for both one's physical and mental well-being. In the face of unexpected occurrences, grief, and uncertainty, COVID-19 has rekindled and reminded everyone of the importance of health and the necessity of enjoying simple joys. If you aren't physically and mentally well, you can't put in the long hours necessary to keep your business afloat and eventually thrive. The authors argue that, regardless of one's position or duty, "self-care" must be everyone's top concern, especially in the context of the COVID-19 crisis we now face. From conducting a SWOT analysis of the business owner, manager,

or decision maker to learning the ins and outs of the business plan, there is a wide range of initiatives to choose from. Give me a rundown of what it's capable of and what it has available. It is normal practice to make reference to a business in one of these ways (Le, H., Nguyen, T., Ngo, C., Pham, T., & Le, T. 2020). The writers argue that a proper reaction to these beliefs must begin with each person. Every business owner/manager needs to undertake a SWOT analysis. This evaluation will take into account the prior conversation regarding how they should collaborate with their support system. Using the objective SWOT technique will make the decision maker more competitive by helping them see things from the eyes of others. In times of crisis, this strategy will also aid in identifying marketable skills that may be quickly deployed.

7. FINDING AND RECOMMENDATION

First, there must be cooperation between all involved parties, with an emphasis on producing outcomes that are beneficial to all. Remembering one's social network is crucial at this time, as it may be used to forge alliances and contribute to the success of the business. Promote locally owned businesses: small and medium-sized enterprises (SMEs), in conjunction with other businesses and local councils, should increase promotion to attract and encourage customers to buy local. Businesses in the food and lodging industries, for example, can easily promote themselves to a neighbourhood clientele .

8. CONCLUSION

The COVID-19 pandemic has changed the structures of various SME businesses around the world. Due to COVID 19, SMEs are highly affected in terms of discontinuation in the manufacturing and supply chain of products and services. Various jobs in SME are at stake in huge quantities, and the closure of SME is a major issue in the economy. Many countries have put in place different policies to help SMEs that were hurt by the COVID-19 pandemic.

REFERENCES

Alves, J. C., Lok, T. C., Luo, Y., & Hao, W. (2020). *Crisis management for small business during the COVID-19 outbreak: Survival, resilience and renewal strategies of firms in Macau.* Academic Press.

Ayedee, N., & Manocha, S. (2020). Role of media (Television) in creating positive atmosphere in COVID 19 during lockdown in India. *Asian Journal of Management, 11*(4), 370–378. doi:10.5958/2321-5763.2020.00057.8

Bartik, A. W., Bertrand, M., Cullen, Z., Glaeser, E. L., Luca, M., & Stanton, C. (2020). The impact of COVID-19 on small business outcomes and expectations. *Proceedings of the National Academy of Sciences of the United States of America, 117*(30), 17656–17666. doi:10.1073/pnas.2006991117 PMID:32651281

Bartik, A. W., Bertrand, M., Cullen, Z., Glaeser, E. L., Luca, M., & Stanton, C. (2020). The impact of COVID-19 on small business outcomes and expectations. *Proceedings of the National Academy of Sciences of the United States of America*, *117*(30), 17656–17666. doi:10.1073/pnas.2006991117 PMID:32651281

Bartik, A. W., Bertrand, M., Cullen, Z. B., Glaeser, E. L., Luca, M., & Stanton, C. T. (2020). *How are small businesses adjusting to COVID-19? Early evidence from a survey (No. w26989)*. National Bureau of Economic Research. doi:10.3386/w26989

Beraha, I., & Đuričin, S. (2020). The impact of COVID-19 crisis on medium-sized enterprises in Serbia. *Economic Analysis*, *53*(1), 14–27.

Bhalerao, K., Mahale, P., Jyothi, N. V., & Yelikar, B. (2021). Technology: A pathway towards sustainability. *Academy of Marketing Studies Journal*, *25*(5), 1–9.

Bhalerao, K., & Patil, V. (2021). Information and communication technology adoption in small and medium enterprises: Post COVID-19 mantra of success. *International Journal of Management and Commerce*, *3*(1), 27–31.

Bhalerao, K., Patil, V., & Swamy, S. (2022). Impact of COVID 19 on small and medium enterprises. *Asian Journal of Management*, *13*(2), 115–119. doi:10.52711/2321-5763.2022.00021

Bhalerao, K., Patil, V., & Swamy, S. (2022). Impact of COVID 19 on small and medium enterprises. *Asian Journal of Management*, *13*(2), 115–119. doi:10.52711/2321-5763.2022.00021

Brown, R., Rocha, A., & Cowling, M. (2020). Financing entrepreneurship in times of crisis: Exploring the impact of COVID-19 on the market for entrepreneurial finance in the United Kingdom. *International Small Business Journal*, *38*(5), 380–390. doi:10.1177/0266242620937464

Brülhart, M., Lalive, R., Lehmann, T., & Siegenthaler, M. (2020). COVID-19 financial support to small businesses in Switzerland: Evaluation and outlook. *Schweizerische Zeitschrift für Volkswirtschaft und Statistik*, *156*(1), 1–13. doi:10.118641937-020-00060-y PMID:33078128

Dai, R., Feng, H., Hu, J., Jin, Q., Li, H., Wang, R., & Zhang, X. (2021). The impact of COVID-19 on small and medium-sized enterprises (SMEs): Evidence from two-wave phone surveys in China. *China Economic Review*, *67*, 101607. doi:10.1016/j.chieco.2021.101607

Dev, S. M., & Sengupta, R. (2020). *Covid-19: Impact on the Indian economy*. Indira Gandhi Institute of Development Research.

Faal, M. L. (2020). Understanding binding constraints to small and medium enterprises (SMEs) in the Gambia: A critical review. *Asian Journal of Management*, *11*(2), 216–221. doi:10.5958/2321-5763.2020.00034.7

Fitriasari, F. (2020). How do Small and Medium Enterprise (SME) survive the COVID-19 outbreak? *Jurnal Inovasi Ekonomi*, *5*(2).

Gerald, E., Obianuju, A., & Chukwunonso, N. (2020). Strategic agility and performance of small and medium enterprises in the phase of Covid-19 pandemic. *International Journal of Financial, Accounting, and Management*, *2*(1), 41–50. doi:10.35912/ijfam.v2i1.163

Hadi, S., & Supardi, S. (2020). Revitalization strategy for small and medium enterprises after Corona virus disease pandemic (covid-19) in Yogyakarta. *J. Xian Univ. Archit. Technol, 12,* 4068–4076.

Haider Syed, M., Khan, S., Raza Rabbani, M., & Thalassinos, Y. E. (2020). *An artificial intelligence and NLP based Islamic FinTech model combining Zakat and Qardh-Al-Hasan for countering the adverse impact of COVID 19 on SMEs and individuals.* Academic Press.

Hebert, D. J. (2021). COVID-19's Impacts on SMEs and Policy Recommendations in Response. *National Law Review, 11*(20). Available at: https://www. natlawreview. com/article/covid-19-s-impacts-smes-and-policy-recommendations-response

Hoorens, S., Hocking, L., & Fays, C. (2020). *How small businesses are coping with the impact of CO-VID-19.* Rand Europe.

Indriastuti, M., & Fuad, K. (2020, July). Impact of covid-19 on digital transformation and sustainability in small and medium enterprises (smes): A conceptual framework. In *Conference on Complex, Intelligent, and Software Intensive Systems* (pp. 471-476). Springer.

Juergensen, J., Guimón, J., & Narula, R. (2020). European SMEs amidst the COVID-19 crisis: Assessing impact and policy responses. *Economia e Politica Industriale, 47*(3), 499–510. doi:10.100740812-020-00169-4

Keogh-Brown, M. R., Jensen, H. T., Edmunds, W. J., & Smith, R. D. (2020). The impact of Covid-19, associated behaviours and policies on the UK economy: A computable general equilibrium model. *SSM - Population Health, 12,* 100651. doi:10.1016/j.ssmph.2020.100651 PMID:33072839

Le, H., Nguyen, T., Ngo, C., Pham, T., & Le, T. (2020). Policy related factors affecting the survival and development of SMEs in the context of Covid 19 pandemic. *Management Science Letters, 10*(15), 3683–3692. doi:10.5267/j.msl.2020.6.025

Liguori, E. W., & Pittz, T. G. (2020). Strategies for small business: Surviving and thriving in the era of COVID-19. *Journal of the International Council for Small Business, 1*(2), 106–110. doi:10.1080/26437015.2020.1779538

McGeever, N., McQuinn, J., & Myers, S. (2020). *SME liquidity needs during the COVID-19 shock (No. 2/FS/20).* Central Bank of Ireland.

Mirza, N., Naqvi, B., Rahat, B., & Rizvi, S. K. A. (2020). Price reaction, volatility timing and funds' performance during Covid-19. *Finance Research Letters, 36,* 101657. doi:10.1016/j.frl.2020.101657 PMID:32837369

Mittal, R. K., Aggarwal, V. S., & Rawat, D. (2017). Enhancing competitiveness of msmes in india through their integration in global supply chain: A study of challenges faced by firms in gurgaon auto–component cluster. *Asian J. Management, 8*(1), 59–67. doi:10.5958/2321-5763.2017.00009.9

Neu, C. R., Carew, D. G., & Shatz, H. J. (2020). *Preserving Small Businesses: Small-Business Owners Speak About Surviving the COVID-19 Pandemic.* RAND. doi:10.7249/PEA317-1

Nyanga, T., & Zirima, H. (2020). Reactions of small to medium enterprises in masvingo, Zimbabwe to covid 19: Implications on productivity. *Business Excellence and Management, 10*(1), 22–32. doi:10.24818/beman/2020.S.I.1-02

Omar, A. R. C., Ishak, S., & Jusoh, M. A. (2020). The impact of Covid-19 Movement Control Order on SMEs' businesses and survival strategies. *Geografia, 16*(2).

Papadopoulos, T., Baltas, K. N., & Balta, M. E. (2020). The use of digital technologies by small and medium enterprises during COVID-19: Implications for theory and practice. *International Journal of Information Management, 55*, 102192. doi:10.1016/j.ijinfomgt.2020.102192 PMID:32836646

Paul, J., & Feliciano-Cestero, M. M. (2021). Five decades of research on foreign direct investment by MNEs: An overview and research agenda. *Journal of Business Research, 124*, 800–812. doi:10.1016/j.jbusres.2020.04.017 PMID:32292218

Pavlendová, G. (2021). *Work from Home during COVID 19 and Gender Differences in Twitter Content Analysis*. Academic Press.

Pedauga, L., Sáez, F., & Delgado-Márquez, B. L. (2022). Macroeconomic lockdown and SMEs: The impact of the COVID-19 pandemic in Spain. *Small Business Economics, 58*(2), 665–688. doi:10.100711187-021-00476-7

Rajagopaul, A., Magwentshu, N., & Kalidas, S. (2020). *How South African SMEs can survive and thrive post COVID-19*. Providing the Right Support to Enable SME Growth Now and Beyond the Crisis.

Ratnasingam, J., Khoo, A., Jegathesan, N., Wei, L. C., Abd Latib, H., Thanasegaran, G., ... Amir, M. A. (2020). How are small and medium enterprises in Malaysia's furniture industry coping with COVID-19 pandemic? Early evidences from a survey and recommendations for policymakers. *BioResources, 15*(3), 5951–5964. doi:10.15376/biores.15.3.5951-5964

Rosado-Serrano, A., Paul, J., & Dikova, D. (2018). International franchising: A literature review and research agenda. *Journal of Business Research, 85*, 238–257. doi:10.1016/j.jbusres.2017.12.049

Saidu, M., & Aifuwa, H. O. (2020). Coronavirus pandemic in Nigeria: How can Small and Medium Enterprises (SMEs) cope and flatten the curve. *European Journal of Accounting, Finance and Investment, 6*(5), 55–61.

Swamy, S. (2022). Impact of COVID 19 on small and medium Enterprises. *Asian Journal of Management, 13*(2), 2.

Chapter 8

COVID–19 and SME Adoption of Social Media in Developing Economies in Africa

Ranson Sifiso Gwala

ⓘD https://orcid.org/0000-0002-1545-2259
University of KwaZulu-Natal, South Africa

Pfano Mashau

ⓘD https://orcid.org/0000-0003-0490-1925
University of KwaZulu-Natal, South Africa

ABSTRACT

This chapter explores how COVID-19 negatively impacted society and small-medium enterprises (SMEs) and how social media marketing, promoting, and influencing played a role in rescuing and resuscitating some of the SMEs during the COVID-19 pandemic. The chapter investigates the use of social media during the hard lockdown due to mitigation measures of COVID-19. It uses a desktop review of literature to qualitatively identify themes. The study aim was to understand how social media could be used by SMEs to improve and grow SMEs. The study identified five key themes during COVID-19, being social media adoption, employees layoffs, falling customer demand, government support, and online business adoption. The social media influencing is being adopted as part of social media marketing, and one of its positives is that it is affordable. The richness of data and literature could lead to the development of a conceptual framework for the use of social media by SMEs in Africa.

INTRODUCTION

Covid-19 was declared a pandemic by the World Health Organisation, (WHO) in March 2020 after the detection of the spread of covid-19 cases in many parts of the world. What followed were lockdowns, with countries locking their citizens in their houses and closing all borders of entry. The spread of co-vid-19, was not easily arrested. It continued to spread. People started to learn to survive in their own

DOI: 10.4018/978-1-6684-5770-2.ch008

limited boundaries. Many families lost their loved ones, many could not even see them when they were buried. Social media came to the fore with live recordings of small events to the broader audience. Video telephoning became a space to connect friends and families. How did this phenomenon extend to small medium enterprises (SME) which were the source of survival as essential services were rendered by these SMEs? Small and medium-sized enterprises (SMEs) are an important contributor to emerging countries' economic growth. However, SMEs have been struggling to sustain their performance in a highly competitive environment.

BACKGROUND AND THE STUDY FOCUS

The emergence of covid-19 brought devastation that is yet to be fully accounted for. Many people lost their lives. Corporations and small, and medium, enterprises, (SMEs) lost their valuable income and were forced to retrench a sizeable number of their workforce. The worst was when some SMEs could no longer meet the bottom line and were forced out of business. The repercussions were dire for both business owners and employees. However, some SMEs were able to survive, learn, adapt and find new ways of doing business under covid-19. As part of small business survival, these SMEs had to adapt and innovate. At the centre of such innovation and adaptation was the adoption of the fourth industrial revolution. The fourth industrial revolution has been around for just over a decade, yet its impact continues to be felt depending on country, organisation and affordability factors.

Social media adoption has been growing in leaps and bounds. However, many organisations have chosen to use less of these social media platforms like websites and Facebook. Platforms like WhatsApp, Instagram, and Twitter have not been effectively used to market businesses. However, during the covid-19, social media adoption by SMEs grew (Patma et al., 2021, Kakumbi and Phiri, 2022). The objectives are as follows:

a)   how the outbreak of COVID-19 affected and influenced SME social media adoption, and,
b)   implications of the COVID-19 pandemic on the adoption, and use of social media in developing economies in Africa.

THE LITERATURE REVIEW

The literature review shall use two models of technology adoption, these are technology, Organisation and Environment model (TOE) and Technology Adoption Model (TAM). Scanning the emergence of covid-19 and how it impacted the SME sector. Further probing how this led to the adoption of technology in the form of social media marketing and other forms brought by the present era of the fourth industrial revolution (4IR). The study utilises the Technology Adoption Model (TAM) as the main theoretical framework.

The Emergence of Covid-19

The World Health Organization (WHO) was informed by the China Health Authority on December 31, 2019, of a large number of pneumonia cases with an unknown cause in Wuhan City, China (Andrews et al., 2020). China reported the first 2019-nCoV fatality on January 11, 2020 (Fang et al., 2020) and the WHO designated 2019-nCoV to be a Public Health Emergency of International Concern on that same day. The emergence of covid-19 brought about lockdowns between nations and countries. Lockdowns brought many industries to a standstill, amongst these were the travel industry, the hotel industry along with their value chains. Many small exotic countries and islands derived substantial amount of their income from tourism. They suffered greatly from the lockdowns. SMEs who survived changed the way they conducted business, some new SMEs were started as a result of the gap or niche identified during covid-19.

The COVID-19 pandemic was not only a medical emergency but also a business emergency that created the need for organisations to be resilient and versatile in managing the impact of the pandemic on their business operations. At the time, (SMEs) were the most vulnerable to the economic disaster caused by the recent crisis, because these companies did not have the necessary resources to absorb losses (Khalil et al., 2022). Digitalisation significantly augments the relationship between the three dynamic capabilities and SME performance. However, digitalisation could only significantly moderate the relationship between transforming capability and SME performance (Martins, 2022). The COVID-19 pandemic has created risks for economies and business operations, with customers stopping, reducing, or postponing purchases, thereby affecting supply chains and resulting in difficulties in sourcing alternative suppliers (Drydakis, 2022). Five significant problems of SMEs during COVID-19 are layoffs of employees, financial crunch, health issues of employees, fall in sales and turnover and fall in customer demands. The adoption of different components of technology, technology 4.0. social media and e-commerce can clarify customer demands, increasing automation, maintaining physical distance and increase in sales and turnover (Kumar and Ayedee, 2021).

The SMEs and Covid-19

Small and mid-size businesses (SMEs) and the COVID-19 as a disabling and enabling mechanism, with an emphasis on how SMEs' crisis management techniques may assist them in navigating the crisis. SMEs could choose a narrowly focused or broad-based strategy, such as retrenchment, perseverance, or innovation (Hossain et al., 2022). Covid-19 restricted movement and lockdowns gave rise to many unintended consequences. Some of these consequences were closure of business, some were forced to scale down production and hence retrenchments. The SME sector was severely affected (Shafi et al., 2020). Developing countries governments could not come up with big business packages that could sustain the whole business value chain leading to foreclosures and retrenchments. In South Africa payment of workers from the Unemployment Insurance Fund, (UIF) mitigated against retrenchments to a certain extent. Many countries in the African continent could not afford exorbitant rescue packages and hence could not impose harsh and strict lockdowns as they could not support SME and the populace.

Challenges of SMEs During the COVID-19 Pandemic

Long-established businesses with a strong market position find it challenging to strike a balance between utilising current business models and exploring new ones in a disruptive business climate (Gupta et al., 2020). Due to the requirement for organisations to consider their core business while pursuing innovation, which frequently goes against organisational routines, combining these two talents is a difficulty. Differences in managers' perceptions of environmental changes can be one of the barriers to changing a business model; it is challenging to establish a convergent manager perspective of environmental changes (Sajjad et al., 2020). However, the COVID-19 epidemic has led practically everyone to assume that the corporate climate has undergone a significant shift. In fact, a lot of people think that these changes won't just happen during the epidemic but would also last after it's over. According to more than half of businesses, the COVID-19 pandemic will have a significant negative impact, necessitating immediate action (Adamowicz, 2022).

Reduced client purchasing power, limitations on engagement and working hours, a lack of raw materials, order cancellations, cash flow issues, and supply chain disruption are just a few of the hurdles that SMEs must contend with. There are, however, some businesses that can profit from the pandemic (Didier et al., 2021). They have the ability to focus resources on establishing economic prospects. When a company model is changed, established companies frequently find themselves in a difficult situation. The implementation of an organisational design that can enable business model change is often used to address these problems. Differences of opinion among top management during the search for a new organisational design may prevent businesses from pursuing radical business model transformation (Priyono et al., 2020).

THE THEORY OF REASONED ACTION

The Theory of Reasoned Action (Fishbein, 1980, Ajzen, 1985) and its extension, the Theory of Planned Behaviour (Fishbein and Ajzen, 1977) are cognitive theories that offer a conceptual framework for understanding human behaviour in specific contexts. In particular, the theory of planned behaviour has been widely used to assist in the prediction and explanation of several health behaviours. The original Theory of Reasoned Action held that the best indicator of whether or not someone will engage in a particular conduct is an individual's intention to do so. Attitudes and arbitrary standards, in turn, predict intentions. To put it another way, a person is more likely to decide to engage in a behaviour or activity if they have a favourable opinion of it and believe that it will benefit their friends, family, or society (LaCaille, 2013).

Figure 1. Theory of reasoned action
Source: (Fishbein and Ajzen, 1977)

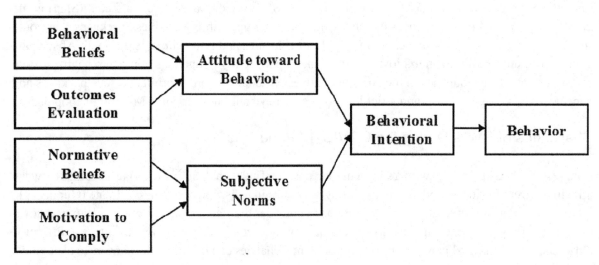

THE THEORY OF PLANNED BEHAVIOUR

The Theory of Planned Behaviour (TPB) was created by (Ajzen, 1985) through expanding the Theory of Reasoned Action (TRA) by adding a new construct called perceived behavioural control (PBC) to account for circumstances in which a person lacks significant control over the targeted behaviour (Tanhan and Young, 2022). A suggestion was made that, in addition to attitudes, use, arbitrary standards, and perceived behavioural controls such the abilities, opportunities, and resources required. The Theory of Planned Behaviour is one of the most significant theories in behavioural science models for forecasting behavioural intentions and actions, and it has been thoroughly validated (Si et al., 2020). The TPB model comes to the conclusion that an individual will be expected to generate the intention to do that action when the opportunity arises if they sense an appropriate level of behavioural control over their behaviour. The three TPB components' direct effects on intention have been studied in several studies. Their study's findings supported the importance of the three TPB components and suggested that intention serves as an important stand-in for explaining pro-environmental behaviour (Liu et al., 2021). Theoretical coherence is still lacking, though. Critics have asserted that, under certain circumstances, the attitude had little discernible effect on intention (Abrahamse and Steg, 2011).

Figure 2. Theory of planned behaviour
Source: (Ajzen, 1985)

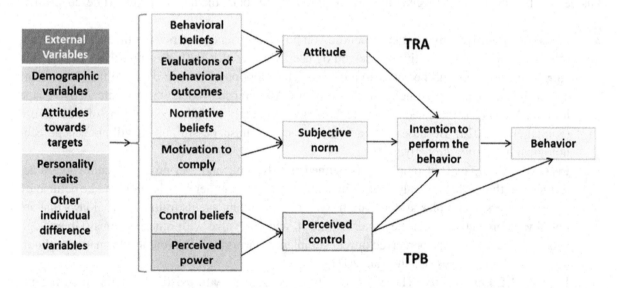

THE TECHNOLOGY, ORGANISATION AND ENVIRONMENT, (TOE) MODEL

The Technology, Organization, and Environment (TOE) model, which was first presented by (Tornatzky et al., 1990). El-Haddadeh (2020) uses the TOE framework to examine aspects such as senior managers' attitudes, IT skills, risk perceptions, and adoption obstacles in order to understand the dynamics of innovation in cloud computing adoption in SMEs. The adoption of technical innovation is ensured through organisational identification using TOE as a foundation. The TOE framework may be used to investigate several innovation settings, such as e-business, e-commerce, and entrepreneurial resource planning, and to gauge how ready SMEs' information technology is in these contexts. The technical context refers to both internal and external elements that might influence an organization's decisions on the adoption of innovations (Sindakis and Aggarwal, 2022). Similarly, the organisational context refers to the characteristics of an organisation, such as its size, the complexity of its management structure, its formalisation, its human resources, a measure of its slack assets, and its connections to presenters who are representative of the organisation (MacLennan and Van Belle, 2014). El-Haddadeh (2020) also uses the TOE framework to examine how senior managers' perspectives, information technology capabilities, risk perceptions, and adoption barriers affect the dynamics of innovation in cloud computing uptake in SMEs. The TOE framework has also been broadly applied as a theory to assess how well SMEs embrace new technologies (Eze et al., 2022). Additionally, TOE has established itself as the preferred paradigm for comprehending technology adoption and the value generation associated with new technology (Saarikko et al., 2020). The use of the TOE framework to examine how factors related to the technology, organisation, and environment dimensions affect the installation, post-implementation, and performance indicators of IT systems and applications is becoming more and more popular in the literature (Dora et al., 2022).

Technological Context

The technological environment emphasises internal and external technology that is advantageous for businesses that talk about the technical skills required to use social media (Klein and Todesco, 2021).

- **Perceived Relative Advantage:** Depending on how user-friendly users view the technology, mobile payments may be positively received by users (Nan et al., 2020). Because users believe that simple technologies will be easier to adjust to. The adoption of mobile payment may be encouraged if it is thought to be simple. The Technology Acceptance Model, which is intended to gauge how well users have adapted to new technology, frequently includes perceptions of ease of use (Kamal et al., 2020). Because if the adaption process is unsuccessful, users will not accept technological innovation properly.
- **Perceived Complexity:** Complexity is defined as a dynamic and ever-emerging collection of activities and things that not only engage in contact with one another but also come to be defined by it. The borders of complex systems are hazy, their interacting agents follow internal laws that are not always predictable, and they interact, adapt, and co-evolve with other systems (Greenhalgh and Papoutsi, 2018). The perceived or real complexity harms the adoption of information technology in small businesses (Ullah et al., 2021).
- **Perceived Compatibility:** The compatibility of innovation with existing systems in an organisational setting is defined by the diffusion of innovation (DOI) hypothesis. Users' perceptions of the consistency of new technology with their values, experiences, and projected requirements are known as perceived compatibility (Badi et al., 2021). The mistakes that some companies commit is developing systems that people are not ready or willing to adopt at the reasonable pace for that technology to make an impact and hence make it viable.

Organisational Context

Researchers posit that further research on social media use in small enterprises is essential (Akpan et al., 2022). Social media's advent has made it simple for small firms to access resources and challenge the dominance of big businesses (Jones, 2022). SMEs have the chance to compete in markets other than the one they are currently in (Baporikar, 2021).

- **Employee Skills:** It is critical that employee's skills are commensurate to the technology complexity in technology and social media adoption. If the employees lack such skills, it makes the adoption costly and longer. It is either you add new employees or train the ones you have to fuse in adoption.
- **Cost Perception:** The initial process to develop the technology or buy into the already established technology will attract some costs. The level of technology skills will also add into the cost factor. Whist training is a must to ensure smooth easing in and adoption by employees. Support becomes a constant factor that will be part of the going costs until the organisation has capacity to deal with the software in-house.
- **Top Management Support:** The top management has greater influence on what is adopted and what is not. If the top management influence technology adoption, they would ensure that they see their vision through.

Environmental Context

The key factor that might encourage or prevent a company from adopting innovation is the business environment (Kazancoglu et al., 2021).The setting in which the firm does business is the external environment. Competition pressure and pressure from trade partners like suppliers and customers are the two main environmental factors influencing the adoption of SME e-commerce (Religia et al., 2021).

- **Competitive Advantage:** The Electronic communications are being used by more and more businesses for marketing purposes on various e-marketing platforms. Social media has displaced traditional marketing tactics with digital ones. The surrounding environment in terms of rival companies and business partners. The ecological context is helpful for forecasting the uptake of information technology by SMEs.
- **Government Support:** The One of the environmental elements that affects technology adoption in the TOE framework is government assistance through legislation. Government regulations can encourage or deter organisations from implementing technology advancements. Adoption is typically hampered when the government introduces unique regulations requiring multiple businesses to possess stringent control and testing equipment for industrial safety.
- **Environmental Uncertainty:** The application of new technologies can be harmed by an uncertain environment. When there are quick, complicated changes, there are environmental uncertainties. Without the backing of their infrastructure and clear operational norms, organisations in a situation of high uncertainty may be unable to implement new technology. This doubt affects people's hesitation to use information technology.

The Technology Acceptance Model (TAM)

Since the technology acceptance model (TAM) initially appeared more than 25 years ago, a considerable amount of work has been done on the topic, which amply demonstrates the model's appeal in the field. The TAM model, which has its roots in the psychological theories of reasoned action and planned behaviour, has developed into a crucial tool for comprehending factors that influence whether people would embrace or reject new technologies. The major goals of the paper are to give a current, well-researched resource of previous and present references to literature that is linked to TAM as well as to suggest potential topics for future TAM study.

Figure 3. The Technology Acceptance Model (TAM)
Source: (Davis, 1985)

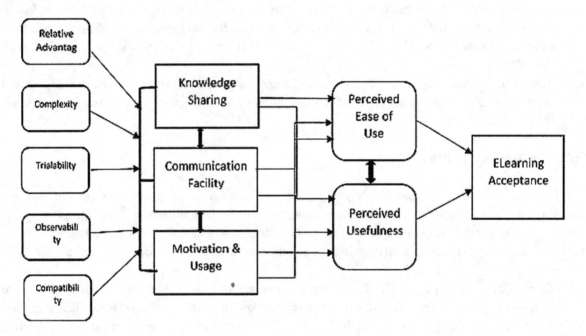

Technology Acceptance Model (TAM) was proposed by (Davis, 1985). Theorizing and comprehending user attitudes and usage patterns of social media sites, such as Twitter, Facebook, Google+, and LinkedIn, is essential for creating future understandings and implementing these new technologies given the increasing popularity of social media. It would be possible to review the technology acceptance model (TAM) in order to address such studies on the factors that influence social media usage behaviour (Rauniar et al., 2014). Usefulness and ease are the two main criteria involved in user adoption of a technology, according to the technology acceptance model (TAM) (Davis, 1989). TAM has been widely used to assess consumer acceptance of general technology, although it has little explanatory value for purposes relating to particular systems (Jansen-Kosterink et al., 2019).

Utilising an example of university students and their perception and adoption of technology, a few terms must be defined. According to Davis, the study's focus on the perceived usefulness (PU) factor is appropriate given that undergraduates think utilising a computer system connects them to a local database or the Internet (Shittu et al., 2011). Instead of using the conventional methods, phones and other electronic gadgets help students with their academic activities. In other words, with technology, students can read and investigate information to complete assignments and research more quickly. Another component of the theory that is pertinent to the investigation is perceived ease-of-use (PEOU) (Bhatiasevi and Naglis, 2016). The simplicity with which students can adopt and employ electronic machine devices will facilitate their usage of digital information resources (DIRs), make learning more convenient for them, and have an impact on their academic activities in daily life.

In other words, using technology automatically makes it easier to find information than using more manual methods. Today instead of taking notes, notes are sent to students before the lecture on their laptops, tablets or even smart phones. This saves students time, even those who were absent can access notes wherever they are. Technology adoption amongst the youth is generally higher than in adults (Zhong et al., 2021). Due to its relevance to the issue under inquiry, the researcher chose this idea. In South Africa when cell phones initially arrived in the early turn of the 21st century, it was argued that it was for the rich. But as cell phones became popular and reasonable cheaper, poor households stopped using home desktop telephones which needed a monthly rental whether you had used it or not. As part of the expansion strategies mobile containers were sold to would be small businesses, to spread, familiarise and expand technology adoption to the rural and urban poor alike.

Social Media Awareness, and SME Social Media Adoption During Covid-19

The ability to create public profiles, specify users when sharing connections with others, and examine a list of links generated by other users in a system are all features of social media (Ebrahim, 2020). In order to realise something, either within of or outside of oneself, one must have consciousness, which is a subjective condition of existence. For continued use of social media, social media awareness is a necessity (Alshehri, 2019). Knowing and comprehending more about something that is happening in the world or around someone is referred to as awareness (Downes, 2022). The use of social media has evolved into a tool for improving and disseminating information (Al-Dmour et al., 2020). According to the survey by(Chowdhury et al., 2020), SMEs impacted by the COVID-19 problem had a high awareness of social media and a strong inclination to embrace it as a channel for marketing their goods and engaging with consumers. Technology, organisational structure, the environment, and social media awareness all have a big impact on people's intentions to use social media. The COVID-19 pandemic may provide an increased incentive for technology adoption and increased use. People have been subjected to a number of public policies such as regional lockdowns, quarantine at home, physical distancing, and restricted travel (Han et al., 2020), which has imposed the need to change traditional communication channels. As crisis information is transmitted across both social and traditional media, the SMCC model enables a distinction between information source and information form (Austin et al., 2012). Information form generally refers to the media through which information is transmitted (e.g. social media, traditional media, or word of mouth). Information source on the other hand refers to origins of information and may include organizations as well as social media and traditional media actors. Figure 4 shows how traditional marketing could function in unison with social media. People are now on their phone for sizeable amount each day and the technology allows for social media ads to be posted and accessed with ease. This allows wider audience reach.

Figure 4. Modified social-mediated crisis communication model
Source: (Austin et al., 2012)

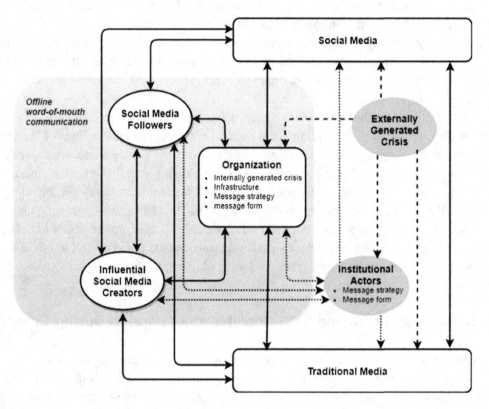

The COVID-19 epidemic has had a significant impact on small and medium-sized businesses (SMEs), and many have had to transition their operations from offline to online in order to survive (Pramudita et al., 2022). The use of social media has evolved into a tool for improving and disseminating information (Akpan et al., 2022).

THE RESEARCH METHODOLOGY

The study shall use a desktop survey of the literature using peer-reviewed articles. Research methodology includes the steps used to define the design, choose methodologies and strategies, process sampling, choose data gathering tools, and perform a systematic analysis of secondary data on the cannabis study topic. The descriptive research approach employed in this chapter is qualitative. The qualitative method is used in the systematic review to assess written and published records as well as theme-based scholarly publications. The qualitative technique helps in comparing South Africa's legalisation and value creation to that of other nations. The main goal of this study's use of past and present data was to perform a literature review and analyse the secondary data that had been gathered. PRISMA protocols were employed, which are a standard protocol and an evidence-based framework for conducting comprehensive review researches. This study used thematic analysis to synthesis the data and consulted leading papers on online services in which social constructionism has been used (Aslam et al., 2018).

THE FINDINGS AND EMERGING THEMES AND TRENDS

The following themes emerged from the qualitative analysis of the data. The challenges that emerged as a result of covid-19 gravitated people towards seeking new solutions, new ways of doing business under trying cobid-19 times. A number of businesses whose business model could not adapt found themselves at the brink of collapse and extinction. The businesses like tourism and related industries were hardest hit as they relied on tourists or physical presence of customers.

Figure 5. Themes emerging from research

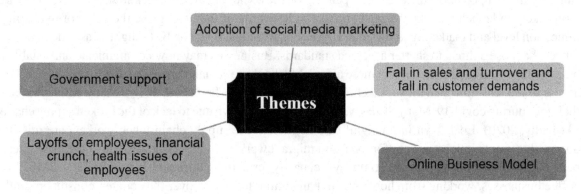

- Adoption of social media marketing
- Layoffs of employees, financial crunch, health issues of employees,
- Fall in customer demands hence fall in sales and turnover
- Government support
- Online business model

Adoption of Social Media Marketing

Social media is considered a dominant platform for ensuring business success and survival, especially in the case of small and medium enterprises businesses (SMEs) (Trawnih et al., 2021).The technological context, organisational context, environmental context, and social media awareness have a substantial impact on the intention to adopt social media (Orji et al., 2020). Covid-19 brought about the necessity to find alternatives to business as usual. Small, medium companies have taken time to adopt mechanisation of their processes unless if their core business needs such machinery (Fonseca, 2018). However, contrary to traditional mediums of marketing which includes radio, newspapers, pamphlets which are costly, social media is slowly taking the marketing space. There are now WhatsApp groups, where small businesses collect data of customer information like cell phone numbers and email addresses to send marketing information. This is relatively cheaper than traditional marketing. Digital or social media marketing has now been adopted as a part of the traditional tools adopted by small, medium and large companies alike. While social media has assumed a critical role in crisis response, organizations are still grappling with how best to leverage its use (Roshan et al., 2016). Recent studies have either sought to compare the relative effectiveness of social media platforms over traditional platforms; examined use and effectiveness of various crises response strategies on particular social media platforms; or explored interactions between crises response strategies and multiple social media platforms (Triantafillidou and Yannas, 2020)One of the key areas of interests among crisis communication scholars relates to how organizations can employ a dialogic communication approach in interacting with their key stakeholders on social media platforms (Wang and Yang, 2020).

Layoffs of Employees

Many SMEs have never treated marketing as a necessary monthly expense to promote their companies. But a significant portion of the SME is dependent on the owner or owners (Eeckhout, 2021). Owners are more likely to launch a marketing push, no matter how little, if they recognise the value of marketing. Education level and marketing knowledge are very important. Crises can be thought of as sudden occurrences that pose a threat to shatter accepted standards. Businesses may now communicate and establish relationships with their stakeholders more affordably thanks to social media, which also provides instant access to the real-time data those stakeholders are creating (Roshan et al., 2016). Many employees lost their jobs during covid-19. Many SMEs were forced to close down due to lack of the broken supply chains (Al-Fadly, 2020). Lockdown has a significant impact on the supply chain when workers are missing due to illness or travel restrictions for local and migrant workers. It has a negative effect on the workers' personal food safety as well as the company's capacity for output (Barman et al., 2021). For SMEs like coffee businesses, working from home was not an option. Instead of over the counter, consumers could order food and beverages through a smartphone app. Customers were allowed to pre-order thanks to the growing online and delivery services by shops and some SMEs. Pre-ordering, reserving tables, placing orders, and paying for beverages in advance all benefited the customers. However, the SMEs without capacity and budget failed.

Fall in Customer Demand Hence Fall in Sales and Turnover

Consumers found themselves in a very difficult situation, as they were locked down and they were only receivers of the available products in the market. They could not go, see, compare and then make informed decisions on which product to purchase, hence some started going online to purchase products (Rydell and Kucera, 2021). Consumers have turned to online channels throughout the pandemic, and businesses have reacted in like (Donthu and Gustafsson, 2020). Regarding commercial activities, the limitations put in place to stop the covid-19 transmission have caused a fall in consumer demand and, as a result, a decline in sales (Nchanji et al., 2021). Different industries have experienced different declines in revenue during the past year as a result of lockdowns, fall in customer demand, and broken supply chains. This has harmed SME investment chances and made their cash flow problems worse (Kejžar et al., 2022). Additionally, a lot of SMEs have been compelled to temporarily halt operations. As a result, employees' workdays were cut short. The gross domestic product (GDP) of many countries fell during covid-19, and it will take time for these countries to recover to pre-covid-19 conditions (Mofijur et al., 2021, Rothengatter et al., 2021).

Government Support

The idea that loans to most SMEs have a larger default risk than what major commercial banks would be accustomed to underwrite has contributed to governments' past, if limited, success in encouraging large commercial banks to issue more loans to SMEs (e.g. relative to loans to State-Owned Enterprises) (Wang et al., 2021). Government-backed bridging loans are useful last-resort options for assisting SMEs to deal with the effects of COVID-19. Governments must promote SMEs and assure their viability since doing otherwise would undermine the nation's economic stability (Hourcade et al., 2021). According to the length of the COVID-19 economic disruption, there is an ideal amount of bridge loan to be given to SMEs, taking into account the opportunity cost of financial support (as they may have been used for other purposes). Government-funded insurance pools for bank loans offer some but insufficient incentives for banks to lend to SMEs because such insurance doesn't actually lower the likelihood of loan default (Hafiz et al., 2020). Different countries utilised different models to support SMEs, some paid workers through the worker's short terms insurance in order to save jobs. Whilst others stimulated the economy by paying rent or interest free loans to save companies from going under, the innovation differed. What is clear is that government support was critical to ameliorate the impact of covid-19 to the economy.

Online Business Model to Leverage Competitive Advantage

Technology advancements in mobile payments make it simpler for users to conduct financial transactions. In addition to making things simpler for users, this transaction is thought to be realistic and supports user performance (Pham and Ho, 2015). By addressing these problems, SMEs should rethink their business plan in order to utilise the Internet to survive the Covid-19 pandemic. Social media marketing has become more popular in the corporate world nowadays as a result of the shift from traditional to online company activities (Ausat and Suherlan, 2021). Companies using social media marketing as a strategic tool to boost their company value, profitability, and competitive advantage are what's driving this. Small and medium-sized businesses (SMEs) in developing economies continue to face numerous obstacles in implementing digital technologies. In contrast, emerging markets have more SME success stories. However, the majority of SMEs in the informal sector in emerging markets and developing economies (EMDEs) suffer comparable difficulties that prevent the adoption of cutting-edge innovations and technology required to enhance business operations and re-engineer processes (Akpan et al., 2022). Even if unintentionally, the use of cutting-edge technologies to direct business operations during the COVID-19 pandemic containment community lockdown shows that technology not only offers competitive advantages but also provides a means for survival by improvising existing business models (Akpan et al., 2021).

IMPLICATIONS OF THE STUDY

Future studies must examine how multinational companies have been involved in collusion, price fixing and unreasonable price increases that were experienced during covid-19. Some of the price increases were justifiable, whilst others were unreasonable. The shortage of input materials, although many countries had agreed to open supply of goods during covid-19, the turnaround time was however negatively impacted. Quantitative studies of how many companies survived and how they survived would form informed studies of the future in order to learn and inform governments what needs to be done during any future pandemics. Covid-19 is not the last pandemic to come, the worsening environmental disasters as a result of global warming poses a clear and present danger. The undiscovered diseases and diseases like Ebola could also present challenges could they be spread worldwide. new markets by utilising the blue ocean and red ocean principles.

CONCLUSION

Many people have not heard about Zoom or any other meeting platform before covid-19 pandemic. Let alone small businesses which were using minimal software to run their businesses. The use of technology in many businesses spiked during covid-19, with many of the users showing clearly their lack of understanding of the use of those platforms. Although WhatsApp, Twitter, Facebook, Instagram, and many other popular social media platforms have been about for some time, but they have been gaining popularity amongst the youth and they were not regarded as mainstream means of marketing of communicating formal business messages. The growth of popularity of these platforms and the growing number of people following superstars and influencers has changed the landscape how business looks at social media. The SMEs have limited marketing budget, and during covid-19, the only open forum to reach the consumer was through social media. The study will seek to understand how SME adopted social media for marketing purposes during covid-19. It will further seek to understand if covid-19 had not come as such a disrupting pandemic, the social media and technology adoption wold have taken place at the same speed as it did during covid-19.

The availability of technology played a major role in aiding SMEs to use these platforms to implement social media marketing, online stock purchasing and opening their online stores. This allowed new markets to thrive, markets like those who adopted transportation of goods directly to customers and using small companies and individuals like influencers to market their businesses. This has introduced new negatives that some SMEs and multinational companies have learnt that they can do more with less workers, hence increasing retrenchments in favour of technology adoption. The fourth industrial revolution has played a critical role in rescuing SMEs but it has also introduced new challenges for the unskilled worker. Governments have a critical role in supporting SMEs and labour in ensuring that workers are reskilled and retrained for the new forms of work post the covid-19 pandemic commensurate to the fourth industrial revolution adoption. The student of the future both at high school and higher institutions of learning must be trained differently from the students of the past. These students must be versatile, easy to train in order to adapt to the fast pace of technology. Therefore legislation is needed in reshaping minds and skilling patterns of the future to produce a workforce of the future

REFERENCES

Abrahamse, W., & Steg, L. (2011). Factors related to household energy use and intention to reduce it: The role of psychological and socio-demographic variables. *Human Ecology Review*, 30–40.

Adamowicz, M. (2022). COVID-19 Pandemic as a Change Factor in the Labour Market in Poland. *Sustainability*, *14*(15), 9197. doi:10.3390u14159197

Ajzen, I. (1985). *From intentions to actions: A theory of planned behavior. In Action control.* Springer.

Akpan, I. J., Soopramanien, D., & Kwak, D.-H. (2021). Cutting-edge technologies for small business and innovation in the era of COVID-19 global health pandemic. *Journal of Small Business and Entrepreneurship, 33*(6), 607–617. doi:10.1080/08276331.2020.1799294

Akpan, I. J., Udoh, E. A. P., & Adebisi, B. (2022). Small business awareness and adoption of state-of-the-art technologies in emerging and developing markets, and lessons from the COVID-19 pandemic. *Journal of Small Business and Entrepreneurship, 34*(2), 123–140. doi:10.1080/08276331.2020.1820185

Al-Dmour, H., Salman, A., Abuhashesh, M., & Al-Dmour, R. (2020). Influence of social media platforms on public health protection against the COVID-19 pandemic via the mediating effects of public health awareness and behavioral changes: Integrated model. *Journal of Medical Internet Research, 22*(8), e19996. doi:10.2196/19996 PMID:32750004

Al-Fadly, A. (2020). Impact of COVID-19 on SMEs and employment. *Entrepreneurship and Sustainability Issues, 8*, 629.

Almqvist, I. (2020). *Medicine of the Imagination: Dwelling in Possibility: An Impassioned Plea for Fearless Imagination.* John Hunt Publishing.

Alshehri, O. (2019). Usage and Perceptions of Social Media Tools among Higher Education Instructor. *International Journal of Information and Education Technology (IJIET), 9*(7), 493–497. doi:10.18178/ijiet.2019.9.7.1252

Andrews, M., Areekal, B., Rajesh, K., Krishnan, J., Suryakala, R., Krishnan, B., Muraly, C., & Santhosh, P. (2020). First confirmed case of COVID-19 infection in India: A case report. *The Indian Journal of Medical Research, 151*(5), 490. doi:10.4103/ijmr.IJMR_2131_20 PMID:32611918

Ausat, A. M. A., & Suherlan, S. (2021). Obstacles and solutions of MSMEs in electronic commerce during covid-19 pandemic: Evidence from Indonesia. *BASKARA: Journal of Business and Entrepreneurship, 4*(1), 11–19. doi:10.54268/baskara.4.1.11-19

Austin, L., Fisher Liu, B., & Jin, Y. (2012). How audiences seek out crisis information: Exploring the social-mediated crisis communication model. *Journal of Applied Communication Research, 40*(2), 188–207. doi:10.1080/00909882.2012.654498

Ayenigbara, G. (2014). Cannabis sativa: A plant with multiple utilities, misunderstood, and a victim of controversial hypocrisy. *Journal of Emerging Trends in Educational Research and Policy Studies, 5*, 54–59.

Badi, S., Ochieng, E., Nasaj, M., & Papadaki, M. (2021). Technological, organisational and environmental determinants of smart contracts adoption: UK construction sector viewpoint. *Construction Management and Economics, 39*(1), 36–54. doi:10.1080/01446193.2020.1819549

Baporikar, N. (2021). *Influence of Business Competitiveness on SMEs Performance. In Research Anthology on Small Business Strategies for Success and Survival.* IGI Global.

Barman, A., Das, R., & De, P. K. (2021). Impact of COVID-19 in food supply chain: Disruptions and recovery strategy. *Current Research in Behavioral Sciences, 2*, 100017. doi:10.1016/j.crbeha.2021.100017

Bhatiasevi, V., & Naglis, M. (2016). Investigating the structural relationship for the determinants of cloud computing adoption in education. *Education and Information Technologies*, *21*(5), 1197–1223. doi:10.100710639-015-9376-6

Chowdhury, M., Sarkar, A., Paul, S. K. & Moktadir, M. (2020). A case study on strategies to deal with the impacts of COVID-19 pandemic in the food and beverage industry. *Operations Management Research*, 1-13.

Collins, J. (2020). A brief history of cannabis and the drug conventions. *The American Journal of International Law*, *114*, 279–284.

Davis, F. D. (1985). *A technology acceptance model for empirically testing new end-user information systems: Theory and results*. Massachusetts Institute of Technology.

Davis, F. D. (1989). Perceived Usefulness, Perceived Ease of Use, and User Acceptance of Information Technology. *Management Information Systems Quarterly*, *13*(3), 319–340. doi:10.2307/249008

Didier, T., Huneeus, F., Larrain, M., & Schmukler, S. L. (2021). Financing firms in hibernation during the COVID-19 pandemic. *Journal of Financial Stability*, *53*, 100837. doi:10.1016/j.jfs.2020.100837

Donthu, N., & Gustafsson, A. (2020). *Effects of COVID-19 on business and research*. Elsevier. doi:10.1016/j.jbusres.2020.06.008

Dora, M., Kumar, A., Mangla, S. K., Pant, A., & Kamal, M. M. (2022). Critical success factors influencing artificial intelligence adoption in food supply chains. *International Journal of Production Research*, *60*(14), 4621–4640. doi:10.1080/00207543.2021.1959665

Downes, S. 2022. Connectivism. *Asian Journal of Distance Education*.

Drydakis, N. (2022). Artificial Intelligence and reduced SMEs' business risks. A dynamic capabilities analysis during the COVID-19 pandemic. *Information Systems Frontiers*, 1–25. PMID:35261558

Ebrahim, R. S. (2020). The role of trust in understanding the impact of social media marketing on brand equity and brand loyalty. *Journal of Relationship Marketing*, *19*(4), 287–308. doi:10.1080/15332667.2019.1705742

Eeckhout, J. (2021). *The Profit Paradox: How Thriving Firms Threaten the Future of Work*. Princeton University Press.

El-Haddadeh, R. (2020). Digital innovation dynamics influence on organisational adoption: The case of cloud computing services. *Information Systems Frontiers*, *22*(4), 985–999. doi:10.100710796-019-09912-2

Eze, S. C., Chinedu-Eze, V. C., Awa, H. O. & Asiyanbola, T. A. (2022). Multi-dimensional framework of the information behaviour of SMEs on emerging information communication technology (EICT) adoption. *Journal of Science and Technology Policy Management*.

Fang, H., Wang, L., & Yang, Y. (2020). Human mobility restrictions and the spread of the novel coronavirus (2019-nCoV) in China. *Journal of Public Economics*, *191*, 104272. doi:10.1016/j.jpubeco.2020.104272 PMID:33518827

Fishbein, M. (1980). Understanding Attitudes and Predicting. *Social Behaviour*.

Fishbein, M., & Ajzen, I. (1977). Belief, attitude, intention, and behavior: An introduction to theory and research. *Philosophy & Rhetoric*, 10.

Fonseca, L. M. (2018). Industry 4.0 and the digital society: concepts, dimensions and envisioned benefits. *Proceedings of the international conference on business excellence*, 386-397. 10.2478/picbe-2018-0034

Greenhalgh, T., & Papoutsi, C. (2018). Studying complexity in health services research: Desperately seeking an overdue paradigm shift. *BMC Medicine*, *16*(1), 95. doi:10.118612916-018-1089-4 PMID:29921272

Gupta, S., Leszkiewicz, A., Kumar, V., Bijmolt, T., & Potapov, D. (2020). Digital analytics: Modeling for insights and new methods. *Journal of Interactive Marketing*, *51*, 26–43. doi:10.1016/j.intmar.2020.04.003

Hafiz, H., Oei, S.-Y., Ring, D. M., & Shnitser, N. (2020). *Regulating in pandemic: evaluating economic and financial policy responses to the coronavirus crisis*. Boston College Law School Legal Studies Research Paper.

Han, E., Tan, M. M. J., Turk, E., Sridhar, D., Leung, G. M., Shibuya, K., Asgari, N., Oh, J., García-Basteiro, A. L., Hanefeld, J., Cook, A. R., Hsu, L. Y., Teo, Y. Y., Heymann, D., Clark, H., McKee, M., & Legido-Quigley, H. (2020). Lessons learnt from easing COVID-19 restrictions: An analysis of countries and regions in Asia Pacific and Europe. *Lancet*, *396*(10261), 1525–1534. doi:10.1016/S0140-6736(20)32007-9 PMID:32979936

Hossain, M. R., Akhter, F. & Sultana, M. M. (2022). SMEs in covid-19 crisis and combating strategies: a systematic literature review (SLR) and A case from emerging economy. *Operations Research Perspectives*, 100222.

Hourcade, J., Glemarec, Y., De Coninck, H., Bayat-Renoux, F., Ramakrishna, K. & Revi, A. (2021). *Scaling up climate finance in the context of Covid-19: A science-based call for financial decision-makers*. Academic Press.

Jansen-Kosterink, S., Dekker-Van Weering, M., & Van Velsen, L. (2019). Patient acceptance of a telemedicine service for rehabilitation care: A focus group study. *International Journal of Medical Informatics*, *125*, 22–29. doi:10.1016/j.ijmedinf.2019.01.011 PMID:30914177

Jones, M. O. (2022). *Digital authoritarianism in the Middle East: Deception, disinformation and social media*. Hurst Publishers.

Kamal, S. A., Shafiq, M., & Kakria, P. (2020). Investigating acceptance of telemedicine services through an extended technology acceptance model (TAM). *Technology in Society*, *60*, 101212. doi:10.1016/j.techsoc.2019.101212

Kazancoglu, I., Sagnak, M., Kumar Mangla, S., & Kazancoglu, Y. (2021). Circular economy and the policy: A framework for improving the corporate environmental management in supply chains. *Business Strategy and the Environment*, *30*(1), 590–608. doi:10.1002/bse.2641

Kejžar, K. Z., Velić, A. & Damijan, J. P. 2022. Covid-19, trade collapse and GVC linkages: European experience. *The World Economy*.

Khalil, A., Abdelli, M. E. A., & Mogaji, E. (2022). Do Digital Technologies Influence the Relationship between the COVID-19 Crisis and SMEs’ Resilience in Developing Countries? *Journal of Open Innovation*, *8*(2), 100. doi:10.3390/joitmc8020100

Klein, V. B., & Todesco, J. L. (2021). COVID-19 crisis and SMEs responses: The role of digital transformation. *Knowledge and Process Management*, *28*(2), 117–133. doi:10.1002/kpm.1660

Kumar, M., & Ayedee, D. (2021). Technology Adoption: A Solution for SMEs to overcome problems during COVID-19. *Forthcoming*. *Academy of Marketing Studies Journal*, 25.

Lacaille, L. (2013). Theory of Reasoned Action. In M. D. Gellman & J. R. Turner (Eds.), *Encyclopedia of Behavioral Medicine*. Springer New York.

Liu, Y., Shi, H., Li, Y. & Amin, A. (2021). Factors influencing Chinese residents' post-pandemic outbound travel intentions: an extended theory of planned behavior model based on the perception of COVID-19. *Tourism Review*.

Maclennan, E., & Van Belle, J.-P. (2014). Factors affecting the organizational adoption of service-oriented architecture (SOA). *Information Systems and e-Business Management*, *12*(1), 71–100. doi:10.100710257-012-0212-x

Martins, A. (2022). Dynamic capabilities and SME performance in the COVID-19 era: the moderating effect of digitalization. *Asia-Pacific Journal of Business Administration*, ahead-of-print.

Merleaux, A. (2020). Drugs, empire, and US foreign policy. *A Companion to US Foreign Relations: Colonial Era to the Present*, 572-595.

Mofijur, M., Fattah, I. R., Alam, M. A., Islam, A. S., Ong, H. C., Rahman, S. A., Najafi, G., Ahmed, S. F., Uddin, M. A. & Mahlia, T. M. I. (2021). Impact of COVID-19 on the social, economic, environmental and energy domains: Lessons learnt from a global pandemic. *Sustainable Production and Consumption*, *26*, 343-359.

Nan, D., Kim, Y., Park, M. H., & Kim, J. H. (2020). What motivates users to keep using social mobile payments? *Sustainability*, *12*(17), 6878. doi:10.3390u12176878

Nchanji, E. B., Lutomia, C. K., Chirwa, R., Templer, N., Rubyogo, J. C., & Onyango, P. (2021). Immediate impacts of COVID-19 pandemic on bean value chain in selected countries in sub-Saharan Africa. *Agricultural Systems*, *188*, 103034. doi:10.1016/j.agsy.2020.103034 PMID:33658743

Orji, I. J., Kusi-Sarpong, S., & Gupta, H. (2020). The critical success factors of using social media for supply chain social sustainability in the freight logistics industry. *International Journal of Production Research*, *58*(5), 1522–1539. doi:10.1080/00207543.2019.1660829

Pham, T.-T. T., & Ho, J. C. (2015). The effects of product-related, personal-related factors and attractiveness of alternatives on consumer adoption of NFC-based mobile payments. *Technology in Society*, *43*, 159–172. doi:10.1016/j.techsoc.2015.05.004

Pramudita, O., Amalia, H. A. M. C., & Savitri, G. A. (2022). SMEs' Adoption of Social Media Consulting During COVID-19 Pandemic. *1st International Conference on Information System & Information Technology (ICISIT)*, 261-266.

Priyono, A., Moin, A., & Putri, V. N. A. O. (2020). Identifying digital transformation paths in the business model of SMEs during the COVID-19 pandemic. *Journal of Open Innovation*, 6(4), 104. doi:10.3390/joitmc6040104

Rauniar, R., Rawski, G., Yang, J., & Johnson, B. (2014). Technology acceptance model (TAM) and social media usage: An empirical study on Facebook. *Journal of Enterprise Information Management*, 27(1), 6–30. doi:10.1108/JEIM-04-2012-0011

Religia, Y., Surachman, S., Rohman, F., & Indrawati, N. (2021). E-commerce adoption in SMEs: A literature review. *Proceedings of the 1st International Conference on Economics Engineering and Social Science, InCEESS 2020*. 10.4108/eai.17-7-2020.2302969

Roshan, M., Warren, M., & Carr, R. (2016). Understanding the use of social media by organisations for crisis communication. *Computers in Human Behavior*, 63, 350–361. doi:10.1016/j.chb.2016.05.016

Rothengatter, W., Zhang, J., Hayashi, Y., Nosach, A., Wang, K., & Oum, T. H. (2021). Pandemic waves and the time after Covid-19–Consequences for the transport sector. *Transport Policy*, 110, 225–237. doi:10.1016/j.tranpol.2021.06.003 PMID:34608362

Rydell, L. & Kucera, J. (2021). Cognitive attitudes, behavioral choices, and purchasing habits during the COVID-19 pandemic. *Journal of Self-Governance & Management Economics*, 9.

Saarikko, T., Westergren, U. H., & Blomquist, T. (2020). Digital transformation: Five recommendations for the digitally conscious firm. *Business Horizons*, 63(6), 825–839. doi:10.1016/j.bushor.2020.07.005

Sajjad, A., Eweje, G., & Tappin, D. (2020). Managerial perspectives on drivers for and barriers to sustainable supply chain management implementation: Evidence from New Zealand. *Business Strategy and the Environment*, 29(2), 592–604. doi:10.1002/bse.2389

Samuel, A.-G. & Edward, B. 2015. The marijuana factor in a university in Ghana: A survey. *Журнал Сибирского федерального университета. Гуманитарные науки*, 8, 2162-2182.

Shafi, M., Liu, J., & Ren, W. (2020). Impact of COVID-19 pandemic on micro, small, and medium-sized Enterprises operating in Pakistan. *Research in Globalization*, 2, 100018. doi:10.1016/j.resglo.2020.100018

Shittu, A. T., Basha, K. M., Abdulrahman, N. S. N., & Ahmad, T. B. T. (2011). Investigating students' attitude and intention to use social software in higher institution of learning in Malaysia. *Multicultural Education & Technology Journal*.

Si, H., Shi, J.-G., Tang, D., Wu, G., & Lan, J. (2020). Understanding intention and behavior toward sustainable usage of bike sharing by extending the theory of planned behavior. *Resources, Conservation and Recycling*, 152, 104513. doi:10.1016/j.resconrec.2019.104513

Sindakis, S., & Aggarwal, S. (2022). *E-business Adoption by Small Businesses: Benefits and Drawbacks. In Small Business Management and Control of the Uncertain External Environment*. Emerald Publishing Limited.

Tanhan, A., & Young, J. S. (2022). Muslims and mental health services: A concept map and a theoretical framework. *Journal of Religion and Health*, 61(1), 23–63. doi:10.100710943-021-01324-4 PMID:34241742

Tornatzky, L. G., Fleischer, M., & Chakrabarti, A. K. (1990). *Processes of technological innovation.* Lexington Books.

Trawnih, A., Yaseen, H., Al-Adwan, A. S., Alsoud, R., & Jaber, O. A. (2021). Factors influencing social media adoption among smes during Covid-19 crisis. *Journal of Management Information and Decision Sciences, 24*, 1–18.

Triantafillidou, A., & Yannas, P. (2020). Social media crisis communication in racially charged crises: Exploring the effects of social media and image restoration strategies. *Computers in Human Behavior, 106*, 106269. doi:10.1016/j.chb.2020.106269

Ullah, F., Sepasgozar, S. M., Thaheem, M. J., & Al-Turjman, F. (2021). Barriers to the digitalisation and innovation of Australian Smart Real Estate: A managerial perspective on the technology non-adoption. *Environmental Technology & Innovation, 22*, 101527. doi:10.1016/j.eti.2021.101527

Wang, S. S., Goh, J. R., Sornette, D., Wang, H., & Yang, E. Y. (2021). *Government support for SMEs in response to COVID-19: Theoretical model using Wang transform.* China Finance Review International.

Wang, Y., & Yang, Y. (2020). Dialogic communication on social media: How organizations use Twitter to build dialogic relationships with their publics. *Computers in Human Behavior, 104*, 106183. doi:10.1016/j.chb.2019.106183

Zhong, Y., Oh, S., & Moon, H. C. (2021). Service transformation under industry 4.0: Investigating acceptance of facial recognition payment through an extended technology acceptance model. *Technology in Society, 64*, 101515. doi:10.1016/j.techsoc.2020.101515

Chapter 9
Efficacy of Social Media Usage on the Performance of SMEs in the Fashion Industry

Barkha
Maharshi Daynand University, India

Deepanshi Aggarwal
Maharshi Dayanand University, India

ABSTRACT

The fashion industry has become more globally competitive as a result of increased globalisation. The recent introduction of new technologies has presented opportunities as well as obstacles for the fashion industry, especially for small and medium-sized businesses (SMEs) whose low resources may make it difficult for them to adopt new technology. But, with the rise of social media, fashion SMEs have new opportunities that can help them become more visible and boost their sales. Accordingly, the present study attempts to analyse the efficacy of social media usage on the performance of SMEs in fashion industry. The study will use both qualitative and quantitative approach to examine the social media usage in terms of reach, richness, affiliation, and influence on SMEs performance. Data will be collected from 400 SMEs in Delhi through questionnaire and their respective social media account (Facebook). Results of the study show that most of the small and medium-sized enterprises used social media for business purpose, and their performance is improved after using social media.

INTRODUCTION

Internet advancements have had a significant impact on business success over the past two decades. Web 2.0 applications give people the chance to bring internet functionality into social settings where they can engage in online social interaction. Social media is a useful cyberspace for finding up-to-date, accurate information. Online learning and information sharing are made easier by the widespread usage of social media. Social media enables people to communicate and create content without the requirement for physi-

DOI: 10.4018/978-1-6684-5770-2.ch009

cal presence. Additionally, social media has been viewed as a powerful advertising tool for businesses to achieve their commercial objectives and improve performance. Most businesses use social media to boost their brand awareness and image, Additionally, eWOM (electronic word of mouth) is influenced by firm branding tactics via social media. As a result, eWOM draws customers and strengthens their intent to buy. Consumers have access to a variety of sources of shared information from other customers regarding their experiences and recommendations by using social media. This has an impact on their shopping choices. As a result, social media's crucial role in building relationships and trust with clients, suppliers, and future partners is a crucial factor for businesses. Participating in social media can benefit a company's brand value (Nisar & Whitehead, 2016), sales growth (Kumar, Bhaskaran, Mirchandani, & Shah, 2013), e-commerce and social commerce (Hajli, 2014), consumer trust and stickiness (Zhang et al., 2017), among other benefits. innovation and new product development (Roberts & Candi, 2014); knowledge sharing (Munar & Jacobsen, 2014); CRM, customer relationship management, (Rosman & Stuhura, 2013), eWOM (Ladhari & Michaud, 2015). Therefore, social media are regarded as one of the contemporary electronic marketing tools that are distinct from other traditional marketing techniques.

Small and medium-sized enterprises (SMEs) are the most often adopted business model in India and are responsible for the economic vitality of the majority of developing and rising economies world-wide. They produce more than 80% of the jobs in India, where they are viewed as engines of economic progress. A number of factors, including the usage of social media, have been linked to the growth of SMEs (Pentina, Koh & Le, 2012). It has not been determined whether the usage of social media directly affects the expansion of SMEs, despite studies showing that they provide value to businesses. Looking at the fashion sector, it was determined that the sector would have expanded more if it had accepted the use of ICT to establish its place in the market. The Indian fashion industry has demonstrated interest in integrating social media into its operations over the past few years, but it's crucial to determine whether this has any impact on the industry's growth. Further, the fashion industry has become more globally competitive as a result of increased globalisation. In addition, the recent introduction of new technologies has presented opportunities as well as obstacles for the fashion industry, especially for small and medium-sized businesses (SMEs) whose low resources may make it difficult for them to adopt new technology. SMEs today operate in a changing environment and must manage a variety of resources to remain competitive. The fashion sector operates in a more complex environment where businesses must quickly react to changing consumer demands. With the rise of social media, fashion SMEs now have new marketing alternatives that can help them become more visible in the marketplace and boost the volume of their sales. Accordingly, the present endeavor attempts analyse the efficacy of Social media usage on the performance of SMEs in fashion industry.

REVIEW OF RELATED LITERATURE

Social marketing is described by Lazer and Kelly's (1973) as "concerning the application of marketing knowledge, concepts, and strategies to enhance social as well as economic purposes." Analysis of the social effects of marketing policies, choices, and actions are also included in its scope. Abu Bashar et al. (2012) examined the extent, social media that helps consumers in buying decision making. This purpose of this study is to suggest strategies to bridge the gap between expectation and performance to improve its effectiveness. The descriptive research design employed in this study. Non-probability convenience sampling techniques were chosen to select the respondents from the population. Primary data was collected from the 150 social networkers through the questionnaire and Google form. Regression analysis technique were used to analyse the data. e medium is growing very fast and holds huge potential but is still in its nascent stage in India. Therefore, it is time for the companies to make effective strategies and execute them to win larger share of business through this revolutionary medium and become the innovative firm of coming future. With the significant development of social media influence, which is altering how consumers obtain information and make purchasing decisions, Benjamin (2013) focused on the evolution of marketing methods used by firms and, more specifically, the evolution of their communication strategies. This study highlighted the need for businesses of all sizes, small and large, to go online, use social media, and alter their business strategies if they want to stay ahead of the competition in their industries. Oztamur et al. (2014) aimed to explore the role of social media for SMEs as a new marketing tool from the perspective of firm performance. Case study approach is employed in the study. This study compares and analyse the Facebook and Twitter accounts in terms of number of likes, followers, richness of content, use of language and the interaction with the customers of four American and Turkish companies between the period of January and February 2014. The results of the study show that American company is more efficient and successful than the Turkish companies in terms of content, use of language and interaction with customers. According to Farzana et al. (2014) organisations are now creating and managing social media public pages to strengthen their social network presence, increase interest in their organisations, and develop interactions with the online public. Social media is utilised in enterprises for a variety of goals, including branding, information search, customer relationship development, advertising and promotion, and many more, according to a study concentrating on the perspectives of social media managers. The findings also demonstrate that social media has a higher impact on firms' performance in terms of improving customer interactions and customer service activities, enhancing information accessibility, and lowering marketing and customer service costs. Tajvidi and Karami (2017) investigated the influence of social media on the performance of smes with mediating role of marketing capabilities in the hotel industry of United Kingdom. This study is entirely based on primary data. Primary data was collected from 384 hotels in the UK by distributing a questionnaire during the year 2015. Sample hotels were collected by employing the stratified random sampling. Structural Equation Modelling was employed to analyse the collected data. Findings of the study demonstrate the significant positive relationship between the social media use and firm performance. D. Lakshmanan and Dr. S. Rabiyathul Basariya (2017) conducted research on the efficiency of social networking site advertising. The study discovers that the calibre of the messages or contents, the company's involvement, and its affiliation with other marketing platforms all have a significant impact on the efficacy of social media marketing. To effectively calculate the return on investment of social media marketing, a comprehensive and in-depth examination of the approach is also required. The survey also reveals that while members of generation Y may be the primary users of social media platforms, they are not the primary target market for social media advertising. Chatterjee and Kar (2020) have investigated the causes and effects of social media marketing use by businesses. The goal of the article was to identify the elements that could enhance the contribution of SMEs to the Indian economy. In order to do this, a theoretical model based on the Technology Adoption Model (TAM) and data gathered from 310 businesses that was subjected to structural equation modelling analysis were produced. The findings demonstrate that social media marketing by SMEs is significantly influenced by elements such as perceived platform compatibility, perceived platform usability, and perceived platform usability by business owners. Adoption of social media negatively influenced by the cost of social media marketing among the small and medium enterprises. Hanafizadeh et al. (2021) aimed to identify the consequence of social media usage on firm performance. The purpose of this study is to develop a conceptual map that demonstrates potential connections between an organization's social media usage maturity level realisation and its corresponding performance effects. The performance theory and the theory of growth and maturity in social media were combined to create the conceptual map, which was then developed by methodical mapping. Following a thorough literature assessment of the impact of social media on corporate performance, the conceptual map was created. This conceptual map states that the organisation will gain from accessing and sharing information once it reaches the initial level of maturity. The realisation of the second stage is expected to result in more customer relationships, and the third stage will be followed by product and new process development. It is expected that by advancing the organisation to the fourth stage, communication with the organization's stakeholders will emerge through social media. Social media will assist with value creation in the fifth stage. Managers and professionals can thus predict what performance benefits they will receive if each stage of maturity is achieved. Emmanuel et al. (2022) aimed to review the effect of social media on business performance. In order to respond this question, "How does the use of SM impact how businesses perform" the paper provides a thorough systematic review. The study studied 70 research papers using the PRISMA and Citation Searching approach. They divided them into seven categories based on themes, adopting and revising the SM adoption state-of-the-art literature review by Dwivedi et al., (2021), and Afful-Dadzie et al (2021). According to the study's results, B2B companies' use of SM has a favourable impact on customer retention, transaction costs, customer relationship management, and financial performance. Additionally, SMEs use SM to interact with clients and develop lasting relationships with them. Additionally, using social media facilitates the development of networks with stakeholders and other possible investors.

Over the last several years, a remarkable shift has occurred in the business sector, with small, medium, and large entrepreneurial firms making the most of the resources available to them on social media platforms with less money and time wasted than on traditional marketing. The majority of earlier research analysed the influence of micro, small, and medium-sized businesses' use of social media on their financial performance. A small number of research looked at how social media usage affected fashion sectors' non-financial performance. That is why, this study will explore the usage of social media platforms among small and medium enterprise under fashion industry in Delhi and its influence on performance. The purpose of this analysis is to give contribution to the existing research on social media and SMEs and to provide a fresh approach on performance evaluation for those studies.

JUSTIFICATION OF THE STUDY

The MSME sector drives the Indian economy. MSME is the second-largest employment sector after agriculture. It accounts for 6% of GDP and 40% of total exports. It is often regarded as the foundation of the country's production, adaptability, and wealth. The use of social media as a marketing tool to interact with potential customers, outperform competitors, and improve firm performance is a growing trend among Indian small enterprises. Small businesses and social media marketing are likely to complement one other. When compared to large worldwide firms, MSME have a smaller fraction of their marketing budget available. These budget constraints, along with the very low expenses of social media marketing. It signifies a significant opportunity for MSME to increase their marketing efforts through social media marketing at a reasonable cost. Despite the fact that many businesses use social media marketing, the use of social media inside MSME in the fashion sector has yet to be properly examined. The goal of this research is to better understand the nature and extent of social media usage among SMEs. This study will attempt to determine the impact of social media usage among SMEs in the Delhi fashion industry.

RESEARCH OBJECTIVE

The purpose of this study is to investigate the influence of social media usage on the performance of SMEs in Fashion Industry.

METHODOLOGY

The overall plan for a study that focuses on how it will be carried out is called the research design. The study will employ a qualitative and quantitative research approach. This research study intends to examine the social media usage in terms of reach, richness and affiliation. *Reach- the firms' access and connection to customers, Richness- depth and detail of two-way information between the SMEs and customer, Affiliation- facilitating useful interaction with customers.* Due to their broad usage and consumer appeal, we focused on the "Facebook" network in this study. The primary methodology for this particular work is qualitative content analysis (Zdemir, 2010), as the ultimate goal is to determine how strategically the businesses use social media, including the contents they select, the frequency with which they update their accounts, the language they employ, and the effectiveness of their communication. A qualitative-exploratory approach was selected to explore how businesses use social media in order to acquire practical insights into effective social media marketing, which frequently relies on qualitative metrics for desirable signs of the tone, quality, and consumer value of the engagement.

In order to examine the performance of SMEs in the fashion industry in Delhi and learn more about how they view social media as a marketing tool, a quantitative research approach is also chosen. This way, new social media strategies that could help these businesses perform better and be recommended to other businesses in a similar industry can be explored (Bulearca and Bulearca, 2010:301). For this reason, the questionnaire for the online and offline survey was created using straightforward language that is simple to grasp. The non-financial performance factors were taken from Ainin et al. (2015) and Qalati et al (2021). Items for financial performance were taken from Ahmad et al. and Qalati et al., both published in 2021. (2018). The five point likert scale of 1 to 5 points (strongly agree, agree, neutral, disagree and strongly disagree) was used for all the variables.

Sample Selection

The population for this study is the social media handlers in SMEs of Delhi. The method used for selecting the sample is purposive sampling. A total of 400 respondents (social media handlers) from Delhi were selected in this study.

FINDINGS

The majority of SMEs have Facebook profiles, but what matters is how well the company performs when using social media as a new marketing strategy tool. Companies should add value for the consumers in order to have a competitive edge. The use of social media may be helpful in this process. As part of the case study, we selected small and medium-sized businesses from the Delhi to compare their social media efforts. In the current year, the Delhi has about 9 lakh micro, small, and medium firms (MSME Annual Report 2021-22). Selected industry and companies were picked for their theoretical significance and unique social network marketing concepts, as well as the suitability of their sizes and industry structure (B2C). All of the businesses that were chosen have strong brands that are well-known to their target audiences, as well as businesses that have social media presences that reflect their sector. This is the main reason why these businesses were picked. The observations and analyses were completed during October and November 2022. We gathered data from the chosen company's social media accounts and concentrated on particulars like the number of likes and followers, frequency of the updates, richness and relevance of the content, interaction of the engagement, and language use.

Fashion Industry Analysis

Initially, medium-sized businesses in Delhi have interesting content for their target clients on their Facebook business page in a variety of ways. To begin, they post various types of surveys, contests, and inquiries in order to pique the interest of their customers. This is a great example of consumer engagement. Second, they post surveys on some clothing and colour. They occasionally publish photos of their designer and staff as stuff. The company not only shares photos, but also high-resolution clips regarding the backstage and the designs. Furthermore, they provide fashion information and advice, which amplifies the content's purpose. They never fail to remember to mark noteworthy occasions. Another significant point is that the company publishes client feedback on their Facebook business page. This is also essential for keeping customers. This SMEs in the fashion sector in Delhi is very active in developing social media content. For example, they participate in numerous activities and upload images on their social media pages to inform their customers. This endeavour can be regarded as an outstanding plan. Because the company refreshes its Facebook business page every day and posts multiple pieces of material that are actually rich, relevant, and eye-catching, the interaction and engagement with customers is quite effective. At the same time, they respond to practically every consumer inquiry and feedback. The responses are not cliche; rather, they virtually always respond in a unique manner. Whether it is a complaint or a compliment, the corporation responds by repeating the customer's name. When we look at how they use language, the corporation is completely different from the other comparative firm in terms of phrasing. To begin with, their language is not stiff; additionally, they respond to inquiries as if both the designer and the owner of the organisation would not do so. Their phrasing is storytelling-like and genuine. Furthermore, they appreciate colourful descriptions, which has a favourable impact on the overall frame of the content.

Table 1. General Overview of the selected firms under Fashion industry social media activity analysis

Firms Profile	Small Sized Firms	Medium Sized Firms
The number of likes	30125*	254123*
The frequency of update	Everyday	Almost Everyday
Richness and relativeness of the content to take attention of target customers:	Quite rich customer oriented content	Product related content as well as customer oriented content
Interaction of the engagement with customers:	Effective (as responding all questions and comments)	Special relevance of interacting for more personal manner
The use of language:	Quite sincere (friendly style)	Quite formal
Punctuation or spelling mistakes:	Well written (there is not any orthographic mistakes)	Well written (there is not any orthographic mistakes)

On the other hand, small sized Fashion Company often shares the photos of their latest fashion collection on the Facebook business page. Besides, they post discount announcements, small surveys and small questions. The company has one video backstage; however, there are some complaints from the customers regarding the low resolution of this video. One of the most important and remarkable point is that; they engage with the followers and form two-way communication through the use of Facebook business page. There are some comments under almost every picture and the content they post. Customer complaints, comments and questions are replied. Meanwhile, the company asks for the contact information of that particular follower in order to keep in touch. In addition to this, whenever a customer asks a question about a size or color of an outfit; they always reply and try to find a solution or if a customer complains about the quality of an outfit; they immediately report the problem. Nevertheless, this Company uses the formal wording in the social-media communication and the answers are given with same words. Besides the all valuable efforts on social media to communicate with target customers, their language still needs more human touch.

Table 2 shows that the majority of SMEs in the sample can be consider moderate adopters of social media. In total, 62.5 percent had started to use social media more than 3 years and 39.5 percent of them made moderate use of social media. 31.5 percent respondents said that they use social media for business pupose extensively. This indicate that they tend to use social media (Facebook) to communicate their relationship with customers and for improving their brand awareness. The majority of the respondents reported that they spent less than 3 hours each day on social media.

Table 3 shows the financial and non-financial performance of SMEs in fashion industry. Firstly, non-financial performance, majority of SMEs agreed that after using the social media platforms such as Facebook improved their relationship with customers, increased their brand awareness and reputation. In case of financial performance, most of smes in Delhi agreed that their profits and sales has increased and their cost of communicating with customers is reduced and also social media is much effective than traditional media.

Table 2. Descriptive analysis

Demographic	Characteristics	Frequency	Percent
Gender	Male	210	52.5%
	Female	190	47.5
Age	Less than 30	110	27.5
	30-40	125	31.25
	40-50	108	27
	Over 50	57	14.25
Education	Secondary	99	24.75
	Diploma	70	17.5
	Graduation	105	26.25
	Post-Graduation	126	31.5
Position	Owner	160	40
	Executive	90	22.5
	Manager	102	25.5
	Senior Manager	48	11.2
Number of years since initial adoption	Less than 2 years	60	15
	2-3 years	90	22.55
	3-4 years	135	33.75
	More than 4 years	115	28.75
Hours spent on social media	Less than 3 hours	179	44.75
	3-6 hours	122	30.5
	6-7 hours	60	15
	More than 7 hours	39	9.7
Level of utilization of social media	Basic	116	27.5
	Moderate	158	39.5
	Extensive	126	31.5

Table 3. Performance of SMEs using Facebook

Performance	Strongly Agree	Agree	Neutral	Disagree	Strongly Disagree	Total
Improved Customer Relationship	189	140	40	10	21	400
Improved brand visibility and Reputation	140	165	29	35	31	400
Increased awareness and market share	170	119	36	52	23	400
Enhanced customer service	155	163	50	22	10	400
Increased sales and profits	140	134	50	47	29	400
Reduced the cost of market communication	156	179	30	17	18	400

CONCLUSION

The purpose of this paper is to investigate the influence of social media usage on the performance of SMEs in Fashion Industry. During a specific time period, the target was to concentrate on certain aspects of their social media accounts, including: the number of likes, the frequency of updates, the richness and relevance of the content, the interaction of engagement, the use of language, and any grammatical or punctuation errors. These are crucial aspects since, in particular, SMEs, may maintain their position and build a following of devoted clients by effectively utilising the aforementioned social network marketing features (SNM). To compare small and medium sized businesses operating in the same industry, the study examined the Facebook accounts of a selected sample of "fashion SMEs" in Delhi. With regard to a new marketing strategy, the findings provide the ability to comment on the various performances and points of view of the firms' usage of social media. From the perspective of a social media marketing network, the research aims to demonstrate how successful and active these firms' social media profiles are. These results suggest that, as compared to small businesses' usage of social media, medium-sized businesses are more likely to implement the necessary strategies and characteristics. After utilising the social media "Facebook" network, both small and medium-sized businesses performed better in terms of enhanced customer relationships, sales, and profitability, among other things. Dynamic businesses, like "fashion SMEs," keep striving than traditional industries on social media, which undoubtedly influences the number of customers they have as followers. Finally, we discovered that even businesses with similar size and scope may choose various strategies for using social media strategically, and these differences become clear when a systematic comparison is done between them. The key suggestion of this paper is that SMEs should invest time in creating engaging content for their social media accounts in order to draw in their target audience if they intend to utilise social media as a competitive marketing tool. Additionally, they should communicate with their target customers with more sincerity, prefer a friendlier tone, and respond promptly to any requests for communication from those customers.

LIMITATIONS AND FUTURE RESEARCH DIRECTIONS

This study has certain limitations, just like every other scientific study does. The first part of this study looks on SMEs involved in the business-to-consumer firm's social media (Facebook account) efforts. The Facebook account of a few targeted sample enterprises was observed as part of the qualitative content analysis chosen as the research methodology. Despite the fact that the questionnaire was designed to collect data from sample enterprises, responsible employees from the chosen businesses tragically declined to participate in our interview. Thus, the conclusions in our research are solely based on our external observations. In order to get more particular and extensive information on the social network marketing initiatives of their companies and to meet their overall marketing objectives, future researchers should interview key informants In the future studies, it's also important to keep an eye on other social media accounts (such Instagram, LinkedIn, Youtube, Twitter, etc.). On the other hand, comprehensive research methodologies with broad industry comparison, diverse geographic location, and high sample size may be designed for future investigations. This sort of study application may be helpful to determine what social network marketing initiatives improve the performance of the businesses in other areas. In order to improve the efficiency of achieving marketing objectives, organisations should consider how to plan their social media activities for various clusters of social media followers.

REFERENCES

Adegbuyi, O. A., Akinyele, F., & Akinyele, S. (2015). Effect of Social Media Marketing on Small Scale Business Performance in Ota-Metropolis, Nigeria. *International Journal of Social Sciences and Management*, 2(3), 275–283. doi:10.3126/ijssm.v2i3.12721

Ahmad, S. Z., Abu Bakar, A. R., Faziharudean, T. M., & Mohamad Zaki, K. A. (2014). An Empirical Study of Factors Affecting e-Commerce Adoption among Small- and Medium-Sized Enterprises in a Developing Country: Evidence from Malaysia. *Information Technology for Development*, 21(4), 555–572. doi:10.1080/02681102.2014.899961

Bajpai, V., Pandey, D. S., & Shriwas, M. S. (2012). Social media marketing: Strategies & its impact. *International Journal of Social Science & Interdisciplinary Research*, 1(7), 214–223.

Bashar, A., Ahmad, I., & Wasique, M. (2021). Effectiveness of social media as a marketing tool: An empirical study. *International Journal of Marketing, Financial Services & Management Research*, 1(11).

Benjamin, A. (2013). *The current development and trends of social media marketing strategies for businesses-Case study on an internet marketing company: Lead Creation* [Bachelor's thesis]. Turku University of Applied Sciences.

Bhanot, S. (2012). Use of social media by companies to reach their customers. *SIES Journal of Management*, 8(1), 47.

Chatterjee, S., & Kar, A. K. (2020). Why do small and medium enterprises use social media marketing and what is the impact: Empirical insights from India. *International Journal of Information Management*, 53, 102103. doi:10.1016/j.ijinfomgt.2020.102103

Chong, S. (2006, August). An Empirical Study of Factors That Influence the Extent of Deployment of Electronic Commerce for Small- and Medium-Sized Enterprises in Australia. *Journal of Theoretical and Applied Electronic Commerce Research*, 1(2), 45–57. doi:10.3390/jtaer1020012

Das, B. B., & Subudhi, R. N. (2016). *Influence of Socio-Economic Factors in Digital and Social Media Marketing: An Empirical Study in India. SSRN Electronic Journal.* doi:10.2139srn.2843076

El-Gohary, H. (2012). Factors affecting E-Marketing adoption and implementation in tourism firms: An empirical investigation of Egyptian small tourism organisations. *Tourism Management*, 33(5), 1256–1269. doi:10.1016/j.tourman.2011.10.013

Emmanuel, B., Zhao, S., Egala, B. S., Mammet, Y., & Godson, K. (2022). Social Media and Its Connection to Business Performance—A Literature Review. *American Journal of Industrial and Business Management*, 12(5).

Farzana, P., Noor, I. J., & Sulaiman, A. (2014). Social media usage and organizational performance: Reflections of Malaysian social media managers. *Science Direct. Telematics and Informatics*, 32, 67–78.

Gumus, N., & Kutahyali. (2017). Perception of social media by small & medium enterprises (SME's) in Turkey. *International Journal of Business Communication*, 12.

Hanafizadeh, P., Shafia, S., & Bohlin, E. (2021). Exploring the consequence of social media usage on firm performance. *Digital Business.*, *1*(2), 100013. Advance online publication. doi:10.1016/j.dig-bus.2021.100013

Illahi, S. (2015). Micro, Small and Medium Enterprises (MSMEs) in Delhi: Problems and Prospects. *International Journal of Research and Development - A Management Review, 4*(4).

Lakshmanan, D., & Rabiyathul Basariya, S. (2017). The Role of Social Media On Enhancing Advertising Effectiveness. *International Journal of Civil Engineering and Technology*, *8*(9), 1042–1047. http://www.iaeme.com/IJCIET/ issues.asp?JType=IJCIET&VType=8 &IType=9

Lazer, W., & Kelley, E. J. (1973). *Social Marketing: Perspectives and Viewpoints*. Richard D. Irwin.

Oztamur, D., & Karakadilar, S. I. (2012). Exploring the role of social media for SMEs: As a new marketing strategy tool for the firm performance perspective. *Procedia: Social and Behavioral Sciences*, 1877–0428.

Sharma, S., & Rehman, A. (2016). Social media marketing: A study of select sectors in India. *International Journal of Management*, *5*(4), 2277–5846.

Sin, S. S., Nor, K. M., & Al-Agaga, A. M. (2012). Factors Affecting Malaysian young consumers' online purchase intention in social media websites. *Procedia: Social and Behavioral Sciences*, *40*, 326–333. doi:10.1016/j.sbspro.2012.03.195

Tajvidi, R., & Karami, A. (2017). The effect of social media on firm performance. *Computers in Human Behavior*, *115*, 105174. doi:10.1016/j.chb.2017.09.026

Chapter 10
Examination of the Effect of New Media in Revolutionizing Entrepreneurship in Bauchi State, Nigeria

Roxie Ojoma Ola-Akuma
Bingham University, Nigeria

Desmond Onyemechi Okocha
https://orcid.org/0000-0001-5070-280X
Bingham University, Nigeria

Josiah Sabo Kente
Nasarawa State University, Nigeria

ABSTRACT

Nano, micro, small, and medium enterprises (NMSMEs) are still heavily reliant on the "brick-and-mortar" system or traditional street-side business methodology, which is no longer as efficient as it once was. In contrast to the foregoing, this study examined the effect of new media on nano and micro enterprises (MSSBs) in Nigeria. Hinged on the technology acceptance model (TAM) and theory of digital divide, the research employed a survey method to generate responses from micro business owners within 36 business categories in Bauchi Metropolis by deploying 100 questionnaires to a random sample size. Chi-Square test calculator and sample median test were used to examine the various hypotheses at a 5% level of significance. The analysis revealed that there was no significant positive relationship between new media products' usage and increased business performance in Bauchi. This is because the majority of NME owners were still unaware of what new media products could offer them. As such, NME owners need to be trained to adopt the new media tools in order to boost NMEs in this region.

DOI: 10.4018/978-1-6684-5770-2.ch010

INTRODUCTION

The need for survival, expansion, customer satisfaction, generation of extraordinary value for customers and other stakeholders, the establishment of new product lines and service offerings, profitability, lower operating costs, and development into a great enterprise are all common business goals for Micro, Small and Medium Scale Enterprises (MSMEs). Although, whether big or small, enterprises continue to depend on government to create an enabling environment where risks are minimised and well managed. In addition, the proper management of customs, laws, regulations, policies, trade agreements and public infrastructure will facilitate ease of movement of a product or service along its value chain (Onyinyechukwu, 2020). With these expectations, the advancements in Information Communication and Technology (ICT), the use of new media tools such as the internet, social media, and digital devices such as mobile smart phones have changed the way and manner in which businesses are now conducted.

According to Appel, Grewal, Hadi et al. (2020), in recent years, the use of new media platforms such as social media by company owners has become an essential platform for promoting their products and services to customers. The media as a tool has long been a visually appealing marketing tactic utilised by huge corporations to engage with prospective consumers. Consequently, the combinations of the Internet and other digital media have caused disruptive innovation in the business space. This development, which is currently ongoing, has resulted in continuity in transactions happening within the online world as it is not limited by the time of the day where traditional businesses would operate between a time-frame daily. When compared to three to four decades ago, there has been a significant shift in how business is conducted nowadays thanks to globalisation. As Quade & Leimstoll (2015) point out, cell phones have ubiquitous uses in many regions of the world as they are utilised for both personal and professional purposes.

It should be noted that, while social media was designed primarily as a means of socialising, some business owners have recognised the commercial prospects that they provide and have opted to use them to promote their enterprises. According to Gielens & Steenkamp (2019) the rise of E-commerce retailers, has taken advantage of new media tools such as social networking sites (Facebook and Instagram), Microblogs (Twitter) and E-commerce sites (Konga and Jumia) as a marketing opportunity. This has helped to cut out the conventional intermediary cost of advertising which middlemen usually profited from as they had previously made connecting businesses directly to customers difficult. In 2019, Chivandi, Samuel, & Muchie posited that the use of these new media products has significantly changed how consumers and marketers communicate and even engage in business transactions.

The challenges surrounding the "brick-and-mortar" system or traditional street-side business that offers products and services to its customers face-to-face either in an office or store that the business owns, or rents include the high cost of maintenance, long travel and delivery times which requires their physical presence to buy and sell. This has made them unable to deliver their products and services except they are present. Also, this long process of activity ends as within the locality of the business owner as opposed to the new media environment that allows businesses to continue globally.

Online media has also enabled customers to survey, select, and purchase products and services from businesses around the world. Peer communication through social media sites like Facebook and Instagram has become a new form of consumer socialisation which has a profound influence on consumer decision making and, consequently, on marketing strategies. The consumer socialisation theory predicts that communication among consumers affects their cognitive, affective, and behavioural attitudes (Al Kailani and Kumar, 2011). New media tools, therefore, might be considered as an important agent of consumer socialisation. In Nigeria, both large and small enterprise owners have also joined millions of internet users, to reach out to customers and new shoppers by promoting and offering their products and services to them online.

The mortality rate among MEs in Nigeria is very high within their first five years of existence. The reasons for the high mortality rate include the following among others: Many prospective entrepreneurs do not have a clear vision and mission of what they intend to do. Many of the SMEs are not business specific and hence have no focus and are easily blown away by the wind. With the dismantling of trade barriers as part of globalisation, SMEs in developing countries such as Nigeria are facing intense competition from industries of other countries, which have enabling environment for production, distribution, and marketing. For instance, the environment in which SMEs in Europe, South East Asia and America operate provides stable power and water supply, standard road and rail network, efficient water and air transport system, advanced technology, modern communication facilities, efficient and responsive financial system and above all good governance. This is not the case in Nigeria where hostile occurrences and policies stifle the survival of SMEs in the global competitive drive.

According to the National policy, an enterprise may be classified by size, sector, organisation, technology, and location. In practice, the number of employees is the most common standard used in National SMEs policies worldwide; in this manner, the classification for small scale businesses or enterprises as adopted by the National Policy on MSMEs earlier, before 2020, had mainly 3 categories as shown in Figure 1.

Figure 1. Data from MSME 2017 survey report

SECTOR	MICRO	SMALL	MEDIUM
Employment Band	1-9	10-49	50-199

From the table above, a micro enterprise is one that is capable of employing a maximum of 9 and minimum of 1 staff – with less than 10,000,000 Naira excluding land and buildings. Small Enterprises are those enterprises whose total assets (excluding land and building) are above 10,000,000 Naira but not exceeding 100, 000,000 Naira with a total workforce of above 10, but not exceeding 49 employees. Medium Enterprises are those enterprises with total assets (excluding land and building) which are above 50,000,000 Naira, but not exceeding 1,000,000,000 Naira with a total workforce of between 50 and 199 employees.

However, the latest report by SMEDAN (2021) revealed a new policy (to run from 2021 – 2025) with a new category *Nano* Enterprise. Hence shown in Figure 2.

Figure 2. Data from MSME 2021 survey report

S/N	CATEGORY	EMPLOYMENT SIZE	TURNOVER (Naira))
1.	Nano/Homestead Enterprises	1-2 persons	Less than 3 million
2.	Micro Enterprises	3-9 Persons	3 < 25 Million
3.	Small Enterprises	10-49 persons	25 < 100 Million
4.	Medium Enterprises	50-199 persons	100 Million < 1 Billion

The table above shows that the MEs have been further divided to accommodate for nano or homestead businesses which were earlier not factored in. A micro enterprise is one that is capable of employing a maximum of 9 and minimum of 3 staff – with less than 25,000,000 Naira excluding lands and buildings. The Nano Enterprise is one that is capable of employing a maximum of 2 staff – with less than 3,000,000 Naira excluding lands and buildings.

For the purpose of this study, Nano, and Micro Enterprises (NMEs) will be the scope. This is because, new media products are a new phenomenon that has changed how their business environment operates even in Nigeria. Medium Enterprises are able to gain access to digital resources that were otherwise not available to them in the past (Eze, Chinedu-Eze, Okike & Bello, 2020), however, it is an alarming issue that some NMEs are not conversant with social media networking apps, mobile and online banking, and E-commerce opportunities as they simply reject any form of payment or contacts which is not physical or cash. New media tools have also helped businesses to increase their worthiness, cultivate strategic partnerships and increase their contact with customers and suppliers.

While the wide acceptance and popular usage of new media products has made it possible for anyone who is interested to set up businesses of different types at any time, NMEs are below the bottom in the competing world regarding earning of profits compared with other business categories mainly because they do not employ modern techniques like digital marketing in their business activities through available new media products. They do not leverage on marketing and advertising campaigns which can be done almost for free online because the NMEs have yet to understand how new media products work as a global communication tool that can significantly improve their business performance. This could be tied to the digital divide which according to Dijk (2012) is the result of inequalities in four successive types: access motivation, physical access, digital skills, and different usage by the business owner. This is further justified by Gorbacheva, Niehaves, Plattfaut, & Becker (2011) who discovered that one of the strongest factors influencing the intention to adopt a technology such as internet banking services is the degree to which an individual believes that it is safe to use such services.

It is against this backdrop, that this study seeks to assess the effect of new media products on the business performance of NMEs across Bauchi State.

OBJECTIVES OF THE STUDY

The general objective or main objective of this study is to investigate the effect of new media tools on the NMEs in Nigeria.

The specific objectives are to:

1. Ascertain the effect of new media products on sales volume of NMEs in Bauchi State
2. Determine the relationship between new media products and business visibility of NMEs in Bauchi State.
3. X-ray the relationship between new media products and profitability of NMEs in Bauchi State.
4. Find out whether new media products are used by NMEs in Bauchi for their business.
5. Examine the knowledge of NMEs in Bauchi in the use of new media products.
6. Identify the challenges faced by NMEs in Bauchi in the use and adoption of new media products.

RESEARCH HYPOTHESES

The following hypotheses have been drawn to match the objectives of this study:

H_0. The use of new media products by NMEs in Bauchi State does not have a significant relationship on their sales volume.

H_1: The use of new media products by NMEs in Bauchi State has a significant relationship on their sales volume.

H_0: There is no significant relationship between new media products and business visibility of NMEs in Bauchi State.

H_1: There is a significant relationship between new media products and business visibility of NMEs in Bauchi State.

H_0: There is no significant relationship between new media products and profitability NMEs in Bauchi State.

H_1: There is a significant relationship between new media products and profitability of NMEs in Bauchi State.

H_0: NMEs in Bauchi do not use new media products for their businesses.

H_1: NMEs in Bauchi use new media products for their businesses.

H_0: NME owners in Bauchi do not know how to use new media products for their businesses.

H_1: NME owners in Bauchi know how to use new media products for their businesses.

THEORETICAL FRAMEWORK

Technology Acceptance Model (TAM)

TAM essentially describes how users of technology come to accept and use the technology. Davis (1989) developed TAM which specifies the causal relationships between system design features, perceived usefulness, perceived ease of use, attitude toward using and actual usage behaviour. When users are presented with a new technology, the decision about how and when to use it is influenced by several factors. These include perceived usefulness; the degree to which a person believes that using a particular system would enhance their job performance, and perceived ease of use; the degree to which a person believes that using a particular system would be free from effort. TAM has been used in a number of researches in new media use (Sheng & Zolfagharian, 2014; Pavlou, 2003; Pentina et al., 2012; Lee et al., 2006; Koufaris, 2002; Gekombe, Tumsifu & Jani, 2019).

Theory of Digital Divide

According to the theory of digital divide, there is an economic and social divide between the inhabitants of a country and their access to information and communication technologies. There are several explanations behind the digital divide. One of the main factors is the rising wealth disparity. As one's money rises, so does one's access to and the use of technology such as the internet. Access to technology and knowledge is hampered by poverty and economic restrictions. Individuals, households, and even geographical units have unequal access to, and use of digital technologies; particularly those intended for information and communications according to Pick & Sarkar (2016). In addition, according to Hartnett (2022), previously documented inequities in access were initially associated to computers, but have since expanded to include the Internet, information, and other digital technologies in current times. Mayhew (2015) also points out that the digital divide is more than just a technology barrier; it also encompasses unequal access to, capacity building in terms of access to resources, and even training in terms of usage and utility.

These theories are relevant to the study as they support the possible effects that new media have on NMEs. Furthermore, they explain why NME owners' select or do not select online media for their businesses.

REVIEW OF RELATED LITERATURE

New Media Tools and Products

According to Cote (2022), new media is any digitally distributed media, from newspaper articles and blogs to music and podcasts. It can also refer to any internet-related form of communication, from a website or email to mobile phones and streaming apps.

New media products such as social media sites, have risen in popularity in recent years, attracting a lot of attention from researchers and practitioners (Appel, Grewal, Hadi, et al., 2020). Edosomwan, Prakasan, Kouame, Watson, and Seymour (2011) define social media as a venue where users can engage with one another, share content, and express their personal opinions. Social media platforms are part of the new media tools which comes in various forms, as shown in the table 1.

Table 1. New media tools

New Media Tools	New Media Products
Social Networking Sites (SNS)	Facebook, Instagram,
Blogs	Blogger, WordPress
Microblogs	Twitter
Collaborative projects	Wikipedia
Content communities and Vlogs	YouTube, Vimeo, Vevo
Virtual game worlds	World of Warcraft
Virtual social worlds	Second Life
Calls	Mobile smart phones
E-commerce Sites	Jumia, Konga, Jiji and Amazon

The table above shows a variety of new media tools against the products. Olsen & Christensen (2015) posit that online technologies have revolutionised the way individuals communicate with one another and even do business. What is evident is that all of these new media tools need Internet connectivity to be accessed and to function through a digital device. With the availability of the range of sites with various features and user groups, consumers have many alternatives when it comes to their purpose to utilise online tools via the internet. The new media arena has evolved into a popular venue for communication, networking, and information exchange. For the purpose of this study, the categories that will be used are –11 Social networking sites specifically: WhatsApp, Twitter, Facebook, Tiktok, YouTube, Pinterest, LinkedIn, Instagram, Likee, Snapchat and Telegram. and E-commerce Sites.

Social Networking Sites, Business Visibility and Sales

While the terms social media and social networking sites or services seem to be used interchangeably, they are different. Social media is a collective term for websites and applications that focus on communication, community-based input, interaction, content-sharing, and collaboration (Lutkevich & Wigmore, 2021). While Social networking sites (SNSs) are virtual communities where users can create individual public profiles, interact with real-life friends, and meet other people based on shared interests using social media (Boyd & Ellison, 2007; Watermeyer, 2012; Griffiths, Kuss & Demetrovics, 2014). Any web site that allows social interaction is considered a social media site, including social networking sites such as Facebook, MySpace, and Twitter; gaming sites and virtual worlds such as Club Penguin, Second Life, and the Sims; video sites such as YouTube; and blogs (O'Keeffe & Clarke-Pearson, 2011).

Due to the varying definitions and the evolving range of stand-alone and built-in social networking services in the online space, Obar & William (2015) came up with four features which they proposed could suffice to for social networking services.

These include:

1. Those with Internet-based applications which can be downloaded on a smart device such as Android or iPhones.

2. Those with user-generated content (UGC) which allows users to create content — photos, video, text, etc. Businesses take advantage of this as when consumers post about a brand on social media, they influence their followers' buying decisions.
3. Users create service-specific profiles for the site or app that are designed and maintained by the SNS companies such as Facebook or WhatsApp that allow users to sign up.
4. A tool that facilitates the development of online social networks by connecting a user's profile with those of other individuals or groups.

Following these suggested features, Qalati, et.al. (2020) posits that with the changing technologies, the number of social media platforms are also increasing, making business owners and their customers to switch and become dynamic in its use. This is also making it quite difficult to place a strict call to just one platform. For example, by engaging on Facebook, Twitter, Instagram, and WhatsApp (all social media) is a routine activity that research has shown benefits people by enhancing communication, social connection, and even technical skills (O'Keeffe & Clarke-Pearson, 2011) which are required to do business in the 21st Century.

According to Petersen (2019) many businesses now effectively use social media to promote their products to make it visible and connect with customers. Although in emerging areas, the cry of fake news has become commonplace and consumer confidence in even traditional media outlets has been significantly eroded. This is because false, misleading, or confusing online sales content can harm the reputation of an enterprise and dissuade people from even considering the purchase of a business' products or services (Petersen, 2019).

SNSs are now a global phenomenon. As at September 2013, 73% of online adults were using an SNS of some kind and 42% were using more than one. In 2019, three scholars: Ojei Harrison Onyijen, Olusesan Michael Awoleye and Titilayo Olubunmi Olaposi went out to test the effectiveness of social media platforms for product marketing in south western Nigeria. Although this was a firm-level analysis, the results revealed that customer loyalty could be gained through the social media platforms by making it imperative for business aspiring to grow their market share to leverage on the available social media tools (Onyijen, Awoleye, & Olaposi, 2019). In another study conducted in South Africa, Iwu, Elvis & Tengeh (2017) resolved that social media is a likely remedy given the variety of the various usable platforms and their capacity for wider customer reach (Iwu, Elvis, & Tengeh, 2017). Kateri (2021) in an empirical study conducted on impact of social media adoption on performance of SMES in Kano State, Nigeria concluded that there was a strong statistical relationship between social media adoption and SMEs performance.

As at the time of this study, Facebook was the most popular platform (with more than 3.1 billion active users), Twitter, which in the previous year had 69.3 million active users, rose to 388 million users worldwide. Based on another report by internet live stats, Nigeria recorded a total of 86,219,965 internet users in 2016. This has moved up to over 109 million internet users - the highest number reported all over Africa as of January 2022 (Statista, 2022).

In parallel to general-purpose SNSs like Facebook and Twitter, online media has provided for businesses specific platforms where users can open Facebook Business or Instagram for Business accounts or WhatsApp Business where they can use marketing tools to run paid adverts to boost their visibility and increase their sales while still maintaining private social accounts for family and friends. The emerging trends are also making today's technologically savvy customers move to other convenient solutions to satisfy their daily needs hence SNS have opened the space to accommodate and target people wanting to access a particular product or service through the same sites.

Ecommerce Growth in Nigeria

E-commerce platforms like Jumia, Konga, Jiji and Fintech companies have brought new dynamics to everyday micro business, as many have been reported to increasingly turn to the internet for a variety of transactions. E-commerce is the use of the internet for marketing, identification, payment and delivery of goods and services. The internet has revolutionized the mode of business transactions by allowing customers to bank, invest, purchase, distribute, interact, explore, and study from nearly anywhere, and any time there is internet connectivity; thanks to E-commerce technologies. E-commerce is one of the many mobile commerce (M-commerce) developments that, to a considerable part, make paying for products and services not only convenient but also flexible for the present day more digitally savvy customer (Osakwe & Okeke, 2016).

Like every online activity, E-commerce activities require internet connectivity for users to access the platforms. According to Statista (2022), Digital Markets E-commerce highlights that revenue in the E-commerce market is projected to reach US$8.52bn in 2022 with a projected market volume of US$12.58bn by 2025. In the E-commerce market, the number of users is expected to amount to 122.5m users by 2025.

User penetration for E-commerce is projected to reach 41.9% in 2022 and further expected to hit 52.5% by 2025. Businesses have also benefited from the internet in respect of the ability to purchase data in any amount. For example, in 2020, the telecoms operator, Airtel, came up with a service designed to enable business enterprises to purchase large data minimum of 1 terabyte. Through this offer, most enterprises can continue to stay online to interact with their customers. During the Covid-19 pandemic in 2020, the telecoms operator Globacom came up with a service plan - *GLOBACOM Work From Home Extra Data Plan.* The plan was a data plan designed for subscribers who were working from home due to the lockdown.

According to (Lancaster, 2019) an analyst, Nigeria is supported by the expansion of national fibre backbone networks, platforms such as E-commerce, online banking and e-payments, e-health, e-learning, and e-government are evolving rapidly. The government had earlier updated its broadband ambitions with the aim to increase penetration from 30% by 2020 to 70% by 2021.

Mobile Phones Penetration in Nigeria

The launch of GSM in 2001 liberated Nigerians from the shackles of the once powerful, but now virtually insignificant, national telecoms monopoly NITEL This was because, the Nigerian telecommunications received a great boost with the coming of the Global System for Communication (GSM) that year (Olaoluwa, 2019). Subsequently in 2003, the Nigerian Communications Commission (NCC) was set up and tasked with the facilitation of investments in and entry into the Nigerian market for provision and supply of communications services, equipment, and facilities.

As of December 2021, there were 195,128,265 active mobile lines in Nigeria.

Figure 3. Active mobile lines in Nigeria
Source: Nigerian Communications Commission 2021

OPERATORS	Jun'21	Sep'21	Dec'21
MTN Nigeria Communication	73,571,192	73,566,926	73,594,682
Globacom Limited	50,130,540	52,934,990	54,817,353
Airtel	50,665,723	51,035,565	53,926,886
EMTS Limited	12,908,092	12,983,433	12,789,344
Sub-Total (GSM)	187,275,547	190,520,914	195,128,265

The data from NCC also shows that 229,248 Voice over Internet Protocol (VoIP) Calls were made as at December 2021. This shows the Facebook calls, WhatsApp calls, Skype calls which basically means calls done via the internet.

According to IWS, the Internet usage statistics shows that Nigeria recorded 92,699,924 Internet users which is 51.1% of the population as at June 2015. According to Lancaster (2019), Nigeria's Internet sector has been hindered by the country's underdeveloped and unreliable fixed-line infrastructure, but this is changing as competition intensifies and new technologies are able to deliver wireless broadband access. Econet was the first telecommunication service to launch its services in Nigeria on August 8, 2001 and has since changed names over 3 times to what we now have as Airtel and going head-to-head with MTN which also began operations in August of the same year (Olaoluwa, 2019).

Through the mobile phones, M-Commerce has been made possible. M-commerce or Mobile Commerce refers to any transaction, involving buying and selling of goods and services, which is initiated and completed by using mobile access to computer-mediated networks with the help of an electronic device. This is a sub dimension of E-commerce.

Classification of Businesses in Nigeria

Micro, Small and medium-sized enterprises (MSMEs) play critical roles in the development and success of varied economies. According to the Macro-Economic Outlook 2022, businesses are the engine of growth of a nation including Nigeria. When properly supported, MSMEs will greatly contribute to the development of Nigeria's National Economic Outcomes. MSMEs are a genuine vehicle for attaining national economic objectives such as employment creation and poverty reduction at an incredibly low investment cost. Small-scale firms in Nigeria as posited by Ayozie & Latinwo (2011) have also helped to build entrepreneurial skills and growth of indigenous technologies.

According to a World Bank data estimate, SMEs account for around 90% of firms and more than 50% of jobs globally. As a result, they account for a fairly large proportion of the overall number of commercial establishments in the country. However, SMEs in Nigeria have not succeeded admirably, and so have not played the expected crucial and active role in Nigeria's economic growth and development. According to Agwu and Emeti (2014), one such confirmation is that start-ups in Nigeria are confronting a financial quagmire.

MSMEs globally are known for the strategic and impactful contributions they make as a stimulus for the industrialisation of national economies.

Small and Medium Scale Enterprises, as posited by Oni & Daniya (2012), constitute an essential ingredient in the lubrication and development of any economy because they dominate the economy. In discussing the factors constraining the growth and survival of SMEs in Nigeria, Okpara (2011) noted that one of such was insufficient profits and low demand for product and services. Ogbo & Nwachukwu (2012) further justifies it through the economic development perspective adding that these factors are thus making SMEs perform below expectation. Yet in looking at MSMEs productivity in Nigeria, these statements are negated by Ajuwon, Ikhide, & Akotey (2017) who discovered that small businesses actually recorded high productivity growth rate in some subsectors of the economy that specialises in product customisation such as garment and furniture.

It should be noted that the Nano Enterprises were also considered under this survey.

Nano and Micro Businesses in Bauchi State

The latest report by Small & Medium Enterprises Development Agency of Nigeria (SMEDAN) and the National Bureau of Statistics (2021) revealed that the total number of MSMEs as at December 2020 stood at 39,654,385 with components as follows, Micro Enterprises – MEs: 38,413,420 (or 96.9%), Small and Medium Enterprises – SMEs: 1,240,965 (or 3.1%). The highest number of enterprises across all the classes was evident in Lagos State Nigeria. This is in contrast with the joint survey on MSMEs which was carried out by SMEDA and NBS in 2017 which recorded over 41,000,000 MSMEs. Statistics show that the drop in number could be tied to so many factors including limited access to innovations, information, access to markets and the covid-19 pandemic (SMEDAN, 2021).

The latest category of Nano businesses are the various "solopreneurs" and home-based businesses such as make-up artists, event planners, battery chargers, independent dispatch riders, vendors, P.O.S agents, call centre agents, fashion designer, vulcanizers, drycleaners, corner shop owners, single retail marketers, repairers, painters, business centre operators, market women and men in the various open markets, among others. Before now, they played an unrecognised but important role across the country. With the recent categorization by SMEDAN they have become the least by classification. With the new data, they are no longer unaccounted as they have also been recognised to constitute a large portion of Nigeria's economy according to investigations.

Report by Engidaw (2022) showed that COVID-19 disruptions did not affect all businesses equally as some were deemed essential and remained open, while others were required to close. Through online media some businesses could shift employees to remote work, while others were ill-equipped for the transition.

METHODOLOGY

This study adopted a survey research technique. The survey approach appears best suited for this work as a pilot study since it is not feasible to interview the entire population of Bauchi State. Furthermore, because there are there are fixed sets of questions, in surveys, the responses can be systematically classified, so that quantitative comparisons can be made.

Relying on the Nigeria Bureau of Statistics (NBC) data shows that the total number of enterprises in Nigeria was estimated at 38,413,420 spread out across the country. Data shows that, Bauchi State had a total of 34,685 NMSMEs with Nano: 6,648, Micro: 12,718 of the total number.

Using a digital sample size calculator with a 95% confidence level and a 4% margin of error, a total of 601were needed across the six-geopolitical zones of the country. To work for the north east, the sample size was divided across 6 with 100 purposively selected from the Bauchi State capital. For a fair representation of all forms of enterprise, the sources of primary data were the structured questionnaire which was administered to 36 identified NMEs drawn from the 365 categories of businesses provided by the Corporate Affairs Commission which is in charge of registering businesses in Nigeria.

Below are the 36 identified categories:

1. Abattoir and meat selling services
2. Bakery services
3. Beauty and salon services
4. Block industry
5. Boutique services
6. Car wash services
7. Carpentry/upholstery services
8. Catering services
9. Chemist /nursing home
10. Creative, art and entertainment activities
11. Deal in soft drinks
12. Dry cleaning and laundry services and industrial cleaning services or training
13. Education
14. Fashion Designing/tailoring services
15. Fishing and aquaculture
16. Gymnasium services
17. Laundry and dry-cleaning service
18. Livestock feeds production and distribution
19. Makeup and makeover services
20. Milling and grinding services
21. Operate fast food outlet
22. Photography services
23. Poultry services
24. Printing and reproduction of recorded media
25. Printing press
26. Sale of agricultural produce
27. Sale of agricultural tools, machine, and allied products
28. Sale of animals
29. Sale of automobile spare parts
30. Sale of computer, laptops, printers, photocopies, and their accessories
31. Sale of dairy products
32. Sale of groceries
33. Sale of mobile phones and accessories

34. Sale of motor vehicle, motorcycles, and other automobile products
35. Sale of sim cards credit/recharge cards
36. Trading

Thus, the SME owners/managers/sales representatives were approached to fill the questionnaire. Literature review provided the secondary data gathered from earlier research work to justify or negate findings.

Data Analysis and Presentation

A total of 100 NME owners participated in the survey. Data shows that of the enterprises surveyed, 67% were owned and supervised by men and 33% were businesses owned and managed by women.

Majority of the businesses were run by those within the age range of 26 – 35 years (49%) followed by those between 36-45 years of age at 33%. 18.4% of the respondents were between the ages of 18 – 25 years.

The entrepreneurs were disaggregated by the level of their educational qualification with majority at 45% being undergraduates. 41% had completed a secondary level education. Out of those surveyed, only 2% of business owners had no form of education.

One of the major disaggregation was by Length of Years of Business. Data shows that majority of the enterprises surveyed had been in business between 4 – 6 years with a 40% response. An average of 30% of the respondents had been in business between 1 -3 years and above 7 years.

57% of the business operating hours were between 9-12 hours while 36% were open between 5 – 8 hours daily. Only 7% were available for 24 hours.

1. Disaggregation by Business Category

Table 2. Source field data

S/N	Category	Frequency
1	Trading	13
2	Sale of groceries	12
3	Beauty and salon services	11
4	Fashion Designing/tailoring services	7
5	Boutique services	6
6	Chemist /nursing home	6
7	Creative, art and entertainment activities	5
8	Abattoir and meat selling services	4
9	Deal in soft drinks	4
10	Livestock feeds production and distribution	3
11	Bakery services	3
12	Photography services	3
13	Catering services	3
14	Sale of sim cards credit/recharge cards	3
15	Laundry and dry-cleaning service	3
16	Sale of agricultural produce	2
17	Makeup and makeover services	2
18	Milling and grinding services	2
19	Operate fast food outlet	2
20	Block industry	1
21	Sale of computer, laptops, printers, photocopies, and their accessories	1
22	Dry cleaning and laundry services and industrial cleaning services or training	1
23	Carpentry/upholstery services	1
24	Printing and reproduction of recorded media	1
25	Fishing and aquaculture	1
	Grand Total	100

The pivot table above describes the category of businesses surveyed with trading 13(13%), sale of groceries 12 (12%), beauty and salon services 11 (11%), fashion designing/tailoring services 7 (7%), chemist /nursing home 6 (6%), boutique services and creative, art and entertainment activities at 5 (5%). The least was a mode of 1 (1%) for the block industry, sale of computer, laptops, printers, photocopies, and their accessories, printing and reproduction of recorded media, dry cleaning and laundry services and industrial cleaning services or training, carpentry/upholstery services and fishing and aquaculture.

2. Number of Staff Employed

Figure 4. Source field data

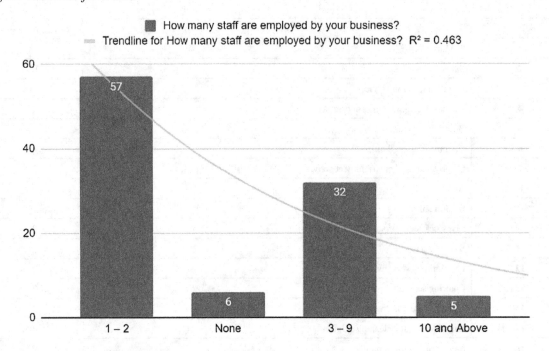

The combo chart above shows that majority of the businesses at 57% response rate had at least one staff employed. This shows that the Nano and Micro Enterprise category are available within the data provided with 57 and 32 respectively. The trendline for the number of staff employed is peaked at $R^2 = 0.463$.

3. Online Media Awareness

Figure 5. Source field data

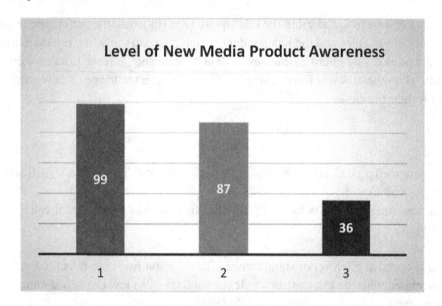

The bar chart above shows that a total of 99 businesses were aware of mobile smart phones while 87% of the sample size said they were aware of social media networks. Only 36% of the respondents admitted that they were aware of E-commerce sites.

4. How Often Do You Use Social Media Personally?

Figure 6. Source field data

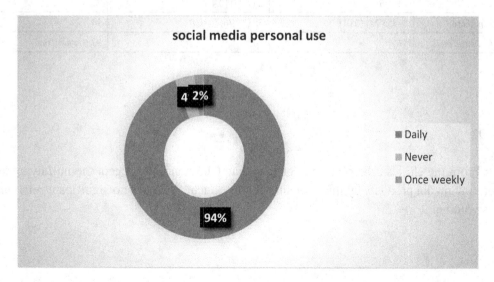

The pie chart above shows that 94% used social media daily.

5. Hypotheses Testing

Hypotheses 1, 2, 3 & 4 were tested using the Chi square (X^2) statistics to examine the relationships between the categorical variables and the independent variable; specifically, the relationship between the use of new media products by micro businesses in Bauchi State and increase in sales volume, visibility, and profitability. Hypothesis 4 was tested using an X^2 to measure the usage of new media products by NME owners for their businesses.

Hypothesis 1

H_0. The use of new media products by NMEs in Bauchi State does not have a significant relationship on their sales volume.

H_1: The use of new media products by NMEs in Bauchi State has a significant relationship on their sales volume.

The hypothesis is tested at 5% level of significance. The decision rule is to reject the null hypothesis if the *p*-value associated with the test statistics is less than 0.05 (5%) level of significance. The result of the hypothesis is presented in the contingency table below.

Contained is the following information:

The observed cell totals, (the expected cell totals) and [the chi-square statistic for each cell].

New Media Products Usage and Sales Volume

Table 3. Source field data

MSP SM	0	1	Marginal Row Totals
Tech in use	1 (1.76) [0.33]	2 (1.24) [0.47]	3
Significant increase	56 (55.24) [0.01]	38 (38.76) [0.02]	94
Marginal Column Totals	57	40	97 (Grand Total)

$X^2 = 0.8261$

$P = .363392.$

Decision: From the chi-test, the p-value is greater than 0.05 hence we accept the null hypothesis that the use of new media products by micro businesses in Bauchi State has no significant relationship on their sales volume.

Hypothesis 2

H_0: There is no significant relationship between new media products and business visibility of micro businesses in Bauchi State.

H_1: There is a significant relationship between new media products and business visibility of micro businesses in Bauchi State.

The contingency table below provides the following information: the observed cell totals, (the expected cell totals) and [the chi-square statistic for each cell].

The chi-square statistic, p-value and statement of significance appear beneath the table 4.

Table 4. Source field data

Dependent Variables	Yes	No	Marginal Row Totals
Visibility	11 (13.50) [0.46]	89 (86.50) [0.07]	100
Profitability	16 (13.50) [0.46]	84 (86.50) [0.07]	100
Marginal Column Totals	27	173	**200 (Grand Total)**

$X^2 = 1.0704$

$p = .300847$

Decision: From the chi-test, the p-value is greater than 0.05 at .300847 hence we accept the null hypothesis that the use of new media products by micro businesses in Bauchi State has no significant relationship on their visibility and profitability. This is because the proportion of respondents who reported they did not use new media tools for visibility (N=89) differed significantly from those who reported they used it to advertise their business.

Hypothesis 4

H_0: NME owners in Bauchi do not use new media products for their businesses.

H_1: NME owners in Bauchi use new media products for their businesses.

The contingency table below provides the following information: the observed cell totals, (the expected cell totals) and [the chi-square statistic for each cell].

The chi-square statistic, p-value and statement of significance appear beneath the table 5.

Table 5. Source field data

Variable	Yes	No	Row Totals
phone for business	10 (8.00) [0.50]	90 (92.00) [0.04]	100
online media for business	6 (8.00) [0.50]	94 (92.00) [0.04]	100
Column Totals	16	184	**200 (Grand Total)**

$X^2 = 1.087$

$p = .297147$

Decision: From the chi-test, the p-value is greater than 0.05 at .297147 which is not significant at p < .05hence we accept the null hypothesis that NME owners in Bauchi do not use new media products for their businesses. This is because the proportion of respondents who reported they did not use their phone and online media for business (N= 90 & N = 94) differed significantly from those who reported they used it their business.

Hypothesis 5

H_0: NME owners in Bauchi do not know how to use new media products for their businesses.
H_1: NME owners in Bauchi know how to use new media products for their businesses.

To examine this hypothesis, a descriptive statistic was used to analyse the items on NME owners' knowledge of how to use new media products for their businesses. The results obtained were presented via median and standard deviation. The recurring mode was used to justify the results. Hence, any item with median score 2 and above was acceptable as a knowledgeable use for business as presented in the table 6.

Table 6. Source SPSS field data

		Mobile Phone Scale	Telegram Scale	Likee Scale	IG Scale	LinkedIn Scale	Pinterest Scale	YouTube Scale	Tiktok Scale	FB Scale	Twitter Scale	WhatsApp Scale	E-comm Scale	Snapchat Scale
N	Valid	100	100	100	100	100	100	100	100	100	100	100	100	100
	Missing	0	0	0	0	0	0	0	0	0	0	0	0	0
Median		5.00	1.00	1.00	1.00	1.00	1.00	1.00	1.00	2.00	1.00	5.00	1.00	1.00
Std. Deviation		1.167	1.060	.716	1.258	.830	.836	1.131	1.304	1.817	1.262	1.739	.937	1.226

Mean = 1.69
Mode = 1

On a scale of 1 – 5, the contingency table above shows an average 1.69 as those knowledgeable on how to use new media products for their businesses. The mode of 1 proves that nano and micro business owners were not knowledgeable about new media products for their businesses.

Decision: Since the average of the hypothesis is less than half, we accept H_0 and conclude that nano and micro business owners in Bauchi do not know how to use new media products for their businesses. Based on the accepted H5 results, the pie chart below justifies the results which shows that 34 businesses (33.32%) were not using online media for business because 50% of them were not aware of any marketing strategies, 15% said they were aware of these platforms but did know how to use them for business. 12% affirmed that they had no interest in using social media for their business. Another 12% said they lacked access to facilities such as a smart phone. Another group of 12% reported that they were not aware of what the various online platforms could offer.

Figure 7. Source field data

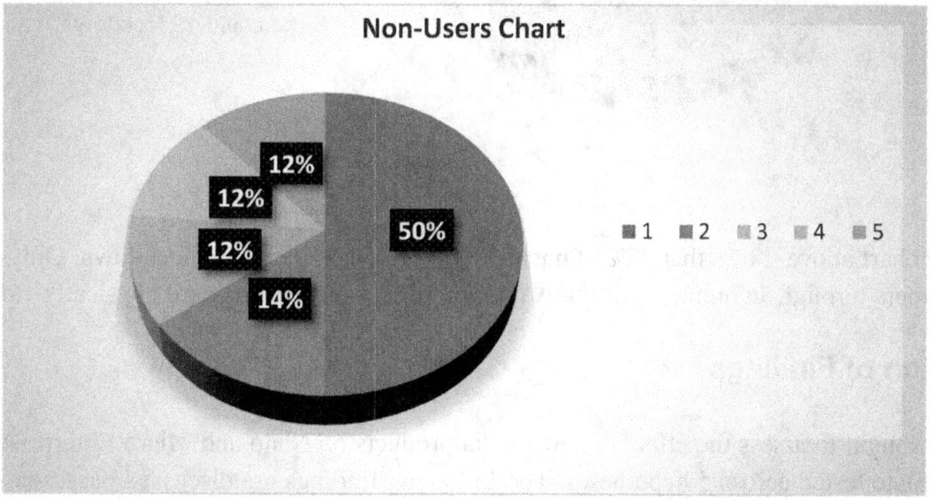

Business Interruptions During Covid-19 Lockdown

To ascertain if there was any effect of the lockdown on NMEs in Bauchi, an additional question was added around business interruptions as shown in the pie chart below

Figure 8. Source field data

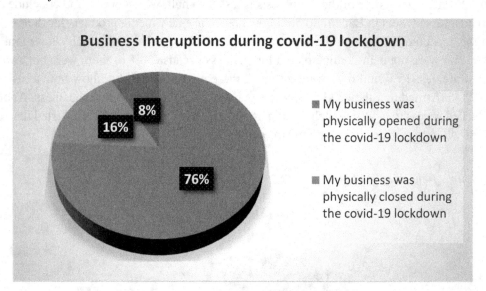

The pie chart above shows that 76% of businesses were open during the lockdown. Only 8% served their customers through an online medium. A total of 16% of businesses were physically closed.

Discussion of Findings

This study sought to assess the effect of new media products on Nano and Micro Enterprises (NMEs) in Bauchi State tested across 5 hypotheses. The following findings are discussed based on hypothesis 1 – 5 examined.

It can be deduced from the results provided during the analysis that the use of new media products by NME owners in Bauchi State has no significant relationship on their sales volume, visibility, and profitability. Although a majority of the sample size were aware of the new media products such as mobile smart phones, social media networks (e.g., Facebook, WhatsApp, Twitter) and E-Commerce the study revealed that it had not significantly translated to usage for business as only 38% reported that they used their smart phone for business. A key finding is that of all the new media products, smart phones, Facebook, and WhatsApp ranked the highest in knowledge and usage by NME owners. This negates the findings of Qalati, et.al. (2020) because the increasing social media platforms were not making NMEs adopt them easily. Some reported that they were distracting.

Worthy of note is that 94% of NMEs did claim that they used new media products especially social media on a daily basis, but these technologies for over 50% of them were for personal and not business purposes. This further justifies that awareness of the tools had not significantly translated to a business tool. Reasons provided for non-usage of new media products for business included: lack of awareness of what the tools could offer, others claimed their smart phone was distracting. Others were pegged on lack of knowledge of marketing strategies offered by new media products. These findings further led to the decision to accept the null hypothesis and conclude that NMEs in Bauchi do not use new media products for their businesses and do not know how to use new media products for their businesses.

Some none-users pegged their reasons along the lack of access to internet and their inability to afford a smart phone or the opportunity to go online. This justifies the theory of digital divide that that there is an economic and social gap between the population of a nation and their access to technologies and technical know-how. This explains why the Technology Acceptance Model also emphasises on the need to consider several factors which include perceived usefulness and affordability that would ensure a user gets the best from a tool.

Now, although only 8% of the respondents reported that they were able to serve their customers online during the lockdown, what is prominent in the data is their educational qualifications which were on the ratio of 50:50 of undergraduates and master's degree holders. Evidence shows that these categories of NME owners were also aware of all 3 new media product categories (mobile phones, social media, and E-commerce). Yet, the study significantly revealed that 98% of respondents doing business had at least a minimum of a primary education. Although 45% of those reported were undergraduates, this additional data did not translate wholly to their awareness of all the new media products listed as only 18% were fully aware which implies that only 2 in every ten undergraduates doing business are aware of all the new media products available for their business.

From the research hypothesis 5, the result obtained showed that all selections by respondents were on a mean of 1 therefore, it can be inferred that the lack of knowledge of the business benefits of new media products by NME owners restricts their use of the products as well. While the use of online technologies has been reported to have revolutionised the way individuals communicate with one another and do business, this study revealed that majority of NMEs in Bauchi performed their businesses oblivious of what new media products could offer.

CONCLUSION

This research took a step towards evaluating the relationship between new media adoption, and business performance of NMEs in Bauchi State. The study also tested the positions of Appel, Grewal, Hadi, et al. (2020); Eze, Chinedu-Eze, Okike & Bello, (2020) along the areas of how social media affects product promotion and visibility. As such, the results discussed here have significant implications in the area of academic learning and business studies. Firstly, this research provides empirical evidence that NMEs in Bauchi though aware of the new media products and tools do not use them to boost their businesses. While empirical tests on NMEs have been tested in filters across Nigeria, (Ndife, 2020; *Daramola, Okolie & Iyiebuniwe. 2021)* these findings are still an imperative task for academics and practitioners, because of the seemingly new evidence which has emerged from a part of the country which had been captured in the theoretical framework as a digital divide. Such theoretical constructs, therefore, make this study a rider for others on the need for an inclusive study that will explore the divide established in this examination. Second, the research contributes to literature by advancing the viewpoint that technological awareness does not translate to usage of product for business. This finding is significant for academics and practitioners alike. Practitioners should take into account that the dependent variables considered for all the constructs in this study were still happening irrespective of new media awareness. While the idea that new media use affects business performance has been the applause received so far, it is important to mention that the manner businesses stayed opened during the 2020 Covid-19 pandemic lockdown in Bauchi State indicates that some regions in Nigeria were not affected by the global effects as reported on the news. This encourages a return to the field to understand this region's dynamics. The researcher believes this study has improved past findings by offering new and useful insights into how businesses could thrive better by improving their knowledge and adoption of innovation of available new media products to achieve a competitive advantage. With so many new media platforms, social media research has recently drawn a lot of interest from academics, stakeholders and governments to practical applications and requires further discussions due to its dynamic nature.

RECOMMENDATIONS

The findings of this study have some recommendations for further analysis:

1 - This study focused on the NMEs in Bauchi State, Nigeria. The findings of the analysis require further research that might triangulate this data for a comparative study across the other geo-political regions of Nigeria. This will provide a basis for generalizability.
2 - There is a need for government bodies and social media platform owners to communicate the benefits of new media tools particularly social media and E-commerce to those businesses that have yet to adopt its usage for their businesses.
3 – Continuous training on the dynamic nature of change new media tools.
4 – NMEs which belong to various associations should, as part of their meetings, involve new media experts that would train and expose them to methods through which they can derive more benefits from their businesses.
5 – To bridge the digital divide, government can subsidize internet and phone costs so the economically disadvantaged can afford it.

REFERENCES

Abu, I. N., & Ezike, J. E. (2012). The role and sustainability of microfinance banks in reducing poverty and development of entrepreneurship in urban and rural areas in Nigeria. *International Journal of Business Administration, 3*(3), 33–40.

Adedoyin, R. (2021). *Nigerian journalism remains vibrant, despite challenges* (A. Nagarajan, Interviewer). International Press Institute (IPI). Retrieved 1 3, 2022, from https://ipi.media/nigerian-journalism-remains-vibrant-despite-challenges

Agwu, M. O., & Emeti, C. I. (2014). Issues, Challenges and Prospects of Small and Medium Scale Enterprises (SMEs) in Port-Harcourt City, Nigeria. *European Journal of Sustainable Development, 3*(1), 101–114. doi:10.14207/ejsd.2014.v3n1p101

Ajuwon, O. S., Ikhide, S., & Akotey, J. O. (2017). MSMEs Productivity in Nigeria. *European Journal of Economics and Business Studies, 7*(1), 114-130. Retrieved 5 6, 2022, from https://journals.euser.org/index.php/ejes/article/view/1788

Augoye, J. (2020, June 5). *Busola Dakolo alleges plot to silence her rape case against Fatoyinbo*. Retrieved 1 25, 2022, from PremiumTimes: https://www.premiumtimesng.com/news/more-news/396222-busola-dakolo-alleges-plot-to-silence-her-rape-case-against-fatoyin bo.html

Ayozie, D. O., & Latinwo, H. K. (2011). Entrepreneurial developments and small scale industry contribution to Nigerian national development- A marketing interface. *Information Management and Business Review*, *1*(2), 51–68. Advance online publication. doi:10.22610/imbr.v1i2.872

Chivandi, A., Samuel, M. O., & Muchie, M. (2019). *Social Media, Consumer Behavior, and Service Marketing* (M. Reyes, Ed.). Consumer Behavior and Marketing., doi:10.5772/intechopen.85406

Cote, J. (2022, February 3). *What is New Media?* Retrieved April 4, 2022, from Southern New Hampshire University: https://www.snhu.edu/about-us/newsroom/liberal-arts/what-is-new-media

Dijk, J. A. (2012). *The Evolution of the Digital Divide - The Digital Divide Turns to Inequality of Skills and Usage*. Retrieved 5 23, 2022, from https://narcis.nl/publication/recordid/oai:ris.utwente.nl:pu blications/a41c16c0-0c0e-4e68-8f74-d43368850914

Edosomwan, S., Prakasan, S. K., Kouame, D., Watson, J., & Seymour, T. (2011). The History of Social Media and its Impact on Business. *The Journal of Applied Management & Entrepreneurship, 16*(3), 79-91. Retrieved 1 24, 2022, from https://www.researchgate.net/publication/303216233_The_histo ry_of_social_media_and_its_impact_on_business

Engidaw, A. E. (2022). Small businesses and their challenges during COVID-19 pandemic in developing countries: In the Case of Ethiopia. *J Innov Entrep, 11*(1), 1. doi:10.118613731-021-00191-3 PMID:35036286

Gielens, K., & Steenkamp, E. J.-B. (2019). Branding in the era of digital (dis)intermediation. *Science Direct, 36*(3), 367-384. Retrieved 1 23, 2022, from doi:10.1016/j.ijresmar.2019.01.005

Gorbacheva, E., Niehaves, B., Plattfaut, R., & Becker, J. (2011). *Acceptance and use of internet banking: A digital divide perspective*. Retrieved 5 23, 2022, from http://aisel.aisnet.org/cgi/viewcontent.cgi?article=1125&con text=ecis2011

Iwu, C. G., Elvis, O. O., & Tengeh, R. K. (2017). Social Media Adoption Challenges of Small Businesses: the Case of Restaurants in the Cape Metropole, South Africa. *African Journal of Hospitality Tourism and Leisure, 6*(4). Retrieved 5 5, 2022, from https://www.researchgate.net/publication/320615314_Social_Me dia_Adoption_Challenges_of_Small_Businesses_the_Case_of_Rest aurants_in_the_Cape_Metropole_South_Africa

Lancaster, H. (2019). *Nigeria - Fixed Broadband Market - Statistics and Analyses*. Retrieved 1 22, 2022, from Budde Comm: https://www.budde.com.au/Research/Nigeria-Fixed-Broadband-Ma rket-Statistics-and-Analyses

Lutkevich, B., & Wigmore, I. (2021, September). *What is social media?* Retrieved 5 10, 2022, from Margaret Rouse: https://whatis.techtarget.com/definition/social-media

O'Keeffe, G., & Clarke-Pearson, K. (2011). The impact of social media on children, adolescents, and families. *Pediatrics, 127*(4), 800–804. Retrieved 2 2, 2022, from http://pediatrics.aappublications.org/content/127/4/800.full

Ogbo, A. I., & Nwachukwu, A. C. (2012). The Role of Entrepreneurship in Economic Development: The Nigerian Perspective. *European Journal of Business and Management, 4*(8), 95-105. Retrieved 5 6, 2022, from https://iiste.org/journals/index.php/ejbm/article/view/1937

Okpara, J. O. (2011). Factors constraining the growth and survival of SMEs in Nigeria. *Management Research Review, 34*(2), 156-171. Retrieved 5 4, 2022, from https://emerald.com/insight/content/doi/10.1108/01409171111102786/full/html

Olaoluwa, J. (2019, October 2). *Then and now: Nigeria's telecommunication history.* Retrieved 1 23, 2022, from Nairametrics: https://nairametrics.com/2019/10/02/then-and-now-nigerias-telecommunication-history/

Olsen, V. N., & Christensen, K. (2015). Social media, new digital technologies and their potential application in sensory and consumer research. *Current Opinion in Food Science, 3*, 23–26. doi:10.1016/j.cofs.2014.11.006

Oni, E. O., & Daniya, A. A. (2012). Development of Small and Medium Scale Enterprises: The role of Government and other Financial Institutions. *Oman Chapter of Arabian Journal of Business and Management Review, 1*(7), 16-29. Retrieved 5 6, 2022, from http://arabianjbmr.com/pdfs/om_vol_1_(7)/2.pdf

Onyijen, O. H., Awoleye, O. M., & Olaposi, T. O. (2019). Effectiveness of Social Media Platforms for Product Marketing in Southwestern Nigeria: A Firm-Level Analysis. *International Journal of Development and Management Review.* Retrieved 5 5, 2022, from https://www.ajol.info/index.php/ijdmr/article/view/186554

Onyinyechukwu, L. (2020). *7 Ways Government Can Create An Enabling Environment for SMEs.* Retrieved 5 15, 2022, from SME360: https://www.sme360.ng/2020/11/02/7-ways-government-can-create-an-enabling-environment-for-smes/

Osakwe, C. N., & Okeke, T. C. (2016). Facilitating mCommerce growth in Nigeria through mMoney usage: A preliminary analysis. *Interdisciplinary Journal of Information, Knowledge, and Management, 11*, 115-139. Retrieved 5 12, 2022, from http://ijikm.org/volume11/ijikmv11p115-139osakwe2222.pdf

Petersen, L. (2019). *The Negative Effect of Social Media on Society and Individuals.* Retrieved 2 4, 2022, from Hearst Communications, Inc.: https://smallbusiness.chron.com/negative-effect-social-media-society-individuals-27617.html

Qalati, S. A., Li, W., Ahmed, N., Mirani, M. A., & Khan, A. (2020, December 23). Examining the Factors Affecting SME Performance: The Mediating Role of Social Media Adoption. *MDPI Sustainability.* doi:10.3390/su13010075

SMEDAN. (2021). *MSME Survey Report.* https://smedan.gov.ng/wp-content/uploads/2022/03/2021-MSME-Survey-Report_1.pdf

Chapter 11
Exploring Social Media Adoption and SME Performance:
Role and Challenges

Riya Wadhwa
Maharashi Dayanand University, Rohtak, India

Rohit Bansal
(iD) https://orcid.org/0000-0001-7072-5005
Vaish College of Engineering, Rohtak, India

Aziza Chakir
FSJES AC, Hassan II University, Casablanca, Morocco

Reena Katyal
Sh. L.N. Hindu College, Rohtak, India

ABSTRACT

Small to medium enterprises (SMEs) are businesses that nourish revenues, assets, or number of employees below an unquestionable threshold. SMEs are the great altruist in developing the economy by employing vast numbers of people and helping in configuration through innovation as well as leading in global development of an economy. In emerging of market economies, SMEs are the engine of economic development because of their great entrepreneurial spirit. These will help to make an enterprise successful as well as bring new innovations for everyone. These days, SME entrepreneurs are coddling themselves on social media for amplifying their achievement, so this chapter will traverse the acquisition of social media and how the performance of SMEs is going while adopting these sites. Associating with these sites are helping people in linking with the world. Roles and challenges will also be narrated in this chapter.

DOI: 10.4018/978-1-6684-5770-2.ch011

INTRODUCTION

The twenty-first century is very unique as well as different as it is coming up with the evolution of old technology with new additions and modifications. It has impacted every area of our lives and become a very pivotal factor in no time and cannot be steer clear of. These digital technologies are attaining with more of the innovations rapidly than before and social media is getting great thrust from everyone as this equates almost half of the entire global population. These platforms can propellant the fragmentation of societies around the world and have the budding to change work grace and made the world a little uncomplicated to work as well to have fun. It is artefact that everyone is appreciating because of its latest innovations. Social media is a communal phrase for websites and applications which crisp on multiple things like communicating, sharing content, collaboration, elevate their product and to stay in touch with their family and friends (Painoli et al, 2021). There are much of popular sites like: Facebook, Whatsapp, Instagram, Youtube, Twitter. These days, in the era of digital world SMEs entrepreneurs are using the different platforms to amplify their performance they are affixing their business with these sites so, that their business outstretch at global level as well as they flatter more successful. So, in this research we are exploring the SME performance while adopting social media. Its roles as well as challenges will using these sites will also be explained. As for many people these things are very unique and different as well as latest marketing tool through which they can bring off goals in a more effective way. Many of the business man take it as a new opportunity for themselves which have a probable to associate as well as popularization of their brand among half of the world. Recently, professional social media campaigns are being instigated for enhancing the performance. As for holding out the right people you need right tools. Best ones tools are being picked out by them to be successful in their business via social media.

LITERATURE REVIEW

Pentina et al (2012) explores the emerging uniformity in the execution of social media marketing by SMEs and segregate the incessant patterns into tactical types. In their research they use verifiable methods of cluster analysis to self reported data by marketing executives and to steer a topology of three presiding social media marketing strategic motif. **Oztamur & Karakadılar (2014)** emphasise in look over the role of social media for SMEs as it is a latest marketing strategy appliance for ameliorating the firm performance. Their research is engrossed on narrating the chronicle including the comparison as well as inspection of four American and Turkish companies. Two platforms were considered i.e. Facebook and Twitter and their studies put forward that Turkish SMEs are cladding problems concerning customer communication summons and unattractive content whereas American SMEs are less operative in using Twitter than Facebook. **Sulaiman et al. (2015)** focuses in probing those factors that sway the use of social media platform i.e. facebook among the SMEs. Their research also scrutinizes the impression of using the FaceBook on economic as well as non-economic performance of SMEs. **Dutot and Burgeron (2016)** aims in developing as well as in trying out the framework of SMEs as strategic inclination and its collision on the staging of the SMEs. In their paper they establish new notion of sales and business development. **Adel et al. (2017)** focuses in investigating the key drivers for acquisition of social media by SME of United Arab Emirates. For researching they made a multiple angles of 3 elements that can affect the SME i.e. technological, organizational and environmental and outcome of their research revealed that organisational as well as environmental was significant rather than technological. **Sha et**

al (2018) describes the role of key factors i.e. social media and corporate communication in setting off the SMEs of Arab World for reaching to the success level. This conceptual study demonstrated the best opportunity for communication with market with lots of benefits and good results. **Gavino et al. (2018)** examines the Latino and Hispanic entrepreneurs while using the social media for professional purpose i.e. business. The ascendancy of culture while using the business and distinctive social networks. The results divulge that Latino owners use personal social networks. **Eze et al. (2020)** focuses in touring the precursor factors that uplift SMEs for embracing the social media marketing. **Sikander et al. (2020)** investigates the footprint of technology organisation and environment as chief factors in the presentation of SME. It also looks into the conciliate role of social media adoption and the discovery nurtured that technology organisation and environment plays great role for improvising SME performance. This study also help organisation in precieving the advantages of using social media and enumerates that investment in social media is rationale by the organization. **Alkateeb & Abdalla (2021)** highlights the impact of adoption of social media on SME execution in the Middle East region i.e. Palestine. In their research they mainly erect the models and by using these models they check the impression of social media platforms. Moreover, they also test the effect level of this assuming on the performance of SME. **Nurfarida et al. (2021)** aims in examining the customer orientation on SME performance. The role of endorsement of the social media is also explained and correlation between customer orientation and SME performance is being also peruses in their research. Results were very pragmatic as these days social media is helping customer inclination as well as in boosting the SME performance. **Oyewobi et al. (2021)** highlights the arbitrate effect of grasping capacity of using the social media on the SMEs as well as on their performance and the findings revealed the positive results between these both learning and performance. These social sites are helping SMEs firms in carrying off great results. **Abddulhai et al. (2022)** focuses in examining the approbation while using the Facebook and their crash on the SMEs performance while ratification of Facebook in the North Western Nigeria.

OBJECTIVES AND METHODOLOGY

This research aims at achieving the following objectives:

1. To explore the Social media adoption in SME Sector
2. To check the performance level of SME while adopting Social Media and role and challenges.

The data for this research is secondary and it has been collected from various sites, journals, books and other e-content that contributes to the existing reviews on exploring social media adoption and SME performance.

EXPLORING SOCIAL MEDIA ADOPTION

Social Media platform means a form of automatic communication, through which they can contribute in information, create online communities, personal message and many more. These are also called as the micro blogging. It is a system for promulgate information over the internet to a hand-pick cluster of followers. There are many of the examples of social media platforms i.e. whatsapp, facebook, youtube, twitter, instagram.

1. **FaceBook:** This is one of the world's largest social media scaffolding which accords the organic content and helps in doing reimbursing social marketing. Many of the adults made the purchases through this app. This app is helping people not only to connect with their friends or family in fact they are helping in uplifting business to connect their business online so, that they can earn huge profits and their brand get more heed. Brands annexing with this platform should sustain their presence and furnishing the organic content to be successful. Monthly active users on this platform is 2.8 billion and most contemporary update is that these days this app is enumerating e-commerce shopping via FaceBook Shops.

2. **WhatsApp:** It is one of the free full featured of messaging. It allows users to swapping messages to an individual or a group of persons. It was founded in 2009. With this platform you can share pictures, videos with each other. These days, modern trait of putting status is also being instituted so, that more and more number of users can access and enjoy this app. It is the 1 messaging app in the world and recently, voted as the world's favourite social media app. As this app introduces WhatsApp business account also which helping the business to grow in a more efficient way and the monthly active users of this platform is 2.0 billion. Every day, 175 million users in almost 180 countries messages one of the 50 million businesses on whatsApp. For businesses this platform is postulating the most appealing ramifications.

3. **Youtube:** This is the video platform where monthly active users are 2.29 billion. On this platforms generally, original videos are being made to exhibit the gratified or information to the users which is the combination of skill, strategy, budget as well as luck. People make their own YouTube channels. People gets benefit through their talent on this platform as best video will have the potential to allure more number of the users towards your channel as subscribers. These days, businesses are get going with their brands to inflate their growth. (Bansal et al, 2014)

4. **Instagram:** This is one of the photo sharing App over past few years. This is acquiring the great drift from the people because of its new features like reels, stories, Instagram Live and many more. On this platform monthly active users are 1.22 billion. Polished feed has lug with the rise of video content and this can be helpful in the more things also. This app was launched in 2010 and which gained popularity among people especially from the "Youth" and later on it was gathered by the Face Book Inc.

In today's world many of people are reckon on these sites. Social Media is getting the lots of productive feedback from all the humans as they are the social flunkey and they in need of the companionship of others to prosper in life. Strength of our relatedness has great footprint on our mental health as well as on our happiness. Being equating socially with people can ease stress, apprehension and depression. In fact these help in shoving the self - worth, lay out comfort and joy. These add many prominent years in our life by making you more positive, happier and healthier. This technology is generally mapping out to make people more close together. These sites now can be easily retrieved on mobile phone which is very fitting to keep in touch. These sites have commentary along with that they keep on computing some more features so, that beguile the heart of audience. These newer tools make them more satisfied as well as happy. Through this they can create a great network for themselves. Many of the videos, pictures and lot of content can be shared at once with lots of public. In India there are lots of users who are recurrently using these sites. These days, it is helping in going forward the economy as many of the SMEs are coupling their business online through these platforms. It is an efficacious social strategy.

Figure 1. Usage of Social media by SMEs
Source: Created by Authors

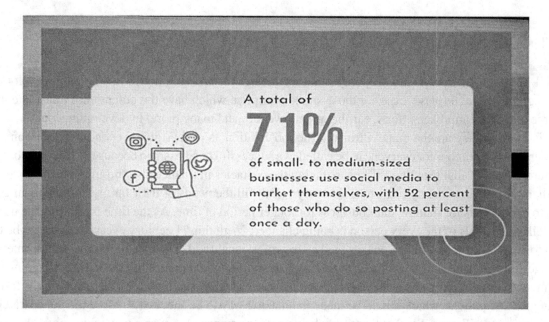

In business these are used to market products, foster brands and equate with customers. These platforms are helping in ameliorating the business reputation as well as builds trust among many of their consumers as they gets the instantaneous response from businessman and their queries are also solved quickly. They can easily associate with many of the people and can make large number of consumers at a particular point of time. They easily get customers feedback also via ratings. Social media is also used for multitude sourcing as this networking is helping people to gather knowledge, goods and services. For promoting their products they split the content either by photos or by videos. These days, videos are manifesting their tremendous results as people think they are more real rather than the pictures and videos recount the goods in a best way. Every platform is providing this facility because this is getting more commending response from the audience. Promoting your brand through these sites are termed as "Social Media Marketing" and to make it triumphant lots of strategies, policies should be sketched in such a way that aims a business to grow rapidly as well as earn huge profits. This is a very authoritative tool for businessman to be successful so, it should be used in a sharp-witted way same as the technology. Digitalisation is helping in amplifying the things in different ways. In business world these social networking sites became a perfect platform for many of the owners as this is helping in generating the new leads, increasing in awareness about the newer products and pilot the website traffic. People view these social media channels and are used by the consumer brands. These can outstandingly benefit B2B and technology companies as well. Although, some people still think that these social media platforms can drive the real business world and help in achieving the good results but if it used as the good strategy then it is helping many of the owners in achieving great heights. Our researchers also said that using of these sites helping in magnifying the market and give of many things. Its conversion rates are also 13 percent higher than the average lead turning rate and which proves that social media is crucial channel and for technology brands. There are many of the tips and more features are coming for doing work in a better way. These days many of the people are working as an influencer also. Being an influencer they have the potential to attract more number of the consumers regarding a particular brand via online.

SME PERFORMANCE

Small Medium Enterprises are very important businesses for an economy as this helps in developing the economy more because these are those small enterprise which have the potential to transmute into a large one by its unbroken efforts, earning great revenues and many more. In developing country, their role is more as they are the major altruist in the job creation as well as global economic development. Earlier, it was strenuous for everyone to be called as a successful businessman because of less technology, resources were available to them. They are facing the obstacles in finance also through which they can't let them grow. They mainly run a business only to full fill the needs of their family and the main goal was to earn profits for running their business for longer period of time. As the time is yielding the needs as well as the goals of the every person is being changed. With this 21 century everyone wants to be the step forward as well best in personal as well as in professional field. The day digital marketing enters it changes the whole scenario as this links each and everything via online. This marketing is helping the business to grow rapidly and achieving their goals very easily in smarter way. This marketing is full of strategies and policies which should be made in amazing way to be successful. More the good strategy, more business will grow. So, that there social channels are managed in such a way which gives the good impact on the people and attracts many more as a satisfied consumers. These days they are targeting their audience, bringing the good content into their post and many more features which help in making their brand shine among other brands. Social media is offering many of the great opportunities for their growth by giving millions of newer tools as well as features. In fact they are changing the whole marketing world in a better way through learning of the marketing skills, accessing the free business on your phone anytime anywhere. Many of the business use these sites for driving the website traffic and sales. These can help in engaging more of the consumers towards your brand and collectively common interest builds a community of a particular product which they mainly like to buy. Many of the potential customers also help in attracting more consumers and these all helps in upgrading the performance of SMEs.

Social Media Marketing is one of form of digital marketing that grip the power of popular social media networks to carry off branding goals. In this business fabricate their profiles and post pictures, videos which constitute the brands as well as enchant the relevant audience. Following and engaging with followers, customers and influencers to build a community around your brand and these all generate the good social networks and all these will help in enlarge the performance of all the small medium enterprises by earning huge profits, customer satisfaction, popularising the brand. These sites never differentiate between the large business and the small business. In fact these attract the audience through their unique content in forms of pictures or videos towards the particular business. These sites act as neutral between the audience and business. Millions of favourable response will be shown via ratings which can help the consumers while selecting the particular product of best brand as lots of business are being done via online so, many of the newer consumer can also feel safe as well as satisfied with a particular business and this act as one of strategy of a businessman. Many of the business man are taking many of the advantages with these sites in one or other way for making their business successful. They are also driving the traffic on their websites of their own business and this gives them chance to convert their visitors into customers. This also helps in building the relations with many of the people and this can help in increasing the brand awareness to more people through word of mouth. SMEs are actually growing and contributing more to the national economy because of achieving higher goals. This is actually increasing the performance of SMEs in a way we can never think. They are measuring their success level through tracking in a different ways. Algorithms are being used for measuring the effectiveness of their work. More the good strategy will help in getting the good fruits of the work. Working online is full of mind work and it is said that great mind gives the great results. With these sites they do not require much finance, cost is lower and the profits are higher and overall awareness of your brand and huge profits is helping SMEs in giving the greater performance through their growth. For the growing of the SMEs every bank as well as government is equipped to help so, that they can be successful and their focal point is to make these enterprises grow and they day business started using these social media is growing.

ROLES OF SOCIAL MEDIA IN SME SECTOR

Every sector is successful because of the good great things or actions which are being played while performing a particular task. These days, social media is playing climacteric role in enhancing the SME performance. Some of the roles of social media in SME sector is being demonstrated below:

1. **Humanize Your Business:** Millions of users are active on these sites on daily basics so, everyone has a powerful network as they are linking globally. If our business is also united with these sites then this will help in enhancing the business in a various ways like promotion of goods on a large scale, brand awareness and the business will be connected globally. This will attract many of the customers which will help in operating the more sales and these will help in donating to the national economy also. With social media everything is ameliorating business, economy and bringing innovations. (Bansal &Minocha, 2021)
2. **Drive Traffic:** After making the particular site on social media it is very obligatory to drive traffic towards your website and this can be possible only when your website is full of fancy products as this come up with the adequate of opportunities to gain the business visitors as well as convert into leads. We have to seize with our target audience consistently, crisp on sharing content, post daily and create a good content which can attract more consumers and ultimately this drives the more traffic to website and this will help our business in assorting as well as cater to growing customer needs around the world not just a local population.
3. **Generate Leads and Customers:** More the traffic more are the possibilities of attracting the consumers towards your business. If the business is getting the favourable retaliation through likes, ratings, feedback then business can easily give rise to leads and it should make efforts to make it more successful through nurturing all with the end goal of converting them into a customer. Through technology, businessman has lots of options for bringing about the leads as well as attracting more and more number of consumers towards your brand. (Bansal &Saini, 2022)
4. **Solidifying Brand Identity:** Conducting your business via online mode will show your business on online. Means your business should be presented online. If your target audience has no knowledge

about your brand or for what it stands for then no amount of online awareness campaigning can rectify that. Through Social media we mainly aware our brand to those who are new as well as it instigating the products in which you are dealing. If our business brought new things then also we have to tell to subsist ones so, that they can get awareness.

5. **Increasing Brand Activity:** Social media is emerging because of its easiness as well as cost-effectiveness to conglomerate content offerings and increase the target visibility of the brand. This helps small business to take part with conglomerates when it comes to reach. These sites have lots of activities to be performed which can strengthen your brand. More features will be used by the business as strategy the best will be the outcomes. Activities like sharing the good content, online streaming, live videos etc.

6. **Provides Many Opportunities:** Social media sites are providing many of the opportunities to all businesses. These build the good community for business which helps to business to grow by giving the great ratings, feedback. Through these business man knows how to make their brand popular. Giving ads of new things is also very trending as well as helpful. This newer opportunity is also helping business to grow their brand. Collaborations with other business can also be possible with these sites. Social sites are big and everything on social sites is connected with each other.

7. **Contribution to Economy:** For every economy it is necessary that everything is going perfect in their area. It can contribute to the national economy also as well as became the way for job creation for the jobseekers. These businesses employ 60 million people. SMEs access to finance and find the innovative solutions to unlock sources of capital also. These contributed 17 percent to the nation's GDP. With these sites their performance is getting better than earlier so, these businesses can contribute more to the economy because of huge profits.

8. **Partnering up With Influencers:** These days, everyone is associating their business online and many of the people are becoming the influencers also. Many of the business man are partnering up with these influencers so, that their business can grow more as these have the budding to influence the buyers of a product or service by recommending the items on social media. These people have specialized knowledge, authority or insight into a specific subject. These promote our brands in a specific and in amazing manner.

9. **Assessing the Competition:** These sites help you to keep track of your competitors. The offers they are running, the products they are selling all of this can be kept track of. In this you could virtually re-strategize our business and the business model to keep up with the changing times. This allows you to potentially offer loyal customers of your competitor to consider looking into an equally better brand. These sites are amazing platforms to make business better.

10. **User-generated Content:** One of the other biggest advantages we can have from these sites is to gauge customer sentiments and buying trends through the data received. People who p are putting their products in the cart potentially shows that something about the deal there were getting could be addressed. Their interest in product or your brand was definitely in place which helps you to strategize your brand's policies via customer feedback. Thereby, improving services offered. (Bansal & Pruthi, 2021)

CHALLENGES OF SOCIAL MEDIA IN SME SECTOR

A new start is very arduous and it is full of pros and cons. So, this social media also have some of the challenges which need to overcome if we have to become successful. Few of the challenges of social media in SME sector is being narrated below:

1. **Mental Health Issues:** Social media is affecting negatively also. As these sites deflect many people by disrupting their sleep and exposing them to bullying, rumour spreading, absurd views of other people's lives and peer pressure. These may create a heightened level of psychological arousal. Many people break down to have a proper diet and limited physical activities which possibly leading to the user experiencing physical as well as mental health problems such as depression, OCD, low family relationships as well as anxieties. Many people face delays in learning as well as in social skills. Many researchers in their research also said that these sites spring back parts of the brain associated with maintaining concentration. People can also have stress because of lack of privacy as everything is transparent as well as constant accessibility of social media.

2. **Polarization:** There are lots of social platforms and due to which customers get decomposition on different platforms according to their choice so it's very hard to keep them stable at one particular site. Every business firms make different policies as well as strategies to captivate towards their brands as there are several brands and everyone wishes to rule over the market by providing most satisfaction to the customers.

3. **Disinformation:** Another challenge faced by people is that they do not get the full information or mislead through stories from people who generally post false kind of content on their websites which is not in the reality. In millions of users we can't differentiate between the genuine and the wrong ones. If the people trusted wrong ones or on fake sites then it can create a big problem for them. This will affect the right one also as people can force into buying from these sites and to show their reality they may have to work more as well as more efforts in proving that they are correct ones. As many people have trust issues.

4. **Security and Retention:** Another big challenge faced by the firms is security and retention of their data because whenever we post on these sites, it becomes public. An happening of data rupture have alarmed many users and forced them to rethink their relationships to social media. These platforms are full of risks because of multiple threats like danger of hackers and m malicious interlopers that undermines personal privacy and in some cases are data is outright stolen.

5. **Offensive Posts:** Combat posts are the ones which has the potential to affect your brand in a negative way as you are connecting with your audience via post only and it should have good content in language, pictures etc. your information should be honest and favourable to the users means only relevant post should be posted among the audience which they likes or shows interest. Many times in the post harsh words, bullies, gestures about place, person or things are being written which can harm the image of our own brand. Placing the right post with the right content is extremely challenging task.

6. **Creating a Particular Strategy that Performs:** There are lots of platforms as well as features on which we can work. For becoming successful through these sites we have to make a good strategy and creating a social strategy can be intimidating. We have to plan as well as execute lots of things. After that we have to show social media presence timely with a great content and then we should

keep reviewing what things are showing the favourable response and which one are showing the unfavourable. So, that wrongs ones can be replaced with the better one for the good performance.

7. **Keeping Up to Date:** Digital world is moving swiftly but for a particular platform it is little harder to keep up as we have to check each and every detail, we have to post fresh and great content on site. Everyone want to see something unique and uniqueness can bring the great outcome otherwise it can show the negative results as there are lots of competitors on other sites. So, to keeping up to date and to compete we can talk to the experts which can help in driving the great results. They also help in applying the relevant things which can improve our results.

8. **Improving Social Media Engagement:** Engagement is one of the crucial for the social media. If the audience does not give their responses through likes or comments then it's very difficult to know about their choices. Their choices can be revealed through many of these kinds of things like views, likes and can help us in making the strategies for popularizing our brand. Engagement is more than just a metric to measure effectiveness and these are used by many of the major platforms and these days algorithms are social media master shudder which helps them in posting relevant content and in deciding which content should be deliver to a user So, that they do not feel irritated.

9. **Building Authentic Connections:** Many of the users now turn to their phones to be a part of the online community to connect with each other, they engage with likes, comments, posting of stories. On these they meet new people also. As a brand operator on these challenge it is important to connect with your target audience in an authentic and personal way. The key to achieve genuine audience and audience engagement, more followers is a very challenging task because of more number of platforms and whosoever have all these things is very appreciable.

10. **Growing your Social Media Following:** Growing of social following lay hand in hand with growing your engagement. The more we reach the more people will discovering our brand. Favourable responses will help in increasing more followers but it is hard to have millions of followers because of increasing number of other social platforms, fulfilling the expectations of the customers. These days, everyone wants to latest things rather than the traditional ones. These newer things have the potential to attract millions of users towards our brand.

CONCLUSION

Modern life is turning into social as well as digital life as people feel more amazing way than earlier life because of the newer innovations as well as ideas. This is escalation the standard of living of people and making their work easy. They are ameliorating each and everything and coming up with the great results in every field. Businesses are vastly expanding because of these technologies. Their advancements provides numerous of features which can be used as the opportunity for many of the businessman. As these can be easily converted into strategy and great strategy gives the great results while achieving the goals of the business. Successful businesses are the ones who achieve the all of their objectives, satisfy their customers, and bring innovation. As customers also wants newer things. This is new era of marketing where businesses indulge themselves in unique and branded products for pleasing their consumers rather than selling the products that they have. More the possible course of action for consumers more will be the loyal consumers and these all helps in achieving the great heights. Earlier, at the initial point of using these sites no one has thought that these will give the tremendous results because they feel that working on these sites are very onerous as well as full of challenges like keeping up to date, growing of social media following, selecting the particular strategy, building authentic connections and many more but with the passage of time they showing their interest in these and start working on these kind of sites for being successful. As there are many of the successful marketers, entrepreneurs and CEOs realise that social media is and leverage it to expose their brands to the masses. They become the role model for the small medium sized enterprises through their success. Lots of great strategies and hard work is required to achieve the great results. For improving their performance they are hiring influencers, tracking their responses and using the newer features. Customer engagement is also increased on these platforms as social media marketing is about identifying the essence of engagement. We have to build engagement as this can't buy. These day social media is about the stories to tell and social media puts the public into PR and the market into marketing. It is being observed that brands which ignore social media will die.

REFERENCES

Abddulhai, I. N., Husin, M. H., Baharudin, A. S., & Abdullah, N. A. (2022). Determinants of Facebook adoption and its impact on service-based small and medium enterprise performance in Northwestern Nigeria. *Journal of Systems and Information Technology, 24*(3).

Adel, H. M., Mahrous, A. A., & Hammad, R. (2020). Entrepreneurial marketing strategy, institutional environment, and business performance of SMEs in Egypt. *Journal of Entrepreneurship in Emerging Economies.*

Ainin, S., Parveen, F., Moghavvemi, S., Jaafar, N. I., & Mohd Shuib, N. L. (2015). Factors influencing the use of Social Media by SMEs and its Performance outcomes. *Industrial Management & Data Systems, 115*(3), 570–588. doi:10.1108/IMDS-07-2014-0205

Alkateeb, M. A., & Abdalla, R. A. (2021). Social Media Adoption and its Impact on SMEs Performance A Case Study of Palestine. *Studies of Applied Economies, 39*(7).

Bansal, R., Masood, R., & Dadhich, V. (2014). Social media marketing-a tool of innovative marketing. *Journal of Organizational Management, 3*(1), 1–7.

Bansal, R., & Minocha, K. (2017). Impact of Social Media on Consumer Attitude Towards A Brand With Special Reference to Hospitality Industry. *International Research Journal of Management and Commerce, 4*(8), 106–120.

Bansal, R., & Pruthi, N. (2021). Developing Customer Engagement Through Social Media: A Review Of Literature. *Marketing 5.0: Putting Up Blocks Together*, 80.

Bansal, R., & Saini, S. (2022). Exploring the Role of Social Media: An Innovative Tool for Entrepreneurs. In Applying Metalytics to Measure Customer Experience in the Metaverse (pp. 34-43). IGI Global.

Bansal, R., & Saini, S. (2022). Leveraging Role Of Social Media Influencers In Corporate World-An Overview. *NOLEGEIN-Journal of Global Marketing, 5*(1), 1–5.

Dutot, V., & Bergeron, F. (2016). From Strategic Orientation to Social Media Orientation: Improving SMEs Performance on Social Media. *Journal of Small Business and Enterprise Development, 23*(4), 1165–1190. doi:10.1108/JSBED-11-2015-0160

Eze, S. C., Chinedu/Eze, V. C., & Bello, A. O. (2020). Some Antecedent Factors that shape SMEs adoption of social media marketing application: A Hybrid Approach. *Journal of* Performance A Case Study of Palestine. *Studies of Applied Economics, 39*(7).

Gavino, M. C., Williams, D. E., Jacobson, D., & Smith, I. (2018). Latino Entrepreneurs and Social Media adoption: Personal and business Social Network Platforms. *Management Research Review*, *42*(4), 469–494. doi:10.1108/MRR-02-2018-0095

Nurfarida, I. N., Sarwoko, E., & Arief, M. (2021). The Impact of Social Media Adoption on Customer Orientation and SME Performance: An Empirical Study in Indonesia. *Journal of Asian Finance, Economics and Business, 8*(6).

Oyewobi, L. O., Adedayo, O. F., Olorunyomi, S. O., & Jimoh, R. (2021). Social Media Adoption and Business Performance: The Mediating Role of Organizational Learning Capacity. *Journal of Facilities Management*, *19*(4), 413–436. doi:10.1108/JFM-12-2020-0099

Oztamur, D., & Karakadilar, I. S. (2014). Exploring the Role of Social Media for SMEs: As a New Marketing Strategy Tool for the Firm Performance Perspective. *Procedia: Social and Behavioral Sciences*, *150*, 511–520. doi:10.1016/j.sbspro.2014.09.067

Painoli, A. K., Bansal, R., Singh, R., & Kukreti, A. (2021). Impact of Digital Marketing on the Buying Behavior of Youth With Special Reference to Uttarakhand State. In Big Data Analytics for Improved Accuracy, Efficiency, and Decision Making in Digital Marketing (pp. 162-182). IGI Global. doi:10.4018/978-1-7998-7231-3.ch012

Pentina, I., Koh, A. C., & Le, T. T. (2012). Adoption of social networks marketing by SMEs: Exploring the role of social influences and experience in technology acceptance. *International Journal of Internet Marketing and Advertising*, *7*(1), 65–82. doi:10.1504/IJIMA.2012.044959

Qalati, S. A., Li, W., Ahmed, N., Mirani, M. A., & Khan, A. (2020). Examining the Factors Affecting SME Performance: The Mediating Role of Social Media Adoption. *Sustainability, 13*(1).

Sha, W., & Basri, M. (2018). Social Media and Corporate Communication Antecedents of SME Sustainability Performance A Conceptual Framework for SMEs of Arab World. *Journal of Economic and Administrative Sciences*, *35*(3).

Chapter 12
SME Survival During the COVID-19 Pandemic:
An Outlook of Threats and Digital Transformation

Shikha Singh
Maharshi Dayanand University, India

Nishita Pruthi
iD https://orcid.org/0000-0002-6094-0972
Maharshi Dayanand University, India

ABSTRACT

There is no denying that worldwide economic and environmental conditions have been affected by the COVID-19 pandemic. Small and medium-sized enterprises (SMEs) have been particularly impacted by the COVID-19 pandemic. With this research, the authors aimed to better comprehend the obstacles faced by small and medium-sized enterprises (SMEs) during a pandemic, the digital reforms that emerged as a result of COVID-19, and the preventive measures that SMEs can take to withstand the crisis. They reviewed a wide range of secondary materials, including scholarly journals, books, internet resources, and blogs. They conclude that small and medium-sized enterprises (SMEs) can benefit from digital transformation because it allows them to rethink their decision-making processes and their use of technology. To overcome the challenges posed by COVID-19 to SMEs, it is necessary to examine a set of policy measures that could aid the recovery of MSMEs.

INTRODUCTION

The epidemic caused by COVID-19 is sending shockwaves across the global economy and causing major disruptions to people's daily lives and the global economy. COVID-19 is a major health emergency but is also much more than that. It is a metabolic jolt with serious short-, intermediate-, and long-term consequences. The quarantines and social isolation enacted in many nations to stop the spread of the

DOI: 10.4018/978-1-6684-5770-2.ch012

virus has delayed production and increased prices for consumers everywhere. Unemployment and work stoppages have increased as firms have closed and individuals have stayed at home, reducing demand for goods and services. Businesses of all sizes have been forced to close their doors because of this epidemic, and tens of millions of people have lost their jobs. Micro, small, and medium-sized businesses serve as the foundation of many global economies, making the significance and value of these businesses crucial. Small and medium-sized enterprises (SMEs) are significant in today's globalized world. The status of the global economy affects both the challenges and opportunities faced by small and medium-sized enterprises (SMEs) that rely on the long-term growth enabled by smartphone applications. Nonetheless, COVID-19 has presented substantial challenges for SMEs across a variety of countries and sectors.

Figure 1. SMEs in covid-19 outbreak
Source: Buchholz, 2020

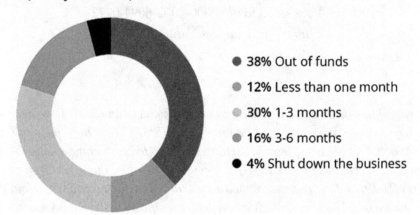

**Half of Indian Startups In
Serious Danger Due to COVID-19**

Self-declared cash reserves of Indian startups and SMEs*
(as of June 2020)

- 38% Out of funds
- 12% Less than one month
- 30% 1-3 months
- 16% 3-6 months
- 4% Shut down the business

In emerging countries like India, SMEs make up the vast bulk of all firms. Numerous governmental and non-governmental organizations (NGOs) have provided various forms of help to SMEs to prevent the collapse of this crucial sector brought on by the COVID-19 crisis. In this chapter, we will delve more into the difficulties encountered by SMEs, the digital changes implemented for their benefit, and the tactics developed by the government during this pivotal time.

LITERATURE REVIEW

Guo et al. (2020) examined how digitalization in small and medium-sized enterprises (SMEs) influenced their public responses to crises using data collected from a survey of 518 SMEs in China. Using their adaptable resources, small and medium-sized enterprises (SMEs) have been able to efficiently respond to public emergencies since digitalization has spread. In addition, SMEs can gain a performance boost from going digital. An overarching theoretical framework of digitization and crisis solutions was presented for SMEs. Behera et al. (2021) aimed to quantify MSMEs' impact on India's economy and identify pre- and post-COVID difficulties. They employed descriptive statistics and correlation and co-integration to measure the link between variables including MSMEs, investment, employment, and production. Variables showed a strong positive association. To boost MSMEs' confidence amid CO-VID-19 uncertainty, the government must establish an ongoing monitoring system and declare urgent relief measures. MSMEs need fiscal stimulus and e-market connections. To attain a Self-reliant India, the Indian government must improve MSMEs. Thukral (2021) discovered that COVID-19's proliferation without treatment has forced governments to lock down vast areas of society and cause behavioral alterations. Creative problem-solving is helping some SMEs survive the crisis. Resilience allows them to identify an opportunity in chaos and endure difficult times, but government actions are needed to revitalize the entrepreneurial environment to turn those prospects into reality. Klein and Todesco (2021) presented the overall benefits and drawbacks of knowledge management (KM) and how it may aid small and medium-sized enterprises (SMEs) in their fight against the epidemic. They developed a conceptual model based on theories of organizational resilience to show how their initial reactions worked and where they may improve. To begin, they looked at the responses of SMEs in similar situations using a literature search. Mass layoffs, temporary and permanent closures, bootstrapping of digitalization, and strategic alliances were some of the ways that businesses responded to the financial repercussions. Belitski et al. (2021) explored the 15 articles in the special issue "Economic implications of the CO-VID-19 epidemic on entrepreneurship and small companies," and presented its findings in four sections: An analysis of four literature streams based on the review of the literature's effect on entrepreneurship and small companies A summary of the articles in this special edition, as well as suggestions for future economic study in the wake of a catastrophic event. Rakshit et al. (2021) explored how developing country SMEs used smartphone apps to boost company productivity during the pandemic. They honored SMEs that used mobile apps to survive the crisis. The study applies the Theory of Consumption Values and the Theory of Planned Behavior to mobile-app-based SMEs, filling a literature gap. 343 Indian SMEs from three IDCs provided data. They tested a SME mobile-app-based business conceptual model using covariance-based structural equation modeling. Consumer choice behavior, perceived behavior control, subjective behavior control, and mobile app attitude affect SMEs' company strategy and decision-making. Bai et al. (2021) used literature study and personal insights to present COVID-19 pandemic digitalization lessons for sustainable MSE development from a technology for social good perspective. "They created a framework for post-COVID-19 digital transformation to maintain SMEs. SME digital transformation should prioritize digital payments, especially mobile money. For business continuity and sustainable production and consumption, institutions must support MSE resources and capacities for digital transformation. MSE management and other stakeholders should incorporate crisis scenarios and business continuity plans to sustain consumers virtually to improve sustainable development." Adam and Alarifi (2021) attempted to construct a theoretical model to explain the relationship between innovative practices, SMEs' performance and survival, and external support. 259 randomly selected Saudi SME managers were surveyed online and evaluated using SmartPLS3. The structural equation modeling results demonstrated that COVID-19-related innovative practices by SMEs improved performance and business survival. PLS-SEM bootstrap results showed that external support boosts SMEs' innovative practices' company survival rather than performance. Caballero-Morales (2021) offered a comprehensive methodological approach to enable small firms to create their products for new markets and make better use of their limited available resources. "As an example of this technique, the research-supported development of a new product for a family-owned SME was undertaken in a zone with high COVID-19 risk. The results gave insight into innovation as a survival mechanism for SMEs during and after the COVID-19 contingency, and the utilization of digital resources is highlighted as the key facilitator for networking and research-based design of new goods within the "social distance" setting." Rupeika-Apoga et al. (2022) believed that a firm with deeper supply chain integration, more diverse customers, and larger revenues would be more economically sustainable. Mediation analysis and survey data from 246 Latvian SMEs were used to test a resource-based theory conceptual framework. The study found that digital orientation and capability directly affect digital transformation, which leads to higher revenue and a more complex business model for SMEs. Tooth et al. (2022) investigated the theoretical foundations of corporate financial culture and its applicability in the context of Hungarian SME industry. This study included a literature review analysis of scholarly articles released over the past decade that covered subjects including "financial literacy," "business risk management," and "corporate financial management." Their findings demonstrated the existence of meaningful and positive connections between business management, risk management, and financial literacy.

OBJECTIVES AND METHODOLOGY

The following are objectives that will be accomplished by conducting this research:

1. To gain insight into the threats that Covid-19 posed to SMEs.
2. To examine the digital reforms implemented by SMEs to deal with the Covid-19 situation.
3. To identify the strategic measures for SMEs in the combat against the Covid-19 disaster.

Secondary data from a variety of sources (websites, journals, books, and other e-content) are used in this study to accomplish the aforementioned objectives.

THREATS IMPOSED IN COVID-19 TO SMEs

The challenges that small and medium-sized enterprises (SMEs) face in maintaining viability, expanding into new markets, and competing globally are significant. It is evident that the global economic crisis brought on by the COVID-19 epidemic poses a greater threat to SMEs. The following are examples of potential threats and difficulties that small and medium-sized enterprises (SMEs) likely encounter in covid-19:

Figure 2. Threats to SMEs in Covid-19
Source: Self-created by authors

Deficiencies in Cash Flow

Nobody knows how long the novel coronavirus will endanger society. Early in the public health crisis, many anticipated the virus would not spread or would be a short-term issue. Most small business owners save for emergencies, but they do not expect them to last months. As the economy deteriorates, many businesses will struggle to meet their financial responsibilities due to a lack of cash flow. "Small and medium-sized enterprises (SMEs) are particularly susceptible to the effects of a financial crisis because of their limited equity reserves, limited adaptation potential and flexibility for downsizing, liquidation problems, excessive reliance on external financial resources, tightened credit lines, payment delays on receivables, and general lack of resources." (Partida, 2020)

Drop in Revenue

Due to a precipitous drop in consumer expenditure, small and medium-sized enterprises saw a sudden drop in revenue. When sales slow, it can be difficult for a small or medium-sized business to make ends meet and stay afloat. For almost a year, these economic repercussions have persisted, wreaking havoc on small and medium-sized enterprises (SMEs). A rise in the unemployment rate is to be expected as firms of all kinds continue to feel the consequences of low demand, reducing their needs for employees. SME operations could be negatively impacted by rising unemployment, which would have a chilling effect on demand and consumer spending. In conclusion, small and medium-sized enterprises (SMEs) are more vulnerable to the negative demand that has been linked to social distancing guidelines and fear of contracting. (Partida, 2020)

Downsides in the Supply Chain

Small and medium-sized enterprises (SMEs) have had fewer people available to work because of illness, quarantines, and a dearth of childcare options. Raw materials, parts, and items needed by SMEs to produce their goods or services were in low supply due to disruptions in the supply chain during the onset of the epidemic. Smaller businesses typically work with fewer vendors than their larger counterparts. When opposed to major corporations, small and medium-sized businesses (SMEs) may find it more challenging to find a replacement supplier in the event of a supplier loss. (Partida, 2020)

Loss of Export Orders

Restricted operations and preventive measures results in loss of export orders to SMEs. 73% of the global trade in goods related to COVID-19 is subject to export prohibitions and other restrictions. A total of 93 nations have temporary export restrictions including bans or limitations on the export of both food and medical supplies. In 2020, the three global supply-chain centers of China, the EU, and the US would collectively lose $126 billion in manufacturing exports as a result of lockdowns.

Insufficient Knowledge

Due to their reliance on tacit knowledge, SMEs are particularly vulnerable to the loss of critical employees (i.e., long-term, experienced, and competent staff) during this pandemic. For small and medium-sized enterprises (SMEs), the loss of important personnel due to natural disasters or the coronavirus can be disastrous. If a small or medium-sized enterprise (SME) loses a key employee, the business could potentially fail. Since many establishments are reopening gradually while others remain closed, it might be confusing for customers to know whether their usual points of purchase are back in operation following the pandemic. (Klein and Todesco, 2021)

DIGITAL TRANSFORMATION OF SMEs

In this context, "digitalization means the acceptance of digital technology within an organization, which leads to the creation of new digital artifacts, platforms, infrastructures, and business and management models." The term "digital technologies refers to a wide range of computerized information and communication technologies, including but not limited to the following 7 technologies: social, mobile, big data, cloud computing, IoT, platform development, and AI-related technologies."

Digital Transformation and SMEs

Most SMEs have expressed curiosity about cutting-edge innovations like the Internet of Things (IoT), cloud computing, big data analysis, and artificial intelligence (AI). The level of interest from SMEs is significantly higher in 2021 than it was in 2019. The trend toward telecommuting over the past year may account for this in part. Technologies like this are crucial for off-site monitoring, data collection, and workforce communication.

Figure 3. Covid-19 SMEs digital transformation
Source: Bielozorov, 2020

Organizations can get various benefits from adopting digital tools. Digitalization contributes to minimize transaction costs in two ways: through improved and quicker information access, and through improved and quicker communication between staff, suppliers, and networks. As a result of the lowered barriers to entry and the increased opportunities for service trade, it can aid small and medium-sized businesses (SMEs) in entering international markets. Since more and more government services are going digital, it is easier to get your hands on resources like money, education, and jobs. It makes it possible to generate data and analyze a company's operations in fresh ways, both of which can improve performance.

When digital technology is applied throughout an entire organization, it may alter processes and increase value for customers. The process of digital transformation is followed by an overhaul of the company model, necessitating the presence of an ecosystem, a specific digital strategy, and digitally savvy personnel. Companies can no longer survive in the long run without the ability to adapt to the digital age. One of the requirements of digital transformation is the cultivation of specialized skill sets, the nature of which varies by industry and business necessity. Capabilities in the digital realm aid in the development of new digital technologies, which in turn help propel the digital transformation process forward.

Important Considerations for a Successful Digital Transformation

The following are the primary factors hindering SMEs from effectively undertaking digital transformation.

- Small and medium-sized business owners (SMEs) often lag behind the digital transformation trend because their executives lack a clear vision and an adequate understanding of the topic.
- There is a high risk of failure among SMEs since they have not yet developed a coherent digital transformation strategy in line with their company strategy and resources, nor have they yet defined appropriate directions for the transformation of technology.
- Due to a focus on short-term gains (i.e., opting to implement numerous changes simultaneously despite a lack of foundational resources), many companies are undergoing digital transformation but have not yet developed a proper roadmap.

The result has been setbacks and delays in digital transformation.

Digitalization Benefits SME Agility

- Firms can benefit from digital transformation by increasing their organizational flexibility and resilience and boosting their dynamic skills, both of which can help them obtain and maintain competitive advantages.
- Due to the enormous advantages of digital resources in terms of volume, velocity, diversity, and value, businesses can buy or retrieve information resources from the outside world at a low cost.
- Digital technology allows businesses to better seize opportunities in the midst of a crisis. Online learning, remote labor, and automated delivery are just a few of the digital innovations that have emerged as promising responses to the COVID-19 pandemic.
- With the help of digitalization, businesses may better reorganize their resources in the face of unexpected challenges. The scope, scale, and adaptability of a company's resources all improve as a result of digitalization.

STRATEGIC MEASURES FOR SMEs TO COMBAT COVID-19

Several governments have already launched measures in response to the pandemic, recognizing that small and medium-sized enterprises (SMEs) would be a crucial engine for the post-crisis economic recovery.

Recommendations to Support SMEs

- **Facilitate Support Access for Small and Medium-Sized Enterprises -** Policymakers should help SMEs find the relevant support programs, apply, and receive aid to boost their response measures participation. Successful countries have created a single, integrated SME contact point. After learning about the best support, SMEs require quick and easy access. For instance, loans, grants, and guarantees that require lengthy applications can inhibit small businesses, which lack the manpower and resources to complete them. Governments can boost SME aid program participation by simplifying administrative processes. (Albaz et al, 2020)

- **Private Sector Development and Supply Chain Disruptions-** Informal sector MSMEs depend on daily sales therefore value chain disruptions are devastating. To prevent short-term insolvencies, these businesses will rely primarily on incentives that lower operating costs and forgive debts. Large, formal firms can partner with tiny, informal businesses to distribute critical commodities to consumers' doorsteps. Stimulus packages should strengthen informal economy workspaces and infrastructure like communal markets to encourage social distancing. They could operate immediately. Long-term private sector development actions could improve firm performance and competitiveness. These should include finance, consultancy, business training, industry-specific networking, laws, standards, innovation, and linkage programs. (Saha, 2020)
- **Policy Frameworks that Foster Resilience-** Policies at the public level that back training and resources, disseminate data, and invest in constructing capacities are crucial to ensuring resilience. Short-term, these measures should facilitate MSMEs' incorporation of remote work, online shopping, and home delivery in response to the new realities of COVID-19. But this calls for customer demand, familiarity with digital platforms, and the presence of fundamental infrastructure (such as an internet connection). Assuring MSMEs can recover robustly requires a medium- to a long-term focus on digital transformation. Digital solutions and training that are simple to implement and do not call for a significant financial investment upfront will facilitate adaptation. (Saha, 2020)

Restoration Strategies

During the COVID-19 pandemic, entrepreneurs benefitted from financial management strategies that increased inflows and decreased outflows. Entrepreneurs have used microfinance banks and government aid to pay rent, keep employees, and meet other overhead costs. During a financial crisis, companies have decreased hours and workers. Entrepreneurial traits affect business performance. Some entrepreneurs have found that launching a COVID-19-related product boosts demand, so they now make sanitizers, masks, PPE kits, etc. Improvisation can mitigate COVID-19 issues for entrepreneurs. Flexibility helps businesses survive. Extreme events benefit from entrepreneurial self-efficacy. Research shows that MSMEs' performance improves when they change business approaches, generate new revenue, prepare for the new regime, stay informed from WHO or the Ministry of Health, identify core products needed to stay operational, and communicate with employees and customers about COVID-19 changes. In times of crisis, restoration strategies include proper health and sanitization, personnel health protection, supply chain preparation, and customer service modification. (Singh et al, 2022)

Policy Measures Dedicated to SMEs (OECD, 2020)

- "Sick leave, shorter work weeks, and temporary layoffs are just a few examples of the policies that several nations have enacted, with some aimed squarely at small and medium-sized enterprises." Governments also often step in to help replace lost wages for workers who have been temporarily laid off or to help businesses keep their doors open. Many nations have enacted policies aimed squarely at the self-employed.
- Many nations have instituted policies that delay payments such as taxes, social security, debt, and rent and utilities in an effort to ease liquidity difficulties. Debt cancellation or tax reduction programs have been instituted in certain situations. There has been action taken on the part of various nations with respect to public procurement and payment delays.

- In an effort to encourage commercial bank lending to small and medium-sized enterprises (SMEs), several nations have adopted, expanded, or simplified the granting of loan guarantees.
- To offset the revenue shortfall, governments in a number of regions are granting businesses in the small and medium enterprise (SME) sector grants and subsidies.
- Non-banking financial support intermediaries are becoming an increasingly common part of the policy support mix for many countries.
- To aid SMEs adapt to the containment measures, many countries are adopting structural policies to promote the use of contemporary methods of production.
- The implementation of telework is one example of how these policies can help with the here and now, but they also help bolster the resilience of small and medium-sized enterprises (SMEs) and promote their further growth.
- To track how the crisis is affecting small and medium-sized enterprises (SMEs) and improve the management of policy responses to their needs, certain nations have implemented unique tracking and management systems.

CONCLUSION

The aforesaid analysis leads us to the conclusion that there is no question in anyone's mind that CO-VID-19 had a significant impact on practically all of the countries that make up the world. The CO-VID-19 epidemic has hit businesses of all sizes, but for a number of reasons, SMEs are particularly prone. Disruptions to the SME sector have significant social and welfare consequences in low-income economies because SMEs are the primary employers and providers of products and services in many countries. Within the scope of this research, we examine the part that COVID-19 played in fostering digital transformation and the ways in which it might help to ensure the continued existence of SMEs. In order to address gaps in their suggested solutions, officials will need to examine the circumstances and be flexible and adaptable. There is a thin balance that governments must tread between intervening to preserve struggling industrial enterprises and putting in place longer-term policies that rebuild better with more robust sectors, better suited to withstand shocks like pandemics.

REFERENCES

Adam, N. A., & Alarifi, G. (2021). Innovation practices for survival of small and Medium Enterprises (smes) in the COVID-19 times: The role of External Support. *Journal of Innovation and Entrepreneurship*, *10*(1), 15. Advance online publication. doi:10.118613731-021-00156-6 PMID:34075328

Albaz, A., Mansour, T., Rida, T., & Schubert, J. (2022, September 1). *Setting up small and medium-size enterprises for restart and recovery*. McKinsey & Company. Retrieved from https://www.mckinsey.com/industries/public-and-social-sector/our-insights/setting-up-small-and-medium-size-enterprises-f or-restart-and-recovery

Bai, C., Quayson, M., & Sarkis, J. (2021). Covid-19 pandemic digitization lessons for sustainable development of micro-and small- enterprises. *Sustainable Production and Consumption, 27*, 1989–2001. doi:10.1016/j.spc.2021.04.035 PMID:34722843

Behera, M., Mishra, S., Mohapatra, N., & Behera, A. R. (2020). Covid-19 pandemic and micro, Small and Medium Enterprises (msmes): Policy response for revival. *SEDME (Small Enterprises Development, Management & Extension Journal): A Worldwide Window on MSME Studies, 47*(3), 213–228. doi:10.1177/09708464211037485

Belitski, M., Guenther, C., Kritikos, A. S., & Thurik, R. (2021). *Economic effects of the covid-19 pandemic on entrepreneurship and small businesses.* SSRN Electronic Journal. doi:10.2139srn.3905065

Bielozorov, A. (2020, May 13). *Covid-19 SME Technology Adoption Assessment* [web log]. Retrieved from https://www.perform-network.eu/covid-19-sme-technology-adoption-assessment/

Blog: Five ways governments can help small businesses in the informal sector survive covid-19. (n.d.). Commonwealth. Retrieved from https://thecommonwealth.org/news/blog-five-ways-governments-can-help-small-businesses-informal-sector-survive-covid-19

Buchholz, K. (2020, June 17). *Half of Indian Startups in Serious Danger Due to COVID-19* [web log]. Retrieved from https://www.statista.com/chart/22027/startup-sme-financial-situation-india/

Caballero-Morales, S.-O. (2021). Innovation as a recovery strategy for smes in emerging economies during the COVID-19 pandemic. *Research in International Business and Finance, 57*, 101396. doi:10.1016/j.ribaf.2021.101396 PMID:33558782

Coronavirus (COVID-19): SME policy responses. (n.d.). OECD. Retrieved from https://www.oecd.org/coronavirus/policy-responses/coronavirus-covid-19-sme-policy-responses-04440101/#section-d1e3087

Digital transformation of small and Medium Enterprises (smes) within the COVID-19 pandemic. (n.d.). Trường Đại học Kinh tế TP. Hồ Chí Minh. Retrieved from https://www.ueh.edu.vn/en/news/digital-transformation-of-small-and-medium-enterprises-smes-within-the-covid-19-pandemic-58518

Guo, H., Yang, Z., Huang, R., & Guo, A. (2020). The digitalization and public crisis responses of small and Medium Enterprises: Implications from a COVID-19 survey. *Frontiers of Business Research in China, 14*(1), 19. Advance online publication. doi:10.118611782-020-00087-1

Hebert, D. J. (2022). *COVID-19's Impacts on SMEs and Policy Recommendations in Response. The National Law Review*, 12.

Karr, J., Loh, K., & Wirjo, A. (2020). *Supporting MSMEs' Digitalization Amid COVID-19.* Asia Pacific Economic Cooperation.

Klein, V. B., & Todesco, J. L. (2021). covid -19 crisis and smes responses: The role of digital transformation. *Knowledge and Process Management*, *28*(2), 117–133. doi:10.1002/kpm.1660

Partida, D. (2020, November 15). *7 covid-19 struggles small businesses are facing and how to overcome them*. Due. Retrieved from https://due.com/blog/small-businesses-struggle-in-pandemic/

Rakshit, S., Islam, N., Mondal, S., & Paul, T. (2021). Mobile apps for SME Business Sustainability during covid-19 and onwards. *Journal of Business Research*, *135*, 28–39. doi:10.1016/j.jbusres.2021.06.005 PMID:34751197

Rupeika-Apoga, R., Petrovska, K., & Bule, L. (2022). *SMEs' digital transformation facilitated by COVID-19*. doi:10.20944/preprints202201.0340.v1

Sannegadu, R. (2021). Managing Local and International Challenges Faced by SMEs of Island States Economies in The Midst of the Covid-19 Pandemic- Evidence from MauritiusRajesh Sannegadu. *Academy of Marketing Studies Journal*, *25*(1).

Singh, S., Chamola, P., Kumar, V., Verma, P., & Makkar, N. (2022). Explaining the revival strategies of Indian msmes to mitigate the effects of covid-19 outbreak. *Benchmarking*. Advance online publication. doi:10.1108/BIJ-08-2021-0497

Thukral, E. (2021). covid -19: Small and medium enterprises challenges and responses with creativity, Innovation, and entrepreneurship. *Strategic Change*, *30*(2), 153–158. doi:10.1002/jsc.2399

Toth, R., Kasa, R., & Lentner, C. (2022). The impact of financial culture on the operation of Hungarian smes before and during COVID-19. *Risks*, *10*(7), 135. doi:10.3390/risks10070135

Chapter 13
The Impact of Social Marketing on SMEs in India:
A Theoretical Perspective

Amandeep Singh
https://orcid.org/0000-0002-0970-5467
Chitkara Business School, Chitkara University, Punjab, India

Amrinder Singh
https://orcid.org/0000-0003-0830-7245
Jain University (Deemed), Bangalore, India

ABSTRACT

The impact of social media can be seen everywhere. Now the success of a business depends upon how successfully it is able to handle its social media marketing. It is a new phenomenon that has changed how the business environment operates. Companies are able to gain access to resources that were otherwise not available to them. It has also helped businesses to increase their worthiness, cultivate strategic partnerships, and increase their contact with customers and suppliers. It has become important for business owners and marketers to understand how social media work as a communication and marketing tool and how they can significantly grow their businesses. The study focused on establishing the effect of social media on the growth of SMEs in India. The present study is theoretical research, based on the various literature available. Additionally, social media allows businesses to communicate speedily and cheaply with customers as well as allow them to construct a database that can be used to generate business leads that may translate to increased sales and thus grow the SMEs.

INTRODUCTION

Small and Medium Enterprise business is based on four resources Land, labour, machine and entrepreneurial ability. Technology and partnership with various other businesses and SMEs can increase the strength of SMEs (Arianty et al., 2018). These days, the improvement of innovation and correspondence

DOI: 10.4018/978-1-6684-5770-2.ch013

are progressively detached, the utilization of online media or internet-based applications has turned into the most compelling thing for SMEs consuming and distributing data. One of the upsides of such methods is having a great deal of potential for the progression of a work.

Accordingly, SME should have the option to fashion themselves following the advancement of innovation through virtual world. Correspondence should be possible through virtual entertainment by organizations to their clients who will affect more noteworthy market access (Samuel & Sarprasatha, 2016). Internet based media is utilized to lead correspondence in business, help advertising items and administrations, speak with clients and providers, supplement brands, lessen costs and for online deals. The quantity of data scattering and the undeniably free rivalry has expanded buyer consciousness of the enormous determination of items to be picked. On the off chance that SMEs don't fix the procedure in that frame of mind for the progression of business, the SME will be compromised bankrupt. Internet based methods and applications are a showcasing device of items or administrations other than as a holder of communications with clients to attempt to tackle their own concerns (Kilgour et al., 2015).

Internet based Social Media marketing likewise offers a ton of advantages for SMEs that is recognizing clients, directing corresponding correspondence, sharing data to have the option to know the items that clients are enjoyed, client participation, connection between clients in view of area and communication designs, and expanded collaboration with different business visionaries to work on the presentation for the headway of SMEs. Social Media that incorporates online channels to share and take part in various exercises, is an undeniably significant way for SMEs to impart intelligently with purchasers. Social media is a gathering of web put together applications constructed based with respect to innovation structure from WEB 2.0, and it permits the making of the substance of trade data from Web clients. WEB 2.0 and can be utilized in SMEs (Jagongo & Kinyua, 2013; Kilgour et al., 2015).

The further examination shows that the advertising directed on the family business. It has not been completely successful, where the money managers who exist in the space isn't yet all Utilizing virtual media. It is seen the business of its items have not been by following the objective, item showcasing has not arrived at a wide region. Showcasing technique is definitely finished by the SMEs to have seriousness and progress one of them is utilizing virtual entertainment. The information possessed by SME entertainers who extremely missing and restricted. So, the item is just endlessly known by the ecological local area around modern assembling alone (Arianty, n.d.; Arianty et al., 2018)..

Internet based communication and person to person communication locales have become pervasive and have gotten a large number of ways for a business to interface with its true capacity and expected purchasers. This study investigates the foundation of SMEs and Social Media Marketing. Overall, the virtual media is consistently acquiring client base and this could interpret as any open doors for organizations to saddle the force of virtual media to make and upgrade purchaser commitment which could thusly mean extension for social media services as a business in itself.

The present study endeavors to see it from three aspects. First is the various alternatives given by Social Media Marketing. The second features the utilization of Social Media Marketing by the various SMEs in India. Next, it examines the elements impacting business venture inside the country. What makes the study relevant is the monetary and social foundations.

SMEs and Social Media Marketing

The advanced media particularly the social media has changed the world and has modified shopper conduct; various types of internet-based engaged have advanced wise shoppers to go with informed decisions. Accordingly, organizations also are advancing and virtual media is acquiring unmistakable quality in their showcasing systems. The range and perceivability of business on friendly media have been abundantly expounded on internationally(Balan et al., 2014). The Virtual Media Advertising Industry Report expressed that over 90% of advertisers pronounced that web-based media was significant for their business, when contrasted with the 86% in previous year (Rugova & Prenaj, 2016). Online media showcasing as a promoting instrument has likewise come to be financial and useful for SMEs who don't have a high showcasing spending plan (Saleh, 2012).

ADVANTAGES OF ONLINE MEDIA FOR SMEs

Aker & Öztürk, (2015) in their paper on A Structure for a Web-based Media Dashboard for Business people rattles off the accompanying open doors for Business people given by Online Media by which it goes about as a significant, in the event that not fundamental piece of business system.

- **Thought Age**

Clients can become engaged with the most common way of gathering the assistance necessities, grasping the requirements furthermore, issues; distinguishing expected arrangements; and assessment of existing administrations. Organizations can likewise reach expected clients with the assistance of online networks by which these clients can give important client input through different means.

- **Thought Refinement**

Clients can support looking into and calibrating thoughts. They can propose upgrades and extra elements; give criticism on ideas through rating frameworks; polls and so on.

- **Framework Plan**

Clients can be taken part in web-based conversations and media content assessment by which they can recommend upgrades, recognize pluses and minuses in framework plan.

- **Help Testing and Pilot Run**

Clients can be a piece of pilot testing gatherings and can be selected through an organization's or a business' social media pages. The potential clients can hence partake in the survey of administration ideas; testing of items and benefits and recommend upgrades.

- **Test Advertising**

Client inputs on promoting plan can be gathered through virtual entertainment. Their degrees of fulfillment on showcasing can be checked alongside social affair ideas for development. Provincial brands across the world have started to understand the capability of advanced and virtual media and are progressively using online media as a component of their computerized promoting efforts to expand their compass and perceivability across nearby and worldwide crowds(Singh et al., 2019; Singh, Singh, et al., 2020a, 2020b; Singh, Singla, et al., 2020; Singh & Kaur, 2021a, 2021b).

SCOPE OF SOCIAL MEDIA FOR SMEs

These external vendors are usually online marketing companies, digital media agencies, creative agencies etc. and the social media services they offer could comprise any or all of the following:

- **Social Media Strategy Planning & Development**

Development of comprehensive social strategies that are based on client's needs, to make their social media platforms into successful brands. This includes audience and Influencer identification and strategies for activation and outreach.

- **Marketing through social media platforms**

Involves marketing through different types of popular social media like Facebook, Twitter, Google +, Linked In, YouTube, Pinterest, Instagram etc.

- **Ad management on social media**

Management of advertisements in the form of banners, display ads and other ads on social media platforms.

- **Social Media Consulting**

Social media consultant offers consultancy services in determining where the opportunities in social media are, specific for each client.

- **Social Media Competitions & campaigns**

Development of highly-targeted social campaigns and competitions to build interaction, grow and engage fans and enhance online presence.

- **Social Media Applications**

Development of applications that work within various social media, in order to further enhance the interaction of customers with a company's brand and products

- **Social copywriting and content development**

Creation of copy and other content specifically for social media promotions

- **Social Media Monitoring**

Monitoring of the social media sphere to discover and analyze what is being said about the client

- **Social ecosystem and competitive analysis**

Performance of in-depth analyses of the social media content and also identify the tactics and create action alerts for current and potential competitors.

- **Measurement & Analytics**

Analyses of the effectiveness of the various strategies, campaigns and social media presence

DISCUSSIONS

In light of exploration acquired there is a positive and huge impact between client relationship the executives to SME propels. This implies that keeping up with client connections can build the advancement of SMEs in various regions, where the administration of solid client relations will uphold the objectives of SMEs, generally the feeble will block or Contrary to SME's objectives. Client relationship the executives can diminish and try and dispense with gathering in a business, and spotlights on individual client needs (Berthon et al., 2008).

Web-based media has turned into a medium that works with and grows Correspondence among SMEs and clients. Web-based media can establish an exceptional climate for SMEs that permits organizations to work available on items, diminish showcasing costs, increment deals, and proposition nearer client relationship the board (Fadhiha Mokhtar et al., 2017) alongside the presence of computerized innovation in the late twentieth hundred years, and the approaching of the virtual media period, SMEs are supposed to focus on clients.

There are two things that make UKM begin to focus on the shoppers, in particular the primary SME gain from past experience that has not done great client relationship the executives through existing web-based media, both absence of understanding the clients in Virtual media use (Michaelson & Stacks, 2011). In keeping the relationship with the client required workers who have Web Authority (Kautz & Nielsen, 2004).

Numerous Web clients who utilize virtual media are a chance for the organization to constantly associate with clients. Having a capable representative in online media dominance can further develop efficiency and effectiveness. expressed that in his examination directed in SMEs get the way that the administration of client relations via virtual media influences the development of SMEs implies SMEs who can lay out a relationship with clients through web-based media can build deals and benefits it will affect the advancement of SMEs.

Social media made by SME entertainers ought to zero in on relationship the board clients, advancing the utilization of virtual media to produce deals, create client data sets, create and find new business thoughts at the end of the day with web-based media expanding the advancement of SMEs, and can open up open doors and effectively draw in associations in managing clients to produce deals and eventually increment benefits(Ines, 2016).

Moreover, the effect of social media on the headway of SMEs is market access. The impact of market admittance to the SME's advancement shows positive worth, intending that there is an immediate impact between market admittance to SME progress. SMEs in directing their business should have a procedure to utilize virtual entertainment to get to the objective market(Hassan et al., 2015). Utilizing online entertainment is the best way SME has in getting to the objective market (Kirtiş & Karahan, 2011). Social media can be a publicizing instrument and access serious areas of strength for a so it can arrive at a more extensive shopper and can draw in and impact customers to buy choices.

Likewise, social media is thought of as fit for assuming a successful part in advertising connections. Market access by utilizing powerful elements permits organizations to discuss reliably with clients in regards to new items and administrations that have to do with deals (Reyneke et al., 2011). With social promoting correspondence and exchanges should be possible whenever and can be in admittance to the remainder of the world, one can likewise see different merchandise over the Web, a large portion of the data about the different items currently accessible in Web, simplicity of requesting and buyer capacity in contrasting one item with another.

CONCLUSION

From the above conversations shows that there is a social media influence on the speed of SMEs in the India, this should be visible in the variable client relationship the executives through the social media massive impact. Underway toward SMEs implies that when client relationship the executives is great it will influence the advancement of SMEs. Notwithstanding the entrance factors of the market through social media critical effect on the advancement of SMEs implies that social media gives adaptability to organizations to lead market and get new business sectors without being upset by geographic area.

The gander at the social media scene across India uncovers that following the worldwide episode of online entertainment social media is progressively acquiring use across the world, in spite of the fact that there are social limitations and restraints. This is likewise valid for India where mechanical availability and cell phone entrance has supported the engendering of web-based entertainment. The rising acknowledgment of social media among its kin has proclaimed an adjustment of the manner in which organizations draw in with them via online entertainment with numerous organizations across the district and in India taking up social media to connect with their neighborhood and worldwide crowd. Notwithstanding, the absence of advanced media abilities in the district, especially inside the country India has blocked neighborhood organizations from completely taking advantage of the capability of this new age media.

This presents amazing open doors in business venture for computerized and online entertainment organizations who grasp the necessities of the organizations and brands and can offer social media related administrations like social media the board and make accessible nearby, applicable substance in numerous dialects to meet the changing requirements of organizations in the India. The rundown of social media related administrations recorded in this study is just characteristic of the all-around the world-famous administrations delivered; there is no restriction to the imagination and drives for online entertainment organizations as the extent of social media related administrations is so immense both in its variety and amount.

Moreover, in spite of the fact that there is an obstacle to be survived, the socio-politic climate in the India appears to help enterprising endeavors and the blast of computerized media joined with the help for pioneering development in the country shows a good situation for the social media business visionaries. The present study suggests further investigation into the accompanying regions:

1. A top to bottom review into the social media goals, discernments, utilization example and conduct of the different socioeconomics that contain India as separated from skillet India, there are no examinations devoted to India that concentrates on the way of behaving, example and inspirations of the overall socioeconomics in India which could add supplemental understanding for advertisers.
2. A top to bottom investigation of the organizations in India relating to their requirement for social media administrations from outer offices and investigating further the ongoing hole in the administrations delivered and their assumptions.
3. Albeit online entertainment and related administrations has been widely examined and expounded on universally, with regards to an emerging country like India, its degree for business venture, open doors and difficulties of this field, future potential stay at this point neglected.

Thusly, this study presumed that a top to bottom gander at the extent of business in the field of social media administrations with regards to the India is feasible and can assist with framing the possibilities and difficulties looked by business people digging in social media administrations. At the point when there is expanding center around advancing business venture consequently enhancing the country's economy, further examination in this space appears to be even more significant.

REFERENCES

Aker, Ç., & Öztürk, Ö. (2015). *Social Media Interactions and the Use of Third-Party Management Applications on Effectiveness and Perception of Information*. doi:10.1007/978-3-319-20889-3_1

Arianty, N. (n.d.). *The Impact of Social Media Use on SME Progress*. Academic Press.

Arianty, N., Fauzi Rambe, M., Bahagia, R., Utara, S., & Kapten Mucthar Basri No, J. (2018). *Increasing Family Revenue Based on Household Industry. Saudi Journal of Business and Management Studies*. SJBMS. doi:10.21276jbms.2018.3.9.10

Balan, N., Skoug, R., Tulasi Ram, S., Rajesh, P. K., Shiokawa, K., Otsuka, Y., Batista, I. S., Ebihara, Y., & Nakamura, T. (2014). CME front and severe space weather. *Journal of Geophysical Research. Space Physics, 119*(12), 10,041–10,058. doi:10.1002/2014JA020151

Berthon, P., Ewing, M. T., & Napoli, J. (2008). Brand Management in Small to Medium-Sized Enterprises*. *Journal of Small Business Management, 46*(1), 27–45. doi:10.1111/j.1540-627X.2007.00229.x

Fadhiha Mokhtar, N., Rosufila, Z., Hasan, A., Sofian, M. A., & Halim, A. (2017). The Social Media and Marketing Strategies: How it Impacts the Small-and Medium-sized Enterprises' Business Performance? *Australasian Journal of Business, Social Science and Information Technology, 3*.

Hassan, S., Nadzim, S. Z. A., & Shiratuddin, N. (2015). Strategic Use of Social Media for Small Business Based on the AIDA Model. *Procedia: Social and Behavioral Sciences, 172*, 262–269. doi:10.1016/j. sbspro.2015.01.363

Ines, J. C. (2016). Social Media as A Marketing Tool: The Case of Small and Medium Enterprise in The Sultanate of Oman. *Intercontinental Journal of Marketing Management, 3*(12), 20–36. www.researchscripts.org

Jagongo, A., & Kinyua, C. (2013). The Social Media and Entrepreneurship Growth (A New Business Communication Paradigm among SMEs in Nairobi). *International Journal of Humanities and Social Science, 3*(10).

Kautz, K., & Nielsen, P. A. (2004). Understanding the implementation of software process improvement innovations in software organizations. *Information Systems Journal, 14*(1), 3–22. doi:10.1111/j.1365-2575.2004.00156.x

Kilgour, M., Sasser, S. L., & Larke, R. (2015). The social media transformation process: Curating content into strategy. *Corporate Communications, 20*(3), 326–343. doi:10.1108/CCIJ-07-2014-0046

Kirtiş, A. K., & Karahan, F. (2011). To Be or Not to Be in Social Media Arena as the Most Cost-Efficient Marketing Strategy after the Global Recession. *Procedia: Social and Behavioral Sciences, 24*, 260–268. doi:10.1016/j.sbspro.2011.09.083

Michaelson, D., & Stacks, D. W. (2011). Standardization in Public Relations Measurement and Evaluation. *The Public Relations Journal, 5*(2).

Reyneke, M., Pitt, L., & Berthon, P. R. (2011). Luxury wine brand visibility in social media: An exploratory study. *International Journal of Wine Business Research, 23*(1), 21–35. doi:10.1108/17511061111121380

Rugova, B., & Prenaj, B. (2016). Social media as marketing tool for SMEs: opportunities and challenges. *Academic Journal of Business, 2*(3). www.iipccl.org

Saleh, S. (2012). Business, barriers and benefits: E-business for SMEs in the sultanate of Oman. *International Journal of Business and Management Studies, 1*(2), 405–422. www.internetworldstats.com

Samuel, B. S., & Sarprasatha, J. (2016). Entrepreneurship in social-media services in Oman - A socio-economic scanning of the Sultanate. *Asian Social Science, 12*(4), 138–148. doi:10.5539/ass.v12n4p138

Singh, A., Jain, A., & Singla, B. (2019). Technological advancement-based paradigm shift: A focus shift from large screen to small screen. *International Journal of Innovative Technology and Exploring Engineering, 8*(10), 48–53. doi:10.35940/ijitee.I8613.0881019

Singh, A., & Kaur, A. (2021). Examining gender differences in the factors affecting ethical leadership: A study of educational institutions. *International Journal of Sociotechnology and Knowledge Development, 13*(4), 153–164. doi:10.4018/IJSKD.2021100110

Singh, A., Singh, A., Singh Vij, T., & Pardesi, A. (2020). An Empirical Study of the Factors Affecting Online Shopping Behavior of the Indian Consumers. *International Journal of Advanced Science and Technology, 29*(8s), 406–411.

Singh, A., Singla, B., & Sharma, S. (2020). An Empirical Study of Factors Affecting the Selection of Point of Purchase Location: A Case of FMCG Industry. *International Journal of Control and Automation, 13*(2s), 72–78.

Chapter 14
Use of Social Media by SMEs in the Tourism Industry

Ankit Dhiraj
Lovely Professional University, India

Sanjeev Kumar
 https://orcid.org/0000-0002-7375-7341
Lovely Professional University, India

Divya Rani
Patliputra University, India

ABSTRACT

The globe is experiencing a significant advancement in modern technology, particularly social networking sites that have been accessible in various industries, including travel and tourism. This makes it more difficult for tourism businesses to give people the best offers on tourist destinations. Tourism SMEs connect with customers, give support, and promotional activity through social media. These new media establish a stronger connection with consumers. Researchers collect data randomly through Google forms of 175 managers or owners from tourism SMEs to achieve their objectives. This chapter discusses the use of social media by tourism SMEs and social media promotion and other aspects like the development and advantages of social media.

1. INTRODUCTION

A total of US$ 194.30 billion, or 6.8 per cent of India's GDP, was contributed by the travel and tourism sector in 2019. India's tourism sector supported about 13% of the nation's overall employment during the 2019 fiscal year. As a result, the share of employment increased marginally from the previous year. The stake went grown more than 1% from the fiscal year 2014 to the current one. In 2019, the tourist sector employed close to 90 million people worldwide. In the industry, there are more indirectly employed workers than directly employed persons (WTTC, 2019). India is not only the second-largest tourism market in Asia after China. According to UNWTO data for the year 2019, In terms of foreign tourism

DOI: 10.4018/978-1-6684-5770-2.ch014

receipts, India Tourism has consistently risen to number 13 and number 22 in the globe, respectively (Tourism, 2021). India is one of the nations that have been most severely impacted by the pandemic. The pandemic has jeopardised the sector's growth possibilities, but it has also led to a serious economic downturn from which the industry will need some time to recover. Social media use in the travel and tourism sector has grown significantly during the covid-19. People were able to connect with friends and family through social media, who were far away. A lot of individuals relied on the internet to keep them entertained throughout the lockdown. These days, the majority of tourists choose their locations and travel plans based on reviews and experiences shared on social media platforms (Alghizzawi et al., 2018). Social media is now widely used by the travel industry. People utilise social media to gather knowledge and decide wisely on their travel plans, which saves them time and money. Additionally, it enables users to communicate about their shared travel-related experiences. They may discuss either a good or bad experience they had at a hotel, airline, restaurant, or some other business. Tourism SMEs companies use social media for

1. **Travel Research**- companies changed their strategies of research for the planning of the trip. They not only conduct practically all of their planning online, but they also frequently ask questions on social media. Although you might not consider websites like TripAdvisor to be the best social media channel, it is undoubtedly social network. Social networking networks have recently developed into fantastic resources for learning about locations, lodging options, activities, restaurants, and other things.
2. **Destination Discovery** - Social media is useful for locating desired destinations. Searchers may find and select you thanks to your strong social media presence. You can encourage the next tourist to book by having current customers post about their enjoyable and thrilling experiences at your establishment.
3. **Customer Service**- Social media communication is two-way. Marketers can hear the criticisms or compliments of their clients and reply with a remark or instant message. Essentially, this acts as a customer service avenue. Your brand will appear to care about its customers if it responds to their online comments, which will help to improve your reputation. Additionally, it humanizes your brand, giving you a more genuine appearance.
4. **Loyalty Programs** - Plans for social sharing are excellent for loyalty programmes at many different travel agencies. Customers can be enticed by attractive benefits or even discounts to post and share their experiences with a brand's goods. By doing this, you may accomplish two goals at once: you can get feedback and reward your fans.
5. **Social Media Channels**- Social media marketing can be done on different platforms, including Facebook, Instagram, Twitter, Linkedin, and Snapchat. You don't have to participate in all of them, but maximizing your brand's exposure and recognition in the most well-liked ones can help. According to surveys, 40% of millennials base their vacation decisions on how attractive their Instagram photographs are.

There is no doubt that social media has significantly changed how we perceive our surroundings. Few industries, meanwhile, have seen it present as important a marketing potential as the tourism sector. Tourism marketing on social media is undoubtedly a match made in digital heaven.

2. LITERATURE REVIEW

Social media usage in the workplace has received a lot of attention recently. The usage of social media by SMEs is the subject of an increasing number of studies. We study a number of current works on SMEs and web 2.0/social media. Recently, there has been a lot of interest in the study surrounding the usage of internal social media apps in the corporate context, sometimes referred to as "Enterprise 2.0". Numerous case studies on the adoption and usage of social media in businesses reveal a wide range of Enterprise 2.0 applications. Social media are internet tools including platforms, apps, and media that promote communication, teamwork, and content sharing (Czekaj, 2017). Social media has evolved into the primary means of expression in the twenty-first century, allowing us to communicate our opinions in novel ways (M. Saravanakumar, 2012). On the other hand, many researchers explained that Social media is a mechanism that enables people to advertise their websites, goods, or services via online social networks as well as to connect with and engage a far bigger population than would have been possible through conventional advertising channels (Thomas D. m ayfiel D iii, 2009), (Greenwood et al., 2016), (Si, 2016). Some researchers defined New web technologies like social media have made it easier for everyone to produce and share content (Zarezadeh et al., 2018).

Figure 1. Definitions of key concepts
Source: *(Nakara et al., 2012)*

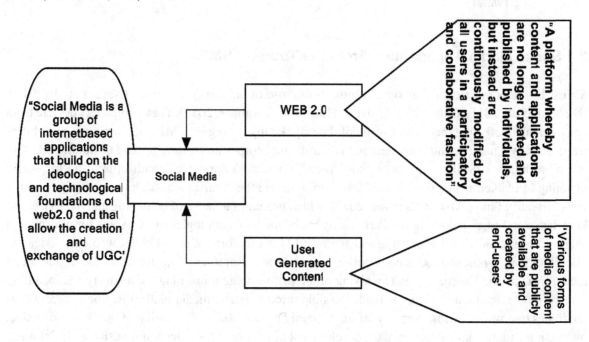

The conventional methods of marketing are being altered by social media. One-way information flow is a feature of traditional marketing, as seen in TV and radio ads. Web-based marketing, on the other hand, makes it possible to maintain push messaging while engaging customers in conversation (Zuhdi et al., 2019). Additionally, social media marketing offers a chance for the timely delivery of information in an informative manner Customers are allowed to contribute to the dissemination of information in this way. Customers are thus no longer just passive receivers of information; actively use and share social media for information(Baumöl et al., 2016).

Figure 2. The characteristics of different types of social media
Source: *(Park & Oh, 2012)*

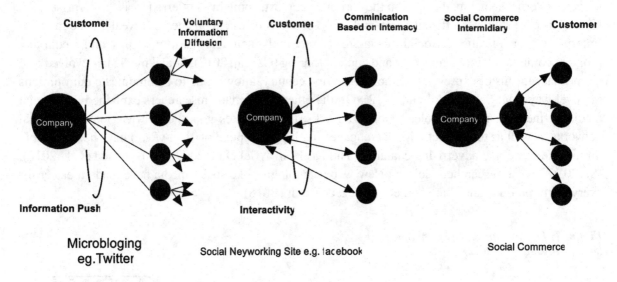

2.1 Social Media Applications From the Tourism SMEs

SMEs' business practices differ significantly from those of larger organizations (Nakara et al., 2012), (Nicholas et al., 2011), (Jansson et al., 2017) (Hrastinski & Aghaee, 2012). They completely deviate from conventional marketing theory as a result of their marketing strategies. SMEs' marketing is straightforward, effective, natural, and consistent with their distinct corporate culture. Instead of traditional "top-down" techniques, SMEs implement "bottom-up," interactive approaches with little to no long-term planning of marketing practices. Web 2.0 technologies are the "human approach to interactivity on the web," (Beatrix Lanyi, Miklos Hornyak, 2021), which promotes a Sense of belonging and the sharing of knowledge and ideas among users. Particularly social media technologies offer a stage for information sharing, communication, Co-creation and Teamwork. Internet forums, social blogs, weblogs, podcasts,, microblogging, wikis, and social bookmarking are just a few examples of the numerous forms that social media (Xu, 2013). The sharing and archiving of interactive content in a range of media types, including as text, image, audio, and video, is made possible through social media platforms. Social media thus facilitates two-way real-time communication (Simmi Dhyani, 2022), the sharing of implicit knowledge, interaction with that knowledge, and the development of relationships. Successful businesses (Camilleri & Kozak, 2022), must "collaborate with and learn from customers and be adaptive to their specific and dynamic demands."

3. OBJECTIVE

The main objectives of this research are

1. To examine the use of social media platforms in the growth of tourism SMEs,
2. To determine the factors that may prevent the adoption of social media in the growth of tourism SMEs,

4. HYPOTHESIS

1. There is a significant relationship between the use of social media platforms and the growth of tourism SMEs
2. There is a significant relationship between factors that may prevent the adoption of social media and the growth of tourism SMEs

5. CONCEPTUAL MODEL

See Figure 3.

Figure 3. Conceptual model

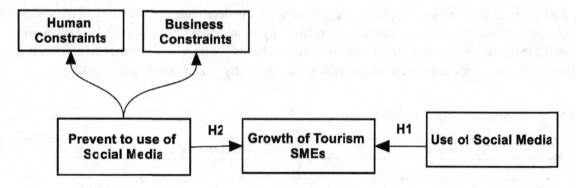

6. METHODOLOGY

Researcher used a quantitative research approach with probability sampling. Simple random sample to make sure the probability of generalizing to the study population (Maree 2013) to fulfil our study goals by conducting a survey of 294 tourism SMEs owners or managers in India asking them to participate in the online survey out of total 1232 registered tourism stakeholders in India. The researcher will contact companies as per Indian law, a small business with an investment in plant and equipment of no more than 10 crore rupees and a revenue of no more than 50 crore rupees, as well as a medium business with an investment in plant and equipment of no more than 50 crore rupees and a turnover of no more than 250 crore rupees (MSME, 2020). Researchers asked participants if their company has already started using social media sites. Firms that have already adopted social media platforms asked to respond to questions about the organization's current state, the adoption process, the applications and advantages of using social media, as well as an evaluation and plans for adopting new platforms.

6.1 Data Collection

Based on the literature study and the data-gathering research questions, a closed-ended structured questionnaire was created. A questionnaire was sent through Google form through e-mail. A statistical expert's recommendations were followed throughout the various stages of building the instrument. A 59.5% response rate was achieved with just 175 surveys being correctly filled out. According to (A Bryman, 2011), attaining a good response rate while surveying a population of small businesses may be challenging. Therefore, 50% response rate is sufficient for analysis.

6.2 Data Analysis

The data gathered from the survey were analysed using SPSS-21. The scope of social media use for both internal and external networking was determined by the study making use of descriptive statistics, such frequency tables. Examining the links between social media and stakeholder indicators required the use of inferential statistics, particularly correlation and regression analysis.

6.3 Reliability of Data

Calculations of the Cronbach's alpha coefficient were used to determine the reliability of the variables. In Table 1, the coefficients are displayed. A trustworthy variable has a Cronbach's alpha value greater than 0.7 (Sharma, 2016). All of the generated variables have Cronbach's alpha coefficients over 0.7, as shown in Table 1, indicating their reliability and the possibility of additional statistical study.

Table 1. Cronbach's alpha's reliability test

Construct	Cronbach Alpha	Item
Use of Social Media	0.756	6
Factors Prevent Adoption of Social media	0.772	7

7. RESULTS AND DISCUSSION

7.1 Demographic Data

Overall 175 respondents were response surveys. This data set included 43 (24.6%) respondent who is Owner of SMEs, 101 (57.7%) a manager of the company and 42 (12%) respondent who are the owner but he plays the role of a manager. This data set indicates that the owner hires a manager to operate a business. The majority of the respondent age ranges between 20 to 40 years means in tourism industries employee are the youngest one. Only 21% of the respondent has below the 12ᵗʰ standard of education. 58.9% of Tourism SMEs have started their operation within 5 years.

Most of the respondent (86) operates social media for up to 10 hours a week while 38.3% spend up to 20 hours. Posting, sharing and other means of social media work doing the owner itself. In some cases, owners hire an agency or recruit employees.

Table 2. Demographic details of respondent

Variable	Category	Freq	Per (%)	Variable	Category	Freq	Per (%)
Age	20-30	67	38.3	Role in the business	Owner	43	24.6
	30-40	67	38.3		Manager	101	57.7
	40-50	22	12.6		Owner/Manager	42	12.6
	50 and above	19	10.9		Other	9	5.1
Education	Below 12th	21	12.0	Support system	I do it myself	84	48.0
	12th	62	35.4		Hired an agency	25	14.3
	Graduation	55	31.4		Family member	23	13.1
	Other	37	21.1		Recruited employee	27	15.4
					Not required	16	9.1
Time spent (Weekly)	0-10	86	49.1	Years of business	0-5	103	58.9
	10-20	67	38.3		05-10	52	29.7
	20-30	3	1.7		10-15	8	4.6
	30-40	16	9.1		15-20	6	3.4
	40 and above	3	1.7		20 and above	6	3.4

Figure 4. Medium to use post on social media

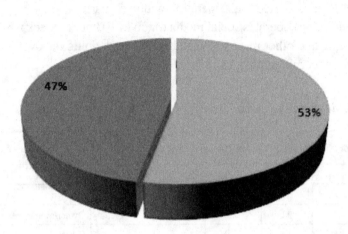

Medium is not important to share or post on social media. 47% of respondents used smartphones while 53% of respondents used smartphones to share and post on social media.

Figure 5. Social media platforms to use post

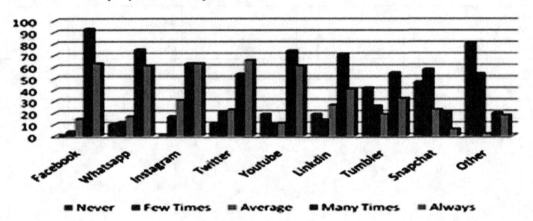

The SMEs in the tourism industry that were surveyed are active on various social media sites. These tourism-related SMEs primarily utilised Facebook, Twitter, Instagram, LinkedIn, and Instagram. Facebook is used far more than any other social media platform, according to our poll. Respondents used Facebook many times to post and Whatsapp, Instagram, Twitter and Linkdin were used frequently.

Table 3. Mean and standard deviation of a variable

Construct	Item	Mean		Std. Deviation	
Use of Social Media	USM1	2.18	14.97	1.21	5.71
	USM2	2.22		1.38	
	USM3	2.15		1.17	
	USM4	3.06		1.9	
	USM5	3.03		1.44	
	USM6	2.42		1.23	
Prevent the adoption of social media	FHC1	3.57	25.8	1.21	4.9
	FHC2	3.73		1.14	
	FHC3	3.37		1.19	
	FHC4	3.3		1.25	
	FBC1	3.99		1.01	
	FBC2	3.84		0.89	
	FBC3	3.83		0.93	

(USM1-receive customer feedback, USM-2- Customer relation management, USM3- getting Like, Share and Followers, USM4- reach new customers, USM-5 advertisement and promotion and USM6-branding, FHC1- Lack of Technological Knowledge, FHC2- Fear of making mistakes while operating social media, FHC3-The Fear of Negative/no Comments, FHC4- Time Constraints, FBC1- The doubtful Return on Investment, FBC2- Lack of Credibility and Reliability as an Information Source, FBC3-Competitive Business Environment)

7.2 Testing the Hypotheses

Hypothesis 1: There is a significant relationship between the use of social media platforms and the growth of tourism SMEs

A multiple regression analysis was done to evaluate this theory, and the outcomes are shown in Table 4.

Table 4. Results of the multiple regression analysis for the use of social media

Beta Coefficient (R)	R^2	F	p-Value
0.990	0.981	1430.275	.000

Table 4 define that the beta coefficient between the use of social media with its variables was (0.990) and (f) statistical value was (1430.275) with a significance level (0.05) and less, which indicates the presence of the effect of the use of social media with their variables (receive customer feedback, Customer relation management, getting Like, Share and Followers, reach new customers, advertisement and promotion and branding). Thus, the alternative hypothesis—that there is a statistically significant effect of using social media with its variables—was accepted and the null hypothesis was rejected.

Table 5. The regression coefficient of the use of social media with their variables

Model		Unstandardized Coefficients		Standardized Coefficients	t	Sig.
		B	Std. Error	Beta		
		.205	.177		1.159	.248
	USM1	.845	.073	.180	11.504	.000
	USM2	.963	.054	.233	17.868	.000
	USM3	.978	.071	.200	13.765	.000
	USM4	.992	.038	.331	26.432	.000
	USM5	1.063	.052	.269	20.429	.000
	USM6	1.006	.056	.217	18.093	.000

It is clear from Table 5 that there are all six dimensions of the use of social media express a statistically significant effect on variables, and the Beta coefficient values were (0.180, 0.233, 0.200, 0.331, 0.269, 0.217) respectively, while the (T) statistical values were (11.504, 17.868, 13.765, 26.432, 20.429, 18.093). These indicated the use of social media is a positive and significant effect on the growth of tourism.

Hypothesis2. There is a significant relationship between factors that may prevent the adoption of social media and the growth of tourism SMEs

Table 6. Results of the multiple regression analysis for the prevention to the adoption of social media

Beta Coefficient (R)	R²	F	p-Value
0.979	0.959	562.480	.000

Table 6 shows that the beta coefficient between prevention to the adoption of social media with its variables was (0.979) and (f) statistical value was (562.480) with a significance level (0.05) and less, which indicates the presence of effect to adoption of social media with their variables (Lack of Technological Knowledge, Fear of making mistakes while operating social media, the fear of negative/no comments, the uncertain return on investment, time Constraints, lack of credibility and reliability as an information Source, competitive business environment). The alternative hypothesis, which asserts that there is a statistically significant effect (=0.05) of preventing the use of social media with its variable for the growth of tourism SMEs, was therefore accepted and the null hypothesis was rejected.

Table 7. The regression coefficient of preventing the adoption of social media with their variables

Model		Unstandardized Coefficients		Standardized Coefficients	t	Sig.
		B	Std. Error	Beta		
		.550	.449		1.226	.222
	FHC1	.887	.106	.225	8.330	.000
	FHC2	1.099	.116	.256	9.488	.000
	FHC3	.708	.100	.173	7.102	.000
	FHC4	.976	.099	.249	9.820	.000
	FBC1	.870	.105	.180	8.301	.000
	FBC2	1.226	.112	.224	10.937	.000
	FBC3	1.099	.118	.210	9.315	.000

Table 7 shows a clear figure that there are all seven dimensions of preventing the adoption of social media that express a statistically significant effect on variables, and the Beta coefficient values were (0.225, 0.256, 0.173, 0.249, 0.180, 0.224, 0.210) respectively, while the (T) statistical values were (8.330, 9.488, 7.102, 9.820, 8.301, 10.937, 9.315). These indicated a fear of adoption of social media is a significant effect on the growth of tourism SMEs.

8. CONCLUSION AND FUTURE IMPLICATION

This study looked at how social media can be used to grow business networks. The fact that tourism SMEs in the study area use social media on an ad hoc and informal basis suggests that there are no explicit policies on the use of these technologies. The results also showed an over-concentration of social media use by SMEs in the travel industry. Tourism SMEs fear mistakes and lack of technological constraints. Perhaps, future studies may also need to do a study on policy effective use of social media without fear or technological constraints.

On the practical side, this research helps a range of tourism-related SMEs by enabling them to better understand tourist decision-making processes and the roles that social media play in those processes. This study is significant because it helps the tourism sector better understand how tourists make decisions and the roles that social media play in those processes.

REFERENCES

Alghizzawi, M., & Salloum, S. (2018). *The role of social media in tourism marketing in Jordan*. Academic Press.

Baumöl, U., Hollebeek, L., & Jung, R. (2016). Dynamics of customer interaction on social media platforms. *Electronic Markets*, *26*(3), 199–202. doi:10.100712525-016-0227-0

Bryman, A. (2011). Research methods in the study of leadership. In The SAGE handbook of leadership. SAGE.

Camilleri, M. A., & Kozak, M. (2022). Interactive engagement through travel and tourism social media groups: A social facilitation theory perspective. *Technology in Society*, *71*, 102098. doi:10.1016/j.techsoc.2022.102098

Czekaj, J. L. (2017). *communicating in the age of social media*. Academic Press.

Greenwood, B. Y. S., Perrin, A., & Duggan, M. (2016). Social Media Update 2016. *Pew Research Center*, *2*(11), 1–18.

Hrastinski, S., & Aghaee, N. M. (2012). How are campus students using social media to support their studies? An explorative interview study. *Education and Information Technologies*, *17*(4), 451–464. doi:10.100710639-011-9169-5

Jansson, J., Nilsson, J., Modig, F., & Hed Vall, G. (2017). Commitment to Sustainability in Small and Medium-Sized Enterprises: The Influence of Strategic Orientations and Management Values. *Business Strategy and the Environment*, *26*(1), 69–83. doi:10.1002/bse.1901

Lanyi, B., Hornyak, M., & Kruzslicz, F. (2021). The effect of online activity on SMEs' competitiveness. *Competitiveness Review*, *31*(3), 477–496. doi:10.1108/CR-01-2020-0022

Mayfield. (2009). A Commander's Strategy for Social Media. *Army Europe and Seventh Army APO*.

MSME. (2020). *Ministry of micro, small and medium enterprises notification* (Vol. 1, Issue D). MSME.

Nakara, W. A., Benmoussa, F. Z., & Jaouen, A. (2012). Entrepreneurship and social media marketing: Evidence from French small business. *International Journal of Entrepreneurship and Small Business*, *16*(4), 386–405. doi:10.1504/IJESB.2012.047608

Nicholas, J., Ledwith, A., & Perks, H. (2011). New product development best practice in SME and large organisations: Theory vs practice. *European Journal of Innovation Management*, *14*(2), 227–251. doi:10.1108/14601061111124902

Park, J., & Oh, I.-K. (2012). A Case Study of Social Media Marketing by Travel Agency: The Salience of Social Media Marketing in the Tourism Industry. *International Journal of Tourism Sciences*, *12*(1), 93–106. doi:10.1080/15980634.2012.11434654

Saravanakumar, T. S. (2012). Social Media Marketing. *Life Science Journal*, *9*(4), 4444–4451.

Sharma, B. (2016). A focus on reliability in developmental research through Cronbach's Alpha among medical, dental and paramedical professionals. *Asian Pacific Journal of Health Sciences*, *3*(4), 271–278. doi:10.21276/apjhs.2016.3.4.43

Si, S. (2016). Social Media and Its Role in Marketing. *Business and Economics Journal*, *7*(1), 1–5. doi:10.4172/2151-6219.1000203

Simmi Dhyani, M. S. (2022). *Effect of communicating corporate social responsibility through social media on brand image, Digital Marketing Outreach*. Routledge India.

Tourism, M. (2021). National Strategy and Roadmap for Sustainable Tourism Ministry of Tourism Government of India. Government of India.

WTTC. (2019). *WTTC_India2019*. WTTC.

Xu, Q. (2013). Social recommendation, source credibility, and recency: Effects of news cues in a social book-marking website. *Journalism and Mass Communication*, *90*(4), 757–775. doi:10.1177/1077699013503158

Zarezadeh, Z. Z., Rastegar, H. R., & Gretzel, U. (2018). Reviewing the Past to Inform the Future: A Literature Review of Social Media in Tourism. *Czech Journal of Tourism*, *7*(2), 115–131. doi:10.1515/cjot-2018-0006

Zuhdi, S., Daud, A., Hanif, R., Nguyen, P. T., & Shankar, K. (2019). Role of social media marketing in the successful implementation of business management. *International Journal of Recent Technology and Engineering, 8*(2), 3841–3844.

Chapter 15
Starting Food Chain as a SME in Canada:
Adopting Social Media for Its Success

Rubina Nabin

Modern College of Business and Science, Muscat, Oman

ABSTRACT

Small and medium enterprises hold an utmost importance while considering any nation's growth, prosperity, and the betterment of its economy. This chapter aims to focus on the SMEs in Canada as a nation and how food chain as a SME can flourish successfully by using social media as a tool for its success. The types of food chain SMEs, the procedures for launching a food chain, acquiring license for food chain, possible challenges that could be faced in food chain SME are also discussed. Social media's adoption and usage to attract customers, promote products and services, market promotions are also intended to be discussed. Social media strategies for food chain SMEs including paid application sponsored advertisements, influencer-promoted paid promotions, food chain SMEs own page posts and promotions, and getting the food chain's social media verified officially will be the foci.

1. INTRODUCTION TO SME IN CANADA

Canada is a very large country with plethora of opportunities. It is a well-known fact that Canada as a country welcomes immigrants, promotes and support the permanent residents and citizens by providing healthcare, education, child tax benefits and so on. Small and Medium Enterprises play a vital role in increasing the Gross Domestic Product also known as GDP of a country (Herwi, 2019).A business in considered as a Small and Medium Enterprise in Canada when the said business is having lesser than five hundred employees. On the other hand, if the business has lesser than one hundred employees, then it is called as a small enterprise in Canada (Vuvor, 2011).

DOI: 10.4018/978-1-6684-5770-2.ch015

2. FOOD CHAIN AS A SME IN CANADA

Canada being a geographically vast nation, is looking for immigrants to promote and enhance the nation's economy. Food chains are a considerably less risky when compared to other fields of business, as we know, food is a basic means of survival.

3. TYPES OF FOOD CHAINS AS A SME IN CANADA

The small enterprises account to overall higher income while considering the Canadian economy. Hence it is advisable to go for the number of employees ranging from 5 to 99 and it is also obvious that the province Ontario can be chosen for successful business. Farm to table is a wonderful concept as food coloring and preservatives are not usually preferred to live healthily.

4. FACTORS INVOLVED IN THE MAJOR DECISIONS ABOUT THE FOOD CHAIN

According to the study (Hendee, 2017) food is not the criteria to decide the success of the restaurant or food chain. The customers who come to eat at a restaurant mainly looks for three qualities:

- **The ambience**

Ambience refers to the atmosphere of the place that people come to eat at. This atmosphere must be made in a way that it is satisfying all categories of people including families with kids, individuals, coupled, group of friends, professional work-related colleagues and peers and others who may just come for uplifting the mood with food.

- **Quality of service**

The quality of service does not just to the quality of the food alone. It can vary from the lighting, furniture, flooring, electricity, internet facility, speediness in delivering order, pleasant handling of customers, ease of payment and so on. People rate the restaurants online and spread the feedback about their views about food to the friends, family, or colleagues. Hence it is important to maintain good quality of service.

- **Simple cuisines**

Rather than having high fi cuisines which the local crowd is unknown to, it is easier to have food menu that is fast moving and easy to reach to the customers. If any new cuisine to be launched, that could be done by choosing to do on a smaller scale first and expand the menu at a later stage depending on the customer liking by adapting to changes.

5. FACTORS TO BE CONSIDERED WHEN DECIDING THE TYPE OF FOOD CHAIN TO BE LAUNCHED IN CANADA

The geographical location in which the food chain is intended to be launched, the food preferences of the people living in that area, the language spoken around in general, the type of individuals, the type of offices, types of educational institutions around are to be considered. As shown in the figure below each factor accounts to various sub factors for growth. It is important to identify them and customize accordingly.

Figure 1. Food chain factors (Massimo F.Marcone)

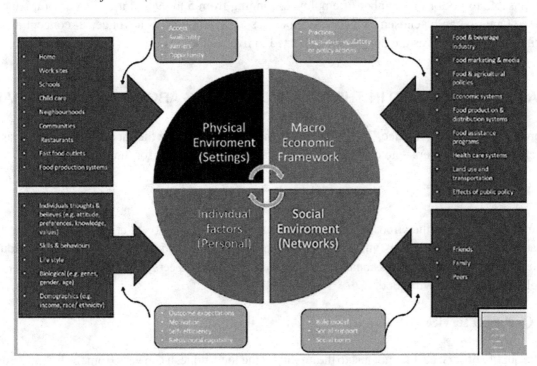

Factors to Be Considered When Deciding the Investment Budget for the Food Chain In Canada

Before investing in the food chain or any business for that matter, there are five aspects to be considered (Pelletier). They are as follows:

- **Analyzing the Existing Market to Know the Possibility of Success**

  Before diving in full swing, it is advisable to watch the other competitors and successful traders in market. There will be many ideas, inspirations, and suggestions to change.

- **Reinvesting the Profit in the Food Business**

The business will require re-investing in a way to improvise the range and quality of products, to maintain the business infrastructure, to upgrade furniture and machinery including tools, cutlery, and kitchen facilities. Opening a new franchise or branch could also be a good option.

- **Balancing the Incoming Cashflow and Borrowed Loans**

It could be challenging to be in debt, and it could be even more depressing to do business knowing that the business is unable to meet the needs of payment to the loan. Therefore, it is important to manage cashflow correctly.

Factors to Be Considered for Acquiring Loan for Supporting the Food Chain SME In Canada

The Small and Medium enterprises account for 99.8% of the country's economy boost (Coe).The general statistical data as shown below brings us to the following inferences

- Education is a priority to acquire loan
- Higher age people have better chances to get loan
- Those with English language as their first language have lesser screening process
- Men SME entrepreneurs apply for more loans than those of women
- The number of years of experience in the field is considered to provide loan

Factors to Be Considered for the Location for the Food Chain

The geographical location, the type of people living around in that area, the food choices of the people, the nationalities of the people, the affordability of rent and maintenance are few of the important factors to be considered while choosing the location for the food chain (Oracle, 2021).

Factors to Be Considered for the Products in the Food Chain

Farm -to-table is becoming more and more of an emerging trend in Canada, like other parts of the world (Alimentarius, n.d.). The drawback being the fact that organic products are priced more when compared to junk food (Elementum, 2018).

Factors to Be Considered in Deciding the Number of Employees in a Food Chain

Figure 2. Graph trend showing the number of employees in food chain in Canada from the year 2012 to 2022 (World)

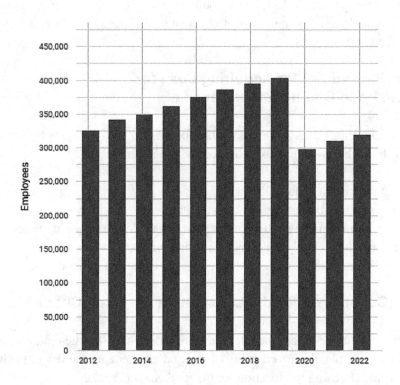

As it is obvious from the above graph. From the year 2020 due to the pandemic there has been a decrease in the number of employees working in the food chain in Canada. However, this situation is continuing to recover with the upcoming years.

A recession is expected to affect Canada starting from the first quarter of the year 2023 (FAN, 2022). This means more people will be losing white collar jobs .Looking at the bright side, if food chain oriented businesses can utilize the situation to their advantage it can prove to be a boom instead of bane.

Factors to Be Considered While Deciding on the Quality Standard Features in the Food Chain in Canada

The way the food safety is features could be established within the food chain begins with certain important practices namely GMP, GRP, GEP, GTrP, GHKP and GNP (Raspor, 2008).The food quality control and standards must be met

- **Good Manufacturing Practice**

The making of products must be done while keeping in mind the health measures, hygiene standards and overall responsibility. Under the measures of Safe Food for Canadians Act (SFCA) and Safe Food for Canadian Regulations (SFCR), a valid license must be obtained to function the food chain. (Canada G. o., n.d.)

- **Good Research Practice**

Before launching a product or service, whether new or as an update to an already existing one, it is important to do the required research for the same.

- **Good Educational Practice**

Before having the services and products launched, it is necessary to be knowledgeable about them. This will come handy in taking the business in a gloriously successful path. Before launching a major business step like acquiring license for example, it is important to know in depth about the requirements and specifications for the same (Canada G. o., Licensing Interactive Tool, n.d.).

- **Good Training Practice**

The employees must be trained properly with the details like the company motto, vision, mission, objectives, logo, work ethics, company practices to name a few.

- **Good Housekeeping Practice**

Having invested in the products and the company, it is only sensible to maintain and take care of it. Things and people when taken care of properly lasts and function better on a longer term. Constant maintenance and interval led quality checks must be a non-negotiable quality improving standard.

Factors to Be Considered to Adhere to the Environmental Safety

Food wastage is a major concern while considering food chain business. In Finland there is an application called as ResQ that collaborates with over two hundred restaurants and collects the leftover food and sells the food at a much-reduced price instead of throwing the food (Timilsina, 2017).Use of plastic, non-biodegradable substances can be avoided and instead environment friendly products can be used. This will make a positive impact when done on a large scale for the overall environment and play a major part in saving mother earth.

6. SOCIAL MEDIA IN CANADA

Canadian spend on an average of fifteen hours and six minutes monthly on Facebook (McKinnon, 2022).

Figure 3. Bar Chart showing the percentage of Canadian adults using social media (McKinnon, 2022)

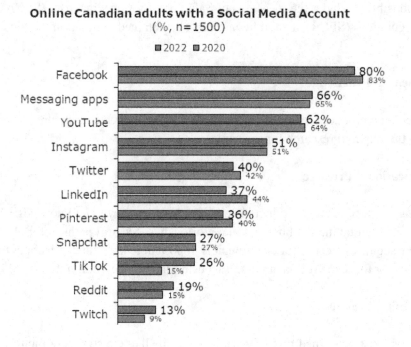

As shown in the figure above, the number of social media users is increasing on a considerable amount.

Types of Social Media in Canada

According to statistics (Statista, 2022), as of March 2022, based on the social media usage, the most prominent and the most used social media platform in Facebook. Nova Scotia province ranks first for the most usage of Instagram.

Table 1. Provincial Social Media Usage Statistics in Canada (S.Dixon, 2022)

Characteristic	British Columbia	Alberta	Saskatchewan	Manitoba	Ontario	Quebec	New Brunswick	Nova Scotia	Prince Edward Island	Newfoundland and Labrador
Facebook	69%	62%	71%	65%	63%	68%	72%	75%	81%	82%
Facebook Messenger	60%	63%	60%	61%	55%	63%	67%	71%	67%	73%
YouTube	56%	58%	54%	51%	55%	43%	46%	66%	65%	63%
Instagram	50%	41%	47%	48%	47%	33%	28%	54%	42%	41%
WhatsApp	49%	39%	39%	35%	49%	23%	20%	31%	20%	22%
LinkedIn	33%	30%	25%	19%	34%	22%	18%	38%	25%	29%
Twitter	29%	25%	30%	19%	29%	16%	18%	35%	26%	39%
Pinterest	16%	17%	32%	22%	18%	17%	21%	28%	25%	28%
Snapchat	18%	17%	35%	20%	16%	14%	14%	20%	25%	18%
TikTok	10%	11%	20%	19%	15%	9%	10%	18%	22%	16%
WeChat	9%	3%	3%	6%	7%	2%	1%	5%	4%	3%
Telegram	4%	3%	10%	6%	5%	3%	2%	4%	8%	4%
Tumblr	4%	4%	4%	3%	2%	2%	1%	5%	1%	3%

Social Media's Role in Helping SMEs

Social Media is not just a means of staying in touch with friends and family but rather it increases the business profit by 77 percentage when compared to those small and medium enterprise-oriented businesses that do not use social media (Peek, 2022).

Types of Promotions Done Using Social Media

There are paid promotions and unpaid, naturally happening promotions. These are called as organic promotions (Patel, n.d.).Depending on the audience and the business to be promoted, the contents must be created to get more likes, views, and shares. The other ways to get noticed are by using hashtags which is meaning symbolically as '#'. Many reels, audios also get famous in a short span of time. Such quick reach of content and marketing through social media is amazing.

Social Media Paid Promotions for Food Chain in Canada

According to a report (Canada, 2018),majority of the food chains in Canada promote the business through electronic marketing or Electronic Commerce or both, depending on the situational needs.

Social Media Promotions Through Influencers

To understand the functioning of promotions of businesses through social media, let us consider the hierarchical diagram of influencers as shown below. Recently there are so many emerging social media influencers. Earning good amount of money through social media by promoting a business is mutually beneficial for the concerned influencer and the said business. In addition, the aim to reach the business to the desired market and customers is done at the right time, in the desired manner.

Figure 4. Influencer importance hierarchy (StarNgage, 2015-2022)

In the above diagram the everyday influencers shown with dotted lines are the most seen influencers who engage the audience or followers by providing stories, reels, and posts daily.

Importance of Individual Social Media Page for a Food Chain

Having a social media page for the business which is verified will add many advantages to the list of success including reliability, fake profiles avoidance and increased dependability (Keenan, 2022).

Procedure for Getting the Food Chain Social Media Page Verified in Canada

Elon Musk, the (Euronews, 2022) CEO of Twitter has made blue tick verified profiles as payment-based subscriptions.

Increased Success Rate in the Food Chain Business with Social Media Usage

As per the statistics as of January 2022, the number of social media user in millions is as shown in the graph below (Statista, 2022)

Figure 5. Number of Social Media Users in Millions as of January 2022

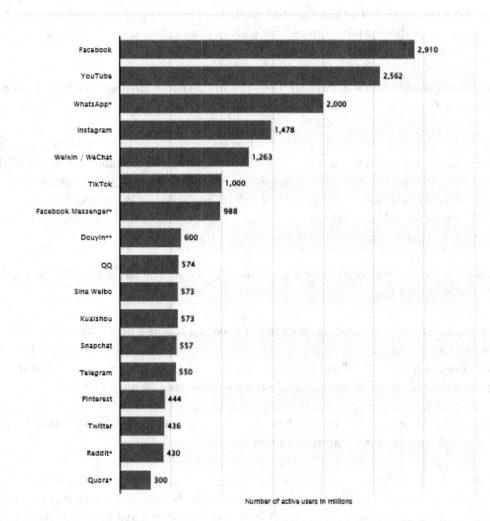

7. CHALLENGES IN LAUNCHING FOOD CHAIN AS A SME IN CANADA

The main challenges faced in small and medium enterprise begin with the capital investment and when approaching the loaners, the responses which are received that do not account to the productivity of the business (Amarjit Gill, 2011).

8. LIMITATIONS IN LAUNCHING FOOD CHAIN AS A SME IN CANADA

According to Gould and Parzen (Gould SK, 1990) there are seven major limitations of difficulties that are commonly faced while starting any business.

- **Unawareness About the Business in The Society**

Before venturing into any new business, it is important to learn about the business. This preliminary research will help in knowing the challenges that might be faced, Analyze the advantages and disadvantages and to know whether the pros outweigh the cons so that the business could be run successfully in a profitable manner.

- **Not Being Considered as A Part Of The Already Existing Businesses Or In Other Words, Being Left Out**

Competition causes conflict in general. However true success comes from having a healthy competition. This healthy competition is when it is possible to compete with the other businesses of the same filed without impacting negatively instead support each other and making profit at the same time by launching exclusive market and customer-based products and services. When asked for help, advice, or support, it is important to lend a helping hand, in any form possible. After all, a little help can make a huge difference potentially, mentally, inter-personally or financially.

- **Loaners Being Partial While Deciding Whom To Loan The Money To Or To Decide How Much Money To Loan**

The private or public form for obtaining loan or financial adapts a heavy screening process which can be very exhausting for the person who is planning on starting the business or a small and medium enterprise. Looking at people of all races, color, and origin equally while only considering the capabilities and possible business prospects can make a positive difference on a societal scale.

- **Seeing Women Small And Medium Enterprise Owners As Less Capable Than That Of The Male Small And Medium Enterprise Owners**

In general women are looked less capable than men in terms of strength and potential. This could be since women in the society's views is mainly seen as child bearers and family care providers when compared to men. Although this view is changing, it is still faced in majority of regions. It is the business proposal, scope of the SME to succeed, and the possible benefits that the business can bring is what is to be considered.

- **Blindly Following The General Stigma And Believing That There Is A Lot Of Competition In The Small And Medium Enterprise Market And Hence Believing The Succeeding Is Difficult**

A mountain peak can be reached by trekking from step to step, an ocean can be crossed by swimming with controlled breathing and meticulous laps of swimming. So many great inventions around us today are a result of grit and determination where the inventors did not give up with some failures in the attempt rather continuously learned from the mistakes kept correcting the mistakes and progressing from strength to strength and eventually achieved success. The same applied to the small and medium enterprises as well. Starting anything new comes with risk. With risk also comes great opportunities. It all depends on strategies, change management, organizational behavior, interpersonal skills, and business planning.

- **Not Believing In The Self-Willpower And Capabilities**

Right from childhood an individual's perspective of life and how things work around forms. If an individual doesn't believe in oneself, there is absolutely no importance in the opinion of others. On the contrary, even if others around have mixed opinions about a person, if this individual believes in oneself, if doesn't matter what others think. Starting a SME, facing difficulties and overcoming them to prove successful requires lot of belief and talent.

9. CONCLUSION

Food chain as a small and medium enterprise business, if done in a way to anticipate and tackle the above-mentioned challenges, is very much possible to be a profitable business. Market analysis, market positioning, product analysis and product impact must all be thoroughly analyzed and implemented. The practical implications of launching food chain as a SME in Canada could provide an exponential growth in invested in the right place, right products, and right people. It can also be concluded that beginning with 5 employees ang going up to 99 employees and choosing Ontario province as a province to establish the business with the help of right tactics of social media promotions will result in a profitable food chin business.

REFERENCES

Alimentarius, C. (n.d.). *Strengthening national food control systems.* Retrieved from https://www.fao.org/3/y8705e/y8705e05.htm

Amarjit Gill, N. B. (2011). Barriers to small business creations in Canada. *International Journal of Entrepreneurship and Small Business, 14*(2), 245–257. doi:10.1504/IJESB.2011.042722

Canada, R. (2018). *Foodservice businesses are increasing attention on social media marketing.* Retrieved from https://www.restaurantscanada.org/foodservice-businesses-increasing-attention-social-media-marketing/

Canada, S. (n.d.). *Full-service restaurants and limited-service eating places - 7225-Businesses - Canadian Industry Statistics.* Government of Canada. Retrieved from https://www.ic.gc.ca/app/scr/app/cis/businesses-entreprises/7225

Canada, G. O. (n.d.). *Food business activities that require a licence under the Safe Food for Canadians Regulations.* Retrieved from Government of Canada: https://inspection.canada.ca/food-licences/food-business-activities/eng/1524074697160/1524074697425

Canada, G. O. (n.d.). *Licensing Interactive Tool.* Retrieved from Government of Canada: https://ca1se.voxco.com/SE/93/SFCR_licence/?&lang=en

Coe, C. (n.d.). *Small Business Financing Program, Small Business Branch Innovation, Science and Economic Development Canada.* Government of Canada. Retrieved from https://ised-isde.canada.ca/site/sme-research-statistics/en/research-reports/sme-profile-canada-small-business-financing-program-borrowers-march-2016/sme-profile-canada-small-business-financing-program-borrowers-march-2016

Dixon, S. (2022, August 16). *Statistics.* Retrieved from https://www.statista.com/statistics/262804/social-networks-used-by-internet-users-in-canada-provinces/

Elementum. (2018, March 28). *Elementum.* Retrieved from Elementum: https://medium.com/age-of-awareness/why-does-eating-healthier-cost-more-82bad6e04ec4

Euronews. (2022). *Elon Musk says Twitter Blue paid-for verification to return despite days of impersonation chaos.* Retrieved from Euronews: https://www.euronews.com/next/2022/11/14/elon-musk-says-twitter-blue-paid-for-verification-to-return-despite-days-of-impersonation-

Fan, N. J. (2022). *Canada Could Be in a Recession as Soon as Early 2023.* Royal Bank of Canada. Retrieved from https://www6.royalbank.com/en/di/hubs/now-and-noteworthy/article/canada-could-be-in-a-recession-as-soon-as-early-2023/l41dzp8q#:~:text=In%20previous%20work%2C%20we%20projected,power%2C%20weighing%20on%20goods%20purchases

Gould, P. J. (1990). Enterprising Women. *Locan initiatives for job creation.*

Hendee, C. (2017). New study reveals what's really important to diners at restaurants. *Denver Business Journal.* Retrieved from https://www.bizjournals.com/denver/news/2017/02/15/new-study-reveals-whats-really-important-to-diners.html?ana=e_me_set3&s=newsletter&ed=2017-02-16&u=Kpsral71P012luK%2Bt8eH0w0f89f49b&t=1487344415&j=77405641

Herwi, S. J. (2019, April). What are SMEs. *Research Gate,* 1-3. Retrieved from https://www.researchgate.net/publication/332539278_What_are_SMEs

Keenan, M. (2022, January 14). *How To Get Verified on Instagram in 2022.* Retrieved from Shopify: https://www.shopify.com/blog/how-to-get-verified-on-instagram

Massimo, F., & Marcone, P. M. (n.d.). An Overview of the Sociological and Environmental Factors Influencing Eating Food Behavior in Canada. *National Library of Medicine.* Retrieved from https://www.ncbi.nlm.nih.gov/pmc/articles/PMC7283517/

McKinnon, M. (2022). *2022 Report: Social Media Use in Canada (Statistics).* Online Business Canada. Retrieved from https://canadiansinternet.com/2022-report-social-media-use-in-canada-statistics/#:~:text=76.9%20percent%20of%20Canadians %20use,dropped%207%20percent%20from%202020

Oracle. (2021, November 10). *Restaurant Location Analysis: How to Choose the Best Restaurant Location.* Retrieved from Oracle Gloria Food: https://www.gloriafood.com/restaurant-location-analysis

Patel, N. (n.d.). *Social Media Marketing: How to do it, Types, Tools & Tips.* Retrieved from Neil Patel What is Social Media Marketing?: https://neilpatel.com/what-is-social-media-marketing/

Peek, S. (2022). *Why Small Businesses Need a Social Media Presence? Considering pausing your social presence? Here's why it still counts for small businesses.* Business.com. Retrieved from https://www.business.com/articles/social-media-small-business-importance/

Pelletier, M. (n.d.). *Five key factors to assess when making an investment decision.* Financial Post. Retrieved from https://financialpost.com/investing/investing-pro/five-key-factors-to-assess-when-making-an-investment-decision

Raspor, P. (2008, August). Total food chain safety: How good practices can contribute? *Elsevier. Trends in Food Science & Technology, 19*(8), 405–412. doi:10.1016/j.tifs.2007.08.009

StarNgage. (2015-2022). *StarNgage.* Retrieved from StarNgage: https://starngage.com/app/ru/page/influencer-marketing-canada

Statista. (2022, January). *Statista.* Retrieved from Statista: https://www.statista.com/statistics/272014/global-social-networks-ranked-by-number-of-users/

Timilsina, M. (2017). *Impacts of social media in restaurant businesses-A case study of restaurants based on Oulu region.* Oulu University of Applied Sciences. Retrieved from https://core.ac.uk/download/pdf/84797241.pdf

Vuvor, J. A. (2011). *The Challenges faced by Small & Medium Enterprises (SMEs) in Obtaining Credit in Ghana.* Blekinge Tekniska Högskola School of Management. Retrieved from https://www.diva-portal.org/smash/get/diva2:829684/FULLTEXT01.pdf;The

World, I. (n.d.). *Fast Food Restaurants in Canada - Employment Statistics 2005–2028.* Industry Statistics Canada. Retrieved from https://www.ibisworld.com/canada/industry-statistics/employment/fast-food-restaurants/

Compilation of References

Abddulhai, I. N., Husin, M. H., Baharudin, A. S., & Abdullah, N. A. (2022). Determinants of Facebook adoption and its impact on service-based small and medium enterprise performance in Northwestern Nigeria. *Journal of Systems and Information Technology*, *24*(3).

Abeza, G., O'Reilly, N., & Reid, I. (2013). Relationship marketing and social media in sport. *International Journal of Sport Communication*, *6*(2), 120–142. doi:10.1123/ijsc.6.2.120

Abrahamse, W., & Steg, L. (2011). Factors related to household energy use and intention to reduce it: The role of psychological and socio-demographic variables. *Human Ecology Review*, 30–40.

Abu, I. N., & Ezike, J. E. (2012). The role and sustainability of microfinance banks in reducing poverty and development of entrepreneurship in urban and rural areas in Nigeria. *International Journal of Business Administration*, *3*(3), 33–40.

Adam, N. A., & Alarifi, G. (2021). Innovation practices for survival of small and Medium Enterprises (smes) in the COVID-19 times: The role of External Support. *Journal of Innovation and Entrepreneurship*, *10*(1), 15. Advance online publication. doi:10.118613731-021-00156-6 PMID:34075328

Adamowicz, M. (2022). COVID-19 Pandemic as a Change Factor in the Labour Market in Poland. *Sustainability*, *14*(15), 9197. doi:10.3390u14159197

Adedoyin, R. (2021). *Nigerian journalism remains vibrant, despite challenges* (A. Nagarajan, Interviewer). International Press Institute (IPI). Retrieved 1 3, 2022, from https://ipi.media/nigerian-journalism-remains-vibrant-despite-challenges

Adegbuyi, O. A., Akinyele, F., & Akinyele, S. (2015). Effect of Social Media Marketing on Small Scale Business Performance in Ota-Metropolis, Nigeria. *International Journal of Social Sciences and Management*, *2*(3), 275–283. doi:10.3126/ijssm.v2i3.12721

Adel, H. M., Mahrous, A. A., & Hammad, R. (2020). Entrepreneurial marketing strategy, institutional environment, and business performance of SMEs in Egypt. *Journal of Entrepreneurship in Emerging Economies*.

Adhikari, D. B., Shakya, B., Devkota, N., Karki, D., Bhandari, U., Parajuli, S., & Paudel, U. R. (2021). Financial hurdles in small business enterprises in Kathmandu Valley. *Modern Economy*, *12*(6), 1105–1118. doi:10.4236/me.2021.126058

Agboh, D. K. (2015). Drivers and Challenges of ICT Adoption by SMES in Accra Metropolis, Ghana. *Journal of Technology Research*, *6*, 1–16.

Agwu, M. O., & Emeti, C. I. (2014). Issues, Challenges and Prospects of Small and Medium Scale Enterprises (SMEs) in Port-Harcourt City, Nigeria. *European Journal of Sustainable Development*, *3*(1), 101–114. doi:10.14207/ejsd.2014. v3n1p101

Ahmad, S. Z., Abu Bakar, A. R., Faziharudean, T. M., & Mohamad Zaki, K. A. (2014). An Empirical Study of Factors Affecting e-Commerce Adoption among Small- and Medium-Sized Enterprises in a Developing Country: Evidence from Malaysia. *Information Technology for Development*, *21*(4), 555–572. doi:10.1080/02681102.2014.899961

Ainin, S., Parveen, F., Moghavvemi, S., Jaafar, N. I., & Mohd Shuib, N. L. (2015). Factors influencing the use of social media by SMEs and its performance outcomes. *Industrial Management & Data Systems*, *115*(3), 570–588. doi:10.1108/IMDS-07-2014-0205

Ajuwon, O. S., Ikhide, S., & Akotey, J. O. (2017). MSMEs Productivity in Nigeria. *European Journal of Economics and Business Studies, 7*(1), 114-130. Retrieved 5 6, 2022, from https://journals.euser.org/index.php/ejes/article/view/1788

Ajzen, I. (1985). *From intentions to actions: A theory of planned behavior. In Action control.* Springer.

Akar, E., & Dalgic, T. (2018). Understanding online consumers' purchase intentions: A contribution from social network theory. *Behaviour & Information Technology*, *37*(5), 473–487. doi:10.1080/0144929X.2018.1456563

Akar, E., & Topçu, B. (2011). An examination of the factors influencing consumers' attitudes toward social media marketing. *Journal of Internet Commerce*, *10*(1), 35–67. doi:10.1080/15332861.2011.558456

Aker, Ç., & Öztürk, Ö. (2015). *Social Media Interactions and the Use of Third-Party Management Applications on Effectiveness and Perception of Information.* doi:10.1007/978-3-319-20889-3_1

Akpan, I. J., Soopramanien, D., & Kwak, D.-H. (2021). Cutting-edge technologies for small business and innovation in the era of COVID-19 global health pandemic. *Journal of Small Business and Entrepreneurship*, *33*(6), 607–617. doi:10.1080/08276331.2020.1799294

Akpan, I. J., Udoh, E. A. P., & Adebisi, B. (2022). Small business awareness and adoption of state-of-the-art technologies in emerging and developing markets, and lessons from the COVID-19 pandemic. *Journal of Small Business and Entrepreneurship*, *34*(2), 123–140. doi:10.1080/08276331.2020.1820185

Albaz, A., Mansour, T., Rida, T., & Schubert, J. (2022, September 1). *Setting up small and medium-size enterprises for restart and recovery.* McKinsey & Company. Retrieved from https://www.mckinsey.com/industries/public-and-social-sector/our-insights/setting-up-small-and-medium-size-enterprises-for-restart-and-recovery

Al-Dmour, H., Salman, A., Abuhashesh, M., & Al-Dmour, R. (2020). Influence of social media platforms on public health protection against the COVID-19 pandemic via the mediating effects of public health awareness and behavioral changes: Integrated model. *Journal of Medical Internet Research*, *22*(8), e19996. doi:10.2196/19996 PMID:32750004

Al-Fadly, A. (2020). Impact of COVID-19 on SMEs and employment. *Entrepreneurship and Sustainability Issues*, *8*, 629.

Alghizzawi, M., & Salloum, S. (2018). *The role of social media in tourism marketing in Jordan.* Academic Press.

Alhajeri, A. S. (2012). *The financing and success factors of small business in Kuwait* [Doctoral dissertation]. University of Portsmouth.

Alimentarius, C. (n.d.). *Strengthening national food control systems.* Retrieved from https://www.fao.org/3/y8705e/y8705e05.htm

Alkateeb, M. A., & Abdalla, R. A. (2021). Social Media Adoption and its Impact on SMEs Performance A Case Study of Palestine. *Studies of Applied Economies*, *39*(7).

Almqvist, I. (2020). *Medicine of the Imagination: Dwelling in Possibility: An Impassioned Plea for Fearless Imagination.* John Hunt Publishing.

Alshehri, O. (2019). Usage and Perceptions of Social Media Tools among Higher Education Instructor. *International Journal of Information and Education Technology (IJIET), 9*(7), 493–497. doi:10.18178/ijiet.2019.9.7.1252

Alshubiri, F., Jamil, S. A., & Elheddad, M. (2019). The impact of ICT on financial development: Empirical evidence from the Gulf Cooperation Council countries. *International Journal of Engineering Business Management, 11,* 1847979019870670. doi:10.1177/1847979019870670

Alves, J. C., Lok, T. C., Luo, Y., & Hao, W. (2020). *Crisis management for small business during the COVID-19 outbreak: Survival, resilience and renewal strategies of firms in Macau.* Academic Press.

Amarjit Gill, N. B. (2011). Barriers to small business creations in Canada. *International Journal of Entrepreneurship and Small Business, 14*(2), 245–257. doi:10.1504/IJESB.2011.042722

Andrade, J. G., & Ruao, T. (2022). *Navigating Digital Communication and Challenges for Organizations.* IGI Global. doi:10.4018/978-1-7998-9790-3

Andrews, M., Areekal, B., Rajesh, K., Krishnan, J., Suryakala, R., Krishnan, B., Muraly, C., & Santhosh, P. (2020). First confirmed case of COVID-19 infection in India: A case report. *The Indian Journal of Medical Research, 151*(5), 490. doi:10.4103/ijmr.IJMR_2131_20 PMID:32611918

Arianty, N. (n.d.). *The Impact of Social Media Use on SME Progress.* Academic Press.

Arianty, N., Fauzi Rambe, M., Bahagia, R., Utara, S., & Kapten Mucthar Basri No, J. (2018). *Increasing Family Revenue Based on Household Industry. Saudi Journal of Business and Management Studies.* SJBMS. doi:10.21276jbms.2018.3.9.10

Ashrafi, R., & Murtaza, M. (2008). Use and impact of ICT on SMEs in Oman. *Electronic Journal of Information Systems Evaluation, 11*(3).

Atanassova, I., & Clark, L. (2015). Social media practices in SME marketing activities: A theoretical framework and research agenda. *Journal of Customer Behaviour, 14*(2), 163–183. doi:10.1362/147539215X14373846805824

Athapaththu, J. C., & Nishantha, B. (2018). Information and Communication Technology Adoption in SMEs in Sri Lanka; Current Level of ICT Usage and Perceived Barriers. *International Journal of E-Entrepreneurship and Innovation, 8*(1), 1–15. doi:10.4018/IJEEI.2018010101

Augoye, J. (2020, June 5). *Busola Dakolo alleges plot to silence her rape case against Fatoyinbo.* Retrieved 1 25, 2022, from PremiumTimes: https://www.premiumtimesng.com/news/more-news/396222-busola-dakolo-alleges-plot-to-silence-her-rape-case-against-fatoyin bo.html

Ausat, A. M. A., & Suherlan, S. (2021). Obstacles and solutions of MSMEs in electronic commerce during covid-19 pandemic: Evidence from Indonesia. *BASKARA: Journal of Business and Entrepreneurship, 4*(1), 11–19. doi:10.54268/baskara.4.1.11-19

Austin, L., Fisher Liu, B., & Jin, Y. (2012). How audiences seek out crisis information: Exploring the social-mediated crisis communication model. *Journal of Applied Communication Research, 40*(2), 188–207. doi:10.1080/00909882.2012.654498

Aydin, G. (2020). Social media engagement and organic post effectiveness: A roadmap for increasing the effectiveness of social media use in hospitality industry. *Journal of Hospitality Marketing & Management, 29*(1), 1–21. doi:10.1080/19368623.2019.1588824

Ayedee, N., & Manocha, S. (2020). Role of media (Television) in creating positive atmosphere in COVID 19 during lockdown in India. *Asian Journal of Management, 11*(4), 370–378. doi:10.5958/2321-5763.2020.00057.8

Ayenigbara, G. (2014). Cannabis sativa: A plant with multiple utilities, misunderstood, and a victim of controversial hypocrisy. *Journal of Emerging Trends in Educational Research and Policy Studies, 5*, 54–59.

Ayozie, D. O., & Latinwo, H. K. (2011). Entrepreneurial developments and small scale industry contribution to Nigerian national development- A marketing interface. *Information Management and Business Review, 1*(2), 51–68. Advance online publication. doi:10.22610/imbr.v1i2.872

Azam, M. S. (2014). *Diffusion of ICT and SME Performance: The Mediating Effects of Integration and Utilisation.* Curtin University.

Azam, M. S. (2013). Towards Digital Communication and transaction: An inquiry into the individuals' Internet acceptance and usage behaviour in Bangladesh. *Journal of International Technology and Information Management, 22*(1), 123–140.

Badi, S., Ochieng, E., Nasaj, M., & Papadaki, M. (2021). Technological, organisational and environmental determinants of smart contracts adoption: UK construction sector viewpoint. *Construction Management and Economics, 39*(1), 36–54. doi:10.1080/01446193.2020.1819549

Bai, C., Quayson, M., & Sarkis, J. (2021). Covid-19 pandemic digitization lessons for sustainable development of micro-and small- enterprises. *Sustainable Production and Consumption, 27*, 1989–2001. doi:10.1016/j.spc.2021.04.035 PMID:34722843

Bajpai, V., Pandey, D. S., & Shriwas, M. S. (2012). Social media marketing: Strategies & its impact. *International Journal of Social Science & Interdisciplinary Research, 1*(7), 214–223.

Bakri, A. A. A. (2017). The impact of social media adoption on competitive advantage in the small and medium enterprises. *International Journal of Business Innovation and Research, 13*(2), 255–269. doi:10.1504/IJBIR.2017.083542

Balan, N., Skoug, R., Tulasi Ram, S., Rajesh, P. K., Shiokawa, K., Otsuka, Y., Batista, I. S., Ebihara, Y., & Nakamura, T. (2014). CME front and severe space weather. *Journal of Geophysical Research. Space Physics, 119*(12), 10,041–10,058. doi:10.1002/2014JA020151

Bansal, R., & Pruthi, N. (2021). Developing Customer Engagement Through Social Media: A Review Of Literature. *Marketing 5.0: Putting Up Blocks Together*, 80.

Bansal, R., & Saini, S. (2022). Exploring the Role of Social Media: An Innovative Tool for Entrepreneurs. In Applying Metalytics to Measure Customer Experience in the Metaverse (pp. 34-43). IGI Global.

Bansal, R., Masood, R., & Dadhich, V. (2014). Social media marketing-a tool of innovative marketing. *Journal of Organizational Management, 3*(1), 1–7.

Bansal, R., & Minocha, K. (2017). Impact of Social Media on Consumer Attitude Towards A Brand With Special Reference to Hospitality Industry. *International Research Journal of Management and Commerce, 4*(8), 106–120.

Bansal, R., & Saini, S. (2022). Leveraging Role Of Social Media Influencers In Corporate World-An Overview. *NOLEGEIN-Journal of Global Marketing, 5*(1), 1–5.

Baporikar, N. (2021). *Influence of Business Competitiveness on SMEs Performance. In Research Anthology on Small Business Strategies for Success and Survival.* IGI Global.

Barman, A., Das, R., & De, P. K. (2021). Impact of COVID-19 in food supply chain: Disruptions and recovery strategy. *Current Research in Behavioral Sciences, 2*, 100017. doi:10.1016/j.crbeha.2021.100017

Barnhart, B. (2021). *Building Your Social Media Marketing Strategy for 2022.* Retrieved July 22, 2022, from https://sproutsocial.com/insights/social-media-marketing-strategy/

Bartik, A. W., Bertrand, M., Cullen, Z. B., Glaeser, E. L., Luca, M., & Stanton, C. T. (2020). *How are small businesses adjusting to COVID-19? Early evidence from a survey (No. w26989).* National Bureau of Economic Research. doi:10.3386/w26989

Bartik, A. W., Bertrand, M., Cullen, Z., Glaeser, E. L., Luca, M., & Stanton, C. (2020). The impact of COVID-19 on small business outcomes and expectations. *Proceedings of the National Academy of Sciences of the United States of America, 117*(30), 17656–17666. doi:10.1073/pnas.2006991117 PMID:32651281

Bashar, A., Ahmad, I., & Wasique, M. (2021). Effectiveness of social media as a marketing tool: An empirical study. *International Journal of Marketing, Financial Services & Management Research, 1*(11).

Basri, W. S., & Siam, M. R. (2017). Maximizing the social media potential for small businesses and startups: A conceptual study. *International Journal of Economic Perspectives, 11*(2), 241–245.

Batista, J. M., Barros, L. S., Peixoto, F. V., & Botelho, D. (2022). Sarcastic or Assertive: How Should Brands Reply to Consumers' Uncivil Comments on Social Media in the Context of Brand Activism? *Journal of Interactive Marketing, 57*(1), 141–158. doi:10.1177/10949968221075817

Baumöl, U., Hollebeek, L., & Jung, R. (2016). Dynamics of customer interaction on social media platforms. *Electronic Markets, 26*(3), 199–202. doi:10.100712525-016-0227-0

Behera, M., Mishra, S., Mohapatra, N., & Behera, A. R. (2020). Covid-19 pandemic and micro, Small and Medium Enterprises (msmes): Policy response for revival. *SEDME (Small Enterprises Development, Management & Extension Journal): A Worldwide Window on MSME Studies, 47*(3), 213–228. doi:10.1177/09708464211037485

Belitski, M., Guenther, C., Kritikos, A. S., & Thurik, R. (2021). *Economic effects of the covid-19 pandemic on entrepreneurship and small businesses.* SSRN Electronic Journal. doi:10.2139srn.3905065

Benjamin, A. (2013). *The current development and trends of social media marketing strategies for businesses-Case study on an internet marketing company: Lead Creation* [Bachelor's thesis]. Turku University of Applied Sciences.

Benoit, I. D., & Miller, E. G. (2017). The mitigating role of holistic thinking on choice overload. *Journal of Consumer Marketing, 34*(3), 181–190. doi:10.1108/JCM-07-2016-1889

Beraha, I., & Ðuričin, S. (2020). The impact of COVID-19 crisis on medium-sized enterprises in Serbia. *Economic Analysis, 53*(1), 14–27.

Berthon, P., Ewing, M. T., & Napoli, J. (2008). Brand Management in Small to Medium-Sized Enterprises*. *Journal of Small Business Management, 46*(1), 27–45. doi:10.1111/j.1540-627X.2007.00229.x

Bhalerao, K., Mahale, P., Jyothi, N. V., & Yelikar, B. (2021). Technology: A pathway towards sustainability. *Academy of Marketing Studies Journal, 25*(5), 1–9.

Bhalerao, K., & Patil, V. (2021). Information and communication technology adoption in small and medium enterprises: Post COVID-19 mantra of success. *International Journal of Management and Commerce, 3*(1), 27–31.

Bhalerao, K., Patil, V., & Swamy, S. (2022). Impact of COVID 19 on small and medium enterprises. *Asian Journal of Management, 13*(2), 115–119. doi:10.52711/2321-5763.2022.00021

Bhanot, S. (2012). Use of social media by companies to reach their customers. *SIES Journal of Management, 8*(1), 47.

Bhatiasevi, V., & Naglis, M. (2016). Investigating the structural relationship for the determinants of cloud computing adoption in education. *Education and Information Technologies, 21*(5), 1197–1223. doi:10.100710639-015-9376-6

Bhattacharya, C. B., Sen, S., Edinger-Schons, L. M., & Neureiter, M. (2022). Corporate Purpose and Employee Sustainability Behaviors. *Journal of Business Ethics*. Advance online publication. doi:10.100710551-022-05090-5

Bhoi, N. K. (2018). Mendeley data repository as a platform for research data management. *Marching Beyond Libraries: Managerial Skills and Technological Competencies*, 481-487.

Bielozorov, A. (2020, May 13). *Covid-19 SME Technology Adoption Assessment* [web log]. Retrieved from https://www.perform-network.eu/covid-19-sme-technology-adoption-assessment/

Bigley, I. P., & Leonhardt, J. M. (2018). Extremity bias in user-generated content creation and consumption in social media. *Journal of Interactive Advertising, 18*(2), 125–135. doi:10.1080/15252019.2018.1491813

Bilro, R. G., Maria, S., & Loureiro, C. (2020). A consumer engagement systematic review : synthesis and research agenda. *Spanish Journal of Marketing, 24*(3), 283–307. doi:10.1108/SJME-01-2020-0021

Block, L., Argo, J., & Kramer, T. (2021). The Science of Consumer Psychology. *Journal of Consumer Psychology, 31*(1), 3–5. doi:10.1002/jcpy.1205

Blog: Five ways governments can help small businesses in the informal sector survive covid-19. (n.d.). Commonwealth. Retrieved from https://thecommonwealth.org/news/blog-five-ways-governments-can-help-small-businesses-informal-sector-survive-covid-19

Blum, K., & Omale, G. (2019). *Gartner Identifies Four Emerging Trends That Will Transform How Marketers Run Their Technology Ecosystems.* https://www.gartner.com/en/newsroom/press-releases/2019-08-29-gartner-identifies-four-emerging-trends-that-will-tra

Bocconcelli, R., Cioppi, M., & Pagano, A. (2017). Social media as a resource in SMEs' sales process. *Journal of Business and Industrial Marketing, 32*(5), 693–709. doi:10.1108/JBIM-11-2014-0244

Bock, G., Zmund, R. W., Kim, Y., & Lee, J. (2005). Behavioral Intention Formation in Knowledge Sharing: Examining the Roles of Extrinsic Motivators, Social- psychological Forces, and Organisational Climate. *Management Information Systems Quarterly, 29*(1), 87–111. doi:10.2307/25148669

Borah, P. S., Iqbal, S., & Akhtar, S. (2022). Linking social media usage and SME's sustainable performance: The role of digital leadership and innovation capabilities. *Technology in Society, 68*, 101900. Advance online publication. doi:10.1016/j.techsoc.2022.101900

Boyd, D. M., & Ellison, N. B. (2007). Social Network Sites: Definition, History, and Scholarship. *Journal of Computer-Mediated Communication, 13*(1), 210–230. doi:10.1111/j.1083-6101.2007.00393.x

Brink, T. (2017). B2B SME management of antecedents to the application of social media. *Industrial Marketing Management, 64*, 57–65. doi:10.1016/j.indmarman.2017.02.007

Broniarczyk, S. M. & Griffin, J. G. (2014). Decision difficulty in the age of consumer empowerment. *Journal of Consumer Psychology, 24*(4), 608-625.

Brown, R., Rocha, A., & Cowling, M. (2020). Financing entrepreneurship in times of crisis: Exploring the impact of COVID-19 on the market for entrepreneurial finance in the United Kingdom. *International Small Business Journal, 38*(5), 380–390. doi:10.1177/0266242620937464

Bruce, E., Shurong, Z., Egala, S. B., Amoah, J., Ying, D., Rui, H., & Lyu, T. (2022). Social media usage and SME firms' sustainability: An introspective analysis from Ghana. *Sustainability (Switzerland)*, *14*(15), 9433. Advance online publication. doi:10.3390u14159433

Brülhart, M., Lalive, R., Lehmann, T., & Siegenthaler, M. (2020). COVID-19 financial support to small businesses in Switzerland: Evaluation and outlook. *Schweizerische Zeitschrift für Volkswirtschaft und Statistik*, *156*(1), 1–13. doi:10.118641937-020-00060-y PMID:33078128

Bryman, A. (2011). Research methods in the study of leadership. In The SAGE handbook of leadership. SAGE.

Buchholz, K. (2020, June 17). *Half of Indian Startups in Serious Danger Due to COVID-19* [web log]. Retrieved from https://www.statista.com/chart/22027/startup-sme-financial-situation-india/

Busch, O. (2016). *Programmatic Advertising: The Successful Transformation to Automated, Data-Driven Marketing in Real-Time*. Springer. doi:10.1007/978-3-319-25023-6

Caballero-Morales, S.-O. (2021). Innovation as a recovery strategy for smes in emerging economies during the COVID-19 pandemic. *Research in International Business and Finance*, *57*, 101396. doi:10.1016/j.ribaf.2021.101396 PMID:33558782

Camilleri, M. A., & Kozak, M. (2022). Interactive engagement through travel and tourism social media groups: A social facilitation theory perspective. *Technology in Society*, *71*, 102098. doi:10.1016/j.techsoc.2022.102098

Canada, G. O. (n.d.). *Food business activities that require a licence under the Safe Food for Canadians Regulations*. Retrieved from Government of Canada: https://inspection.canada.ca/food-licences/food-business-activities/eng/1524074697160/1524074697425

Canada, G. O. (n.d.). *Licensing Interactive Tool*. Retrieved from Government of Canada: https://ca1se.voxco.com/SE/93/SFCR_licence/?&lang=en

Canada, R. (2018). *Foodservice businesses are increasing attention on social media marketing*. Retrieved from https://www.restaurantscanada.org/foodservice-businesses-increasing-attention-social-media-marketing/

Canada, S. (n.d.). *Full-service restaurants and limited-service eating places - 7225-Businesses - Canadian Industry Statistics*. Government of Canada. Retrieved from https://www.ic.gc.ca/app/scr/app/cis/businesses-entreprises/7225

Cao, D., Maureen, M., Donna, W., & Senmao, X. (2021). Understanding consumers' social media engagement behaviour: An examination of the moderation effect of social media context. *Journal of Business Research*, *122*, 835–846. doi:10.1016/j.jbusres.2020.06.025

Cao, Y., Ajjan, H., Hong, P., & Le, T. (2018). Using social media for competitive business outcomes: An empirical study of companies in China. *Journal of Advances in Management Research*, *15*(2), 211–235. doi:10.1108/JAMR-05-2017-0060

Capriotti, P. (2017). The World Wide Web and the Social Media as Tools of CSR Communication. In Handbook of Integrated CSR Communication (pp. 193–210). doi:10.1007/978-3-319-44700-1_11

Cheng, C. C., & Shiu, E. C. (2019). How to enhance SMEs customer involvement using social media: The role of Social CRM. *International Small Business Journal*, *37*(1), 22–42. doi:10.1177/0266242618774831

Chen, Y. S., & Lin, H. H. L. (2021). Effect of Social Media Marketing Strategies on Competitive Advantage Among the SMEs in China. *Journal of Marketing Communications*, *4*(1), 14–23.

Chernev, A. (2003). When more is less and less is more: The role of ideal point availability and assortment in consumer choice. *The Journal of Consumer Research, 30*(2), 170–183. doi:10.1086/376808

Chernev, A., Böckenholt, U., & Goodman, J. (2015). Choice overload: A conceptual review and meta-analysis. *Journal of Consumer Psychology, 25*(2), 333–358. doi:10.1016/j.jcps.2014.08.002

Chien, F., Ngo, Q. T., Hsu, C. C., Chau, K. Y., & Iram, R. (2021). Assessing the mechanism of barriers towards green finance and public spending in small and medium enterprises from developed countries. *Environmental Science and Pollution Research International, 28*(43), 60495–60510. doi:10.100711356-021-14907-1 PMID:34156623

China Internet Network Information Center. (2022). *The 49th Statistical Report on the Development of the Internet in China.* http://www.cnnic.cn/hlwfzyj/hlwxzbg/hlwtjbg/202202/P020220407403488048001.pdf

ChinaLiterature. (2022). *ChinaLiterature Annual Report 2021.* https://max.book118.com/html/2022/0419/5111024204004214.shtm

Chinese Academy of Social Sciences. (2022). *2021 Research Report on the Development of Online Literature in China.* http://lit.cssn.cn/wx/wx_yczs/202204/t20220407_5402451.shtml

Chittithaworn, C., Islam, M. A., Keawchana, T., & Yusuf, D. H. M. (2011). Factors affecting business success of small & medium enterprises (SMEs) in Thailand. *Asian Social Science, 7*(5), 180–190. doi:10.5539/ass.v7n5p180

Chivandi, A., Samuel, M. O., & Muchie, M. (2019). *Social Media, Consumer Behavior, and Service Marketing* (M. Reyes, Ed.). Consumer Behavior and Marketing., doi:10.5772/intechopen.85406

Cho, C. K., & Johar, G. V. (2011). Attaining satisfaction. *The Journal of Consumer Research, 38*(4), 622–631. doi:10.1086/660115

Choi, I., Koo, M., & Choi, J. A. (2007). Individual differences in analytic versus holistic thinking. *Personality and Social Psychology Bulletin, 33*(5), 691–705. doi:10.1177/0146167206298568 PMID:17440200

Cho, M., Furey, L. D., & Mohr, T. (2017). Communicating corporate social responsibility on social media: Strategies, stakeholders, and public engagement on corporate facebook. *Business and Professional Communication Quarterly, 80*(1), 52–69. doi:10.1177/2329490616663708

Chong, S. (2006, August). An Empirical Study of Factors That Influence the Extent of Deployment of Electronic Commerce for Small- and Medium-Sized Enterprises in Australia. *Journal of Theoretical and Applied Electronic Commerce Research, 1*(2), 45–57. doi:10.3390/jtaer1020012

Chowdhury, M., Sarkar, A., Paul, S. K. & Moktadir, M. (2020). A case study on strategies to deal with the impacts of COVID-19 pandemic in the food and beverage industry. *Operations Management Research,* 1-13.

Chu, S. C., Chen, H. T., & Sung, Y. (2016). Following brands on twitter: An extension of theory of planned behavior. *International Journal of Advertising, 35*(3), 421–437. doi:10.1080/02650487.2015.1037708

Clevenger, M. R., & Macgregor, C. J. (2019). Stakeholder Management and Corporate Social Responsibility (CSR). *Business and Corporation Engagement with Higher Education,* 67–81. doi:10.1108/978-1-78754-655-420191003

CNNIC. (2015). *Ten highlights of China's Internet development in the 12th Five-Year Plan.* http://www.cnnic.com.cn/AU/MediaC/rdxw/2015n/201511/t20151105_52985.htm

Coe, C. (n.d.). *Small Business Financing Program, Small Business Branch Innovation, Science and Economic Development Canada.* Government of Canada. Retrieved from https://ised-isde.canada.ca/site/sme-research-statistics/en/research-reports/sme-profile-canada-small-business-financing-program-borrowers-march-2016/sme-profile-canada-small-business-financing-program-borrowers-march-2016

Collins, J. (2020). A brief history of cannabis and the drug conventions. *The American Journal of International Law*, *114*, 279–284.

Coronavirus (COVID-19): SME policy responses. (n.d.). OECD. Retrieved from https://www.oecd.org/coronavirus/policy-responses/coronavirus-covid-19-sme-policy-responses-04440101/#section-d1e3087

Cote, J. (2022, February 3). *What is New Media?* Retrieved April 4, 2022, from Southern New Hampshire University: https://www.snhu.edu/about-us/newsroom/liberal-arts/what-is-new-media

Czekaj, J. L. (2017). *communicating in the age of social media.* Academic Press.

Dai, R., Feng, H., Hu, J., Jin, Q., Li, H., Wang, R., & Zhang, X. (2021). The impact of COVID-19 on small and medium-sized enterprises (SMEs): Evidence from two-wave phone surveys in China. *China Economic Review*, *67*, 101607. doi:10.1016/j.chieco.2021.101607

Dalkir, K. (2011). Measuring the impact of social media: Connection, communication and collaboration. In *Social knowledge: using social media to know what you know* (pp. 24–36). IGI Global.

Das, B. B., & Subudhi, R. N. (2016). *Influence of Socio-Economic Factors in Digital and Social Media Marketing: An Empirical Study in India. SSRN Electronic Journal.* doi:10.2139srn.2843076

Das, S., & Mondal, S. R. (2020). *Innovations in Digital Branding and Content Marketing.* IGI Global.

Davis, F. D. (1985). *A technology acceptance model for empirically testing new end-user information systems: Theory and results.* Massachusetts Institute of Technology.

Davis, F. D. (1989). Perceived Usefulness, Perceived Ease of Use, and User Acceptance of Information Technology. *Management Information Systems Quarterly*, *13*(3), 319–340. doi:10.2307/249008

Dessart, L., Veloutsou, C., & Morgan-Thomas, A. (2015). Consumer engagement in online brand communities: A social media perspective. *Journal of Product and Brand Management*, *24*(1), 28–42. doi:10.1108/JPBM-06-2014-0635

Dev, S. M., & Sengupta, R. (2020). *Covid-19: Impact on the Indian economy.* Indira Gandhi Institute of Development Research.

Devereux, E., Grimmer, L., & Grimmer, M. (2020). Consumer engagement on social media: Evidence from small retailers. *Journal of Consumer Behaviour*, *19*(2), 151–159. doi:10.1002/cb.1800

Devkota, N., Paudel, U. R., & Bhandari, U. (2020). Does westernization influence the business culture of a touristic city? *Economia e Sociologia*, *13*(4), 154–172. doi:10.14254/2071-789X.2020/13-4/10

Devkota, N., & Phuyal, R. K. (2018). Adoption practice of climate change adaptation options among Nepalese rice farmers: Role of information and communication technologies (ICTs). *American Journal of Climate Change*, *7*(2), 135–152. doi:10.4236/ajcc.2018.72010

Devkota, N., Shreebastab, D. K., Korpysa, J., Bhattarai, K., & Paudel, U. R. (2022). Determinants of successful entrepreneurship in a developing nation: Empirical evaluation using an ordered logit model. *Journal of International Studies*, *15*(1), 181–196. doi:10.14254/2071-8330.2022/15-1/12

Didier, T., Huneeus, F., Larrain, M., & Schmukler, S. L. (2021). Financing firms in hibernation during the COVID-19 pandemic. *Journal of Financial Stability*, *53*, 100837. doi:10.1016/j.jfs.2020.100837

Digital transformation of small and Medium Enterprises (smes) within the COVID-19 pandemic. (n.d.). Trường Đại học Kinh tế TP. Hồ Chí Minh. Retrieved from https://www.ueh.edu.vn/en/news/digital-transformation-of-small-and-medium-enterprises-smes-within-the-covid-19-pandemic-58518

Dijk, J. A. (2012). *The Evolution of the Digital Divide - The Digital Divide Turns to Inequality of Skills and Usage*. Retrieved 5 23, 2022, from https://narcis.nl/publication/recordid/oai:ris.utwente.nl:publications/a41c16c0-0c0e-4e68-8f74-d43368850914

Dixon, S. (2022, August 16). *Statistics*. Retrieved from https://www.statista.com/statistics/262804/social-networks-used-by-internet-users-in-canada-provinces/

Donthu, N., & Gustafsson, A. (2020). *Effects of COVID-19 on business and research*. Elsevier. doi:10.1016/j.jbusres.2020.06.008

Dora, M., Kumar, A., Mangla, S. K., Pant, A., & Kamal, M. M. (2022). Critical success factors influencing artificial intelligence adoption in food supply chains. *International Journal of Production Research*, *60*(14), 4621–4640. doi:10.1080/00207543.2021.1959665

Downes, S. 2022. Connectivism. *Asian Journal of Distance Education*.

Drydakis, N. (2022). Artificial Intelligence and reduced SMEs' business risks. A dynamic capabilities analysis during the COVID-19 pandemic. *Information Systems Frontiers*, 1–25. PMID:35261558

Dutot, V., & Bergeron, F. (2016). From strategic orientation to social media orientation: Improving SMEs' performance on social media. *Journal of Small Business and Enterprise Development*, *23*(4), 1165–1190. doi:10.1108/JSBED-11-2015-0160

Du, Y. (2018). *A Study on Jinjiang Literature City IP Operation*. Shanxi Teacher Training University.

Dweck, C. S. (1988). Goals: An approach to motivation and achievement. *Journal of Personality and Social Psychology*, *54*(1), 5–12. doi:10.1037/0022-3514.54.1.5 PMID:3346808

Dweck, C. S. (2000). *Self-theories: Their role in motivation, personality, and development*. Psychology Press.

Dweck, C. S., & Yeager, D. S. (2019). Mindsets: A view from two eras. *Perspectives on Psychological Science*, *14*(3), 481–496. doi:10.1177/1745691618804166 PMID:30707853

Dwivedi, Y. K., Ismagilova, E., Hughes, D. L., Carlson, J., Filieri, R., Jacobson, J., Jain, V., Karjaluoto, H., Kefi, H., Krishen, A. S., Kumar, V., Rahman, M. M., Raman, R., Rauschnabel, P. A., Rowley, J., Salo, J., Tran, G. A., & Wang, Y. (2020). Setting the future of digital and social media marketing research: Perspectives and research propositions. *International Journal of Information Management*, *102168*. Advance online publication. doi:10.1016/j.ijinfomgt.2020.102168

Ebrahim, R. S. (2020). The role of trust in understanding the impact of social media marketing on brand equity and brand loyalty. *Journal of Relationship Marketing*, *19*(4), 287–308. doi:10.1080/15332667.2019.1705742

Economist. (2009). *Small business, big problem.* Retrieved July 20, 2022, from https://www.economist.com/leaders/2009/12/10/small-business-big-problem

Edosomwan, S., Prakasan, S. K., Kouame, D., Watson, J., & Seymour, T. (2011). The History of Social Media and its Impact on Business. *The Journal of Applied Management & Entrepreneurship, 16*(3), 79-91. Retrieved 1 24, 2022, from https://www.researchgate.net/publication/303216233_The_history_of_social_media_and_its_impact_on_business

Eeckhout, J. (2021). *The Profit Paradox: How Thriving Firms Threaten the Future of Work.* Princeton University Press.

Effing, R., & Spil, T. A. (2016). The social strategy cone: Towards a framework for evaluating social media strategies. *International Journal of Information Management, 36*(1), 1–8. doi:10.1016/j.ijinfomgt.2015.07.009

Eggers, F., Kraus, S., Hughes, M., Laraway, S., & Snycerski, S. (2004). Implications of customer and entrepreneurial orientations for SME growth. *ICT, E-Business and Small*, (86). doi:10.1787/232556551425

Elementum. (2018, March 28). *Elementum.* Retrieved from Elementum: https://medium.com/age-of-awareness/why-does-eating-healthier-cost-more-82bad6e04ec4

El-Gohary, H. (2012). Factors affecting E-Marketing adoption and implementation in tourism firms: An empirical investigation of Egyptian small tourism organisations. *Tourism Management, 33*(5), 1256–1269. doi:10.1016/j.tourman.2011.10.013

El-Haddadeh, R. (2020). Digital innovation dynamics influence on organisational adoption: The case of cloud computing services. *Information Systems Frontiers, 22*(4), 985–999. doi:10.100710796-019-09912-2

Emerson, T., Ghosh, R., & Smith, E. (2012). Case study: Using the social share of voice to predict events that are about to happen. *Practical text mining and statistical analysis for non-structured text data applications,* 127-131.

Emmanuel, B., Zhao, S., Egala, B. S., Mammet, Y., & Godson, K. (2022). Social Media and Its Connection to Business Performance—A Literature Review. *American Journal of Industrial and Business Management, 12*(5).

Engidaw, A. E. (2022). Small businesses and their challenges during COVID-19 pandemic in developing countries: In the Case of Ethiopia. *J Innov Entrep, 11*(1), 1. doi:10.118613731-021-00191-3 PMID:35036286

Epede, M. B., & Wang, D. (2022). Global value chain linkages: An integrative review of the opportunities and challenges for SMEs in developing countries. *International Business Review, 31*(5), 101993. doi:10.1016/j.ibusrev.2022.101993

Erkan, I., & Evans, C. (2016). The influence of eWOM in social media on consumers' purchase intentions: An extended approach to information adoption. *Computers in Human Behavior, 61*, 47–55. doi:10.1016/j.chb.2016.03.003

Eteokleous, P. P., Leonidou, L. C., & Katsikeas, C. S. (2016). Corporate social responsibility in international marketing: review, assessment, and future research. In International Marketing Review (Vol. 33, Issue 4). doi:10.1108/IMR-04-2014-0120

Euronews. (2022). *Elon Musk says Twitter Blue paid-for verification to return despite days of impersonation chaos.* Retrieved from Euronews: https://www.euronews.com/next/2022/11/14/elon-musk-says-twitter-blue-paid-for-verification-to-return-despite-days-of-impersonation-

Eze, S. C., Chinedu/Eze, V. C., & Bello, A. O. (2020). Some Antecedent Factors that shape SMEs adoption of social media marketing application: A Hybrid Approach. *Journal of* Performance A Case Study of Palestine. *Studies of Applied Economics, 39*(7).

Eze, S. C., Chinedu-Eze, V. C., Awa, H. O. & Asiyanbola, T. A. (2022). Multi-dimensional framework of the information behaviour of SMEs on emerging information communication technology (EICT) adoption. *Journal of Science and Technology Policy Management.*

Faal, M. L. (2020). Understanding binding constraints to small and medium enterprises (SMEs) in the Gambia: A critical review. *Asian Journal of Management, 11*(2), 216–221. doi:10.5958/2321-5763.2020.00034.7

Fadhiha Mokhtar, N., Rosufila, Z., Hasan, A., Sofian, M. A., & Halim, A. (2017). The Social Media and Marketing Strategies: How it Impacts the Small-and Medium-sized Enterprises' Business Performance? *Australasian Journal of Business, Social Science and Information Technology, 3.*

Fan, N. J. (2022). *Canada Could Be in a Recession as Soon as Early 2023.* Royal Bank of Canada. Retrieved from https://www6.royalbank.com/en/di/hubs/now-and-noteworthy/article/canada-could-be-in-a-recession-as-soon-as-early-2023/l41dzp8q#:~:text=In%20previous%20work%2C%20we%20projected,power%2C%20weighing%20on%20goods%20purchases

Fan, W. (2017). The Sense of Internet of Online Literature is Important in the IP Era. *International Publishing Weekly*, 11.

Fang, G. G., Qalati, S. A., Ostic, D., Shah, S. M. M., & Mirani, M. A. (2021). Effects of entrepreneurial orientation, social media, and innovation capabilities on SME performance in emerging countries: A mediated–moderated model. *Technology Analysis and Strategic Management*, 1–13.

Fang, H., Wang, L., & Yang, Y. (2020). Human mobility restrictions and the spread of the novel coronavirus (2019-nCoV) in China. *Journal of Public Economics, 191*, 104272. doi:10.1016/j.jpubeco.2020.104272 PMID:33518827

Farache, F., Tetchner, I., & Kollat, J. (2014). CSR Communications on Twitter: An Exploration into Stakeholder Reactions. In Corporate Responsibility and Digital Communities. Palgrave Studies in Governance, Leadership and Responsibility (pp. 145–163). Academic Press.

Farzana, P. T., Noor, I. J., & Sulaiman, A. (2016). Social media's impact on organizational performance and entrepreneurial orientation in organizations. *Management Decision, 54*(9), 22080–22234.

Farzana, P. T., Noor, I. J., & Sulaiman, A. (2018). Understanding the impact of social media usage among organizations. *Information & Management, 55*(3), 308–321. doi:10.1016/j.im.2017.08.004

Farzana, P., Noor, I. J., & Sulaiman, A. (2014). Social media usage and organizational performance: Reflections of Malaysian social media managers. *Science Direct. Telematics and Informatics, 32*, 67–78.

Fasolo, B., McClelland, G. H., & Todd, P. M. (2007). Escaping the tyranny of choice: When fewer attributes make choice easier. *Marketing Theory, 7*(1), 13–26. doi:10.1177/1470593107073842

Favaretto, J. E. R. (2015). *Stage level measurement of information and communication technology in organizations* (Doctoral dissertation).

Feng, S.S., & Xiao, Y.Y. (2018). Internet thinking in the production of Daylight Entertainment TV series. *Film and Television Production, 24*(12), 79-82.

Fishbein, M. (1980). Understanding Attitudes and Predicting. *Social Behaviour.*

Fishbein, M., & Ajzen, I. (1977). Belief, attitude, intention, and behavior: An introduction to theory and research. *Philosophy & Rhetoric*, 10.

Fitriasari, F. (2020). How do Small and Medium Enterprise (SME) survive the COVID-19 outbreak? *Jurnal Inovasi Ekonomi, 5*(2).

Fleischer, H. (2021). Corporate Purpose : A Management Concept and its Implications for Company Law. European Corporate Governance Institute.

Fonseca, L. M. (2018). Industry 4.0 and the digital society: concepts, dimensions and envisioned benefits. *Proceedings of the international conference on business excellence*, 386-397. 10.2478/picbe-2018-0034

Foroudi, P., Jin, Z., Gupta, S., Foroudi, M. M., & Kitchen, P. J. (2018). Perceptional components of brand equity: Configuring the Symmetrical and Asymmetrical Paths to brand loyalty and brand purchase intention. *Journal of Business Research, 89*(January), 462–474. doi:10.1016/j.jbusres.2018.01.031

Gartenberg, C., Prat, A., & Serafeim, G. (2019). Corporate purpose and financial performance. *Organization Science, 30*(1), 1–18. doi:10.1287/orsc.2018.1230

Gavino, M. C., Williams, D. E., Jacobson, D., & Smith, I. (2018). Latino Entrepreneurs and Social Media adoption: Personal and business Social Network Platforms. *Management Research Review, 42*(4), 469–494. doi:10.1108/MRR-02-2018-0095

Geho, P. R., & Dangelo, J. (2012). The evolution of social media as a marketing tool for entrepreneurs. *The Entrepreneurial Executive, 17*, 61.

Georgescu, M., & Popescul, D. (2015). Social Media–the new paradigm of collaboration and communication for the business environment. *Procedia Economics and Finance, 20*, 277–282. doi:10.1016/S2212-5671(15)00075-1

Gerald, E., Obianuju, A., & Chukwunonso, N. (2020). Strategic agility and performance of small and medium enterprises in the phase of Covid-19 pandemic. *International Journal of Financial, Accounting, and Management, 2*(1), 41–50. doi:10.35912/ijfam.v2i1.163

Gesenhues, A. (2020). How real is your real-time marketing? *MarTech*, 1–9. https://martech.org/how-real-is-your-real-time-marketing/

Ghimire, R. (2011). Micro and Small Level Enterprises in Nepal. *Journal of Finance and Management Review, 2*(2), 257–269.

Gielens, K., & Steenkamp, E. J.-B. (2019). Branding in the era of digital (dis)intermediation. *Science Direct, 36*(3), 367-384. Retrieved 1 23, 2022, from doi:10.1016/j.ijresmar.2019.01.005

Gironda, J. T., & Korgaonkar, P. K. (2014). Understanding consumers' social networking site usage. *Journal of Marketing Management, 30*(5–6), 571–605. doi:10.1080/0267257X.2013.851106

Google Trends. (2022). *Dia Internacional da Mulher*. Google.

Gorbacheva, E., Niehaves, B., Plattfaut, R., & Becker, J. (2011). *Acceptance and use of internet banking: A digital divide perspective*. Retrieved 5 23, 2022, from http://aisel.aisnet.org/cgi/viewcontent.cgi?article=1125&context=ecis2011

Gould, P. J. (1990). Enterprising Women. *Locan initiatives for job creation*.

Grandi, B., & Cardinali, M. G. (2021). Choice Overload in the Grocery Setting: Results from a Laboratory Experiment. *International Business Research, 14*(1), 1–94.

Greenhalgh, T., & Papoutsi, C. (2018). Studying complexity in health services research: Desperately seeking an overdue paradigm shift. *BMC Medicine, 16*(1), 95. doi:10.118612916-018-1089-4 PMID:29921272

Greenwood, B. Y. S., Perrin, A., & Duggan, M. (2016). Social Media Update 2016. *Pew Research Center, 2*(11), 1–18.

Greenwood, E., & Ramjaun, T. R. (2020). Exploring choice overload in online travel booking. *Journal of Promotional Communications, 8*(1), 86–104.

Grégoire, Y., Salle, A., & Tripp, T. M. (2015). Managing social media crises with your customers: The good, the bad, and the ugly. *Business Horizons, 58*(2), 173–182. doi:10.1016/j.bushor.2014.11.001

Grosser, K., & Moon, J. (2005). The role of corporate social responsibility in gender mainstreaming. *International Feminist Journal of Politics, 7*(4), 532–554. doi:10.1080/14616740500284524

Grosser, K., & Moon, J. (2019). CSR and Feminist Organization Studies: Towards an Integrated Theorization for the Analysis of Gender Issues. *Journal of Business Ethics, 155*(2), 321–342. doi:10.100710551-017-3510-x

Gruber, D. A., Smerek, R. E., Thomas-Hunt, M. C., & James, E. H. (2015). The real-time power of Twitter: Crisis management and leadership in an age of social media. *Business Horizons, 58*(2), 163–172. doi:10.1016/j.bushor.2014.10.006

Gummerus, J., Liljander, V., Weman, E., & Pihlström, M. (2012). Customer engagement in a Facebook brand community. In Management Research Review (Vol. 35, Issue 9). doi:10.1108/01409171211256578

Gumus, N., & Kutahyali. (2017). Perception of social media by small & medium enterprises (SME's) in Turkey. *International Journal of Business Communication, 12.*

Guo, H., Yang, Z., Huang, R., & Guo, A. (2020). The digitalization and public crisis responses of small and Medium Enterprises: Implications from a COVID-19 survey. *Frontiers of Business Research in China, 14*(1), 19. Advance online publication. doi:10.118611782-020-00087-1

Gupta, S., Leszkiewicz, A., Kumar, V., Bijmolt, T., & Potapov, D. (2020). Digital analytics: Modeling for insights and new methods. *Journal of Interactive Marketing, 51*, 26–43. doi:10.1016/j.intmar.2020.04.003

Hadi, S., & Supardi, S. (2020). Revitalization strategy for small and medium enterprises after Corona virus disease pandemic (covid-19) in Yogyakarta. *J. Xian Univ. Archit. Technol, 12*, 4068–4076.

Hafiz, H., Oei, S.-Y., Ring, D. M., & Shnitser, N. (2020). *Regulating in pandemic: evaluating economic and financial policy responses to the coronavirus crisis.* Boston College Law School Legal Studies Research Paper.

Haider Syed, M., Khan, S., Raza Rabbani, M., & Thalassinos, Y. E. (2020). *An artificial intelligence and NLP based Islamic FinTech model combining Zakat and Qardh-Al-Hasan for countering the adverse impact of COVID 19 on SMEs and individuals.* Academic Press.

Hall, C., & Jay, P. (2022, June 9). *Unpacking Uniqlo's India Strategy.* The Business of Fashion.

Hamzah, Z. L., Wahab, H. A., & Waqas, M. (2021). Unveiling drivers and brand relationship implications of consumer engagement with social media brand posts. *Journal of Research in Interactive Marketing, 15*(2), 336–358. doi:10.1108/JRIM-05-2020-0113

Hanafifizadeh, P., Shafifia, S., & Bohlin, E. (2021). Exploring the consequence of social media usage on firm performance. *Digital Business, 1*(2).

Hanafizadeh, P., Shafia, S., & Bohlin, E. (2021). Exploring the consequence of social media usage on firm performance. *Digital Business., 1*(2), 100013. Advance online publication. doi:10.1016/j.digbus.2021.100013

Han, E., Tan, M. M. J., Turk, E., Sridhar, D., Leung, G. M., Shibuya, K., Asgari, N., Oh, J., García-Basteiro, A. L., Hanefeld, J., Cook, A. R., Hsu, L. Y., Teo, Y. Y., Heymann, D., Clark, H., McKee, M., & Legido-Quigley, H. (2020). Lessons learnt from easing COVID-19 restrictions: An analysis of countries and regions in Asia Pacific and Europe. *Lancet*, *396*(10261), 1525–1534. doi:10.1016/S0140-6736(20)32007-9 PMID:32979936

Hardey, M. (2011). Generation C: Content, creation, connections and choice. *International Journal of Market Research*, *53*(6), 749–770. doi:10.2501/IJMR-53-6-749-770

Hassan, S., Nadzim, S. Z. A., & Shiratuddin, N. (2015). Strategic Use of Social Media for Small Business Based on the AIDA Model. *Procedia: Social and Behavioral Sciences*, *172*, 262–269. doi:10.1016/j.sbspro.2015.01.363

Haudi, H., Handayani, W., Suyoto, M. Y. T., Praseti, T., Pitaloka, E., Wijoyo, H., Yonata, H., Koho, I. R., & Cahyono, Y. (2022). The effect of social media marketing on brand trust, brand equity and brand loyalty. *International Journal of Data and Network Science*, *6*(3), 961–972. doi:10.5267/j.ijdns.2022.1.015

Hebert, D. J. (2021). COVID-19's Impacts on SMEs and Policy Recommendations in Response. *National Law Review, 11*(20). Available at: https://www. natlawreview. com/article/covid-19-s-impacts-sm es-and-policy-recommendations-response

Hebert, D. J. (2022). *COVID-19's Impacts on SMEs and Policy Recommendations in Response. The National Law Review*, 12.

Hendee, C. (2017). New study reveals what's really important to diners at restaurants. *Denver Business Journal*. Retrieved from https://www.bizjournals.com/denver/news/2017/02/15/new-study -reveals-whats-really-important-to-diners.html?ana=e_me_set3 &s=newsletter&ed=2017-02-16&u=Kpsral71P012luK%2Bt8eH0w0f89f4 9b&t=1487344415&j=77405641

Hervás-Oliver, J. L., Parrilli, M. D., Rodríguez-Pose, A., & Sempere-Ripoll, F. (2021). The drivers of SME innovation in the regions of the EU. *Research Policy*, *50*(9), 104316. doi:10.1016/j.respol.2021.104316

Herwi, S. J. (2019, April). What are SMEs. *Research Gate*, 1-3. Retrieved from https://www.researchgate.net/publication/332539278_What_are_ SMEs

He, W., Tian, X., Chen, Y., & Chong, D. (2016). Actionable social media competitive analytics for understanding customer experiences. *Journal of Computer Information Systems*, *56*(2), 145–155. doi:10.1080/08874417.2016.1117377

He, W., Wu, H., Yan, G., Akula, V., & Shen, J. (2015). A novel social media competitive analytics framework with sentiment benchmarks. *Information & Management*, *52*(7), 801–812. doi:10.1016/j.im.2015.04.006

Hong, H., & Kim, Y. (2021). What makes people engage in civic activism on social media? *Online Information Review*, *45*(3), 562–576. doi:10.1108/OIR-03-2020-0105

Hong, J., Edler, J., & Massini, S. (2022). Evolution of the Chinese intellectual property rights system: IPR law revisions and enforcement. *Management and Organization Review*, *18*(4), 755–787. Advance online publication. doi:10.1017/mor.2021.72

Hoorens, S., Hocking, L., & Fays, C. (2020). *How small businesses are coping with the impact of COVID-19*. Rand Europe.

Hossain, M. R., Akhter, F. & Sultana, M. M. (2022). SMEs in covid-19 crisis and combating strategies: a systematic literature review (SLR) and A case from emerging economy. *Operations Research Perspectives*, 100222.

Hourcade, J., Glemarec, Y., De Coninck, H., Bayat-Renoux, F., Ramakrishna, K. & Revi, A. (2021). *Scaling up climate finance in the context of Covid-19: A science-based call for financial decision-makers*. Academic Press.

Hrastinski, S., & Aghaee, N. M. (2012). How are campus students using social media to support their studies? An explorative interview study. *Education and Information Technologies*, *17*(4), 451–464. doi:10.100710639-011-9169-5

Huotari, L., Ulkuniemi, P., Saraniemi, S., & Mäläskä, M. (2015). Analysis of content creation in social media by B2B companies. *Journal of Business and Industrial Marketing*, *30*(6), 761–770. doi:10.1108/JBIM-05-2013-0118

Hurth, V., Ebert, C., & Prabhu, J. (2018). Organisational purpose: The construct and its antecedents and consequences. *Cambridge Judge Business School*. https://www.jbs.cam.ac.uk/fileadmin/user_upload/research/workingpapers/wp1802.pdf

Hur, W. M., Kim, H., & Jang, J. H. (2016). The Role of Gender Differences in the Impact of CSR Perceptions on Corporate Marketing Outcomes. *Corporate Social Responsibility and Environmental Management*, *23*(6), 345–357. doi:10.1002/csr.1380

Hur, W. M., Kim, H., & Woo, J. (2014). How CSR Leads to Corporate Brand Equity: Mediating Mechanisms of Corporate Brand Credibility and Reputation. *Journal of Business Ethics*, *125*(1), 75–86. doi:10.100710551-013-1910-0

Illahi, S. (2015). Micro, Small and Medium Enterprises (MSMEs) in Delhi: Problems and Prospects. *International Journal of Research and Development - A Management Review, 4*(4).

Inbar, Y., Botti, S., & Hanko, K. (2011). Decision speed and choice regret: When haste feels like waste. *Journal of Experimental Social Psychology*, *47*(3), 533–540. doi:10.1016/j.jesp.2011.01.011

Indriastuti, M., & Fuad, K. (2020, July). Impact of covid-19 on digital transformation and sustainability in small and medium enterprises (smes): A conceptual framework. In *Conference on Complex, Intelligent, and Software Intensive Systems* (pp. 471-476). Springer.

Ines, J. C. (2016). Social Media as A Marketing Tool: The Case of Small and Medium Enterprise in The Sultanate of Oman. *Intercontinental Journal of Marketing Management*, *3*(12), 20–36. www.researchscripts.org

Iwu, C. G., Elvis, O. O., & Tengeh, R. K. (2017). Social Media Adoption Challenges of Small Businesses: the Case of Restaurants in the Cape Metropole, South Africa. *African Journal of Hospitality Tourism and Leisure, 6*(4). Retrieved 5 5, 2022, from https://www.researchgate.net/publication/320615314_Social_Media_Adoption_Challenges_of_Small_Businesses_the_Case_of_Restaurants_in_the_Cape_Metropole_South_Africa

Iyengar, S. S., & Lepper, M. R. (2000). When choice is demotivating: Can one desire too much of a good thing? *Journal of Personality and Social Psychology*, *79*(6), 995–1006. doi:10.1037/0022-3514.79.6.995 PMID:11138768

Iyengar, S. S., Wells, R. E., & Schwartz, B. (2006). Doing better but feeling worse: Looking for the "best" job undermines satisfaction. *Psychological Science*, *17*(2), 143–150. doi:10.1111/j.1467-9280.2006.01677.x PMID:16466422

Jagongo, A., & Kinyua, C. (2013). The Social Media and Entrepreneurship Growth (A New Business Communication Paradigm among SMEs in Nairobi). *International Journal of Humanities and Social Science*, *3*(10).

Jagongo, A., & Kinyua, C. (2013). The social media and entrepreneurship growth. *International Journal of Humanities and Social Science*, *3*(10), 213–227.

Jaini, A., Md Dahlan, J., Suhadak, N., & Zainuddin, N. A. (2023). *Leveraging digital marketing to empower SME competency: A conceptual paper*. doi:10.1007/978-3-031-08093-7_4

Jain, S. P., & Weiten, T. J. (2020). Consumer psychology of implicit theories: A review and agenda. *Counselling Psychology Review*, *3*(1), 60–75. doi:10.1002/arcp.1056

Jansen-Kosterink, S., Dekker-Van Weering, M., & Van Velsen, L. (2019). Patient acceptance of a telemedicine service for rehabilitation care: A focus group study. *International Journal of Medical Informatics*, *125*, 22–29. doi:10.1016/j.ijmedinf.2019.01.011 PMID:30914177

Jansson, J., Nilsson, J., Modig, F., & Hed Vall, G. (2017). Commitment to Sustainability in Small and Medium-Sized Enterprises: The Influence of Strategic Orientations and Management Values. *Business Strategy and the Environment*, *26*(1), 69–83. doi:10.1002/bse.1901

Jimenez, D., Franco, I. B., & Smith, T. (2021). A review of corporate purpose: An approach to actioning the sustainable development goals (SDGs). *Sustainability (Switzerland)*, *13*(7), 3899. Advance online publication. doi:10.3390u13073899

Jinjiang Literature. (2022). www.jjwxc.net

Jones, M. O. (2022). *Digital authoritarianism in the Middle East: Deception, disinformation and social media.* Hurst Publishers.

Juergensen, J., Guimón, J., & Narula, R. (2020). European SMEs amidst the COVID-19 crisis: Assessing impact and policy responses. *Economia e Politica Industriale*, *47*(3), 499–510. doi:10.100740812-020-00169-4

Jurado, T., & Battisti, M. (2019). The evolution of SME policy: The case of New Zealand. *Regional Studies. Journal of Regional Science*, *6*(1), 32–54.

Kahneman, D. (2013). *Thinking, fast and slow*. Farrar, Straus and Giroux.

Kallier Tar, S. M., & A Wiid, J. (2021). Consumer perceptions of real-time marketing used in campaigns for retail businesses. *International Journal of Research in Business and Social Science, 10*(2), 86–105. doi:10.20525/ijrbs.v10i2.1075

Kallier, S. M. (2017). International Review of Management and Marketing The Influence of Real-time Marketing Campaigns of Retailers on Consumer Purchase Behavior. *International Review of Management and Marketing*, *7*(3), 126–133. http:www.econjournals.com

Kamal, S. A., Shafiq, M., & Kakria, P. (2020). Investigating acceptance of telemedicine services through an extended technology acceptance model (TAM). *Technology in Society*, *60*, 101212. doi:10.1016/j.techsoc.2019.101212

Kaplan, A. M., & Haenlein, M. (2010). Users of the world, unite! The challenges and opportunities of social media. *Business Horizons*, *53*(1), 59–68. doi:10.1016/j.bushor.2009.09.003

Karimi, S., & Naghibi, H. S. (2015). Social media marketing (SMM) strategies for small to medium enterprises (SMEs). *International Journal of Information, Business and Management*, *7*(4), 86.

Karki, D., Upreti, S., Bhandari, U., Rajbhandari, S., Devkota, N., Parajuli, S., & Paudel, U. R. (2021). Does the Formal Financial Sector Enhance Small Business Employment Generation in Nepal: Evidence from Cross-Sectional Data. *Journal of Social Economics Research*, *8*(2), 155–164. doi:10.18488/journal.35.2021.82.155.164

Karr, J., Loh, K., & Wirjo, A. (2020). *Supporting MSMEs' Digitalization Amid COVID-19*. Asia Pacific Economic Cooperation.

Kautz, K., & Nielsen, P. A. (2004). Understanding the implementation of software process improvement innovations in software organizations. *Information Systems Journal*, *14*(1), 3–22. doi:10.1111/j.1365-2575.2004.00156.x

Kazancoglu, I., Sagnak, M., Kumar Mangla, S., & Kazancoglu, Y. (2021). Circular economy and the policy: A framework for improving the corporate environmental management in supply chains. *Business Strategy and the Environment*, *30*(1), 590–608. doi:10.1002/bse.2641

Keenan, M. (2022, January 14). *How To Get Verified on Instagram in 2022*. Retrieved from Shopify: https://www.shopify.com/blog/how-to-get-verified-on-instagram

Kejžar, K. Z., Velić, A. & Damijan, J. P. 2022. Covid-19, trade collapse and GVC linkages: European experience. *The World Economy*.

Kelleher, T., & Sweetser, K. (2012). Social media adoption among university communicators. *Journal of Public Relations Research*, *24*(2), 105–122. doi:10.1080/1062726X.2012.626130

Keller, K. L., & Brexendorf, T. O. (2019). Measuring Brand Equity. In S. R. Wirtschaft (Ed.), *Handbuch Markenführung*. Springer Gabler. doi:10.1007/978-3-658-13342-9_72

Keller, K. L., & Staelin, R. (1987). Effects of quality and quantity of information on decision effectiveness. *The Journal of Consumer Research*, *14*(2), 200–213. doi:10.1086/209106

Keogh-Brown, M. R., Jensen, H. T., Edmunds, W. J., & Smith, R. D. (2020). The impact of Covid-19, associated behaviours and policies on the UK economy: A computable general equilibrium model. *SSM - Population Health*, *12*, 100651. doi:10.1016/j.ssmph.2020.100651 PMID:33072839

Khalil, A., Abdelli, M. E. A., & Mogaji, E. (2022). Do Digital Technologies Influence the Relationship between the COVID-19 Crisis and SMEs’ Resilience in Developing Countries? *Journal of Open Innovation*, *8*(2), 100. doi:10.3390/joitmc8020100

Kharel, S., K C, A., Devkota, N., & Paudel, U. R. (2022). Entrepreneurs' Level of Awareness on Knowledge Management for Promoting Tourism in Nepal. *Journal of Information & Knowledge Management*, *21*(02), 2250023. doi:10.1142/S021964922250023X

Kilgour, M., Sasser, S. L., & Larke, R. (2015). The social media transformation process: Curating content into strategy. *Corporate Communications*, *20*(3), 326–343. doi:10.1108/CCIJ-07-2014-0046

Killian, G., & McManus, K. (2015). A marketing communications approach for the digital era: Managerial guidelines for social media integration. *Business Horizons*, *58*(5), 539–549. doi:10.1016/j.bushor.2015.05.006

Kim, H., Kulow, K., & Kramer, T. (2013). The interactive effect of beliefs in malleable fate and fateful predictions on choice. *The Journal of Consumer Research*, *40*(6), 1139–1148. doi:10.1086/674196

Kim, P., Vaidyanathan, R., Chang, H., & Stoel, L. (2018). Using brand alliances with artists to expand retail brand personality. *Journal of Business Research*, *85*, 424–433. doi:10.1016/j.jbusres.2017.10.020

Kim, S. (2021). Mapping social media analytics for small business: A case study of business analytics. International Journal of Fashion Design. *Technology and Education*, *14*(2), 218–231.

Kirtiş, A. K., & Karahan, F. (2011). To Be or Not to Be in Social Media Arena as the Most Cost-Efficient Marketing Strategy after the Global Recession. *Procedia: Social and Behavioral Sciences*, *24*, 260–268. doi:10.1016/j.sbspro.2011.09.083

Klein, V. B., & Todesco, J. L. (2021). COVID-19 crisis and SMEs responses: The role of digital transformation. *Knowledge and Process Management*, *28*(2), 117–133. doi:10.1002/kpm.1660

Knox, S., & Maklan, S. (2004). Corporate Social Responsibility: Moving Beyond Investment Towards Measuring Outcomes. *European Management Journal, 22*(5), 508–516. doi:10.1016/j.emj.2004.09.009

Kozinets, R. V. (2002). The Field Behind the Screen: Using Netnography For Marketing Research in Online Communities. *JMR, Journal of Marketing Research, 39*(1), 61–72. doi:10.1509/jmkr.39.1.61.18935

Kozinets, R. V., & Gambetti, R. (2021). *Netnography Unlimited - Understanding Technoculture Using Qualitative Social Media Research*. Routledge.

Kozinets, R. V., Scaraboto, D., & Parmentier, M. A. (2018). Evolving netnography: How brand auto-netnography, a netnographic sensibility, and more-than-human netnography can transform your research. *Journal of Marketing Management, 34*(3–4), 231–242. doi:10.1080/0267257X.2018.1446488

Krisch, U., & Grabner-kra, S. (2017). Insights into the Impact of CSR Communication Source on Trust and Purchase Intention. In *Handbook of Integrated CSR Communication* (pp. 449–469). CSR, Sustainability, Ethics & Governance. doi:10.1007/978-3-319-44700-1_25

Kumar, A., & Ayedee, N. (2018). Social media tools for business growth of SMEs. *Journal of Management, 5*(3), 137–142.

Kumar, B., & Sharma, A. (2022). Examining the research on social media in business-to-business marketing with a focus on sales and the selling process. *Industrial Marketing Management, 102*, 122–140. doi:10.1016/j.indmarman.2022.01.008

Kumar, M., & Ayedee, D. (2021). Technology Adoption: A Solution for SMEs to overcome problems during COVID-19. *Forthcoming. Academy of Marketing Studies Journal, 25*.

Kuokkanen, H., & Sun, W. (2019). Companies, Meet Ethical Consumers : Strategic CSR Management to Impact Consumer Choice. *Journal of Business Ethics*. doi:10.1007/s10551-019-04145-4

Kwon, E. S., & Sung, Y. (2011). Follow Me! Global Marketers' Twitter Use. *Journal of Interactive Advertising, 12*(1), 4–16. doi:10.1080/15252019.2011.10722187

Kwon, J., Seo, Y., & Ko, D. (2016). Effective luxury-brand advertising: The ES–IF matching (Entity–Symbolic versus Incremental–Functional) model. *Journal of Advertising, 45*(4), 459–471. doi:10.1080/00913367.2016.1226995

Lacaille, L. (2013). Theory of Reasoned Action. In M. D. Gellman & J. R. Turner (Eds.), *Encyclopedia of Behavioral Medicine*. Springer New York.

Lacho, K. J., & Marinello, C. (2010). How small business owners can use social networking to promote their business. *The Entrepreneurial Executive, 15*, 127.

Lakshmanan, D., & Rabiyathul Basariya, S. (2017). The Role of Social Media On Enhancing Advertising Effectiveness. *International Journal of Civil Engineering and Technology, 8*(9), 1042–1047. http://www.iaeme.com/IJCIET/ issues.asp?JType=IJCIET&VType=8&IType=9

Lancaster, H. (2019). *Nigeria - Fixed Broadband Market - Statistics and Analyses*. Retrieved 1 22, 2022, from Budde Comm: https://www.budde.com.au/Research/Nigeria-Fixed-Broadband-Market-Statistics-and-Analyses

Lanyi, B., Hornyak, M., & Kruzslicz, F. (2021). The effect of online activity on SMEs' competitiveness. *Competitiveness Review, 31*(3), 477–496. doi:10.1108/CR-01-2020-0022

Lazer, W., & Kelley, E. J. (1973). *Social Marketing: Perspectives and Viewpoints*. Richard D. Irwin.

Lee, I. (2018). Social media analytics for enterprises: Typology, methods, and processes. *Business Horizons, 61*(2), 199–210. doi:10.1016/j.bushor.2017.11.002

Lee, S. (2010).. . *The Electronic Library, 34*(1), 1–5.

Le, H., Nguyen, T., Ngo, C., Pham, T., & Le, T. (2020). Policy related factors affecting the survival and development of SMEs in the context of Covid 19 pandemic. *Management Science Letters, 10*(15), 3683–3692. doi:10.5267/j.msl.2020.6.025

Leonardi, P. M., & Vaast, E. (2016). Social media and their affordances for organizing: A review and agenda for research. *The Academy of Management Annals, 11*(1), 150–188. doi:10.5465/annals.2015.0144

Li, Y. Q. (2018). Virtual Experience and Literary Imagination - New Essays on Chinese Internet Literature. *Chinese Social Sciences,* (1), 156-178+207-208.

Liguori, E. W., & Pittz, T. G. (2020). Strategies for small business: Surviving and thriving in the era of COVID-19. *Journal of the International Council for Small Business, 1*(2), 106–110. doi:10.1080/26437015.2020.1779538

Lim, W. M. (2015). Antecedents and consequences of e-shopping: An integrated model. *Internet Research, 25*(2), 184–217. doi:10.1108/IntR-11-2013-0247

Lim, W. M. (2018). Dialectic antidotes to critics of the technology acceptance model: Conceptual, methodological, and replication treatments for behavioural modelling in technology-mediated environments. *AJIS. Australasian Journal of Information Systems, 22,* 22. doi:10.3127/ajis.v22i0.1651

Lim, W. M. (2021). Toward an agency and reactance theory of crowding: Insights from COVID-19 and the tourism industry. *Journal of Consumer Behaviour, 20*(6), 1690–1694. doi:10.1002/cb.1948

Lim, W. M. (2021a). A marketing mix typology for integrated care: The 10 Ps. *Journal of Strategic Marketing, 29*(5), 453–469. doi:10.1080/0965254X.2020.1775683

Lim, W. M., & Weissmann, M. A. (2021). Toward a theory of behavioral control. *Journal of Strategic Marketing,* 1–27. doi:10.1080/0965254X.2021.1890190

Liu, Y., Shi, H., Li, Y. & Amin, A. (2021). Factors influencing Chinese residents' post-pandemic outbound travel intentions: an extended theory of planned behavior model based on the perception of COVID-19. *Tourism Review.*

Liu, S. Q., & Mattila, A. S. (2017). Airbnb: Online targeted advertising, sense of power, and consumer decisions. *International Journal of Hospitality Management, 60,* 33–41. doi:10.1016/j.ijhm.2016.09.012

Lu, J., Ren, L., Zhang, C., Rong, D., Ahmed, R. R., & Streimikis, J. (2020). Modified Carroll's pyramid of corporate social responsibility to enhance organizational performance of SMEs industry. *Journal of Cleaner Production, 271,* 122456. doi:10.1016/j.jclepro.2020.122456

Lutkevich, B., & Wigmore, I. (2021, September). *What is social media?* Retrieved 5 10, 2022, from Margaret Rouse: https://whatis.techtarget.com/definition/social-media

Ma, L. J., & Zhang, X. N. (2020). An analysis of the reasons for the success of Daylight Entertainment TV series. *Contemporary Television, 2020*(3), 94-96. DOI:. doi:10.16531/j.cnki.1000-8977.2020.03.025

Maclennan, E., & Van Belle, J.-P. (2014). Factors affecting the organizational adoption of service-oriented architecture (SOA). *Information Systems and e-Business Management, 12*(1), 71–100. doi:10.100710257-012-0212-x

Malone, T., & Lusk, J. L. (2019). Mitigating choice overload: An experiment in the US beer market. *Journal of Wine Economics, 14*(1), 48–70. doi:10.1017/jwe.2018.34

Manolică, A., Guță, A. S., Roman, T., & Dragăn, L. M. (2021). Is Consumer Overchoice a Reason for Decision Paralysis? *Sustainability*, *13*(11), 5920. doi:10.3390u13115920

Margues, S., & Simon, S. C. L. (2007). The adoption of e-business and knowledge management in SMEs. *Benchmarking*, *14*(1), 37–58. doi:10.1108/14635770710730928

Marolt, M., Zimmermann, H. D., & Pucihar, A. (2018). Exploratory study of social CRM use in SMEs. *The Engineering Economist*, *29*(4), 468–477.

Martins, A. (2022). Dynamic capabilities and SME performance in the COVID-19 era: the moderating effect of digitalization. *Asia-Pacific Journal of Business Administration,* ahead-of-print.

Martin, W. J. (2017). *The global information society*. Routledge. doi:10.4324/9781315239385

Massimo, F., & Marcone, P. M. (n.d.). An Overview of the Sociological and Environmental Factors Influencing Eating Food Behavior in Canada. *National Library of Medicine*. Retrieved from https://www.ncbi.nlm.nih.gov/pmc/articles/PMC7283517/

Mathur, P., Jain, S. P., Hsieh, M.-H., Lindsey, C. D., & Maheswaran, D. (2013). The influence of implicit theories and message frame on the persuasiveness of disease prevention and detection advocacies. *Organizational Behavior and Human Decision Processes*, *122*(2), 141–151. doi:10.1016/j.obhdp.2013.05.002

Mayfield. (2009). A Commander's Strategy for Social Media. *Army Europe and Seventh Army APO*.

McCabe, S., Li, C., & Chen, Z. (2016). Time for a radical reappraisal of tourist decision making? Toward a new conceptual model. *Journal of Travel Research*, *55*(1), 3–15. doi:10.1177/0047287515592973

McCann, M., & Barlow, A. (2015). Use and measurement of social media for SMEs. *Journal of Small Business and Enterprise Development*, *22*(2), 273–287. doi:10.1108/JSBED-08-2012-0096

Mccarthy, L. (2017). Empowering Women Through Corporate Social Responsibility: A Feminist Foucauldian Critique. *Business Ethics Quarterly*, *27*(4), 603–631. doi:10.1017/beq.2017.28

McGeever, N., McQuinn, J., & Myers, S. (2020). *SME liquidity needs during the COVID-19 shock (No. 2/FS/20)*. Central Bank of Ireland.

McKenna, R. (1995). Real-Time Marketing. *Harvard Business Review*.

McKinnon, M. (2022). *2022 Report: Social Media Use in Canada (Statistics)*. Online Business Canada. Retrieved from https://canadiansinternet.com/2022-report-social-media-use-in-canada-statistics/#:~:text=76.9%20percent%20of%20Canadians%20use,dropped%207%20percent%20from%202020

Meinhold, K., & Darr, D. (2019). The processing of non-timber forest products through small and medium enterprises—A review of enabling and constraining factors. *Forests*, *10*(11), 1026. doi:10.3390/f10111026

Merleaux, A. (2020). Drugs, empire, and US foreign policy. *A Companion to US Foreign Relations: Colonial Era to the Present*, 572-595.

Meske, C., & Stieglitz, S. (2013, June). Adoption and use of social media in small and medium-sized enterprises. In *Working conference on practice-driven research on enterprise transformation* (pp. 61-75). Springer.

Meske, C., & Stieglitz, S. (2013). Adoption and use of social media in small and medium-sized enterprises. *Working Conference on Practice-Driven Research on Enterprise Transformation*, 61-75. 10.1007/978-3-642-38774-6_5

Michaelidou, N., Siamagka, N. T., & Christodoulides, G. (2011). Usage, barriers and measurement of social media marketing: An exploratory investigation of small and medium B2B brands. *Industrial Marketing Management, 40*(7), 1153–1159. doi:10.1016/j.indmarman.2011.09.009

Michaelson, D., & Stacks, D. W. (2011). Standardization in Public Relations Measurement and Evaluation. *The Public Relations Journal, 5*(2).

Mills, A. J., & Plangger, K. (2015). Social media strategy for online service brands. *Service Industries Journal, 35*(10), 521–536. doi:10.1080/02642069.2015.1043277

Ming, T., & Lam, E. (2012). The Creativity of Social Media On Smes Brand Building. *ICSB World Conference Proceeding, 2*(1), 1.

Mirza, N., Naqvi, B., Rahat, B., & Rizvi, S. K. A. (2020). Price reaction, volatility timing and funds' performance during Covid-19. *Finance Research Letters, 36*, 101657. doi:10.1016/j.frl.2020.101657 PMID:32837369

Misirlis, N., & Vlachopoulou, M. (2018). Social media metrics and analytics in marketing–S3M: A mapping literature review. *International Journal of Information Management, 38*(1), 270–276. doi:10.1016/j.ijinfomgt.2017.10.005

Misuraca, R., Ceresia, F., Teuscher, U., & Faraci, P. (2019). The role of the brand on choice overload. *Mind & Society, 18*(1), 57–76. doi:10.100711299-019-00210-7

Misuraca, R., & Teuscher, U. (2013). Time flies when you maximize—Maximizers and satisficers perceive time differently when making decisions. *Acta Psychologica, 143*(2), 176–180. doi:10.1016/j.actpsy.2013.03.004 PMID:23584103

Misuraca, R., Teuscher, U., & Faraci, P. (2016). Is more choice always worse? Age differences in the overchoice effect. *Journal of Cognitive Psychology, 28*(2), 242–255. doi:10.1080/20445911.2015.1118107

Mittal, R. K., Aggarwal, V. S., & Rawat, D. (2017). Enhancing competitiveness of msmes in india through their integration in global supply chain: A study of challenges faced by firms in gurgaon auto–component cluster. *Asian J. Management, 8*(1), 59–67. doi:10.5958/2321-5763.2017.00009.9

Mofijur, M., Fattah, I. R., Alam, M. A., Islam, A. S., Ong, H. C., Rahman, S. A., Najafi, G., Ahmed, S. F., Uddin, M. A. & Mahlia, T. M. I. (2021). Impact of COVID-19 on the social, economic, environmental and energy domains: Lessons learnt from a global pandemic. *Sustainable Production and Consumption, 26*, 343-359.

Monga, A. B., & John, D. R. (2010). What makes brands elastic? The influence of brand concept and styles of thinking on brand extension evaluation. *Journal of Marketing, 74*(3), 80–92. doi:10.1509/jmkg.74.3.080

Monitor, C. (2022). *Which Social Media Platform is Best for Marketing a Business*. Retrieved July 20, 2022, from https://www.campaignmonitor.com/resources/knowledge-base/which-social-media-platform-is-best-for-marketing-a-business/

MSME. (2020). *Ministry of micro, small and medium enterprises notification* (Vol. 1, Issue D). MSME.

Murphy, M. C., & Dweck, C. S. (2016). Mindsets and consumer psychology: A response. *Journal of Consumer Psychology, 1*(26), 165–166. doi:10.1016/j.jcps.2015.06.006

Myovella, G., Karacuka, M., & Haucap, J. (2020). Digitalization and economic growth: A comparative analysis of Sub-Saharan Africa and OECD economies. *Telecommunications Policy, 44*(2), 101856. doi:10.1016/j.telpol.2019.101856

Nakara, W. A., Benmoussa, F. Z., & Jaouen, A. (2012). Entrepreneurship and social media marketing: Evidence from French small business. *International Journal of Entrepreneurship and Small Business, 16*(4), 386–405. doi:10.1504/IJESB.2012.047608

Nan, D., Kim, Y., Park, M. H., & Kim, J. H. (2020). What motivates users to keep using social mobile payments? *Sustainability*, *12*(17), 6878. doi:10.3390u12176878

Narayanaswamy, R., & Heiens, R. A. (2022). Finding the optimal social media marketing mix to drive customer attraction and sales performance: An exploratory study. *International Journal of Electronic Marketing and Retailing*, *13*(1), 65–82. doi:10.1504/IJEMR.2022.119248

National People's Congress Standing Committee. (2020). The Copyright Law.

Nchanji, E. B., Lutomia, C. K., Chirwa, R., Templer, N., Rubyogo, J. C., & Onyango, P. (2021). Immediate impacts of COVID-19 pandemic on bean value chain in selected countries in sub-Saharan Africa. *Agricultural Systems*, *188*, 103034. doi:10.1016/j.agsy.2020.103034 PMID:33658743

Neu, C. R., Carew, D. G., & Shatz, H. J. (2020). *Preserving Small Businesses: Small-Business Owners Speak About Surviving the COVID-19 Pandemic*. RAND. doi:10.7249/PEA317-1

Ngai, E. W., Tao, S. S., & Moon, K. K. (2015). Social media research: Theories, constructs, and conceptual frameworks. *International Journal of Information Management*, *35*(1), 33–44. doi:10.1016/j.ijinfomgt.2014.09.004

Ngammoh, N., Atthaphon, M., Sujinda, P., & Achariya, I. (2021). Enabling social media as a strategic capability for SMEs through organizational ambidexterity. *Journal of Small Business and Entrepreneurship*, 1–21. doi:10.1080/082 76331.2021.1980682

Nguyen, T. H. (2009). Information technology adoption in SMEs: an integrated framework. International *Journal of Entrepreneurial Behavior & Research*.

Nguyen, A. T. H., Nguyen, P. V., & Do, H. T. S. (2022). The effects of entrepreneurial orientation, social media, managerial ties on firm performance: Evidence from Vietnamese SMEs. *International Journal of Data and Network Science*, *6*(1), 243–252. doi:10.5267/j.ijdns.2021.9.004

Nicholas, J., Ledwith, A., & Perks, H. (2011). New product development best practice in SME and large organisations: Theory vs practice. *European Journal of Innovation Management*, *14*(2), 227–251. doi:10.1108/14601061111124902

Noguchi, T., & Hills, T. T. (2016). Experience-based decisions favor riskier alternatives in large sets. *Journal of Behavioral Decision Making*, *29*(5), 489–498. doi:10.1002/bdm.1893

Nurfarida, I. N., Sarwoko, E., & Arief, M. (2021). The Impact of Social Media Adoption on Customer Orientation and SME Performance: An Empirical Study in Indonesia. *Journal of Asian Finance, Economics and Business, 8*(6).

Nurfarida, I. N., & Sudarmiatin, S. (2021). Use of social media marketing in SMEs: Driving factors and impacts. *Management and Entrepreneurship: Trends of Development*, *2*(16), 70–81. doi:10.26661/2522-1566/2021-1/16-06

Nyangarika, A., & Ngasa, Z. J. (2020). *Profitability of ICT Usage towards Productivity of Small Business Enterprises in Tanzania*. Academic Press.

Nyanga, T., & Zirima, H. (2020). Reactions of small to medium enterprises in masvingo, Zimbabwe to covid 19: Implications on productivity. *Business Excellence and Management*, *10*(1), 22–32. doi:10.24818/beman/2020.S.I.1-02

O'Keeffe, G., & Clarke-Pearson, K. (2011). The impact of social media on children, adolescents, and families. *Pediatrics, 127*(4), 800–804. Retrieved 2 2, 2022, from http://pediatrics.aappublications.org/content/127/4/800.full

O'Regan, N., & Ghobadian, A. (2006). Perceptions of generic strategies of small and medium sized engineering and electronics manufacturers in the UK: The applicability of the Miles and Snow typology. *Journal of Manufacturing Technology Management*, *17*(5), 603–620. doi:10.1108/17410380610668540

Öberseder, M., Schlegelmilch, B. B., & Murphy, P. E. (2013). CSR practices and consumer perceptions. *Journal of Business Research, 66*(10), 1839–1851. doi:10.1016/j.jbusres.2013.02.005

Odoom, R., Anning-Dorson, T., & Acheampong, G. (2017). Antecedents of social media usage and performance benefits in small- and medium-sized enterprises (SMEs). *Journal of Enterprise Information Management, 30*(3), 383–399. doi:10.1108/JEIM-04-2016-0088

Ogbo, A. I., & Nwachukwu, A. C. (2012). The Role of Entrepreneurship in Economic Development: The Nigerian Perspective. *European Journal of Business and Management, 4*(8), 95-105. Retrieved 5 6, 2022, from https://iiste.org/journals/index.php/ejbm/article/view/1937

Okpara, J. O. (2011). Factors constraining the growth and survival of SMEs in Nigeria. *Management Research Review, 34*(2), 156-171. Retrieved 5 4, 2022, from https://emerald.com/insight/content/doi/10.1108/01409171111102786/full/html

Olaoluwa, J. (2019, October 2). *Then and now: Nigeria's telecommunication history.* Retrieved 1 23, 2022, from Nairametrics: https://nairametrics.com/2019/10/02/then-and-now-nigerias-telecommunication-history/

Olsen, V. N., & Christensen, K. (2015). Social media, new digital technologies and their potential application in sensory and consumer research. *Current Opinion in Food Science, 3*, 23–26. doi:10.1016/j.cofs.2014.11.006

Omar, A. R. C., Ishak, S., & Jusoh, M. A. (2020). The impact of Covid-19 Movement Control Order on SMEs' businesses and survival strategies. *Geografia, 16*(2).

Oni, E. O., & Daniya, A. A. (2012). Development of Small and Medium Scale Enterprises: The role of Government and other Financial Institutions. *Oman Chapter of Arabian Journal of Business and Management Review, 1*(7), 16-29. Retrieved 5 6, 2022, from http://arabianjbmr.com/pdfs/om_vol_1_(7)/2.pdf

Onyijen, O. H., Awoleye, O. M., & Olaposi, T. O. (2019). Effectiveness of Social Media Platforms for Product Marketing in Southwestern Nigeria: A Firm-Level Analysis. *International Journal of Development and Management Review.* Retrieved 5 5, 2022, from https://www.ajol.info/index.php/ijdmr/article/view/186554

Onyinyechukwu, L. (2020). *7 Ways Government Can Create An Enabling Environment for SMEs.* Retrieved 5 15, 2022, from SME360: https://www.sme360.ng/2020/11/02/7-ways-government-can-create-an-enabling-environment-for-smes/

Oracle. (2021, November 10). *Restaurant Location Analysis: How to Choose the Best Restaurant Location.* Retrieved from Oracle Gloria Food: https://www.gloriafood.com/restaurant-location-analysis

Orji, I. J., Kusi-Sarpong, S., & Gupta, H. (2020). The critical success factors of using social media for supply chain social sustainability in the freight logistics industry. *International Journal of Production Research, 58*(5), 1522–1539. doi:10.1080/00207543.2019.1660829

Osakwe, C. N., & Okeke, T. C. (2016). Facilitating mCommerce growth in Nigeria through mMoney usage: A preliminary analysis. *Interdisciplinary Journal of Information, Knowledge, and Management, 11*, 115-139. Retrieved 5 12, 2022, from http://ijikm.org/volume11/ijikmv11p115-139osakwe2222.pdf

Oyewobi, L. O., Adedayo, O. F., Olorunyomi, S. O., & Jimoh, R. (2021). Social Media Adoption and Business Performance: The Mediating Role of Organizational Learning Capacity. *Journal of Facilities Management, 19*(4), 413–436. doi:10.1108/JFM-12-2020-0099

Ozkazanc-Pan, B. (2018). CSR as Gendered Neocoloniality in the Global South. *Journal of Business Ethics*, 1–14. doi:10.100710551-018-3798-1

Oztamur, D., & Karakadilar, I. S. (2014). Exploring the Role of Social Media for SMEs: As a New Marketing Strategy Tool for the Firm Performance Perspective. *Procedia: Social and Behavioral Sciences*, *150*, 511–520. doi:10.1016/j.sbspro.2014.09.067

Oztamur, D., & Karakadilar, S. I. (2012). Exploring the role of social media for SMEs: As a new marketing strategy tool for the firm performance perspective. *Procedia: Social and Behavioral Sciences*, 1877–0428.

Painoli, A. K., Bansal, R., Singh, R., & Kukreti, A. (2021). Impact of Digital Marketing on the Buying Behavior of Youth With Special Reference to Uttarakhand State. In Big Data Analytics for Improved Accuracy, Efficiency, and Decision Making in Digital Marketing (pp. 162-182). IGI Global. doi:10.4018/978-1-7998-7231-3.ch012

Papadopoulos, T., Baltas, K. N., & Balta, M. E. (2020). The use of digital technologies by small and medium enterprises during COVID-19: Implications for theory and practice. *International Journal of Information Management*, *55*, 102192. doi:10.1016/j.ijinfomgt.2020.102192 PMID:32836646

Park, J., & Oh, I.-K. (2012). A Case Study of Social Media Marketing by Travel Agency: The Salience of Social Media Marketing in the Tourism Industry. *International Journal of Tourism Sciences*, *12*(1), 93–106. doi:10.1080/15980634.2012.11434654

Partida, D. (2020, November 15). *7 covid-19 struggles small businesses are facing and how to overcome them.* Due. Retrieved from https://due.com/blog/small-businesses-struggle-in-pandemic/

Patel, N. (n.d.). *Social Media Marketing: How to do it, Types, Tools & Tips.* Retrieved from Neil Patel What is Social Media Marketing?: https://neilpatel.com/what-is-social-media-marketing/

Paudel, U. R., & Devkota, N. (2018). Socio-Economic influences on small business performance in Nepal-India open border: Evidence from cross-sectional analysis. *Economia e Sociologia*, *11*(4), 11–30. doi:10.14254/2071-789X.2018/11-4/1

Paudel, U. R., Devkota, N., & Bhandari, U. (2018). Socio-cultural and economic factors in cross-border purchase: A study of customers' perspective in Sunauli-Nepal/India Border. *Modern Economy*, *9*(6), 1089–1102. doi:10.4236/me.2018.96070

Paul, J., & Feliciano-Cestero, M. M. (2021). Five decades of research on foreign direct investment by MNEs: An overview and research agenda. *Journal of Business Research*, *124*, 800–812. doi:10.1016/j.jbusres.2020.04.017 PMID:32292218

Paul, J., Lim, W. M., O'Cass, A., Hao, A. W., & Bresciani, S. (2021). Scientific procedures and rationales for systematic literature reviews (SPAR-4-SLR). *International Journal of Consumer Studies*, *45*(4), O1–O16. doi:10.1111/ijcs.12695

Paul, J., & Mas, E. (2020). Toward a 7-P framework for international marketing. *Journal of Strategic Marketing*, *28*(8), 681–701. doi:10.1080/0965254X.2019.1569111

Pavlendová, G. (2021). *Work from Home during COVID 19 and Gender Differences in Twitter Content Analysis.* Academic Press.

Pedauga, L., Sáez, F., & Delgado-Márquez, B. L. (2022). Macroeconomic lockdown and SMEs: The impact of the COVID-19 pandemic in Spain. *Small Business Economics*, *58*(2), 665–688. doi:10.100711187-021-00476-7

Peek, S. (2022). *Why Small Businesses Need a Social Media Presence? Considering pausing your social presence? Here's why it still counts for small businesses.* Business.com. Retrieved from https://www.business.com/articles/social-media-small-business-importance/

Pelletier, M. (n.d.). *Five key factors to assess when making an investment decision.* Financial Post. Retrieved from https://financialpost.com/investing/investing-pro/five-key-f actors-to-assess-when-making-an-investment-decision

Pentina, I., Koh, A. C., & Le, T. T. (2012). Adoption of social networks marketing by SMEs: Exploring the role of social influences and experience in technology acceptance. *International Journal of Internet Marketing and Advertising, 7*(1), 65–82. doi:10.1504/IJIMA.2012.044959

Pereira, T., Loureiro, S. M. C., & Sarmento, E. M. (2022). Achieving Brand Engagement and Brand Equity Through Co-creation Process. *Journal of Creative Communications*, (3), 303–318. Advance online publication. doi:10.1177/09732586221083862

Pérez-González, D., Trigueros-Preciado, S., & Popa, S. (2017). Social media technologies' use for the competitive information and knowledge sharing, and its effects on industrial SMEs' innovation. *Information Systems Management, 34*(3), 291–301. doi:10.1080/10580530.2017.1330007

Pervin, M. T., & Sarker, B. K. (2021). Benefits and challenges in adopting social media for SMEs: A case from Bangladesh. *Journal of Sustainable Tourism and Entrepreneurship, 2*(3), 171–185. doi:10.35912/joste.v2i3.783

Petersen, L. (2019). *The Negative Effect of Social Media on Society and Individuals.* Retrieved 2 4, 2022, from Hearst Communications, Inc.: https://smallbusiness.chron.com/negative-effect-social-media -society-individuals-27617.html

Pfister, P., & Lehmann, C. (2021). Returns on digitisation in SMEs—A systematic literature review. *Journal of Small Business and Entrepreneurship*, 1–25. doi:10.1080/08276331.2021.1980680

Pham, T.-T. T., & Ho, J. C. (2015). The effects of product-related, personal-related factors and attractiveness of alternatives on consumer adoption of NFC-based mobile payments. *Technology in Society, 43*, 159–172. doi:10.1016/j.techsoc.2015.05.004

Pilli, L. E., & Mazzon, J. A. (2016). Information overload, choice deferral, and moderating role of need for cognition: Empirical evidence. *Revista de Administração (São Paulo), 51*(1), 36–55. doi:10.5700/rausp1222

Polman, E. (2012). Effects of self–other decision making on regulatory focus and choice overload. *Journal of Personality and Social Psychology, 102*(5), 980–993. doi:10.1037/a0026966 PMID:22429272

Popli, Rishi, & Mathew. (2021). *Contemporary Marketing Regaining Ground: Perspectives from Research & Practice.* IMTG Report.

Popli, S., & Rishi, B. (2021). Customer Experience Management – The Road Ahead. In Crafting Customer Experience Strategy. Emerald Publishing Limited. doi:10.1108/978-1-83909-710-220211011

Pramudita, O., Amalia, H. A. M. C., & Savitri, G. A. (2022). SMEs' Adoption of Social Media Consulting During COVID-19 Pandemic. *1st International Conference on Information System & Information Technology (ICISIT)*, 261-266.

Priyono, A., Moin, A., & Putri, V. N. A. O. (2020). Identifying digital transformation paths in the business model of SMEs during the COVID-19 pandemic. *Journal of Open Innovation, 6*(4), 104. doi:10.3390/joitmc6040104

Qalati, S. A., Li, W., Ahmed, N., Mirani, M. A., & Khan, A. (2020). Examining the Factors Affecting SME Performance: The Mediating Role of Social Media Adoption. *Sustainability, 13*(1).

Qalati, S. A., Ostic, D., Shuibin, G., & Mingyue, F. (2022). A mediated–moderated model for social media adoption and small and medium-sized enterprise performance in emerging countries. *Managerial and Decision Economics, 43*(3), 846–861. doi:10.1002/mde.3422

Qalati, S. A., Ostic, D., Sulaiman, M. A. B. A., Gopang, A. A., & Khan, A. (2022). Social media and SMEs' performance in developing countries: Effects of technological-organizational-environmental factors on the adoption of social media. *SAGE Open*, *12*(2). Advance online publication. doi:10.1177/21582440221094594

Qalati, S. A., Yuan, L. W., Khan, M. A. S., & Anwar, F. (2021). A mediated model on the adoption of social media and SMEs' performance in developing countries. *Technology in Society*, *64*, 101513. doi:10.1016/j.techsoc.2020.101513

Qalati, S., Li, W., Ahmed, N., Ali Mirani, M., & Khan, A. (2020). Examining the factors affecting SME performance: The mediating role of social media adoption. *Sustainability*, *13*(1), 75. doi:10.3390u13010075

Rahman, K. T. (2021a). Applications of Blockchain Technology for Digital Marketing: A Systematic Review. *Blockchain Technology and Applications for Digital Marketing*, 16-31.

Rahman, K. T. (2021b). Driving Engagement on Instagram: A Comparative Analysis of Amazon Prime and Disney+. *SEISENSE Business Review*, *1*(3), 1–11. doi:10.33215br.v1i3.676

Rahmawati, T. Y., Dewi, M. K., & Ferdian, I. R. (2020). Instagram: Its roles in management of Islamic banks. *Journal of Islamic Marketing*, *11*(4), 841–861. doi:10.1108/JIMA-11-2018-0213

Rajagopaul, A., Magwentshu, N., & Kalidas, S. (2020). *How South African SMEs can survive and thrive post COVID-19*. Providing the Right Support to Enable SME Growth Now and Beyond the Crisis.

Rakshit, S., Islam, N., Mondal, S., & Paul, T. (2021). Mobile apps for SME Business Sustainability during covid-19 and onwards. *Journal of Business Research*, *135*, 28–39. doi:10.1016/j.jbusres.2021.06.005 PMID:34751197

Ramya, V. (2019). Corporate Social Responsibility Towards Women Empowerment. *Quarterly Journal*, *22*(4), 10732–10739.

Raspor, P. (2008, August). Total food chain safety: How good practices can contribute? *Elsevier. Trends in Food Science & Technology*, *19*(8), 405–412. doi:10.1016/j.tifs.2007.08.009

Ratheeswari, K. (2018). Information Communication Technology in Education. *Journal of Applied and Advanced Research*, *3*(S1), 45. doi:10.21839/jaar.2018.v3iS1.169

Ratnasingam, J., Khoo, A., Jegathesan, N., Wei, L. C., Abd Latib, H., Thanasegaran, G., ... Amir, M. A. (2020). How are small and medium enterprises in Malaysia's furniture industry coping with COVID-19 pandemic? Early evidences from a survey and recommendations for policymakers. *BioResources*, *15*(3), 5951–5964. doi:10.15376/biores.15.3.5951-5964

Rauniar, R., Rawski, G., Yang, J., & Johnson, B. (2014). Technology acceptance model (TAM) and social media usage: An empirical study on Facebook. *Journal of Enterprise Information Management*, *27*(1), 6–30. doi:10.1108/JEIM-04-2012-0011

Read, W., Robertson, N., McQuilken, L., & Ferdous, A. S. (2019). Consumer engagement on Twitter: Perceptions of the brand matter. *European Journal of Marketing*, *53*(9), 1905–1933. doi:10.1108/EJM-10-2017-0772

Reece, M. (2010). *Real-Time Marketing for Business Growth*. FT Press.

Religia, Y., Surachman, S., Rohman, F., & Indrawati, N. (2021). E-commerce adoption in SMEs: A literature review. *Proceedings of the 1st International Conference on Economics Engineering and Social Science, InCEESS 2020*. 10.4108/eai.17-7-2020.2302969

Reyneke, M., Pitt, L., & Berthon, P. R. (2011). Luxury wine brand visibility in social media: An exploratory study. *International Journal of Wine Business Research*, *23*(1), 21–35. doi:10.1108/17511061111121380

Richter, A., & Riemer, K. (2013). *The contextual nature of enterprise social networking: A multi-case study comparison*. ECIS.

Rietveld, R., Van Dolen, W., Mazloom, M., & Worring, M. (2020). What you feel, is what you like. Influence of message appeals on customer engagement on Instagram. *Journal of Interactive Marketing, 49*(1), 20–53. doi:10.1016/j.intmar.2019.06.003

Rishi, B., & Kuthuru, N. R. (2021a). A Review for Managerial Guidelines for Social Media Integration of IMC in Digital Era. In Digital Entertainment (pp. 187-212). Palgrave Macmillan. doi:10.1007/978-981-15-9724-4_10

Rishi, B., & Mohammed, J. (n.d.). Design, Execute, and Manage Promotions: Study on Social Media Platforms. In Promotional Practices and Perspectives from Emerging Markets (pp. 226-245). Routledge India.

Rishi, B., & Popli, S. (2021). Getting Into the Customers, Shoes: Customer Journey Management. In Crafting Customer Experience Strategy. Emerald Publishing Limited. doi:10.1108/978-1-83909-710-220211002

Rishi, B., & Bandyopadhyay, S. (Eds.). (2017). *Contemporary issues in social media marketing*. Routledge. doi:10.4324/9781315563312

Rishi, B., & Kuthuru, N. R. (2021b). Leveraging Social Media to Create Socially Responsible Consumers. In *Social and Sustainability Marketing* (pp. 415–432). Productivity Press. doi:10.4324/9781003188186-15

Rosado-Serrano, A., Paul, J., & Dikova, D. (2018). International franchising: A literature review and research agenda. *Journal of Business Research, 85*, 238–257. doi:10.1016/j.jbusres.2017.12.049

Roshan, M., Warren, M., & Carr, R. (2016). Understanding the use of social media by organisations for crisis communication. *Computers in Human Behavior, 63*, 350–361. doi:10.1016/j.chb.2016.05.016

Rothengatter, W., Zhang, J., Hayashi, Y., Nosach, A., Wang, K., & Oum, T. H. (2021). Pandemic waves and the time after Covid-19–Consequences for the transport sector. *Transport Policy, 110*, 225–237. doi:10.1016/j.tranpol.2021.06.003 PMID:34608362

Roy, A., & Dionne, C. (2015). How SMEs evaluate their performance in reaching and attracting customers with social media. In *ECSM2015-Proceedings of the 2nd European Conference on Social Media* (390-397). Academic Press.

Rucker, D. D., & Galinsky, A. D. (2016). Growing beyond growth: Why multiple mindsets matter for consumer behavior. *Journal of Consumer Psychology, 26*(1), 161–164. doi:10.1016/j.jcps.2015.06.009

Rugova, B., & Prenaj, B. (2016). Social media as marketing tool for SMEs: opportunities and challenges. *Academic Journal of Business, 2*(3). www.iipccl.org

Rugova, B., & Prenaj, B. (2016). Social media as marketing tool for SMEs: Opportunities and challenges. *Academic Journal of Business, 2*(3), 85–97.

Rupeika-Apoga, R., Petrovska, K., & Bule, L. (2022). *SMEs' digital transformation facilitated by COVID-19*. doi:10.20944/preprints202201.0340.v1

Rydell, L. & Kucera, J. (2021). Cognitive attitudes, behavioral choices, and purchasing habits during the COVID-19 pandemic. *Journal of Self-Governance & Management Economics, 9*.

Saarikko, T., Westergren, U. H., & Blomquist, T. (2020). Digital transformation: Five recommendations for the digitally conscious firm. *Business Horizons, 63*(6), 825–839. doi:10.1016/j.bushor.2020.07.005

Saidu, M., & Aifuwa, H. O. (2020). Coronavirus pandemic in Nigeria: How can Small and Medium Enterprises (SMEs) cope and flatten the curve. *European Journal of Accounting, Finance and Investment, 6*(5), 55–61.

Sajjad, A., Eweje, G., & Tappin, D. (2020). Managerial perspectives on drivers for and barriers to sustainable sup-ply chain management implementation: Evidence from New Zealand. *Business Strategy and the Environment*, *29*(2), 592–604. doi:10.1002/bse.2389

Saleh, S. (2012). Business, barriers and benefits: E-business for SMEs in the sultanate of Oman. *International Journal of Business and Management Studies*, *1*(2), 405–422. www.internetworldstats.com

Salesforce Research. (2020). *State of thee connect-ed customer*. https://www.salesforce.com/content/dam/web/pt_br/www/documen ts/e-books/stateoftheconnectedcustomer/Salesforce State of t he Connected Customer 4th Ed_BR.pdf

Saltsman, T. L., Seery, M. D., Ward, D. E., Lamarche, V. M., & Kondrak, C. L. (2021). Is satisficing really satisfying? Satisficers exhibit greater threat than maximizers during choice overload. *Psychophysiology*, *58*(1), e13705. doi:10.1111/psyp.13705 PMID:33107043

Samuel, A.-G. & Edward, B. 2015. The marijuana factor in a university in Ghana: A survey. *Журнал Сибирского федерального университета. Гуманитарные науки, 8*, 2162-2182.

Samuel, B. S., & Sarprasatha, J. (2016). Entrepreneurship in social-media services in Oman - A socio-economic scan-ning of the Sultanate. *Asian Social Science*, *12*(4), 138–148. doi:10.5539/ass.v12n4p138

Sannegadu, R. (2021). Managing Local and International Challenges Faced by SMEs of Island States Economies in The Midst of the Covid-19 Pandemic- Evidence from MauritiusRajesh Sannegadu. *Academy of Marketing Studies Journal*, *25*(1).

Saravanakumar, T. S. (2012). Social Media Marketing. *Life Science Journal*, *9*(4), 4444–4451.

Saura, J. R. (2021). *Advanced Digital Marketing Strategies in a Data Driven Era*. IGI Global. doi:10.4018/978-1-7998-8003-5

Savlovschi, L. I., & Robu, N. R. (2011). The role of SMEs in modern economy. *Economia*. *Seria Management*, *14*(1), 277–281.

Scheibehenne, B., Greifeneder, R., & Todd, P. M. (2010). Can there ever be too many options? A meta-analytic review of choice overload. *The Journal of Consumer Research*, *37*(3), 409–425. doi:10.1086/651235

Schivinski, B., Langaro, D., Fernandes, T., & Guzmán, F. (2020). Social media brand engagement in the context of collaborative consumption: The case of AIRBNB. *Journal of Brand Management*, *27*(6), 645–661. doi:10.105741262-020-00207-5

Schmeltz, L. (2012). Consumer-oriented CSR communication: Focusing on ability or morality? *Corporate Communica-tions*, *17*(1), 29–49. doi:10.1108/13563281211196344

Schwartz, B. (2004). *The paradox of choice: why more is less*. Harper Perennial.

Scott, D. M. (2011). *Real-Time Marketing and PR: How to Instantly Engage Your Market, Connect with Customers, and Create Products That Grow Your Business Now*. John Wiley & Sons.

Scott, D. M., & Scott, R. (2020). *Fanocray: Turning Fans into Customers and Customers into Fans*. Portfolio.

Sedalo, G., Boateng, H., & Kosiba, J. P. (2022). Exploring social media affordance in relationship marketing practices in SMEs. *Digital Business, 2*(1).

Sedalo, G., Boateng, H., & Kosiba, J. P. (2022). Exploring social media affordance in relationship marketing practices in SMEs. *Digital Business*, *2*(1), 100017. doi:10.1016/j.digbus.2021.100017

Settle, R. B., & Golden, L. L. (1974). Attribution theory and advertiser credibility. *JMR, Journal of Marketing Research*, *11*(2), 181–185. doi:10.1177/002224377401100209

Sewanyana, J., & Busler, M. (2007). Adoption and usage of ICT in developing countries: Case of Ugandan firms. *International Journal of Education and Development using ICT*, *3*(3), 49-59.

Shafi, M., Liu, J., & Ren, W. (2020). Impact of COVID-19 pandemic on micro, small, and medium-sized Enterprises operating in Pakistan. *Research in Globalization*, *2*, 100018. doi:10.1016/j.resglo.2020.100018

Sharifi, S. S., & Palmeira, M. (2017). Customers' reactions to technological products: The impact of implicit theories of intelligence. *Computers in Human Behavior*, *77*, 309–316. doi:10.1016/j.chb.2017.09.013

Sharma, B. (2016). A focus on reliability in developmental research through Cronbach's Alpha among medical, dental and paramedical professionals. *Asian Pacific Journal of Health Sciences*, *3*(4), 271–278. doi:10.21276/apjhs.2016.3.4.43

Sharma, S. (2019). Article. *Descriptive Statistics.*, *18*(5). Advance online publication. doi:10.32964/tj18.5

Sharma, S., & Rehman, A. (2016). Social media marketing: A study of select sectors in India. *International Journal of Management*, *5*(4), 2277–5846.

Sha, W., & Basri, M. (2018). Social Media and Corporate Communication Antecedents of SME Sustainability Performance A Conceptual Framework for SMEs of Arab World. *Journal of Economic and Administrative Sciences*, *35*(3).

Shen, H., & Wen, X. (2016). The reform of the Chinese intellectual property trial system. *Global Journal of Comparative Law*, *5*(1), 68–90. doi:10.1163/2211906X-00501004

Sherman, B., & Bently, L. (1999). *The making of modern intellectual property law: the British experience, 1760–1911*. Cambridge University Press.

Sheshadri, C., & Arpan, K. K. (2020). Why do small and medium enterprises use social media marketing and what is the impact: Empirical insights from India. *International Journal of Information Management*, *53*, 1–42.

Shiels, H., McIvor, R., & O'Reilly, D. (2003). Understanding the implications of ICT adoption: Insights from SMEs. *Logistics Information Management*, *16*(5), 312–326. doi:10.1108/09576050310499318

Shittu, A. T., Basha, K. M., Abdulrahman, N. S. N., & Ahmad, T. B. T. (2011). Investigating students' attitude and intention to use social software in higher institution of learning in Malaysia. *Multicultural Education & Technology Journal*.

Shi, Z. M. (2021). From Literary Creation to Copyright Sale: A Study of the Platform Ecology of Jinjiang Literature City in the New Media Perspective. *New Media Research*, *7*(05), 49–52. doi:10.16604/j.cnki.issn2096-0360.2021.05.015

Shu, J. Y. (2019). 20 Years of Jinjiang Literature. *China Reading News*, 17.

Si, H., Shi, J.-G., Tang, D., Wu, G., & Lan, J. (2020). Understanding intention and behavior toward sustainable usage of bike sharing by extending the theory of planned behavior. *Resources, Conservation and Recycling*, *152*, 104513. doi:10.1016/j.resconrec.2019.104513

Simmi Dhyani, M. S. (2022). *Effect of communicating corporate social responsibility through social media on brand image, Digital Marketing Outreach*. Routledge India.

Sindakis, S., & Aggarwal, S. (2022). *E-business Adoption by Small Businesses: Benefits and Drawbacks. In Small Business Management and Control of the Uncertain External Environment*. Emerald Publishing Limited.

Singh, A., Jain, A., & Singla, B. (2019). Technological advancement-based paradigm shift: A focus shift from large screen to small screen. *International Journal of Innovative Technology and Exploring Engineering, 8*(10), 48–53. doi:10.35940/ijitee.I8613.0881019

Singh, A., & Kaur, A. (2021). Examining gender differences in the factors affecting ethical leadership: A study of educational institutions. *International Journal of Sociotechnology and Knowledge Development, 13*(4), 153–164. doi:10.4018/IJSKD.2021100110

Singh, A., Singh, A., Singh Vij, T., & Pardesi, A. (2020). An Empirical Study of the Factors Affecting Online Shopping Behavior of the Indian Consumers. *International Journal of Advanced Science and Technology, 29*(8s), 406–411.

Singh, A., Singla, B., & Sharma, S. (2020). An Empirical Study of Factors Affecting the Selection of Point of Purchase Location: A Case of FMCG Industry. *International Journal of Control and Automation, 13*(2s), 72–78.

Singh, S., Chamola, P., Kumar, V., Verma, P., & Makkar, N. (2022). Explaining the revival strategies of Indian msmes to mitigate the effects of covid-19 outbreak. *Benchmarking*. Advance online publication. doi:10.1108/BIJ-08-2021-0497

Sin, S. S., Nor, K. M., & Al-Agaga, A. M. (2012). Factors Affecting Malaysian young consumers' online purchase intention in social media websites. *Procedia: Social and Behavioral Sciences, 40*, 326–333. doi:10.1016/j.sbspro.2012.03.195

Si, S. (2016). Social Media and Its Role in Marketing. *Business and Economics Journal, 7*(1), 1–5. doi:10.4172/2151-6219.1000203

SMEDAN. (2021). *MSME Survey Report*. https://smedan.gov.ng/wp-content/uploads/2022/03/2021-MSME-Survey-Report_1.pdf

Song, Y. A., Lee, S. Y., & Kim, Y. (2019). Does mindset matter for using social networking sites?: Understanding motivations for and uses of Instagram with growth versus fixed mindset. *International Journal of Advertising, 38*(6), 886–904. doi:10.1080/02650487.2019.1637614

StarNgage. (2015-2022). *StarNgage*. Retrieved from StarNgage: https://starngage.com/app/ru/page/influencer-marketing-canada

Statista. (2022, January). *Statista*. Retrieved from Statista: https://www.statista.com/statistics/272014/global-social-networks-ranked-by-number-of-users/

Sterbenk, Y., Champlin, S., Windels, K., & Shelton, S. (2021). Is Femvertising the New Greenwashing? Examining Corporate Commitment to Gender Equality. *Journal of Business Ethics, 2015*. Advance online publication. doi:10.100710551-021-04755-x

Suryani, T., Fauzi, A. A., & Nurhadi, M. (2021). SOME-Q: A model development and testing for assessing the Consumers' perception of social media quality of small medium-sized enterprises (SMEs). *Journal of Relationship Marketing, 20*(1), 62–90. doi:10.1080/15332667.2020.1717277

Sutto, G. (2021). *As 25 marcas mais valiosas do Brasil em 2021, segundo a Interbrand*. InfoMoney. https://www.infomoney.com.br/negocios/as-25-marcas-mais-valiosas-do-brasil-em-2021-segundo-a-interbrand/

Swamy, S. (2022). Impact of COVID 19 on small and medium Enterprises. *Asian Journal of Management, 13*(2), 2.

Tajvidi, R., & Karami, A. (2021). The effect of social media on firm performance. *Computers in Human Behavior, 115*, 105174. doi:10.1016/j.chb.2017.09.026

Tanhan, A., & Young, J. S. (2022). Muslims and mental health services: A concept map and a theoretical framework. *Journal of Religion and Health, 61*(1), 23–63. doi:10.100710943-021-01324-4 PMID:34241742

Tasci, A. D. A. (2021). A critical review and reconstruction of perceptual brand equity. *International Journal of Contemporary Hospitality Management, 33*(1), 166–198. doi:10.1108/IJCHM-03-2020-0186

Thai, N. T., & Yuksel, U. (2017). Choice overload in holiday destination choices. *International Journal of Culture, Tourism and Hospitality Research, 11*(1), 53–66. doi:10.1108/IJCTHR-09-2015-0117

The Ministry of Human Resources and Social Security & the Ministry of Culture and Tourism. (2020). *Guiding Opinions of the Ministry of Human Resources and Social Security, the Ministry of Culture and Tourism on Deepening the Reform of the Title System for Artistic Professionals.* http://www.mohrss.gov.cn/SYrlzyhshbzb/rencairenshi/zcwj/zhua nyejishurenyuan/202009/t20200928_391837.html

The State Administration of Radio Film and Television of China. (2014). *Circular of the State Administration of Press, Publication, Radio, Film and Television on Printing and Distributing the Guiding Opinions on Promoting the Healthy Development of Internet Literature.* https://www.nppa.gov.cn/nppa/contents/772/76567.shtml

Thukral, E. (2021). covid -19: Small and medium enterprises challenges and responses with creativity, Innovation, and entrepreneurship. *Strategic Change, 30*(2), 153–158. doi:10.1002/jsc.2399

Timilsina, M. (2017). *Impacts of social media in restaurant businesses-A case study of restaurants based on Oulu region.* Oulu University of Applied Sciences. Retrieved from https://core.ac.uk/download/pdf/84797241.pdf

Tiwasing, P. (2021). Social media business networks and SME performance: A rural-urban comparative analysis. *Growth and Change, 52*(3), 1892–1913. doi:10.1111/grow.12501

Toffler, A. C. (1971). Learning to Live with Future Shock. *College and University Business, 51*(3), 55–57.

Tornatzky, L. G., Fleischer, M., & Chakrabarti, A. K. (1990). *Processes of technological innovation.* Lexington Books.

Toth, R., Kasa, R., & Lentner, C. (2022). The impact of financial culture on the operation of Hungarian smes before and during COVID-19. *Risks, 10*(7), 135. doi:10.3390/risks10070135

Tourism, M. (2021). National Strategy and Roadmap for Sustainable Tourism Ministry of Tourism Government of India. Government of India.

Trawnih, A., Yaseen, H., Al-Adwan, A. S., Alsoud, R., & Jaber, O. A. (2021). Factors influencing social media adoption among smes during Covid-19 crisis. *Journal of Management Information and Decision Sciences, 24*, 1–18.

Triantafillidou, A., & Yannas, P. (2020). Social media crisis communication in racially charged crises: Exploring the effects of social media and image restoration strategies. *Computers in Human Behavior, 106*, 106269. doi:10.1016/j.chb.2020.106269

Tsimonis, G., & Dimitriadis, S. (2014). Brand strategies in social media. *Marketing Intelligence & Planning, 32*(3), 328–344. doi:10.1108/MIP-04-2013-0056

Ullah, F., Sepasgozar, S. M., Thaheem, M. J., & Al-Turjman, F. (2021). Barriers to the digitalisation and innovation of Australian Smart Real Estate: A managerial perspective on the technology non-adoption. *Environmental Technology & Innovation, 22*, 101527. doi:10.1016/j.eti.2021.101527

United Nation. (2022). *Goal 5: Achieve gender equality and empower all women and girls.* Sustainable Development Goals. https://www.un.org/sustainabledevelopment/gender-equality/

Vieira, V. A., Severo de Almeida, M. I., Gabler, C. B., Limongi, R., Costa, M., & Pires da Costa, M. (2022). Optimising digital marketing and social media strategy: From push to pull to performance. *Journal of Marketing Management*, *38*(7-8), 709–739. doi:10.1080/0267257X.2021.1996444

von Hoffen, M., Hagge, M., Betzing, J. H., & Chasin, F. (2018). Leveraging social media to gain insights into service delivery: A study on Airbnb. *Information Systems and e-Business Management*, *16*(2), 247–269. doi:10.100710257-017-0358-7

Vuvor, J. A. (2011). *The Challenges faced by Small & Medium Enterprises (SMEs) in Obtaining Credit in Ghana*. Blekinge Tekniska Högskola School of Management. Retrieved from https://www.diva-portal.org/smash/get/diva2:829684/FULLTEXT01.pdf;The

Wang, S. S., Goh, J. R., Sornette, D., Wang, H., & Yang, E. Y. (2021). *Government support for SMEs in response to COVID-19: Theoretical model using Wang transform*. China Finance Review International.

Wang, W. Y., Pauleen, D. J., & Zhang, T. (2016). How social media applications affect B2B communication and improve business performance in SMEs. *Industrial Marketing Management*, *54*, 4–14. doi:10.1016/j.indmarman.2015.12.004

Wang, Y. (2016). What are the biggest obstacles to growth of SMEs in developing countries?–An empirical evidence from an enterprise survey. *Borsa Istanbul Review*, *16*(3), 167–176. doi:10.1016/j.bir.2016.06.001

Wang, Y., & Yang, Y. (2020). Dialogic communication on social media: How organizations use Twitter to build dialogic relationships with their publics. *Computers in Human Behavior*, *104*, 106183. doi:10.1016/j.chb.2019.106183

Wanyoike, J., & Kithae, P. P. (2019). Social media networks and SME performance in the international arena: A case of SMEs operating in Kamukunji area of Nairobi County, Kenya. *European Journal of Business & Management Research*, *4*(5). Advance online publication. doi:10.24018/ejbmr.2019.4.5.122

Wei, J. (2021). An interpretation of the innovative thinking of Daylight Entertainment's TV series. *News Enthusiasts*, *2021*(01), 49–51. doi:10.16017/j.cnki.xwahz.2021.01.013

Wheeler, S. C., & Omair, A. (2015). Potential growth areas for implicit theories research. *Journal of Consumer Psychology*, *26*(1), 137–141. doi:10.1016/j.jcps.2015.06.008

Wibawa, B. M., Baihaqi, I., Nareswari, N., Mardhotillah, R. R., & Pramesti, F. (2022). Utilization of social media and its impact on marketing performance: A case study of SMEs in Indonesia. *International Journal of Business and Society*, *23*(1), 19–34. doi:10.33736/ijbs.4596.2022

Willemsen, L. M., Mazerant, K., Kamphuis, A. L., & van der Veen, G. (2018). Let's Get Real (Time)! The potential of real-time marketing to catalyze the sharing of brand messages. *International Journal of Advertising*, *37*(5), 828–848. doi:10.1080/02650487.2018.1485214

Williams, J., & Chinn, S. J. (2010). Meeting relationship-marketing goals through social media: A conceptual model for sport marketers. *International Journal of Sport Communication*, *3*(4), 422–437. doi:10.1123/ijsc.3.4.422

Wood, J., & Khan, G. F. (2016). Social business adoption: An empirical analysis. *Business Information Review*, *33*(1), 28–39. doi:10.1177/0266382116631851

World Bank. (2020). *Small and Medium Enterprises (SMEs) Finance*. https://www. worldbank.org/en/topic/smefinance

World Bank. (2022). *Small and Medium Enterprises (SMEs) Finance*. Retrieved July 20, 2022, from https://www. worldbank.org/en/topic/smefinance

World, I. (n.d.). *Fast Food Restaurants in Canada - Employment Statistics 2005–2028.* Industry Statistics Canada. Retrieved from https://www.ibisworld.com/canada/industry-statistics/employment/fast-food-restaurants/

WTTC. (2019). *WTTC_India2019.* WTTC.

Wu, S. (2022). Television adaptation in the age of media convergence: Chinese intellectual property shows and the case of all is well. *Adaptation, 15*(2), 187–206. doi:10.1093/adaptation/apab002

Xiao, J., Chen, D., Tang, Q., Suo, L., Zhou, X., Wang, W., Zheng, W., & Zhou, M. (2022). 2020 Report on the development of Chinese Internet literature. *New Techno Humanities, 2*(1), 1–12. doi:10.1016/j.techum.2022.100004

Xu, Q. (2013). Social recommendation, source credibility, and recency: Effects of news cues in a social bookmarking website. *Journalism and Mass Communication, 90*(4), 757–775. doi:10.1177/1077699013503158

Yadav, M. S. (2014). Enhancing theory development in marketing. *AMS Review, 4*(1-2), 1–4. doi:10.100713162-014-0059-z

Yasmin, A., Tasneem, S., & Fatema, K. (2015). Effectiveness of Digital Marketing in the Challenging Age: An Empirical Study. *The International Journal of Management Science and Business Administration, 1*(5), 69–80. doi:10.18775/ijmsba.1849-5664-5419.2014.15.1006

Yazdanfar, D., & Öhman, P. (2018). Growth and job creation at the firm level: Swedish SME data. *Management Research Review, 41*(3), 345–358. doi:10.1108/MRR-03-2017-0093

Yoo, B., & Donthu, N. (2001). Developing and validating a multidimensional consumer-based brand equity scale. *Journal of Business Research, 52*(1), 1–14. doi:10.1016/S0148-2963(99)00098-3

Yu, P. K. (2018). When the Chinese intellectual property system hits 35. *Queen Mary Journal of Intellectual Property, 8*(1), 3–14. doi:10.4337/qmjip.2018.01.01

Yu, P., Liao, Y., & Mahendran, R. (2022). Research on Social Media Advertising in China: Advertising Perspective of Social Media Influencers. In I. Krom (Ed.), *Handbook of Research on Global Perspectives on International Advertising* (pp. 88–122). IGI Global. doi:10.4018/978-1-7998-9672-2.ch006

Yu, P., Tang, H., Tang, H., & Hanes, E. (2022). Using "Digitalization + Intellectual Property" Management to Realize Cultural Economy: Case Study of Chinese Museums. In R. Pettinger, B. Gupta, A. Roja, & D. Cozmiuc (Eds.), *Handbook of Research on Digital Transformation Management and Tools* (pp. 236–264). IGI Global. doi:10.4018/978-1-7998-9764-4.ch011

Zajas, J., & Zotz, L. Jr. (1995). Integrating Customer Satisfaction into the Strategic Marketing Plan. *Journal of Customer Service in Marketing & Management, 1*(3), 51–66. doi:10.1300/J127v01n03_05

Zarezadeh, Z. Z., Rastegar, H. R., & Gretzel, U. (2018). Reviewing the Past to Inform the Future: A Literature Review of Social Media in Tourism. *Czech Journal of Tourism, 7*(2), 115–131. doi:10.1515/cjot-2018-0006

Zeng, X., Xu, X., & Wu, Y. J. (2022). Learning social media content optimization: How can SMEs draw the users' attention on official WeChat accounts? *Frontiers in Psychology, 12*, 783151. Advance online publication. doi:10.3389/fpsyg.2021.783151 PMID:35095669

Zeng, Y. G., & Du, Z. W. (2021). Rethinking IP Adaptation of Online Literature in the Era of Digital Media. *Chinese Editorials, 6*, 75–78.

Zhang, H. (2020, June 18). "SwordNet 2020" to combat online piracy. *People's Daily Online.* http://politics.people.com.cn/n1/2020/0618/c1001-31750923.html

Zhang, H., Zang, Z., Zhu, H., Uddin, M. I., & Amin, M. A. (2022). Big data-assisted social media analytics for business model for business decision making system competitive analysis. *Information Processing & Management, 59*(1), 102762. doi:10.1016/j.ipm.2021.102762

Zhang, L. Y. (2021). Analysis and lessons learned from the experience model of Daylight Entertainment's film & TV drama production. *Western Radio and Television, 42*(14), 99–101.

Zhang, L., & Bruun, N. (2017). Legal transplantation of intellectual property rights in china: Resistance, adaptation and reconciliation. *IIC International Review of Intellectual Property and Competition Law, 48*(1), 4–41. doi:10.100740319-016-0542-1

Zhang, T., Lu, C., & Kizildag, M. (2018). Banking "on-the-go": Examining consumers' adoption of mobile banking services. *International Journal of Quality and Service Sciences, 1*(1), 1–20. doi:10.1108/IJQSS-07-2017-0067

Zhong, Y., Oh, S., & Moon, H. C. (2021). Service transformation under industry 4.0: Investigating acceptance of facial recognition payment through an extended technology acceptance model. *Technology in Society, 64*, 101515. doi:10.1016/j.techsoc.2020.101515

Zou, H., Xie, X., Meng, X., & Yang, M. (2018). The diffusion of corporate social responsibility through social network ties: From the perspective of strategic imitation. *Corporate Social Responsibility and Environmental Management, 26*(1), 186–198. doi:10.1002/csr.1670

Zuhdi, S., Daud, A., Hanif, R., Nguyen, P. T., & Shankar, K. (2019). Role of social media marketing in the successful implementation of business management. *International Journal of Recent Technology and Engineering, 8*(2), 3841–3844.

About the Contributors

Sikandar Ali Aqlati is a motivated Assistant Professor with excellent educational credentials and hands-on experience in activities/event management, education, and research field. Skilled at performing quality control and managing several projects, while meeting deadlines under pressure. Creates, develops, and fine-tunes various experimental study designs. Demonstrates excellent problem-solving skills with a keen eye for details; collaborate with faculty and students across different departments to conduct interdisciplinary research. Superb facilitator thrives in making maximum use of managerial, interpersonal, communication, presentation, and persuasive abilities, to conduct training programs and organize high-end professional courses.

Dragana Ostic is an assistant professor at Jiangsu University, China. Her area of interest includes digital marketing, e-commerce, and academic collaboration.

Rohit Bansal is working as Associate Professor in Department of Management Studies in Vaish College of Engineering, Rohtak, India. He has authored & edited 19 books with renowned national & international publishers. In addition to, he has published 130 research papers and chapters in journals of repute including Scopus indexed as well as edited books. He has also presented papers in 50 conferences and seminars. His area of interest includes organizational behaviour, marketing management, human resource management, social media marketing and service marketing. He is on the editorial advisory board as a member in 110 national and international peer reviewed journals. He served as a member of advisory committee in many international conferences. He has acted as session chair in many international conferences. He has been awarded many times for contribution to academics and research.

* * *

Deepanshi Aggarwal is a research scholar in Department of Commerce at Maharshi Dayanand University, Rohtak, India. She has done her graduation and post graduation from Department of Commerce at Maharshi Dayanand University, Rohtak, India and became the Gold Medalist of the respective programmes. She has also presented many papers in national and international conferences and seminars. She has published research papers in reputed journals.

Anushka Anand is a senior at Shiv Nadar University where she is majoring in Management studies. Passionate and Insightful, she has the ability to stay calm even in the most difficult situations. She believes that her problem solving, and detail-oriented mindset helps her in making the right decisions. She is a resourceful individual who is ready to accept challenges and explore new avenues.

Belem Barbosa received her PhD in Business and Management Studies – Specialisation in Marketing and Strategy from the University of Porto, Portugal. She is Assistant Professor at the School of Economics and Management of the University of Porto. She is full researcher at GOVCOPP, the Research Unit of Governance, Competitiveness, and Public Policies, and Invited Researcher at cef.up Center for Economics and Finance at the University of Porto. Her research interests lie primarily in the areas of digital marketing and consumer behavior.

Barkha is a research scholar in Department of Commerce at Maharshi Dayanand University, Rohtak, India. she has done her graduation from Bhagat Phool Singh Mahila Vishwavidyalya, khanpur, Sonepat and post graduation from Maharshi Dayanand University, Rohtak, India. she has also presented many papers in national and international conferences and seminars. she has published research papers in reputed journals.

Devid Basyal is a Ph.D. in Public Administration (South Korea) with e- government major. Previously he gained MPhil/MA in Economics (TU/Nepal) and MBA from UoG, UK. He has more than 15 years of teaching experience at the graduate and undergraduate levels. E-government, Development Economics, Public Policy and Administration, and Marketing are areas of his interest.

Melanie Bobik, MBA, M.A., is a marketing communications expert, researcher, trend analyst and linguist. Her research areas cover digital marketing, consumer behaviour, branding, mass media, intercultural communication and the consumer market in China. Her international work experience includes managerial roles in Europe and Asia. She was officially awarded for the branding and marketing concept of famous polar bear cub "Knut" of the Berlin zoo. Her book "Thirst for Wine – Inside China`s Wine Industry" was the first one to outline successful marketing strategies for imported wine in China. Further, she is a presenter and lecturer and engagements include universities in Germany and China. An Austrian native, she has an MBA in European-Asian Management and graduated from Free University Berlin with a master's in Communications and English Linguistics.

Cássia Carvalho graduated in Social Communication - Journalism with post graduation in Marketing Strategies and MBA in Organizational Communication from the University of Caxias do Sul, Brazil. Master's in marketing from the University of Aveiro, Portugal.

Aziza Chakir is a Senior Lecturer, Keynote Speaker and currently serve as a researcher professor in Hassan II university. Her research interests include in the area of Computer Engineering, Information Systems, Digital culture, Software Engineering, Knowledge Transfer Technology, IT Governance, Cloud Computing, Suitable Development (Green IT), Machine Learning, Big Data, Data mining... She is currently working on many projects such as "Green computing", "Ecological frameworks".

Niranjan Devkota is an economist with the special focus on cross border activities and climate change related issues focusing adaptation. He has over 10 years of experience in the field of economics related research with varietal dynamics. His recent research focuses ranges from development economics especially in cross-border activities and agriculture. He received his PhD degree from Tribhuvan University Nepal. He has experience in impact analysis and model building. He has worked in terms to prepare strategic and implementation plans of several economic issues as a research associates. He has received high level training and capacity building workshop on international co-operation, natural resource management and trade related activities from several international agencies like SANDEE (ICI-MOD), NDRC (China), Hi-Aware (ICIMOD), SANEM (Bangladesh) and from esteemed organizations and universities (online mode). He has command over STATA and basic knowledge of R.

Ankit Dhiraj is working in SOHMT, LPU as a research scholar and qualified JRF. Area of the specialization of tourism (Buddhist Tourism).

Ranson Sifiso Gwala is a PhD Candidate at the University of KwaZulu Natal (UKZN) studying towards a Doctor of Business Administration (DBA). He is working for the Department of Agriculture and Rural Development (DARD). He is a Provincial Executive Committee (PEC) member of the South African Communist Party (SACP) in KwaZulu Natal. He has co-published one peer reviewed article titled, "Corporate governance and firm performance in the fourth industrial revolution: A systematic Literature review", in the Corporate Governance and Organizational Behaviour Review and Covid-19 and "The future of migration and mobility in Africa: A systematic literature review", in the Journal of Nation-building & Policy Studies. He also attended and presented a paper to the International Conference on Migration, Development and Emerging New Order, titled, Covid-19 and the future of migration and mobility in Africa. He also attended 1st International Engaged Scholarship Conference 2022 and presented a paper titled, Framework for corporate governance and firm performance in the fourth industrial revolution. He is an avid reader and an enthusiastic academic want to be. He was born in Ndwedwe, KwaZulu Natal but now resides between Durban and Pietermaritzburg.

Reena Katyal is working as an assistant professor at Sh. LN Hindu College, Rohtak, Haryana.

Sanjeev Kumar has pursued Ph.D. from Amity University Rajasthan Jaipur. He is currently associated with Lovely Professional University. His areas of interests are data analysis, LR in Hospitality area, Food and Beverages.

Chenghai Li is an independent researcher. Her research interests include FinTech, finance and Chinese economy.

Ramya Mahendran is a managed innovation consultant. She is certified in design thinking, business modeling and jobs to be done. She has over 10 years of experience in the fields of managed innovation, startup incubation and acceleration, crowd sources idea management systems, design thinking and sustainability. She works with student entrepreneurs to build their business ideas into a successful business model. She works with some of India's leading Technology and Business Incubators, Institution Innovation Councils and Entrepreneurship Cells. She specializes in setting up innovation strategy, opportunity identification, large scale ideation campaigns and facilitating rapid prototyping events like design service jams and hackathons, organizing large-scale Innovation summits and global idea crowdsourcing events. Her current ares of research is - how can empathy be taught with the help of design tools for product, service and policy designers.

Rubina Nabin has 7 + years of teaching experience in Jazan University (KSA) and Modern College of Business and Science (Oman) in the field of Business Administration specialized in Management Information Systems and Computer Applications for Business. Passionate for research. Believes in the "Publish or Perish" motto!

Desmond Onyemechi Okocha, PhD, is a Social Scientist with specialisation in management and mass communication. He has over 15 years experience in consulting, Research and lecturing. He obtained his B.A degree in Management from the United Kingdom, holds a M.A and PhD in Journalism and Mass Communication, both from India. Additionally, has PGDs in Education Management and Leadership and another in Logistics and Supply Chain Management. He was the pioneer National Knowledge Management and Communication Coordinator for the International Fund for Agricultural Development project in the Niger Delta. He is presently, a Senior Lecturer, Department of Mass Communication, Bingham University, Nigeria. He is the Founder of Institute for Leadership and Development Communication, Nigeria. As an international voice, Dr. Okocha is a frequent speaker in conferences across continents. In 2018, he was invited to speak at Harvard University, USA, Vienna University, Austria, and at the MIRDEC-8th, International Academic Conference on Social Sciences, Portugal.

Roxie Ola-Akuma is an author passionate about using existing media tools to contribute value to society. She holds a master's degree in media and communication from Pan-Atlantic University in Lagos, Nigeria, as well as a bachelor's degree in television and journalism from the famed NTA Television College in Jos Plateau State. Roxie is currently a PhD candidate in Development Communication at Bingham University Nigeria. Her research interests includes emerging trends in new and digital media. Some of her publications include: Journalistic Metamorphosis: Robot Journalism Adoption in Nigeria in a Digital Age (2022); Netizens Perception of Nigerian Security Agencies' Representation in the New Media (2022); Drone Journalism: The Empirical Arguments for its Utilization in Investigative Journalism in Nigeria (2021). As a training expert, she's involved in training students and corporate professionals in the use of digital tools to create their works. Additionally, she runs a solar community campaign and consultancy to support families and institutions in accessing uninterrupted power supply in Nigeria. Roxie is currently the Country Information and Communication Officer for the MEDA Youth Entrepreneurship and Women's Empowerment Project in Nigeria, with a responsibility for designing, implementing and integrating the project's communication strategy into all activities with partners and stakeholders. Her hobbies include, hiking, swimming, running and travelling.

Rabin Paudel is an MBA graduate from Quest International College.

Nishita Pruthi is research scholar at Institute of Management Studies and Research, Maharshi Dayanand University, Rohtak. Her area of interest is social media, digital marketing, and customer engagement. She has contributed 6 chapters in international edited books. She has also published 3 research papers in reputed journals. She has participated in many national as well as international conferences.

Kazi Turin Rahman is a published researcher in the field of marketing and technology. He is an Editorial Review Board Member at International Journal of Strategic Decision Sciences (IJSDS). Moreover, he obtained his MBA from Coventry University, UK with distinction.

Divya Rani is a research scholar of University Department of Economics, Patliputra University Patna, Bihar, India. The main area of research is study of economic impact of tourism. She was published paper in Web of Science and IGI Global.

Bikramjit Rishi is a Professor in Marketing at the School of Management & Entrepreneurship (SME) at Shiv Nadar University (SNU) – Delhi (NCR). He has spent nearly 2 decades making significant contributions to the success and growth of the marketing discipline. His research work has been published in several A league journals such as the Marketing Intelligence and Planning, Journal of Brand Management, and Australasian Marketing Journal. He has also published several edited books in the area of social media marketing, marketing research, and consumer behaviour and a textbook in the domain of social media marketing. He has been a faculty fellow at the doctoral consortiums supported by the American Marketing Association (AMA) and Academy of Indian Marketing (AIM). He serves on the Editorial and Review Board of several journals and international conferences.

Josiah Sabo Kente is Associate Professor and Head, Department of Mass Communication, Nasarawa State University.

Claudia Amaral Santos has a PhD in Linguistics/Terminology from the University of Aveiro (UA) and NOVA Social School of Sciences and Humanities (NOVA-FCSH). She has been an Adjunct Professor at the Aveiro Institute of Accounting and Administration (ISCA-UA) since 2001 where she lectures Languages for Specific Purposes. She coordinates the Languages and Social Sciences team and International Mobility programs in her department. Claudia Amaral Santos is a member of the research unit on Governance, Competitiveness and Public Policy (GOVCOPP) and a collaborator of the research unit on Languages, Literatures and Cultures (CLLC) at the University of Aveiro. She participates regularly in several international projects and her main research interests are focused on education and internationalization, consumer behaviour, tourism, innovation and sustainability.

Tejasvi Sharma is a management and marketing enthusiast from Shiv Nadar University who has a minor in Management and is pursuing a major in Mechanical Engineering. He accepts challenges with alacrity and motivation which helps in broadening his preview. His zeal to explore different horizons helps him to build a strong network. He has the sine qua non for marketing and management roles. His communication skills inter alia help him to better understand the situation and customer's needs which helps him to relate with them with complete ease. He is currently engrossed in the field of marketing research and always tries to find new avenues to use his thinking cap and do research to comprehend society and the market in more depth.

Amandeep Singh holds a Doctorate in Management specializing in Marketing and he is also UGC-NET qualified. He holds more than 16 years of teaching experience. His main area of research is Consumer Sciences and Business Innovations. Currently, he is working as Professor at Chitkara Business School, Chitkara University, Punjab, India. He has published 48 research papers in various journals and conferences which are indexed in Scopus, Web of Science and Google Scholar. He has edited 7 books published by IGI Global, De Gruyter and Wiley. He has also chaired many National and International Conferences. He is on the editorial board of 3 International Journals. He was awarded the Best Teacher in 2008. He is also part of the Board of Studies of various B-Schools and leading universities in Northern India.

Amrinder Singh is currently holding the position of Associate Professor at Jain University, Bangalore. He has a master's in Business Administration and Doctorate in Business Studies from Punjabi University, Patiala. Having teaching experience of more than 15 years under his belt, he is a personality to reckon with in the field of Marketing and Research. He has about more than 30 research papers published to his credit in various National and International journals of repute. He has also published one book. He is a member of academic and administrative bodies of various Universities and Institutions nationally and internationally.

Ram Singh is a new Age Innovative Educationist working as an Associate Professor and the Head, Department of Commerce & Finance, Quantum University Roorkee. Dr. Singh has a vast teaching and research experience of more than 11 years at the UG & PG courses. Being a researcher, Dr. Singh holds multifarious positions in the field of academics, for instance, he is a member and secretary of the Research Council of Quantum University, member of Editorial Board of various reputed journals in the domain of Accounting, Finance & General Management, Reviewer in IGI Global, Inderscience Journals, member and Chairperson of the Board of Faculty & Board of Study (Commerce & Management), member in Board of Management etc. Besides, Dr. Singh has also been awarded the „Excellent Reviewer Award-2020" by Bilingual Publishing Company Singapore, „Best Doctoral Thesis Award-2022" by International Association of Research & Developed Organization, Ghaziabad India, and „National Elite Teacher Award-2022" by International Institute of Organized Research (I2OR) Chennai. Currently his professional affiliation includes a member of four National & International academic organizations, i.e., Life Member of the Indian Commerce Association (ICA), Life Member in the International Association of Academic plus Corporate Society (IAACS), Life Member in the Indian Academic Researchers Association (IARA), Life Member in the International Institute of Organized Research (I2OR). He has published 6 Books, 25 Research Papers, 20 Chapters and 10 Proceedings in Conferences.

Shikha Singh earned her bachelor's degree in commerce with honors from Delhi University and master's degree in commerce from Maharshi Dayanand University. She has been a faculty member at Delhi University's Non Collegiate Women's Education Board for three years. Her current academic affiliation is with the IMSAR at Maharshi Dayanand University, where she is working on a doctorate degree. Her wide-ranging interests include both the financial sector and the rise of digital technology.

Vinay Singh is Sr. Assistant Professor in the Department of Commerce and Management at Quantum University Roorkee, he has more than 10 Years a rich experience in teaching and research. He has completed his PhD in Finance from CCSU Meerut. Besides this he has published 8 Research Papers, 4 Book Chapters, 2 Conference proceedings and 2 Patents in his credentials.

Sahadeb Upretee earned a PhD in Mathematics (Specializations: Actuarial Science; Statistics) from the University of Wisconsin Milwaukee, USA. Dr. Upretee is an assistant professor at the Department of Mathematics, Central Washington University, Ellensburg, WA. He teaches undergraduate courses in Mathematics, Statistics, and Actuarial Science. His research interest includes Data Science, Applied Statistics, Actuarial Science, Loss Data Analytics, Financial Economics, Structural Equations Modeling, Business Analytics, Model Uncertainty, Risk Measures, and Math Education. He collaborates with faculty members and researchers across different countries for scholarly activities.

Riya Wadhwa is a research scholar and pursuing PhD from Institute of Management Studies and Research and working as an assistant professor in Sh. L.N Hindu college, Rohtak and She had published chapters in international as well as in national edited book. She had attended 6 international conferences and published two papers in UGC CARE list.)

Poshan (Sam) Yu is a Lecturer in Accounting and Finance in the International Cooperative Education Program of Soochow University (China). He is also an External Professor of FinTech and Finance at SKEMA Business School (China), a Visiting Professor at Krirk University (Thailand) and a Visiting Researcher at the Australian Studies Centre of Shanghai University (China). Sam leads FasterCapital (Dubai, UAE) as a Regional Partner (China) and serves as a Startup Mentor for AIC RAISE (Coimbatore, India). His research interests include financial technology, regulatory technology, public-private partnerships, mergers and acquisitions, private equity, venture capital, start-ups, intellectual property, art finance, and China's "One Belt One Road" policy.

Pan Yue is an independent researcher. Her research interests include media, Chinese economy and business analytics.

Index

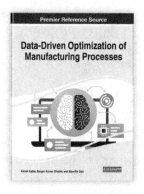
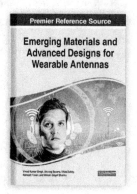
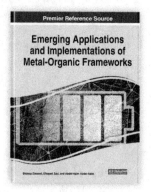
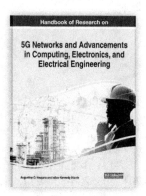
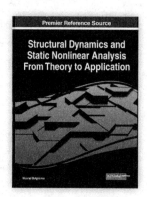

Ensure Quality Research is Introduced to the Academic Community

Become an Evaluator for IGI Global Authored Book Projects

Premier Reference Source

Stabilizing Currency and Preserving Economic Sovereignty Using the Grondona System

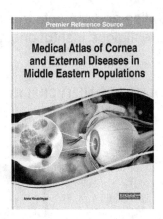

Premier Reference Source

Medical Atlas of Cornea and External Diseases in Middle Eastern Populations

Premier Reference Source

Examining Biophilia and Societal Indifference to Environmental Protection

Premier Reference Source

Using Narratives and Storytelling to Promote Cultural Diversity on College Campuses

The overall success of an authored book project is dependent on quality and timely manuscript evaluations.

Applications and Inquiries may be sent to:
development@igi-global.com

Applicants must have a doctorate (or equivalent degree) as well as publishing, research, and reviewing experience. Authored Book Evaluators are appointed for one-year terms and are expected to complete at least three evaluations per term. Upon successful completion of this term, evaluators can be considered for an additional term.

If you have a colleague that may be interested in this opportunity, we encourage you to share this information with them.

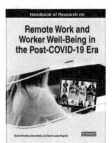

Printed in the United States
by Baker & Taylor Publisher Services